Herbert A. Grueber

**Exhibition of the Royal House of Guelph**

(From George I. to William IV.) under the patronage of her majesty the queen

Herbert A. Grueber

**Exhibition of the Royal House of Guelph**
*(From George I. to William IV.) under the patronage of her majesty the queen*

ISBN/EAN: 9783742841711

Manufactured in Europe, USA, Canada, Australia, Japa

Cover: Foto ©ninafisch / pixelio.de

Manufactured and distributed by brebook publishing software (www.brebook.com)

Herbert A. Grueber

**Exhibition of the Royal House of Guelph**

THE NEW GALLERY,
*Regent Street.*

1891.

## Arrangement of the Exhibition.

### WEST GALLERY.
THE ROYAL ROOM.

### NORTH GALLERY.
STATESMEN AND COMMANDERS.

### SOUTH GALLERY.
ARTS, LETTERS, AND SCIENCE.

### CENTRAL HALL.
HISTORICAL COLLECTION OF CHINA, &c.

### BALCONY.
PICTURES, DRAWINGS, AND MANUSCRIPTS.

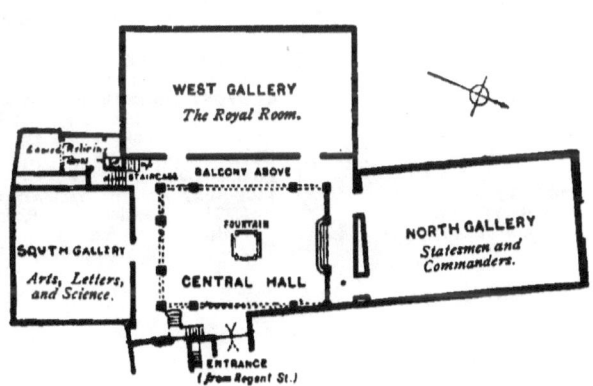

### Patron.
HER MAJESTY THE QUEEN.

### Vice-Patrons.
H.R.H. THE PRINCE OF WALES.    H.R.H. THE DUKE OF CAMBRIDGE.

### The General Committee.

*President:*

THE MARQUESS OF LOTHIAN, K.T., LL.D.,
SECRETARY FOR SCOTLAND.

*Vice-President:*

THE EARL OF WHARNCLIFFE.

THE EARL OF ALBEMARLE, F.S.A., F.R.G.S.
W. R. BAKER, Esq.
GENERAL THE VISCOUNT BRIDPORT, DUKE OF BRONTE, K.C.B.
E. A. BOND, Esq., C.B., LL.D., F.S.A.
SIR ALGERNON BORTHWICK, Bart., M.P.
THE EARL BROWNLOW.
THE DUKE OF BUCCLEUCH, K.T.
THE DUCHESS OF BUCKINGHAM AND CHANDOS.
SIR FREDERICK W. BURTON, Knt., R.H.A., F.S.A., Director of the National Gallery.
CHARLES BUTLER, Esq., F.R.G.S.
THE LORD CARLINGFORD, K.P.
THE EARL OF CARLISLE.
*J. COMYNS CARR, Esq.
THE EARL OF CHICHESTER.
J. W. CLARK, Esq., F.S.A.
SIDNEY COLVIN, Esq.
W. M. CONWAY, Esq., F.S.A.
THE BARONESS BURDETT-COUTTS.
THE EARL OF CRAWFORD, LL.D., F.R.S., F.S.A.
THE VISCOUNT CROSS, G.C.B., F.R.S., Secretary of State for India.
*G. MILNER-GIBSON-CULLUM, Esq., F.S.A.
*LIONEL CUST, Esq., F.S.A.

THE LORD DE LISLE AND DUDLEY.
THE DUKE OF DEVONSHIRE, K.G., LL.D., F.R.S.
*THE HON. HAROLD DILLON, Secretary Society of Antiquaries.
LIEUT.-GEN. SIR MARTIN DILLON, K.C.B., C.S.I.
HENRY AUSTIN DOBSON, Esq.
THE LORD DONINGTON.
HENRY E. DOYLE, Esq., C.B., R.H.A., Director of the National Gallery of Ireland.
THE LADY LOUISA EGERTON.
*JOHN EVANS, Esq., D.C.L., Treas. R.S., President of the Society of Antiquaries.
THE HON. SIR SPENCER PONSONBY FANE, K.C.B.
THE DUKE OF FIFE, K.T.
BASIL FITZHERBERT, Esq.
C. DRURY FORTNUM, Esq., D.C.L., F.S.A.
A. W. FRANKS, Esq., C.B., F.R.S., Litt.D., V.P. Society of Antiquaries.
EDMUND GOSSE, Esq.
LORD RONALD GOWER.
VICE-ADMIRAL SIR WILLIAM GRAHAM, K.C.B., President of Royal Naval College, Greenwich.
THE MARQUESS OF GRANBY, M.P.

J. M. GRAY, Esq., F.S.A. Scotland, Curator of the Scottish National Portrait Gallery.
*EVERARD GREEN, Esq., F.S.A.
RIGHT HON. SIR WILLIAM GREGORY, K.C.M.G., F.R.S.
ARTHUR E. GRIFFITHS, Esq., M.A.
*H. A. GRUEBER, Esq., F.S.A.
*C. E. HALLÉ, Esq.
THE DUKE OF HAMILTON, K.T.
RIGHT HON. LORD GEORGE HAMILTON, M.P., First Lord of the Admiralty.
THE VISCOUNT HARDINGE, F.S.A.
THE MARQUESS OF HARTINGTON, M.P.
THE HON. CLAUDE G. HAY.
BIRKBECK HILL, Esq.
*R. R. HOLMES, Esq., F.S.A., Librarian, Windsor Castle.
THE VISCOUNT HOOD.
*W. H. ST. JOHN HOPE, Esq., Assistant Secretary of the Society of Antiquaries.
J. M. HOWDEN, Esq., F.S.A., Scotland.
GENERAL THE EARL HOWE, C.B.
THE EARL OF ILCHESTER
HENRY IRVING, Esq.
*HENRY JENNER, Esq., F.S.A.
E. BURNE-JONES, Esq., A.R.A.
FELIX JOSEPH, Esq.
W. E. HARTPOLE LECKY, Esq.
SIR FREDERICK LEIGHTON, Bart., President of the Royal Academy.
THE EARL OF LICHFIELD.
THE HON. SCHOMBERG K. MCDONNELL.
MAJOR G. E. W. MALET.
COLONEL H. E. MALET.
H. C. MAXWELL LYTE, Esq., C.B., F.S.A., Deputy Keeper of the Public Records.
C. TRICE MARTIN, Esq., F.S.A.
SIR JOHN E. MILLAIS, Bart., R.A., D.C.L.
LADY MILLAIS.
F. D. MILLET, Esq.
ALFRED MORRISON, Esq., F.R.G.S.
H. MONTAGU, Esq., F.S.A.

THE DUKE OF NORFOLK, K.G., Earl-Marshal.
THE LORD NORTH.
THE DUKE OF NORTHUMBERLAND, K.G., LL.D., D.C.L.
*F. M. O'DONOGHUE, Esq., F.S.A.
THE EARL OF ORFORD.
R. W. COCHRAN PATRICK, Esq., LL.D., F.S.A., Under-Secretary for Scotland; Hon. Sec. Soc. of Antiquaries, Scotland.
THE HON. WILLIAM A. PONSONBY.
THE DUKE OF PORTLAND.
EDWARD J. POYNTER, Esq., R.A.
J. L. PROPERT, Esq., M.D.
C H. READ, Esq., F.S.A.
THE LORD REAY, LL.D., G.C.I.E.
SIR J. C. ROBINSON, F.S.A., H.M. Surveyor of Pictures.
THE EARL OF ROSEBERY, LL.D., F.R.S., F.S.A.
THE LORD ROTHSCHILD.
ALFRED DE ROTHSCHILD, Esq.
THE LORD SACKVILLE.
THE MARQUESS OF SALISBURY, K.G., D.C.L., LL.D.
THE EARL OF SANDWICH.
*GEORGE SCHARF, Esq., C.B., F.S.A., Director and Secretary of the National Portrait Gallery.
THE HON. MRS. MAXWELL-SCOTT.
W. BARCLAY SQUIRE, Esq., F.S.A.
*ISIDORE SPIELMANN, Esq., F.S.A.
J. ASHBY STERRY, Esq.
L. ALMA-TADEMA, Esq., R.A., F.S.A.
THE EARL TEMPLE.
E. MAUNDE THOMPSON, Esq., D.C.L., F.S.A., Principal Librarian of the British Museum.
H. D. TRAILL, Esq.
T. HUMPHREY WARD, Esq.
THE DUKE OF WELLINGTON.
THE DUKE OF WESTMINSTER, K.G.

Secretary, LEONARD C. LINDSAY, F.S.A.

*The names with an asterisk form the Executive Committee.*

# PREFATORY NOTE.

THE President and Members of the Committee of the Guelph Exhibition take this opportunity to offer their most grateful thanks to all those who have so kindly responded to their call, and have rendered the Exhibition possible by intrusting their valuable possessions to their care. It is impossible to exaggerate the debt of gratitude which the Committee owe to the Lenders of the objects of which this is the Catalogue.

The Committee have also to express their gratitude to Mr. G. Scharf, C.B., for the ready assistance he has afforded them in tracing the principal portraits of the period ; to Mr. H. Jenner, who has supplied the notes on the manuscripts and autographs, together with the historical notice of the House of Guelph ; and especially to Mr. H. A. Grueber, who, apart from the constant help he has rendered in the organization of the Exhibition, has made himself responsible for the compilation of the Catalogue and for the biographical notices of the historical personages whose portraits are represented on the walls. For valuable assistance in the arrangement of the collection they have also to offer their thanks to Mr. I. Spielmann, Mrs. Grueber, the Hon. Harold Dillon, Mr. Lionel Cust, Mrs. H. Jenner, Mr. F. M. O'Donoghue: to the Directors of the Gallery and their Secretary: and to Mr. Leonard C. Lindsay, the Secretary of the Guelph Exhibition, for his continued and valuable services in the organization and control of every department.

The Exhibition will remain open to the public till the 4th April, from 10 to 6 daily.

The Directors of the New Gallery hope this extremely interesting series of Historical Exhibitions may be continued in the winter of next year, when it is proposed to illustrate the Reign of her Majesty the Queen.

# THE HOUSE OF GUELPH.

THE HOUSE OF GUELPH became extinct in the male line in 1047. Its line may be traced in a shadowy manner from the Dukes of Alsace or earlier from certain of the Frankish Mayors of the Palace down to a more certain Warinus, Lord of Altdorf in Suabia, who lived about the year 750, and was one of the Counts of the Court of Carloman. His son Isenbart married Irmentrude, daughter of Childbrand, Duke of Suabia, and sister of Hildegarde, wife of Charles the Great. To her is attributed the legendary origin of the name of the House. It is said that, seeing a woman nursing twins, she expressed a doubt as to the possibility of twins by the same father. For her strange physiological theory she was punished by herself having twelve children at a birth. Being naturally annoyed at this, she directed the nurse to destroy eleven of them; Isenbart, meeting her on her way to obey the command, asked her what she was carrying, to which she replied, "Whelps for drowning." Isenbart, however, discovered what they were and saved their lives, and from them descend many of the great German Houses. The eldest was called Welf or Guelph, to commemorate the incident, and with him, who died in 820, the House of Guelph *eo nomine* begins. By grants, inheritance, and marriage, the Guelphs acquired very large dominions in Bavaria, and after two centuries more the main line ended in an heiress, Cunigunda, daughter of Guelph III., who married in 1040, Azo d'Este, Marquis of Este, Milan, &c., whose descendants by her adopted the surname of Guelph. Thus it is that the Royal House of Hanover is in the male line the House of Este, and undoubtedly its proper name is "Guelph d'Este."

The House of Este claims very high antiquity. It professes to descend from Actius (hence the name *Azo*) in the reign of the elder Tarquin. The pedigree, however, remains vague and improbable for the first thousand years or more, and the earliest certain ancestor of the House seems to be Albert of Este, who died in 938. He was Count of Este (a place some twenty miles to the south-west of Padua) and also Marquis of Tuscany. It was his great-grandson who married the heiress of the Guelphs.

Azo Guelph d'Este married a second time Garsenda or Ermengarda, daughter of Hugh, Count of Maine, and from Fulk, the son of this marriage, descended that line of Este, Dukes of Modena and Ferrara, to which the wife of King James II. belonged, which became extinct in the male line at the death in 1803 of Ercole Rinaldo, whose representative in the female line, curiously enough, represents also the Royal House of Stuart. Guelph, the son of the first marriage, was the ancestor of the House of Brunswick, which is therefore the elder branch of the House of Este.

More and more did the House of Guelph acquire power and sovereignty. Through the marriage of Henry, son of Guelph, with Wolfhilda, daughter of Magnus, Duke of Old Saxony, and of his son, Henry the Proud, with Gertrude, heiress of Brunswick, they added the great dominions of the Houses of Witekind and Billung in North Germany to their Bavarian lands, until the next of the line, Henry the Lion, could say:—

> "Heinrich der Löwe bin ich genannt,
> In aller Welt und Weit bekannt;
> Von der Elbe bis an den Rhein,
> Vom Harz bis an die See war mein."

Henry the Lion, however, for opposing the Emperor Frederick Barbarossa was deprived of his Bavarian and Saxon dominions and driven into exile at the Court of Henry II. of England, whose daughter Matilda he had married. His son Otto became Emperor in 1198, but was deposed in 1212. It is curious that though a Guelph by family he seems to have sided with the Ghibelline faction against the Pope as soon as he became Emperor. His abdication was caused by his defeat by Philip Augustus of France at the

Battle of Bouvines, where the help of John of England was of no avail to him. William of Winchester, called Longsword, the brother of Otto, continued the line, through his son Albert, who became Duke of Brunswick, and died in 1279. The custom of subdivision of territory seems to have become systematic in his time, though several separated lines subsequently became extinct and their territories were reunited. Two sons of Albert, Henry and Albert, founded the two branches of Grubenhagen and Hanover, the first becoming extinct in 1596, and the second receiving the dominions of Wolfenbüttel on the death of a third brother William. The line of the second, Albert, continued, and Magnus Torquatus, his grandson, at his death in 1373, gave Wolfenbüttel to his son Henry and Luneburg to his son Bernard. The line of Henry became extinct in 1634. and Wolfenbüttel reverted to Augustus, son of Henry, eldest son of Ernest of Brunswick-Luneburg, the descendant of the above-mentioned Bernard while the possessions of Luneburg were held by the descendants of Ernest's second son, William. From this time the two Houses of Brunswick-Luneburg and Brunswick-Wolfenbüttel remained distinct, until by the death of the last Duke of Brunswick-Wolfenbüttel, in 1884, the heirship of his dominions reverted to Ernest, King of Hanover, and Duke of Cumberland, the head of the House of Brunswick-Luneburg. William, the son of Ernest of Brunswick-Luneburg, was the father of George, Duke of Brunswick-Luneburg, whose son Ernest was created Elector of Hanover in 1692 and married Sophia, youngest child of Frederick, Elector Palatine and King of Bohemia, and Elizabeth, daughter of King James I. of Great Britain and Ireland. As all the senior descendants of James I. were Roman Catholics, the Act of Settlement excluded them, and entailed the Crown of Great Britain and Ireland on the descendants of the Electress Sophia. The excluded lines were those of James II., of Henrietta of Orleans, daughter of Charles I., and of the elder children of Elizabeth of Bohemia. The Electress Sophia died on the 8th of June, 1714, losing by not quite two months the succession to the Crown of England. Her son, George I., succeeded on the first of August, 1714. In 1816 the title of Elector of Hanover was changed to that of King, and in 1837, in consequence of the Salic form of succession in Hanover, the Crown of that country was separated from that of England, and given to Ernest, Duke of Cumberland, whose son, George V., was deprived of his kingdom by the Prussians in 1867, and the possessions of the House of Brunswick-Luneburg were incorporated in those of the House of Hohenzollern. In 1860 the head, in the female line, of the younger branch of the House of Este, Francis V., Duke of Modena, was deprived of his Italian possessions, so that now this great House, the possessor of one of the most magnificent pedigrees in Europe, has lost absolutely all of its hereditary dominions.

NOTE ON THE GUELPHS AND GHIBELLINES.—The origin of these party names is somewhat curious. In Suabia the rival to the House of Guelph was that of Weiblingen, which, according to some, was a branch of the same family. The rivalry had nothing to do with Italian parties, but when Frederick (Barbarossa) of Hohenstauffen, the descendant of Frederick, Freiherr of Weiblingen and Hohenstauffen, became Emperor in 1152, and Henry the Lion, his hereditary enemy, took the Pope's side against him, the names of the two families noted for their hostility in their own country were adopted in Italy—Guelph for the Papal party, and Weiblingen, Italianized into Ghibelline, for the Imperial. These names continued long after the fall of the House of Suabia had taken the Weiblingen family away from the contests, and it was not until the rise of the House of Visconti at the end of the fourteenth century united Italy against a common enemy that the parties and their names ceased to exist.

# CHRONOLOGY OF REMARKABLE EVENTS FROM 1714—1837.

### GEORGE I. (1714-1727).

1714. Townshend Prime Minister.
1715. Jacobite Rising. The Chevalier in Scotland.
1717. Stanhope Prime Minister.
1718. The Spanish fleet defeated at Cape Passaro by Byng.
1720. The South Sea Bubble.
1721. Death of Stanhope. Walpole Prime Minister.
1727. Death of the King.

### GEORGE II. (1727-1760).

1739. War declared against Spain.
,, Capture of Porto Bello.
,, Anson begins his voyage round the world.
1741. Retirement of Walpole. Lord Wilmington Prime Minister.
1743. Battle of Dettingen.
,, Pelham Prime Minister.
1745. Battle of Fontenoy.
,, Rising in Scotland.
1746. Battle of Culloden.
1751. Death of Frederick, Prince of Wales.
1754. Death of Pelham. Duke of Newcastle Prime Minister.
1756. Minorca captured by the French.
1757. Execution of Admiral Byng.
,, Pitt's first Administration.
1759. Hawke's victory at Quiberon.
,, Quebec taken. Death of Wolfe.
1760. Canada conquered. Death of George II.

### GEORGE III. (1760-1820).

1761. Resignation of Pitt.
1762. Lord Bute Prime Minister.
1763. Resignation of Lord Bute. George Grenville Prime Minister.
,, Arrest of Wilkes on "a general warrant."
1765. Resignation of Grenville. Marquess of Rockingham Prime Minister.
1766. Resignation of Rockingham. Pitt created Earl of Chatham. His second Ministry. Duke of Grafton Prime Minister.
1768. Resignation of Pitt.
1770. Resignation of the Duke of Grafton. Lord North Prime Minister.
1775. Commencement of the American War of Independence.
1778. Death of Chatham.
1779. War with Spain.
1780. Rodney's Victory at Cape St. Vincent.
1782. Resignation of Lord North. Marquess of Rockingham's second Administration.
,, Rodney's Victory over De Grasse in the West Indies.
,, Relief of Gibraltar by Lord Howe.
1783. Resignation of Shelburne.
,, Coalition Ministry.
,, Pitt Prime Minister.
1786. Impeachment of Warren Hastings.
1797. Victory of Jervis off Cape St. Vincent.
,, Victory of Duncan off Camperdown.
1798. French Expedition to Egypt.
,, Nelson's Victory at the Nile.
1801. Resignation of Pitt. Addington Prime Minister.

1801. Battle of Copenhagen.
  ,,   Battle of Alexandria.
1804. Pitt's Second Administration.
1805. Battle of Trafalgar, and death of Nelson.
1806. Death of Pitt.
  ,,   Lord Grenville Prime Minister.
  ,,   Death of Fox.
1807. Duke of Portland Prime Minister.
  ,,   Bombardment of Copenhagen.
1808. Battle of Vimiera, and occupation of Lisbon by the British troops.
1809. Battle of Corunna, and death of Sir John Moore.
  ,,   Battle of Talavera.
1809. Perceval Prime Minister.
1810. Battle of Busaco. Lines of Torres Vedras occupied.
1811. The Regency.
  ,,   Battle of Fuentes de Onoro and Albuera.
1812. Assassination of Perceval. Lord Liverpool Prime Minister.
  ,,   Capture of Ciudad Rodrigo and Badajoz.
  ,,   Battle of Salamanca.
1813. Battle of Vittoria and the Pyrenees.
  ,,   Capture of St. Sebastian. Wellington enters France.
1814. Battle of Toulouse.
  ,,   Abdication of Napoleon.

1815. Battle of Waterloo.
  ,,   Peace of Paris.
1816. Bombardment of Algiers.
1817. Death of Princess Charlotte.
1820. Death of George III.

GEORGE IV. (1820-1830).

1820. Trial of Queen Caroline.
1821. Death of Queen Caroline.
1827. Canning Prime Minister, his death. Lord Goderich Prime Minister.
1828. Duke of Wellington Prime Minister.
1830. Death of George IV.

WILLIAM IV. (1830-1837).

1831. Resignation of the Duke of Wellington. Earl Grey Prime Minister.
1832. Reform Bill passed.
1833. Abolition of Slavery.
1834. Lord Melbourne Prime Minister.
  ,,   Sir Robert Peel Prime Minister.
1835. Lord Melbourne's Second Administration.
1837. Death of William IV.

# CATALOGUE

*The Numbers commence in the West Gallery, and continue from left to right.*

*\*\*\* Throughout the Catalogue, in describing the pictures and medals, the* RIGHT *and the* LEFT *mean those of the spectator facing the portrait. His or her apply strictly to the persons represented.*

*The works are catalogued under the names given to them by the Contributors. The Committee can accept no responsibility as to their authenticity.*

## WEST GALLERY.

### THE ROYAL ROOM.

**1.** SOPHIA, ELECTRESS OF HANOVER (1630–1714).

Daughter of Frederick, King of Bohemia, and Elizabeth, daughter of James I. Born at the Hague, October 13, 1630; married in 1658, Ernest Augustus, Elector of Hanover, and was the mother of George I. By the Act of Settlement she was declared heir to the English crown in succession to Queen Anne, whom she pre-deceased by a few weeks, June 8, 1714. She was a woman of masculine intellect and of uncommon beauty, preserving even at the age of seventy-three all the comeliness and vigour of youth.

Three-quarter length, life-size, seated facing, head to left, in pale pink dress and blue mantle lined with ermine; her hair is arranged in large curls over the temples; landscape in background. Canvas 54 × 47 in.

Lent by The DUKE OF MARLBOROUGH.

B

## 2. HENRY ST. JOHN, VISCOUNT BOLINGBROKE (1678-1751).

Statesman, diplomatist, &c. Son of Henry, Viscount St. John, educated at Eton and Christ Church, Oxford; entered Parliament for Wootton Basset, and, attaching himself to Robert Harley, became Secretary for War during the period of Marlborough's most brilliant victories, 1704-1707. When Harley was again at the head of affairs in 1710, St. John became Secretary of State, took a prominent part in settling the peace of Utrecht, and in 1712 was raised to the peerage as Viscount Bolingbroke. On the accession of George I. he was deprived of office, impeached and attainted, and retiring to the Continent, openly served the Pretender. Being restored in blood in 1723 he returned to England, bitterly opposed Walpole, and espoused the cause of Frederick Prince of Wales. He was an intimate friend of Pope and Dean Swift. To Bolingbroke Pope dedicated his *Essay on Man*.

Three-quarter length, life-size, to right, head facing, in peer's robes, lace cravat and wig; left hand resting on table on which is coronet, left on his hip; architectural background. Canvas 50 × 40 in.

By POMPEO BATTONI.  Lent by The LORD BAGOT.

## 3. CHARLES MORDAUNT, 3RD EARL OF PETERBOROUGH, K.G. (1658-1735).

Son of John, Lord Mordaunt, whom he succeeded in 1675; entered the navy and distinguished himself against the Moors in Tangier, 1680. He accompanied the Prince of Orange to England; was created Earl of Monmouth in 1689, and succeeded to the earldom of Peterborough on the death of his uncle in 1697. He was appointed in 1705 Commander-in-Chief of the English forces in Spain; took Barcelona, and drove the French out of the kingdom. For this service he received the thanks of Parliament, and in 1713 was created a K.G. During the reign of George I. he was made General of the Marines. He died on his passage to Lisbon.

Three-quarter length, life-size, nearly full-face, in Garter robes, collar, &c., and wig; thumb of right hand thrust into his belt, left arm rests on table on which is placed his plumed hat. Canvas 48 × 38 in.

By M. DAHL.  Lent by The EARL OF CARLISLE.

## 4. SARAH JENNINGS, DUCHESS OF MARLBOROUGH, AND LADY FITZ-HARDING.

The Duchess was the second daughter of Richard Jennings of Sandridge, Hertford. At twelve years old she was received with her sister into the household of Mary, Duchess of York, and became attendant to Princess Anne. Married in 1678 Col. John Churchill, afterwards Duke of Marlborough; appointed Lady of the Bedchamber to the Princess and accompanied her in her flight on the landing of the Prince of Orange. A correspondence was carried on by the Princess and her under the names of Mrs. Morley and Mrs. Freeman. On the accession of Queen Anne she interfered much in political matters: was supplanted by her cousin Mrs. Masham, and finally left the Court in 1710. Wrote memoirs of her Court life: and died October, 1744.

Lady Fitzharding, daughter of Sir Edward Villiers, was governess to William, Duke of Gloucester, and assisted the Princess Anne in making her escape in 1688. She married John, Viscount Fitzharding, and died in 1708, in her 52nd year.

Three-quarter length, life-size figures; the Duchess and Lady Fitzharding playing at cards; the latter holds the nine of diamonds conspicuously to the spectator, the former rests her left hand upon a pedestal, inscribed *G. Kneller ft.* 1691. Canvas 58 × 43 in.

The Duchess, in her "Account of her Conduct," admits her partiality to cards, and says of Lady Fitzharding that she was more than anybody in Queen Mary's favour, and one "for whom it was well known I had a singular affection."

By SIR G. KNELLER. Lent by The DUKE OF MARLBOROUGH.

**5. ADMIRAL JOHN BYNG (1704–1757).**

Son of George, Viscount Torrington, entered the Navy under his father's auspices, rose to be Admiral, prevented supplies coming from France to Scotland in 1745, and rendered other services. His attempts to relieve Fort St. Philip in Minorca in 1756, when blockaded by the French fleet, proved abortive, and his hesitation in engaging the enemy, when a bold attack might perhaps have led to victory, drew the clamours of the nation against him. He was tried by court-martial, condemned and shot at Portsmouth, March 14, 1757, meeting death with calm resignation.

Three-quarter length, life-size, to right, head facing; in naval uniform and wig; his right arm rests on a gun, the hand holding a baton; under his left arm, his hat; in the background, naval engagement. Canvas 50 × 40 in.

Lent by The EARL OF STRAFFORD.

**6. GEORGE I. (1660–1727).**

Son of Ernest Augustus, Elector of Hanover, and Sophia, daughter of Frederick, Elector Palatine, and granddaughter of James I. of England; born at Osnaburg, May 28, 1660, succeeded to the electorate on the death of his father in 1698, and ascended the throne of England on the death of Queen Anne, August 1, 1714. Died at Osnaburg, June 11, 1727. Married Sophia Dorothea of Zelle, November 21, 1682, by whom he had two children, George Augustus (George II.), and Sophia Dorothea, Queen of Prussia.

Full-length, life-size, facing; red coat and hose, full brown wig; in right hand his hat; his left thrust in his coat; in background landscape through open window. Canvas 87 × 52 in.

By SIR G. KNELLER. Lent by The DUKE OF FIFE, K.T.

**7. ROBERT HARLEY, 1ST EARL OF OXFORD (1661–1724).**

Statesman. Son of Sir Edward Harley; at the Revolution was returned as M.P. for Tregony, Cornwall; appointed Speaker 1700-5, and Secretary of State 1704-8, when he was forced to resign, being accused of correspondence with Prince James, the Chevalier. In 1710 he was constituted a Commissioner of the Treasury, and in the same year narrowly escaped assassination from the hands of a Frenchman, the Marquis de Guiscard; was raised to the peerage as 1st Earl of Oxford in 1711, and Prime Minister,

1711-14. In 1715 he was impeached by the House of Commons, committed to the Tower for two years, but acquitted by his peers in 1717. Died May 21, 1724.

Three-quarter length, life-size, to right, in Chancellor's robes, holding in right hand a copy of the Succession Bill; left resting on his hip. Canvas 49 × 39 in.

Lent by The DUKE OF PORTLAND.

**8.** GEORGE I., AS ELECTOR (1660–1727). Dated 1705.

Three-quarter length, life-size, in steel armour, with red mantle and white fur, and ribbon of the Garter, holding truncheon in right hand, the Electoral cap on the rock at his elbow; blue sky background. Canvas 54 × 45 in.

This picture was probably the work of Hirschmann. There is a fine mezzotint engraving after a similar picture by John Smith.

By HIRSCHMANN. Lent by The DUKE OF MARLBOROUGH.

**9.** CHARLES FITZROY, 2ND DUKE OF GRAFTON, K.G. (1683–1767).

Grandson of King Charles II. and Barbara Villiers, Duchess of Cleveland, succeeded to the Dukedom on the death of his father, who was killed at the siege of Cork in 1690, and after extensive travelling on the Continent, held several appointments in the royal household, and in 1720 was appointed Lord-Lieutenant of Ireland. He was elected a K.G. in the following year, and on all occasions of George I. quitting his dominions was nominated one of the Chief Justices of Great Britain. In 1724 he was appointed Lord Chamberlain of the Household, and retained the office till his death in 1767.

Half length, life-size, facing, head to left, red coat, blue cap; right hand holding his coat. Canvas 35 × 27 in.

By SIR G. KNELLER. Lent by R. B. BAKER, ESQ.

**10.** JOHN CHURCHILL, 1ST DUKE OF MARLBOROUGH, K.G. (1650–1722).

Pre-eminent as a general and statesman. Son of Sir Winston Churchill; born at Ashe, Devonshire; was page of honour to the Duke of York; obtained an ensigncy in the Guards, served at Tangiers in 1671; under the Duke of Monmouth, against the Dutch in 1672; and under the influence of the Duke of York was created Lord Churchill in 1682. At James's accession he was advanced to a barony; aided in the defeat of Monmouth, then joined the Prince of Orange, and voted in the "Convention" Parliament, and was created Earl of Marlborough in 1689. Appointed by Queen Anne Captain-General of the Forces in the Low Countries, he gained the victory of Blenheim in 1704; Ramillies, in 1706; Oudenarde, in 1708; and Malplaquet in 1709. He was created a Duke for his first campaign of 1702. He subsequently lost the favour of Queen Anne and retired abroad, but was reinstated by George I. He married Sarah, daughter of R. Jennings (see No. 4).

The Duke is on horseback holding his Marshal's baton, crowned by Victory, and surrounded by figures of Justice, Discord, Hercules, an emblematical female figure of Lille offering model of city, above Amorini in clouds. Canvas 35 × 28 in.

By SIR G. KNELLER and PRICE RYAT. Lent by The EARL OF CHICHESTER.

**11. SOPHIA DOROTHEA, WIFE OF GEORGE I. (1666–1726).**

Daughter of George William, Duke of Zelle; born September 15, 1666; married November 21, 1682, George Lewis, hereditary Prince of Brunswick-Luneberg, afterwards Elector and King of England. Being accused of adultery with the Count of Konigsmark, she was separated from her husband in 1694, confined in a fortress, where she died, November 13, 1726.

Full-length, life-size, to left, in blue ermine-lined gown and mantle, over white satin gold embroidered petticoat; jewels in her hair; in right hand she holds the orb which, with the crown, is placed on the table before her; with her left she holds her mantle. Canvas 87 × 52 in.

Lent by The DUKE OF FIFE, K.T.

**12. SIMON, 1ST VISCOUNT HARCOURT, LORD CHANCELLOR (1660–1727).**

Son of Sir Philip Harcourt and Anne, daughter of Sir William Wallis, the Parliamentarian General, studied at Pembroke College, Oxford, and was called to the bar in 1683. He was elected M.P. for Abingdon in 1690, named Solicitor-General and knighted in 1702, and being advanced to the Attorney-Generalship in 1707, framed the bill for the Union with Scotland. In 1710 he was appointed Lord Keeper, and in the following year raised to the peerage as Baron Harcourt of Stanton Harcourt. Early in 1713 he became Lord Chancellor, but being suspected of favouring the House of Stuart, he was deprived of office at the accession of George I. He afterwards rose to favour with the King, and in 1721 was created Viscount Harcourt. He was the intimate friend of Bolingbroke, Gay, Prior, and Pope, and it was in a house belonging to him at Stanton Harcourt that the latter translated the *Iliad*. Died July 25, 1727.

Three-quarter length, life-size, standing to left, in Chancellor's robes and wig; on left purse of the great seal. Canvas 50 × 40 in.

By SIR G. KNELLER. Lent by E. W. HARCOURT, ESQ.

**13. JAMES, 1ST EARL STANHOPE (1671–1721).**

General and statesman. Son of Alexander Stanhope, brother of the 2nd Earl of Chesterfield; born at Paris, entered the military service in 1694, served in the Spanish Peninsula from 1702-1704, and as brigadier-general shared the glory of Lord Peterborough's brilliant campaign of 1705. He was sent as envoy-extraordinary to Spain in 1706, and as commander of the British forces in that country from 1708-1711, took Minorca, and gained the battle of Almenara, in which engagement he slew with his own hand, Amezaga, the general of the Spanish cavalry; but in January 1711, he was taken prisoner at Brihuega, and remained in captivity until the peace of Utrecht. During the reign of George I. he filled in succession the offices of Secretary of State and First Lord of the Treasury, and being raised to the peerage in 1717 as Viscount Stanhope, was promoted to the earldom in the following year. Died February 5, 1721.

Three-quarter length, life-size, seated to right; red coat, black wig; in right hand pen; his left rests on table, and holds paper. Canvas 50 × 40 in.

By SIR G. KNELLER. Lent by The EARL STANHOPE.

**14. RICHARD BOYLE, 3RD EARL OF BURLINGTON AND 4TH EARL OF CORK (1695–1753).**

Celebrated for his architectural tastes. Was the only son of Charles, 3rd Earl of Cork, succeeded to the titles and estates of his father in 1704, appointed Lord High Treasurer of Ireland in 1715, and installed a Knight Companion of the Garter in June 1730. Died in 1753. In his early days Lord Burlington became an enthusiastic admirer of the architectural genius of Palladio, and in 1716 began to reconstruct Burlington House, Piccadilly, built by his grandfather, the 1st Earl of Burlington. The building figures in a print by Hogarth, intended to satirize the Earl and his friends, entitled *Taste of the Town*, and in another one entitled *The Man of Taste*, in which Pope is represented as washing Burlington House and bespattering the Duke of Chandos; Lord Burlington appears as a mason mounting a ladder. He also rebuilt Chiswick House, which Lord Hervey described as "being too small to live in, and too large to hang to a watch."

Three-quarter length, life-size, seated to left, in wig, brown coat, ribbon and star of the Garter; right hand holds volume of Inigo Jones, resting on console, which also supports a bust of the architect. Canvas 50 × 40 in.

By G. KNAPTON.   Lent by The MARQUESS OF HARTINGTON, M.P.

**15. PRINCESS SOPHIA DOROTHEA, QUEEN OF PRUSSIA (1684–1757).**

Only dau. of George I. married November 28, 1706, Frederick William of Brandenburg, who shortly after became King of Prussia, and by whom she was inhumanly treated, her children separated from her, and herself provided with an income which barely sufficed to supply the ordinary necessaries of subsistence. She was the mother of Frederick the Great.

Three-quarter length, life-size, to right; dark blue dress embroidered in silver, light blue stomacher and ermine-lined mantle; her left hand rests on her crown, placed on cushion, her right holds up her mantle; crimson curtain in background. Canvas 54 × 41 in.

Lent by HER MAJESTY THE QUEEN
(Buckingham Palace).

**16. EDWARD WORTLEY MONTAGU (d. 1761).**

Grandson of the 1st Earl of Sandwich. Represented, at different periods, the cities of Westminster and Peterborough, and the boroughs of Huntingdon and Bossiney, in Parliament; distinguished himself by the introduction of several useful bills; was appointed a Lord of the Treasury in 1714, and in 1716 went as ambassador to the Porte, but was recalled in 1717. Died 1761. He married Lady Mary, the eldest daughter of Evelyn, 1st Duke of Kingston.

Three-quarter length, life-size, to left, plum-coloured coat and wig; right hand extended; left resting on pedestal; landscape background. Canvas 50 × 40 in.

By SIR G. KNELLER.   Lent by The EARL OF WHARNCLIFFE.

**17. Sir Robert Walpole, 1st Earl of Orford, K.G. (1676–1745).**

One of the most eminent of our great Parliamentary leaders. Born at Houghton, in Norfolk; was educated at Eton and King's College, Cambridge. In 1708 he was appointed Secretary-at-War, and Prime Minister in 1715; but it was not till 1722, after the deaths of Stanhope and Sunderland, that he attained the highest power in the administration, and he continued in office with great success and great renown as First Lord of the Treasury and Chancellor of the Exchequer till 1742. Upon his retirement he was created Earl of Orford. In 1725 he had received the Order of the Bath, and in 1726 the Order of the Garter, being one of the very few commoners in modern times who have ever been invested with the latter. Died March 18, 1745.

Three-quarter length, life-size, to right, in robes of Chancellor of the Exchequer and wig, and ribbon of the Garter; his right hand rests on the purse of Lord High Treasurer; in left, paper. Canvas 49 × 39 in.

By J. B. Van Loo.  Lent by H. Spencer Walpole, Esq.

**18. Frederick, Prince of Wales, his brother the Duke of Cumberland, and their Sisters.**

Son of George II. and Caroline of Brandenburg Anspach; born at Hanover, January 20, 1707, created Duke of Gloucester in 1717, K.G. in 1718, and Duke of Edinburgh in 1726. In the twenty-second year of his age he first came to this country, and shortly after his arrival was made Earl of Chester, Prince of Wales, and a Member of the Privy Council. He soon became exceedingly popular, but lost credit at Court in betraying a strong bias towards the Opposition, of which he eventually became the head. In 1736 he married Augusta, daughter of Frederick, Duke of Saxe-Gotha, by whom he had four sons (the eldest being George III.) and two daughters. Died March 20, 1751. Princess Anne, his eldest sister, married, in 1734, William, Prince of Orange, died in 1759; Princess Amelia, died unmarried in 1786; Princess Elizabeth, died unmarried in 1758; William, Duke of Cumberland, who commanded at Fontenoy and Culloden, born in 1721, died in 1765; Princess Mary, married Frederick, Landgrave of Hesse-Cassel, in 1740, died in 1771; and Princess Louise, the youngest, married Frederick V. of Denmark in 1743, and died in 1751.

The Prince of Wales stands in the centre, in red coat and ribbon of the Garter, and points to a celestial globe on which is a chart with representation of an eclipse of the sun; on his left are grouped the Princesses Anne (seated), Amelia, and Elizabeth, and the Duke of Cumberland; on his right are his two youngest sisters, the Princesses Mary and Louisa, one of whom plays with a dog; architectural background. Canvas 110 × 147 in.

Lent by The Marquess of Hartington, M.P.

**19. George II. on Horseback (1683–1760).**

Son of George I. and Sophia Dorothea of Zelle: born at Hanover, October 30, 1683; married, 1705, Wilhelmina Carolina, dau. of the Margrave of Brandenburg-Anspach; succeeded to the throne, June 11, 1727; died at Kensington, October 25, 1760. At his accession he is described as being of a pleasing and expressive countenance, with prominent eyes and a Roman nose. In person he was well-proportioned, but below the middle size.

Small equestrian figure, to right, King in armour, holds baton in right hand, behind an attendant who carries his helmet, architectural and landscape background. Canvas 29 × 24 in.

By J. HIGHMORE.  Lent by The DUKE OF RICHMOND AND GORDON, K.G.

**20.** MISS ANNE HOGARTH.

Half-length, life-size, to right, head facing; in cap, brown dress, and white bodice; in right hand she holds a flower. Canvas 30 × 24 in.

Hogarth painted pictures of his two sisters, Mary and Anne, about 1746. They were done in profile so as to face each other. That of Mary Hogarth is in the National Gallery. Both pictures were sold at Mr. Hogarth's death in 1790.

By W. HOGARTH.  Lent by MISS REID.

**21.** CHARLOTTE, COUNTESS OF WARWICK (d. 1731).

Daughter of Sir Thomas Middleton, married first to Edward Rich, 4th Earl of Holland and 6th Earl of Warwick, and secondly, in 1716, to Joseph Addison, the essayist, poet, &c. This second marriage is generally said to have been uncomfortable. Johnson says that it resembled the marriages in which a sultan gives his daughter a man to be a slave, and there is a report that Addison used to escape from his uncomfortable splendour at Holland House to a coffee-house at Kensington.

Half-length, life-size, to right, head facing; in an oval; red dress, showing white bodice, black mantle. Canvas 30 × 25 in.

By SIR G. KNELLER.  Lent by W. ADDISON, ESQ.

**22.** GENERAL JAMES WOLFE (1726-1759).

Son of Lieut.-Gen. Edward Wolfe. Born at Westerham in Kent; entered the army at an early age, and distinguished himself at Dettingen, in the campaign of Fontenoy, and at Falkirk, Culloden, and Minden. In 1751 he joined Boscawen and Amherst in the reduction of Louisburg, from whence he had just returned when he was appointed to command the expedition to Quebec. The enterprise was hazardous, but Wolfe surmounted all difficulties and encountered the enemy on the heights of Abraham, September 13, 1759. In the moment of victory he received a ball in the wrist and another in the body. In his last agonies he was roused by the cry, "They run," on which he eagerly asked, "Who runs?" and on being told the French, he said, "I thank God, I die content," and expired. His body was brought to England and buried at Greenwich.

Small full-length, standing in a landscape, facing, in military uniform; right hand extended, holding hat; left on hilt of his sword. Canvas 29 × 24 in.

Lent by CLIFFORD CHAPLIN, ESQ.

**23.** RICHARD, 3RD EARL OF BURLINGTON, AFTERWARDS 4TH EARL OF CORK, AND HIS THREE SISTERS, ELIZABETH, JULIANA, AND HENRIETTA, WHEN YOUNG.

Richard, 3rd Earl of Burlington, see No. 14. His eldest sister, Elizabeth, married in 1719 Sir Henry Arundel Bedingfeld, Bart. His second, Juliana, married in 1719 Charles, Lord Bruce, son and heir of Thomas, Earl of Aylesbury. Died without issue in 1739. His youngest, Henrietta, married in 1726 Henry Boyle, of Castle Martyr, co. Cork, who was created Earl of Shannon.

Four full-length, life-size figures. The Earl stands pointing with his right hand, head to right; in blue dress, with red coat, white stockings, and classical sandals; on his left a dog. His eldest sister, in blue and yellow, is seated with her hand on the shoulder of the second sister, who holds a dog. At their feet sits the youngest child, who holds a basket of flowers. Architectural background. Canvas 76 × 70 in.

Lent by The MARQUESS OF HARTINGTON, M.P.

**24.** FRANCIS, 2ND EARL OF GODOLPHIN (1678–1766).

Only child of Sidney, 1st Earl; was educated at Eton and King's College, Cambridge, sat in Parliament for various constituencies from 1701 to 1712, when he succeeded to the family titles and estates, and during that period held several minor offices. He was a Lord of the Bedchamber to George I. and II., Groom of the Stole, and in 1728 appointed Governor of the Scilly Islands. During the king's absences from England in 1723–1727 he acted as one of the justices of the United Kingdom. Dying without issue, most of his titles became extinct.

Half length, life-size, to right, head to left, in grey coat and wig; right arm rests on pedestal. Canvas 35 × 27 in.

By SIR G. KNELLER.                            Lent by R. B. BAKER, ESQ.

**25.** JOHN, 2ND DUKE OF MONTAGU, K.G. (1688–1749).

Third son of Ralph, 1st Duke. Succeeded to the title in 1709; officiated as High Constable of England at the Coronation of George I., and during that reign filled several offices of high honour. Was elected a K.G. in 1718, and a K.B. in 1725, and at the Coronation of George II. carried the sceptre with the cross. In 1733 he was made Governor of the Isle of Wight, Master-General of the Ordnance in 1740, and was one of the Lord Justices for the administration of the Government during the absences of the King in 1745 and 1748. Married, 1705, Mary, daughter of the Great Duke of Marlborough.

Half length, life-size, to right, head to left, red coat and wig; right hand holding stick. Canvas 35 × 27 in.

By SIR G. KNELLER.                            Lent by R. B. BAKER, ESQ.

**26.** PHILIP YORKE, 1ST EARL OF HARDWICKE, LORD CHANCELLOR (1690-1764).

Born at Dover, entered at the Middle Temple, and was called to the bar in 1715. Elected M.P. for Lewes, and afterwards for Seaford, he was appointed Solicitor-General in 1720, Attorney-General in 1724, Chief Justice of the King's Bench in 1733, and in the same year created Baron Hardwicke. In 1737 he became Lord Chancellor, and presided as Lord High Steward at the trials of Lords Kilmarnock, Balmerino, &c., in 1746-7. Created Earl of Hardwicke in 1754. He resigned office with the Duke of Newcastle in 1756, and died March 6, 1764. He stood very high in reputation as an equity judge, and so great confidence was placed in his uprightness and his professional ability that of all his decisions as Chancellor not one was set aside. Walpole describes him as being "a most comely personage with a fine voice."

Three-quarter length, life-size, seated to right, in Chancellor's robes; on right table, on which purse of the Great Seal. Canvas 50 × 40 in.

By A. RAMSAY?  Lent by The EARL OF CHICHESTER.

**27.** QUEEN CAROLINE, WITH HER SON WILLIAM, DUKE OF CUMBERLAND.

Caroline, daughter of John Frederick, Margrave of Brandenburg-Anspach, born 1682, married at Hanover, George, the Electoral Prince of Hanover, afterwards George I. of England; became Queen on his accession, and died November 20, 1737. She was universally admired for her beauty and superior endowments, and was a munificent patroness of learning and genius. Her son, William, Duke of Cumberland, born in 1721, was wounded at Dettingen in 1743, and commanded at Fontenoy in 1745; but his fame principally rests on the active measures which he adopted for the suppression of the Scottish Rebellion, and his decisive victory at Culloden in 1746. Died suddenly in London in 1765.

Three-quarter length figures, life-size; the Queen to the right, in gold brocaded dress and ermine train; her left hand rests on the shoulder of her son, who wears the ribbon of the Garter, on which his right hand rests; to left, head of dog. Canvas 49 × 40 in.

By T. HUDSON.  Lent by The MARQUESS OF HARTINGTON, M.P.

**28.** PRINCESS AMELIA IN HUNTING COSTUME (1711-1786).

Second daughter of George II. Although highly accomplished she passed her life in celibacy, but apparently not without attachments. The Dukes of Grafton and Newcastle it was said, paid her great attention, and according to Walpole, the wooings of the former were so far from being disagreeable that the Princess and the Duke hunted two or three times a week together, and on one occasion stayed out unusually late, lost their attendants, and went together to a private house in Windsor Forest, to the great indignation of the Queen. She was Ranger of Richmond Park, and her manners and dress were exceedingly masculine, even to taking immense quantities of snuff. It was her custom to pass much time in her stables, and she usually wore a round hat and a riding habit in the German fashion. She died October 31, 1786.

Bust to left, life-size, in hunting costume. Canvas 20 × 16 in. Signed *D. Burlington*.
The painter wrote under the portrait
" Let others seek the Royal maid to prize,
See what Emilia is in Saville's eyes."
By DOROTHY, COUNTESS OF BURLINGTON.
Lent by The MARQUESS OF HARTINGTON, M.P.

**29.** GEORGE II. (1727-1760).

Life-size, equestrian portrait, to left, in scarlet military uniform; ribbon and Star of the Garter; cocked hat; in the background view of the Battle of Dettingen. Canvas 113 × 94 in.
By J. WOOTTON and PYNE.  Lent by HER MAJESTY THE QUEEN
(St. James's Palace).

**30.** PRINCESS ANNE (PRINCESS ROYAL), DAUGHTER OF GEORGE II. (d. 1759).

She married in 1734 William IV., Prince of Orange, and on his death became Regent of Holland. Died January 12, 1759.
Small full-length figure, in white satin brocade dress, and figured black shawl; standing in a garden at a tea-table, on which is a dog, which she touches with both hands. Canvas 29 × 22 in.
By T. NETSCHER.  Lent by ALFRED DE ROTHSCHILD, ESQ.

**31.** PRINCESS ANNE, DAUGHTER OF GEORGE II. (1709-1758).

Half-length, life-size, to left, nearly full-face; black dress, green and white striped-sleeves, cloak over right shoulder; set in an oval. Canvas 30 × 24 in.
By A. RAMSAY.  Lent by J. P. BOYCE, ESQ.

**32.** PHILIP DORMER STANHOPE, 4TH EARL OF CHESTERFIELD, K.G. (1694-1773).

One of the most shining characters of his time; was educated at Cambridge, made the tour of Europe, and appointed in 1715 Lord of the Bedchamber to the Prince of Wales. He entered Parliament for St. German's before the legal age, succeeded to the Earldom in 1722, appointed Ambassador to Holland in 1728, created a K.G., and made Lord Steward in 1730, but having opposed Walpole was compelled to resign his office. In 1745 he went to Ireland as Lord-Lieutenant, and by his exertions preserved tranquillity there, though a civil war was raging in England and Scotland. He returned in the following year to fill the office of Secretary of State which he resigned in 1748, and retiring into private life devoted himself to literary leisure. He wrote some letters in the *World*, took an active part in the reformation of the Calendar, but he is principally known for the letters addressed to his illegitimate son, Philip Stanhope. Lord Hervey (*Mem.* i., p. 96) describes his personal appearance as "very short, disproportioned, thick and clumsy made, had a broad rough-featured ugly face with black teeth, and a head long enough for a 'Polyphemus.'"

Half-length, life-size to left, head facing ; red coat, ribbon and star of the Garter, and wig. Canvas 26 × 20 in.

By T. HUDSON. Lent by The DUKE OF FIFE, K.T.

**33. SIR ROBERT WALPOLE, K.B., A.D. 1725, AFTERWARDS 1ST EARL OF ORFORD, K.G. (1676–1745).**

Three-quarter length, life-size, to left, wearing dark blue coat, wig, and the ribbon and star of the order of the Bath ; right hand holding paper rests on table, his left on his hip ; purse of the great seal on table. Canvas 50 × 40 in.

By CHARLES JERVAS. Lent by HENRY SPENCER WALPOLE, ESQ.

**34. GEORGE, LORD ANSON (1697–1762).**

Admiral. Son of William Anson, of Colwich, Staffordshire ; entered the navy and was made post-captain in 1724. In 1739 he was appointed commander of the expedition against the Spanish Settlements in the Pacific Ocean, and, departing in the following year, in the course of his voyage circumnavigated the globe, took several prizes, including the Acapulco galleon laden with silver bullion, from which coins bearing the name of LIMA were afterwards struck, and arrived again in England in 1744, having in a fog sailed through the midst of the French fleet then cruising in the Channel. In 1747, for his capture of six French men of war and for his previous services, Anson was created a peer, and in 1751 was appointed First Lord of the Admiralty. Died at Moor Park, Hertfordshire, June 6, 1762.

Three-quarter length, life-size, facing, in naval dress ; right hand extended holds baton, in left his hat ; sea and ship in background. Canvas 50 × 40 in.

By G. ROMNEY. Lent by The DUKE OF RICHMOND AND GORDON, K.G.

**35. FREDERICK, PRINCE OF WALES, AS A CHILD (1707–1751).**

Three-quarter length, life-size, to right, head to left ; red frock, Ribbon and Star of the Garter. Canvas 30 × 24 in.

Lent by The REV. J. E. WALDY.

WEST GALLERY.] *Portraits.* 13

**36. PRINCESS AUGUSTA, WIFE OF FREDERICK, PRINCE OF WALES, AND HER CHILDREN, PRINCESS AUGUSTA, PRINCE GEORGE, PRINCE EDWARD, AND OTHERS.**

Princess Augusta was the youngest daughter of Frederick, Duke of Saxe-Gotha. She was born in 1719, married Frederick Lewis, Prince of Wales, in 1736, and died at Carlton House, February 8, 1772. Her sons, Prince George (1738—1820), afterwards succeeded as George III., and Prince Edward (1739—1767) was created Duke of York and Albany. Her daughter, Princess Augusta, married Charles, Duke of Brunswick.

Life-size group; the Princess Augusta, in crimson-gold brocade dress, is seated in the centre; rests her right arm on a table, and with left holds her daughter, who stands at her side. On the Princess's right, seated on a table, is Prince George. The Lady Anne Hamilton holds Prince Edward in her arms, and near her is Mrs. Herbert. To the left of the Princess stands Lord Boston. Canvas 86 × 77 in.

By J. ZOFFANY, R.A.        Lent by HER MAJESTY THE QUEEN
(Buckingham Palace).

**37. CHARLOTTE SOPHIA, BARONESS KIELMANSEGG, COUNTESS OF DARLINGTON (d. 1730).**

Wife of Baron Kielmansegg, Master of the Horse to George I. when Elector; was mistress of George I., who created her Countess of Platen in Germany, and in 1721 Countess of Leinster in England, and in 1722 Countess of Darlington. Died 1730.

Half-length, life-size, to left, in puce dress. Canvas 31 × 26 in.

By SIR G. KNELLER.        Lent by The COUNT KIELMANSEGG.

**38. HENRY FOX, 1ST LORD HOLLAND (1705–1774).**

Statesman. Second son of Sir Stephen Fox; entered Parliament for Hendon in 1735, was made Surveyor-General of the Board of Trade, in 1743 a Commissioner of the Treasury, in 1746 Secretary for War, and in 1757 Paymaster of the Forces, in which office his conduct brought him into great obloquy. His wife, Georgiana Caroline, eldest daughter of Charles, 2nd Duke of Richmond, was created Baroness Holland of Holland, co. Lincoln, in 1762, and the next year he was raised to the Peerage as Lord Holland of Foxley, Wilts.

Bust, to right, nearly full face; gold edged brown coat and wig. Canvas 23½ × 19 in.

Nichols (works of Hogarth) does not give any date to this picture. It was probably one of his latest works. It formerly belonged to Mr. Samuel Ireland. The etching by Joseph Haynes, was done from an unfinished sketch by Hogarth. The painter introduced a portrait of Lord Holland, then Mr. Fox, in Plate II. of *The Harlot's Progress*, and again in Plate II. of *The Times*, where he appears on the platform in the act of removing the garden pots.

By W. HOGARTH.        Lent by The EARL OF ILCHESTER.

14     *Exhibition of the Royal House of Guelph.*

**39.** BARON KIELMANSEGG, MASTER OF THE HORSE TO GEORGE I.

Half-length figure, to left, in armour, and wig.   Canvas 30 × 25 in.   (See No. 37.)

By SIR G. KNELLER.     Lent by The COUNT KIELMANSEGG.

**40.** HOUSE OF COMMONS : SPEAKER ONSLOW (1730).

View of interior of the House. According to a paper at back, signed A.O., the figures are :—(1) The Speaker, Arthur Onslow ; (2) Sir Robert Walpole (blue ribbon); (3) Sidney Godolphin (in red) ; (4) Col. R. Onslow, M.P. (in front row) ; (5) Sir J. Thornhill, M.P. (front row).

By SIR J. THORNHILL and W. HOGARTH.     Lent by The EARL OF ONSLOW.

**41.** THOMAS PELHAM HOLLES, DUKE OF NEWCASTLE, K.G. (1693-1768).

Son of Thomas, 1st Lord Pelham and Grace, sister of John Duke of Newcastle. Inherited great wealth both from his father whom he succeeded in the title in 1712, and from his uncle the Duke of Newcastle. Being a strong adherent of the House of Hanover he filled many important offices during the reign of George I. and George II. He was made a K.G. in 1718, appointed Secretary of State in 1724, and on the death of his brother, Sir William Pelham in 1754, succeeded him as First Lord of the Treasury. He was created Duke of Newcastle-under-Lyne November 13, 1756. His reputation as a statesman was not of the highest order, and the loss of Port Mahon and the death of Admiral Byng led to his resignation in 1756, but he resumed office in the following year and resigned to Lord Bute in 1762.

Three-quarter length, life-size, seated nearly facing, in robes of the Garter, collar and badge ; his right hand extended ; left, gloved, rests on his hip.  Canvas 50 × 40 in.

By W. HOARE, R.A.     Lent by The EARL OF CHICHESTER.

**42.** LIONEL SACKVILLE, 1ST DUKE OF DORSET K.G. (1688-1765).

Son of Charles 6th Earl of Dorset; succeeded as 7th Earl in 1706, was sent to Hanover to announce the death of Queen Anne to George I., elected a K.G. in 1714, and in 1720 created Duke of Dorset. He was one of the Lord Justices of England during the King's absence in 1727, and Lord-Lieutenant of Ireland from 1730-1737, and again from 1750-1755.

Full-length, life-size, to left, in robes of the Garter ; in right hand plumed hat ; his left rests on his hip ; architectural background.   Canvas 93 × 57 in.

By SIR G. KNELLER.     Lent by The LORD SACKVILLE.

WEST GALLERY.] *Portraits.* 15

**43.** SIR RICHARD STEELE, KNT. (1671–1729).

Half-length, life-size, head to left; blue gown and cap. Canvas 30 × 24 in.
This picture was formerly in the collection of Edward Harley, Earl of Oxford.
By SIR G. KNELLER. Lent by The STATIONERS' COMPANY.

**44.** "THE MALL."

View of St. James's Park, various groups, some strolling, others seated; the two figures to the right of the centre of the picture acing and wearing the ribbon and star of the Garter, are supposed to be Frederick Prince of Wales and his brother the Duke of Cumberland; in the distance Westminster Abbey. Canvas 54 × 40½ in.

This picture was first exhibited in the British Gallery in 1814. Nichols describes it as a very fine subject for a first-rate engraver. It is not mentioned either by Walpole or Ireland amongst the works of Hogarth. John Galt was of opinion that it was really painted by Jeminiani an Italian artist. Another suggestion is that it is the work of Samuel Wale, R.A.

By W. HOGARTH (?) Lent by HER MAJESTY THE QUEEN
(Windsor).

**45.** ANNE LUTTRELL, MRS. HORTON, AFTERWARDS DUCHESS OF CUMBERLAND (d. 1803).

Daughter of Simon Luttrell, afterwards Earl of Carhampton; married, 1st, Christopher Horton, Esq., of Colton Hall, Derbyshire, and 2ndly, Henry Frederick, Duke of Cumberland, brother of King George III. Survived her husband, and died, 1803.

Three-quarter length, life-size, to left, in white and red dress, hair powdered; left arm crossed in front. Canvas 50 × 40 in.

This is a sketch made probably about 1777, in which year Gainsborough exhibited at the Royal Academy his finished picture of the Duchess and her husband.
By T. GAINSBOROUGH, R.A. Lent by HER MAJESTY THE QUEEN
(Windsor).

**46.** EDWARD HARLEY, SECOND EARL OF OXFORD (1689–1741).

Son of Robert, 1st Earl; eminent for his literary tastes. Was the friend of Pope, Swift, Prior, and others. Made valuable additions to the library formed by his father, and also brought together a large collection of pictures, medals, and miscellaneous curiosities.

Half-length, life-size, to left, head facing, red coat and cap.
By J. RICHARDSON. Lent by The EARL OF KINNOULL.

**47.** RIGHT HON. HENRY PELHAM, M.P. (1696–1754).

Statesman. Was the brother of Thomas Holles Pelham, Duke of Newcastle; served as a volunteer at Preston in 1715, and entering Parliament for Seaford, Sussex, in 1718, as a follower of Sir Robert Walpole, was made a Lord of the Treasury in 1721, Secretary for War in 1724, and Paymaster of the Forces in 1730. On the union of the parties in 1743 he was placed at the head of the administration, reserving for himself the offices of Prime Minister and Chancellor of the Exchequer. Died in office, March 6, 1754. The period of his ascendency in the Cabinet is generally known as the "Pelham Administration."

> Three-quarter length, life-size, seated to right, in robes of the Exchequer, and wig; in left hand paper, right resting on chair. Canvas 50 × 40 in.
> Painted in 1752.

By WILLIAM HOARE, R.A.      Lent by The EARL OF CHICHESTER.

**48.** ROBERT, LORD CLIVE, K.C.B. (1725-1774).

The founder of the British Empire in India. Born at Styche in Shropshire, entered the Civil Service of the East India Company in 1741, but in 1747 quitted it for the military service; distinguished himself at Pondicherry and at the taking of Devicota in Tanjore. In 1751 he took Arcot, and his subsequent defence of that place was as remarkable as his capture of it. After visiting England for his health he returned to India in 1755, and in 1757 recovered Calcutta from Suraj-ud-Daulah, and on June 23 of that year gained the victory of Plassey. It was under the title of "Baron Clive of Plassey" that in 1762 he was raised to the Irish peerage. In 1764 he was appointed Governor-General of India, and after his return to England in 1769 was made a K.C.B. His health, both of body and mind, having been undermined by his exertions and by the bitter attacks in Parliament, he died by his own hand at his house in Berkeley Square, November 22, 1714.

> Three-quarter length, life-size, to right, head turned to left; in military dress, ribbon of the Bath, and wig; right hand pointing, left holding hilt of sword; landscape background, with military camp in the distance. Canvas 44 × 37 in.

By SIR N. DANCE, R.A.      Lent by The REV. J. E. WALFORD.

**49.** GEORGE III. (1738-1820).

Eldest son of Frederick Prince of Wales, succeeded 1760, married 1761, Charlotte, daughter of Charles, Duke of Mecklenburg-Strelitz, was mentally deranged during the later years of his reign. Died 29th Jan. 1820.

> Three-quarter length, life-size, to right, blue gold-embroidered coat, red mantle lined with ermine, ribbon of the Garter; right hand on hip, crown on cushion to right. Canvas 50 × 40 in.
>
> Painted in January, 1759, as this was the first and only sitting which the Prince of Wales gave to Reynolds before his accession.

By SIR J. REYNOLDS, P.R.A.      Lent by HER MAJESTY THE QUEEN
                                                         (St. James's Palace).

## Portraits.

**50. RICHARD BRINSLEY SHERIDAN (1751–1816).**

Bust facing; head to right; close-shaven; blue coat, yellow waistcoat. Canvas 24 × 20 in.

By A. HICKEL.                                  Lent by HER MAJESTY THE QUEEN
                                                              (Hampton Court).

**51. GEORGE III. (1760–1820).**

Full-length, life-size, turned slightly to the right, blue coat with gold braid, buff waistcoat and breeches, and wig; his right hand rests on the ribbon of the Garter; in left his hat; in background, portico of a palace and park. Canvas 95 × 61 in.

Exhibited at the Royal Academy in 1781.

By T. GAINSBOROUGH, R.A.                      Lent by HER MAJESTY THE QUEEN
                                                              (Buckingham Palace).

**52. PRINCESS CHARLOTTE, AFTERWARDS QUEEN OF WÜRTEMBERG (1766–1828).**

Princess Royal, eldest dau. of George III.; married May 18, 1797, Frederick Charles William, then Duke (but subsequently King) of Würtemberg, by whom she had no issue.

Three-quarter length, life-size; seated to right; blue dress and red sash, order of Würtemberg; her right elbow rests on the sofa on which she is seated. Canvas 35 × 27½ in.

The series of portraits by Sir William Beechey of the children of George III. exhibited by permission of Her Majesty the Queen, were executed by the painter during his residence at Court in the capacity of instructor to the princesses, who, with the King and Queen, entertained for him the strongest regard to the end of his life.

By SIR W. BEECHEY, R.A.                       Lent by HER MAJESTY THE QUEEN
                                                              (Buckingham Palace).

**53. PRINCESS AMELIA, 6TH DAUGHTER OF GEORGE III. (b. 1783; d. unm. 1810).**

Three-quarter length, life-size, seated facing, head to right, white dress and blue sash, the arms crossed on her lap; before her on a table is a book; the fingers of the left hand are inserted in a portfolio. Canvas 35 × 27½ in.

By SIR W. BEECHEY, R.A.                       Lent by HER MAJESTY THE QUEEN
                                                              (Buckingham Palace).

18    Exhibition of the Royal House of Guelph.

**54.** GEORGE IV. AS PRINCE OF WALES (1762-1830).

Eldest son of George III.; married, 1795, Princess Caroline, second daughter of Charles, Duke of Brunswick Wolfenbüttel; appointed Regent 1811, succeeded to the throne 1820. Died 1830.

Half-length, life-size, to right, head turned to left, green coat with gold trimmings, powdered hair. Canvas (oval) 28 × 22 in.

Probably painted in 1782, and exhibited in the Royal Academy that year.

By T. GAINSBOROUGH, R.A.    Lent by The MARQUESS OF LOTHIAN, K.T.


**55.** PRINCESS SOPHIA, DAUGHTER OF GEORGE III., (b. 1777; d. *unm.* 1848).

Three-quarter length, life-size; seated to left; white dress, blue sash, and ribbon in her hair, arms folded on her lap. Canvas 35 × 27½ in.

By SIR W. BEECHEY, R.A.    Lent by HER MAJESTY THE QUEEN
(Buckingham Palace).


**56.** JOHN, MARQUESS OF GRANBY (1721-1770).

General. Eldest son of John, 3rd Duke of Rutland, entered the army, and in 1745 raised a regiment of foot at his own expense. He obtained high military reputation as Commander-in-Chief of the British Forces, serving under Prince Ferdinand of Brunswick in the Seven Years' War in Germany. After the peace of 1763, he was named Master-General of the Ordnance, and in 1766 Commander-in-Chief. He represented Cambridge in Parliament, and was twice re-elected.

Full-length, life-size, to left, in military dress, steel cuirass; resting his left arm on the withers of his horse, on the other side of which stands a negro; battle scene in the distance. Canvas 96 × 80 in.

By SIR J. REYNOLDS, P.R.A.    Lent by HER MAJESTY THE QUEEN
(St. James's Palace).


**57.** QUEEN CHARLOTTE (1744-1818).

Second daughter of Charles Louis Frederick, Duke of Mecklenburg-Strelitz; married George III. September 8, 1761, by whom she had fifteen children; died November 17, 1818.

Full-length, life-size, to right, head to left, white dress embroidered in gold, powdered

hair; arms crossed, right hand holding fan; dog at her feet; architectural background and landscape. Canvas 95 × 61 in.
Exhibited at the Royal Academy in 1781.
By T. GAINSBOROUGH, R.A.     Lent by HER MAJESTY THE QUEEN
(Buckingham Palace).

**58.** PRINCESS ELIZABETH (1770–1840).

3rd daughter of George III.; married 7th April, 1818, Frederick, Landgrave and Prince of Hesse-Homburg. Died 10th June, 1840. In her childhood she was lively, intelligent, and remarkably beautiful. She was an accomplished artist, and many of her drawings were engraved.

Three-quarter length, life-size, seated to left at a table with drawing-pencil in right hand; her head rests on her left hand; red dress with slashed sleeves; flowers on table. Canvas 35 × 27½ in.
By SIR W. BEECHEY, R.A.     Lent by HER MAJESTY THE QUEEN
(Buckingham Palace).

**59.** MARGARET GEORGIANA, COUNTESS SPENCER (1737–1814).

Daughter of the Right Hon. Stephen Poyntz, of Midgham, Berks; married in 1775 John first Earl Spencer, by whom she had issue George John, second Earl, and two daughters, Georgiana, who became Duchess of Devonshire, and Henrietta, afterwards Countess of Bessborough, both remarkable for their beauty.

Half-length, life-size, facing, left hand supporting head; black dress, white cap with blue ribbon. Canvas (oval) 24 × 19½ in.
    Lent by The DUKE OF DEVONSHIRE, K.G.

**60.** HENRY, 12TH EARL OF SUFFOLK AND 5TH EARL OF BERKSHIRE K.G. (1739–1779).

Son of William, Lord Andover. Was educated at Eton and Magdalen College, Oxford; succeeded as 12th Earl in 1757; appointed bearer of the second sword at the Coronation of George III., deputy Earl-Marshal of England, 1763-65, Lord Keeper of the Privy Seal, 1771, and elected a K.G. June 3, 1778. Died March 7, 1779, "an absolute cripple to gout."

Three-quarter length, life-size; seated facing in a library, head to right; light-brown coat, grey vest, hair powdered *en perruque*; ribbon and star of the Garter; his right hand rests on papers, his left on his knee. Canvas 50 × 40 in.
By SIR J. REYNOLDS, P.R.A.     Lent by The EARL OF SUFFOLK AND BERKSHIRE.

**61.** EDWARD, 12TH EARL OF DERBY (1752-1834).

Son of John, Lord Stanley, and grandson of the 11th Earl; married June 23, 1774, Lady Elizabeth Hamilton, only daughter of James VI., Duke of Hamilton. Succeeded his grandfather in the Earldom in 1776; held the office of Chancellor of the Duchy of Lancaster in 1783, and again in 1806. He married 2ndly, in 1797, Miss Elizabeth Farren, the actress.

Three-quarter length, life-size, to left, head facing; blue coat, buff waistcoat and breeches, hair *en perruque;* right hand resting on parapet holds a glove; in his left a hat. Canvas 50 × 40 in.

By T. GAINSBOROUGH, R.A.      Lent by The EARL OF DERBY, K.G.

**62.** GEORGE, VISCOUNT SACKVILLE (1716-1785).

Soldier and statesman. Son of the 1st Duke of Dorset, born June 26, 1716, was present at Dettingen and Fontenoy, and served under the Duke of Cumberland in the Rebellion of '45. At the battle of Minden, August 1, 1759, he commanded the allied cavalry, and for his failure to execute the commander-in-chief's order to charge the retiring French cavalry he was court-martialled and dismissed the service. Restored to favour by George III., he entered the Cabinet of Lord North, as Secretary of State for the Colonies, retaining office during the American revolutionary war. Created a viscount February 11, 1782. Died August 26, 1785. In his person, which was to nearly six feet, he was muscular, and capable of enduring much bodily as well as mental fatigue. His countenance indicated intellect, particularly his eye, the motion of which was quick and piercing (Wraxall, *Hist. Mem.*).

Three-quarter length, life-size, seated to left; blue gold-embroidered coat, white satin waistcoat and wig; in his right hand he holds a paper; his left rests on the arm of his chair. Canvas 50 × 40 in.

By T. GAINSBOROUGH, R.A.      Lent by The LORD SACKVILLE.

**63.** WILLIAM WYNDHAM, LORD GRENVILLE (1759-1834).

Statesman. Son of George Grenville; entered Parliament for Buckingham in 1782, and through his friendship with Pitt was appointed Paymaster-General in 1783, Speaker of the House of Commons and Home Secretary in 1789, and being removed to the House of Lords in 1790 by a patent of peerage, became thus the echo of William Pitt. He resigned with Pitt on the Catholic Emancipation question in 1801, afterwards joined the Opposition, and was Prime Minister of " All the Talents," 1806-7. After this time he held no public appointments, but continued his efforts for Catholic Emancipation. Died without issue, 1834.

Three-quarter length, life-size, to left, in peer's robes and wig; in left hand papers; right rests on hip. Canvas 50 × by 40 in.

By GAINSBOROUGH DUPONT.      Lent by The EARL FORTESCUE.

**64. FRANCIS, 2ND EARL OF GODOLPHIN (1678-1766).**

Half-length, life-size, to right; brown coat and wig. Canvas 29 × 25½ in. (see No. 24).

Lent by The DUKE OF LEEDS.

**65. PRINCESS MARY, DUCHESS OF GLOUCESTER (1776-1857).**

4th dau. of George III; married in 1816 her cousin William Frederick, Duke of Gloucester, by whom she had no issue.

Three-quarter length, life-size, seated to right; white dress; the arms folded on her lap; in left hand a drawing, and before her on a table the bust of a child which she has been copying. Canvas 35 × 27½ in.

By SIR W. BEECHEY, R.A.  Lent by HER MAJESTY THE QUEEN (Buckingham Palace).

**66. PRINCESS AUGUSTA SOPHIA, 2ND DAUGHTER OF GEORGE III. (b. 8 Nov. 1768; d. unm. 1840).**

Three-quarter length, life-size, to left, seated, white dress and yellow girdle; she holds in her two hands a drawing-book; on a table to right is a bust. Canvas 35 × 27½ in.

By SIR W. BEECHEY, R.A.  Lent by HER MAJESTY THE QUEEN (Buckingham Palace).

**67. CHILDREN OF GEORGE III.**

The portraits are those of Princess Mary, born in 1776, afterwards Duchess of Gloucester; the Princess Sophia, born in 1777, died 1848; and the Princess Amelia, born in 1783, died in 1810; the last was the youngest and the favourite child of the King; her death, it has always been said, brought on the sad malady with which the monarch was afflicted shortly after her decease.

Princess Mary, in yellow and white dress, holds aloft a tambourine in left hand, and with right draws a little carriage in which are seated her two sisters; Princess Sophia, in pink dress and blue hat and sash, holds her younger sister's right hand, and has an umbrella in her left; the baby wears white frock, blue sash, and white hat and cap, and holds on to her sister with both hands; dogs and flowers in foreground; columns with wreaths of vine, in which are perched two macaws; distant view of Windsor. Canvas 104 × 73 in.

This is one of Copley's finest pictures in arrangement and colour. It was formerly at Windsor. "Copley painted so slowly and tediously, and required such long sittings, that when he was at Windsor painting this picture the attendants, children, dogs, and parrots became equally wearied. The attendants complained to the Queen, the Queen complained to the King, and the King complained to West, who

had obtained the commission for Copley, and who succeeded in convincing the King that the painter must be allowed to go on his own way, and take his own time."
By J. S. COPLEY, R.A.  Lent by HER MAJESTY THE QUEEN
(Buckingham Palace).

**68.** MARIA WALPOLE, COUNTESS WALDEGRAVE AND DUCHESS OF GLOUCESTER (1737-1807).

Second illegitimate daughter of Sir Edward Walpole, K.B. Married first, James, 2nd Earl Waldegrave; and secondly, William Henry, Duke of Gloucester, 1st son of Frederick, Prince of Wales, by whom she was the mother of William Frederick, 2nd Duke of Gloucester and Princesses Sophia and Caroline. Died August 22, 1807.

Three-quarter length, life-size, to right; white dress, red mantle; left arm rests on pedestal; landscape background. Canvas 48 × 40. in.

Lent by H.R.H. The DUKE OF CAMBRIDGE, K.G.

**69.** RIGHT HON. GEORGE GRENVILLE (1712–1770).

Statesman. Younger brother of Richard Grenville, Earl Temple, sat in Parliament for Buckingham from 1741 till his death. Appointed in 1754 Treasurer of the Navy, in 1763 First Lord of the Admiralty, and in the same year Prime Minister. During his administration the contest with Wilkes began, and the American Stamp Act was introduced. In 1765 he resigned his office to the Marquess of Rockingham. His grandson was created, in 1822, Duke of Buckingham and Chandos.

Three-quarter length, life-size, seated to left, in robes of Chancellor of the Exchequer and wig; in right hand, paper, his left rests on arm of chair. Inscribed RT. HONBLE. GEORGE GRENVILLE, 1764. Canvas 50 × 40 in.

By A. RAMSAY.  Lent by CHRIST CHURCH, OXFORD.

**70.** CHARLES, 3RD DUKE OF RICHMOND, K.G. (1735-1806).

Half-length, life-size, to left, blue coat and wig. Canvas 29 × 24 in.

By G. ROMNEY.  Lent by The BARONESS BURDETT-COUTTS.

**71.** WILLIAM HENRY, 1ST DUKE OF GLOUCESTER, K.G. (1743-1805).

Third son of Frederick, Prince of Wales, born November 25, 1743, served in several continental expeditions, and by gradations attained the rank of senior Field-Marshal; created Duke of Gloucester on his majority, and shortly after married Maria, Countess Dowager of Waldegrave, September 6, 1766, thereby incurring the displeasure of George III. (see No. 68). In consequence the Duke and Duchess resided in Italy till 1776, when a reconciliation took place. Died August 26, 1805.

Half-length, life-size, facing, head to left, in military uniform, and star of the Garter. Canvas 30 × 24 in.

Lent by H.R.H. The DUKE OF CAMBRIDGE, K.G.

### 72. AUGUSTUS FREDERICK, DUKE OF SUSSEX, K.G. (1773–1843).

Sixth son of George III.; born January 27, 1773, studied at Göttingen; married when a minor Lady Augusta de Ameland, daughter of John (Murray) 4th Earl of Dunmore, whereby he incurred the King's displeasure, and the marriage being deemed a violation of the Royal Marriage Act, was declared null and void. Created Duke of Sussex in 1798. He is known as a friend of Science and Art; was elected P.R.S. in 1838; died April 21, 1843, and buried at his special desire at Kensal Green.

Half-length, life-size, to left, in black coat, and star of the Garter. Canvas 30 × 24 in.

Lent by H.R.H. The DUKE OF CAMBRIDGE, K.G.

### 73. FREDERICK, DUKE OF YORK (1763–1827).

Second son of George III., born August 16, 1763; entered the army in 1780, studied military science at Berlin, created Duke of York in 1784; was Commander-in-Chief in Flanders in 1794, but was recalled and nominated Field-Marshal and Commander-in-Chief of the Army. He served again in Holland in 1799, this being his last command. He was popular as the "Soldiers' Friend."

Full-length, life-size, to right, in Garter robes; left hand on sword, right on his hip, plumed cap on table to left; architectural background. Canvas 92 × 58 in.

Lent by HER MAJESTY THE QUEEN
(St. James's Palace).

### 74. QUEEN CAROLINE, WIFE OF GEORGE IV. (1768–1821).

Second daughter of Charles William Ferdinand, Duke of Brunswick-Wolfenbüttel. Born at Brunswick; married in 1795, her cousin George, Prince of Wales. The marriage was not pleasing to him, and a separation took place after the birth of Princess Charlotte in 1796. Having obtained leave to travel on the Continent she left England in 1814, and did not return till the accession of George IV., when she was proceeded against by Bill of Pains and Penalties in the House of Lords, which, on account of the splendid defence of Brougham, the ministry were obliged to abandon. She was prevented from occupying her position as Queen, was refused coronation, and died August 7, 1821. Buried at Brunswick.

Three-quarter length, life-size; seated, to right, in black dress, ermine cloak and ewelled diadem; in right hand she holds a letter inscribed "For His Majesty the King;" left rests on arm of chair; on left crown on cushion. Canvas 55 × 43 in.

Presented to the Corporation of London by Her Majesty Queen Caroline in 1820.

By J. LONSDALE. Lent by The CORPORATION OF THE CITY OF LONDON.

### 75. QUEEN CHARLOTTE (1744–1818).

Half-length, life-size, facing, head to left, white dress, blue sleeves, ermine tippet, pearl necklace and ornaments. Pastel 23 × 17 in.

By MISS READ. Lent by The EARL OF CHICHESTER.

**76. GEORGE IV. AS PRINCE REGENT (1762-1830).**

By RICHARD COSWAY, R.A.   Lent by The HON. and REV. E. V. BLIGH.

**77. WILLIAM FREDERICK, 2ND DUKE OF GLOUCESTER, K.G. (1776-1834).**

Son of William Henry, 1st Duke of Gloucester, born at Rome, January 15, 1776, served under the Duke of York in Holland, and was made a Field-Marshal in the army, married July 22, 1816, his first cousin Princess Mary, daughter of George III., and died without issue. November 30, 1834.

Half-length, life-size, to right, in military uniform, and ribbon and star of the Garter, and badge and star of the Guelphs; hat in right hand. Canvas 36 × 28 in.

Lent by H.R.H., The DUKE OF CAMBRIDGE., K.G.

**78. VICTORIA MARY LOUISA, DUCHESS OF KENT (1786-1861).**

Youngest child of Francis, Duke of Saxe-Coburg, born at Coburg 17 Aug. 1786; married first in 1803 Emich Carl, Prince of Leiningen, who left her a widow in 1814: she then married in May, 1818, Edward Duke of Kent, and became mother of Her Majesty the Queen; was left a widow Jan. 1820, and devoted herself to the education of her daughter, with whom she continued to live from her accession to her marriage. Died at Frogmore 16 Jan. 1861.

Three-quarter length, life-size, seated to right, her hands on her lap, black dress; coronet on her head. Canvas 35 × 27 in.

By G. DAWE, R.A.   Lent by HER MAJESTY THE QUEEN
(Windsor).

**79. GEORGE IV. AS PRINCE OF WALES (1762-1832).**

Half-length, life-size, head to left, in Hussar uniform, with badge of the Garter; hair powdered *en perruque.* Canvas 30 × 24 in.

By J. HOPPNER, R.A.   Lent by H.R.H. THE PRINCESS LOUISE
(Marchioness of Lorne).

**80. EDWARD, DUKE OF KENT, K.G. (1767-1820).**

Fourth son of George III. and father of Her Majesty the Queen; born November 2, 1767, educated at Göttingen and Hanover; served with distinction in the army, in Canada, and the West Indies, and attained the rank of Field-Marshal; was Governor of Gibraltar in

1802; married Victoria Mary Louisa, widow of the Prince of Leiningen, May 20, 1818, who gave birth to Her Majesty the Queen, May 24, 1819. Died suddenly at Sidmouth, January 23, 1830.

Half-length, life-size, to left, in military uniform, ribbon and star of the Garter and other orders; left hand on hip. Canvas 35 × 30 in.

*Lent by* H.R.H. The DUKE OF CAMBRIDGE, K.G.

**81.** ERNEST AUGUSTUS, DUKE OF CUMBERLAND, KING OF HANOVER, K.G. (1771–1851).

Fifth son of George III., born June 5, 1771, created Duke of Cumberland in 1799, married Princess Frederica, 3rd daughter of the Duke of Mecklenburg-Strelitz in 1815, and succeeded to the Crown of Hanover on the accession of Her Majesty Queen Victoria in 1837; died November 18, 1851.

Half-length, life-size, to left, in Hussar uniform, and ribbon of the Garter, busby in left hand. Canvas 36 × 28 in.

*Lent by* H.R.H. The DUKE OF CAMBRIDGE, K.G.

**82.** PRINCESS CHARLOTTE AUGUSTA OF WALES (1796–1817).

Only child of George IV. and Queen Caroline, married 1816 Prince Leopold of Coburg, afterwards King of the Belgians. Died in childbirth 1817.

Three-quarter length, life-size, seated to right, head turned to left; blue dress trimmed with gold, white bodice and sleeves; her left arm rests on portfolio; her left hand holds drapery, which lies over the back of the couch; curtain and landscape background. Canvas 55 × 43 in.

*Lent by* H.R.H. The DUKE OF CAMBRIDGE, K.G.

**83.** WILLIAM PITT, 1ST EARL OF CHATHAM (1708–1778).

This great statesman and orator, known as "the Great Commoner," born November 15, 1708, was educated at Eton and Oxford, entered Parliament in 1735 for Old Sarum, and enlisted early in the ranks of the opposition against Walpole. In 1746 he was appointed Vice-Treasurer for Ireland, and soon after Paymaster of the Army; Secretary of State in 1755, and Prime Minister from 1757-1761, a period of glorious victories to British Arms. In 1766 Pitt returned to office having received the royal commission to form a Ministry. He chose for himself the office of Privy Seal, with a seat in the House of Lords as Viscount Pitt and Earl of Chatham. Ill health compelled his retirement in 1768, but he still took an active part in public affairs, strongly opposing the Government with all his powers of eloquence in its harsh policy towards the American colonies. It was on one of these occasions, on April 7, 1778, whilst addressing the House, that he was seized with a fit, falling into the arms of those who were near him. Died May 11 following, and was buried in Westminster Abbey.

Half-length, life-size, to left, brown coat and wig. 23½ × 17½ in.
Purchased at the Stowe Sale.

Lent by The EARL FORTESCUE.

**84. ADOLPHUS FREDERICK, DUKE OF CAMBRIDGE, K.G. (1774–1850).**

Youngest son of George III.; born February 24, 1774; educated at Göttingen; served under the Duke of York in Flanders in 1793; created Duke of Cambridge in 1795; appointed Colonel-in-Chief of the King's German Legion in 1803, Field-Marshal in 1813, and, on the restoration of Hanover, its Viceroy, 1815-1837. He married in 1818 Princess Wilhelmina Louise of Hesse, by whom he had issue H.R.H. the present Duke of Cambridge and the Princess Mary. Died July 8, 1850.

Half-length, life-size, to left, in black coat, and star of the Garter. Canvas 30 × 24 in.
By SIR W. BEECHEY, R.A.    Lent by H.R.H. The DUKE OF CAMBRIDGE, K.G.

**85. MRS. MARIA ANNA FITZHERBERT (1756–1837).**

Youngest daughter of Walter Smythe of Bambridge, Hants; married 1st, Edward Weld of Lulworth Castle, who died the same year, 1775; 2ndly, Thomas Fitzherbert of Swinnerton, county Stafford, who died in 1781. Soon afterwards her beauty and fascinating manners attracted the particular attention of the Prince of Wales (George IV.), and she consented to a marriage with him according to the rite of the Roman Church. At the command of the Prince, Fox denied the marriage in the House of Commons. Mrs. Fitzherbert died at Brighton, March 27, 1837.

Three-quarter length, life-size, to left, brown bodice, grey lace shawl; right hand raised to the face; powdered hair. Canvas 29 × 24 in.
Left by Mrs. Fitzherbert to the Hon. Mrs. Dawson Damer, and by her to the late Countess Fortescue.

By T. GAINSBOROUGH, R.A.    Lent by The EARL FORTESCUE.

**86. ELIZABETH, LADY CRAVEN, MARGRAVINE OF ANSPACH (d. 1828).**

Daughter of Augustus, 4th Earl Berkeley. Married first 18 May, 1767, William, 6th Baron Craven, and secondly, Christian Frederick, Margrave of Brandenburg Anspach and Bayreuth. Died 1828.

Full length, life-size, walking to left, white satin dress and cap with gold trimming; architectural and landscape background. Canvas 94 × 57 in.

By G. ROMNEY.    Lent by The FISHMONGERS' COMPANY.

## 87. WILLIAM IV. AS DUKE OF CLARENCE (1765-1837).

Third son of George III. Born August 21, 1765; entered the Royal Navy in 1778, attained the rank of Post-Captain in 1786, and was created Duke of Clarence and St. Andrews, and Earl of Munster in 1789. Having passed through the grades of Rear-Admiral and Admiral, his Royal Highness succeeded Sir Peter Parker as Admiral of the Fleet in 1811, and was appointed Lord High Admiral of England in 1827. Succeeded to the throne June 26, 1830, died June 20, 1837. His Majesty married, July 11, 1818, Princess Adelaide, eldest daughter of George, Duke of Saxe-Meiningen.

Three-quarter length, life-size, facing; head to right, in blue coat, white waistcoat and grey trousers, and Star of the Garter; left hand holds glove and stick; hat in right; sea and rock in the background. Canvas 50 × 40.

By SIR THOMAS LAWRENCE, P.R.A.    Lent by The LORD DE L'ISLE AND DUDLEY.

## 88. QUEEN ADELAIDE, CONSORT OF WILLIAM IV. (1792-1849).

Eldest child of George, Duke of Saxe-Meiningen, and Louisa, daughter of Christian Albert, Prince of Hohenlohe Langenburg; born August 13, 1792; married the Duke of Clarence July 11, 1818; became Queen of England on the accession of the Duke of Clarence as William IV. in 1830; Queen Dowager in 1837. Died at Bentley Priory, near Stanmore, Middlesex, December 2, 1849.

Half-length, life-size, to right, head facing; brown dress, with deep lace collar and cap; with both hands she holds vase of flowers. Canvas 30 × 24 in.

By E. PARRIS.    Lent by JOHN CLELAND, ESQ., of Stormont.

## 89. PRINCESS SOPHIA MATILDA OF GLOUCESTER, DAUGHTER OF WILLIAM, 2ND DUKE (1773-1844).

Three-quarter length, life-size, seated to left; left elbow on table, white dress; curtain behind. Canvas 30 × 24½ in.

By J. HOPPNER, R.A.    Lent by H. L. BISCHOFFSHEIM, ESQ.

## 90. GEORGE IV. (1820-1827).

Small, full-length, standing to left, in Coronation robes; his right hand rests on table, his left on his hip. Canvas 34 × 26 in.

By SIR T. LAWRENCE, P.R.A.    Lent by JOHN CLELAND, ESQ., of Stormont.

**91.** WILLIAM WILBERFORCE (1759–1833).

Philanthropist. Born at Hull; was educated at St. John's College, Cambridge, and on coming of age was elected M.P. for his native place. In 1787 he began to distinguish himself by his exertions for the abolition of the slave trade, which, after a severe contest, was finally decreed in 1807. Wilberforce at first approved the principles of the French Revolution, and in 1792 was voted the right of French citizenship, but in 1801 he denounced the designs of Buonaparte, and supported the Government in its vigorous measures against France. Died in London, July 29, 1833.

Three-quarter length, life-size, seated in red chair, facing, at a table on which are an open book and papers; he wears black coat, and holds pen in right hand and scroll in left. Canvas, 48 × 38.

This picture was painted for Lord Muncaster.

By J. RISING. Lent by the EARL OF CRAWFORD.

## NORTH GALLERY.

### STATESMEN AND COMMANDERS.

**92.** FREDERICK HOWARD, 5TH EARL OF CARLISLE, K.G. (1748-1825), AND GEORGE AUGUSTUS SELWYN (1719-1791).

Frederick Howard succeeded his father as 5th Earl in 1758; was created a K.T. in 1768; appointed Treasurer of the Royal Household in 1777, and Lord-Lieutenant of Ireland, 1780-1782. He subsequently held various offices: was elected a K.G. June 12, 1793.

George Augustus Selwyn. Statesman and wit. Was educated at Oxford, represented Gloucester in Parliament, and afterwards Ludgershall; obtained through the interest of his friends many lucrative posts under government, and though very dissipated amassed a large fortune. He was a man of so much wit that nearly all the current *bon-mots* of his day were attributed to him.

Three-quarter length figures, life-size, seated at a table; the Earl is facing; in brown coat, star and ribbon of the Garter, his left hand resting on a book, holds a paper; Selwyn turned to the right, in red coat and waistcoat, and wig, caresses a pug dog; landscape and architectural background. Canvas 59 × 70 in.

By SIR J. REYNOLDS, P.R.A.   Lent by The EARL OF CARLISLE.

**93.** GEORGIANA SPENCER, DUCHESS OF DEVONSHIRE (1757-1806)

Daughter of John, 1st Earl Spencer, married, in 1774, William, 5th Duke of Devonshire. Celebrated for her beauty and accomplishments, and for the prominent part she took in the party politics of her time.

Half-length, life-size, to left, wearing large hat, hair powdered.   Canvas 30 ×

This is an unfinished portrait. It was probably painted about the time that the Duchess was sitting to Reynolds for her portrait representing her with her daughter, and exhibited at the Royal Academy in 1786.

By SIR J. REYNOLDS, P.R.A.   Lent by The DUKE OF DEVONSHIRE, K.G.

**94.** JOHN COUTTS (1699-1751).

    Merchant and banker. Born at Montrose, the eldest son of Patrick Coutts, a tradesman of Edinburgh; began life as a commission agent and dealer in grain, and acquiring capital, became a negotiator of bills, a business which bankers had not yet taken up. In 1742 he was elected Lord Provost of Edinburgh, and held that office till 1744, having been once re-elected. He was a great encourager of the fine arts. Died at Nola, near Naples, in 1751.

    Half-length, life-size, to right; blue coat and wig. Canvas 30 × 24 in.

By SIR J. REYNOLDS, P.R.A.      Lent by The BARONESS BURDETT-COUTTS.

**95.** RIGHT HON. CHARLES JAMES FOX ADDRESSING THE HOUSE DURING THE MINISTRY OF LORD NORTH (1770-1782).

    Scene in the old House of Commons. To right (to left of the Speaker) Fox, clad in blue coat, yellow vest and knee breeches is addressing the House, his right hand extended. Canvas 20 × 29 in.

    This picture in its colouring and grouping closely resembles that by Hickel in the National Portrait Gallery representinng Pitt addressing the House of Commons. It is therefore not improbable that this may be a companion picture, thus representing the two most celebrated personages of the time, each on his own side of the House of Commons.

    Lent by MAJ.-GEN. SIR CLAUD ALEXANDER, BART.

**96.** MARIA WALPOLE, COUNTESS WALDEGRAVE, DUCHESS OF GLOUCESTER (1737-1807), AND HER DAUGHTER, PRINCESS SOPHIA (1773-1844).

    Second natural daughter of Sir Edward Walpole, K.B.; married first in 1759, James, 2nd Earl Waldegrave, and secondly in 1766, William Henry, Duke of Gloucester, 3rd son of Frederick, Prince of Wales. By her second marriage she had issue William Frederick, 2nd Duke of Gloucester, and Princesses Sophia Matilda and Caroline Augusta Maria. As the marriage took place before the passing of the Royal Marriage Act, it was acknowledged by George III., but a reconciliation with his brother did not take place till 1776. The Duchess was niece to Horace Walpole, who frequently refers to her extreme beauty. He also mentions her being mobbed on a Sunday in the park when in company with Lady Coventry. She sat often to Reynolds, and there are at least four portraits of her by his hand.

    Three-quarter length, life-size, to left, of the Duchess, who holds by both hands the child who stands on the arm of the chair, the head facing spectator, holding her mother's chin with her right hand. The Duchess wears a white dress and blue scarf; the child is in white frock, and cap with blue ribbons; architectural background. Canvas (arched top) 50 × 40 in.

    Exhibited at the Royal Academy in 1774.

By SIR J. REYNOLDS, P.R.A.      Lent by The REV. B. GIBBONS.

## 97. JOHN LEE (1733-1793).

A popular lawyer, known as "Honest Jack Lee." Was Member of Parliament for Higham Ferrers, one of the counsel engaged in the defence of Admiral Keppel in 1779, Solicitor-General in 1782, in the Rockingham Ministry, and Attorney-General, in 1782, in the Coalition Ministry. Died August 5, 1793, and was buried at Staindrop, Durham.

Three-quarter length, life-size, seated to right in an arm-chair, in wig and gown, with long lace bands; his right hand on the arm of the chair; behind, a curtain, books, &c. Canvas 50 × 40 in.

Painted in 1786, and exhibited at the Royal Academy in that year, where it hung in company with twelve other pictures by Sir Joshua, amongst which were the portraits of Erskine, Lee's colleague in the Keppel court-martial, the Duke of Orleans, the Duchess of Devonshire and her daughter Lady Spencer, John Hunter, &c. It was a year of triumph to the painter.

By SIR J. REYNOLDS, P.R.A.  Lent by The HON. F. B. MASSEY MAINWARING.

## 98. AUGUSTUS, VISCOUNT KEPPEL (1725-1786).

Admiral. Second son of William, Earl of Albemarle; went with Anson round the world, and after a long course of distinguished service in various parts of the world, obtained in 1778 the rank of Admiral of the Blue. In the same year, as Commander of the Channel Fleet, he had a partial engagement with the French off Ushant, July 12, but nothing decisive being effected, the nation was dissatisfied. Charges and counter-charges were brought against each other by Keppel and Sir Hugh Palliser, his second in command, when the former was acquitted and the latter censured. In 1782 Keppel was rewarded with a Peerage, and twice named First Lord of the Admiralty.

Three-quarter length, life-size, to left, in naval uniform, right hand resting on sword, left on hip; sea in the background. Canvas 50 × 40 in.

Painted in 1799. After his trial by court-martial at Portsmouth and acquittal, Keppel presented bank-notes for £1000 to each of his counsel for their professional assistance. These were John Lee, the Solicitor-General, John Dunning, afterwards Lord Ashburton, and Thomas Erskine, afterwards Lord Chancellor. Lee and Dunning returned the money; Erskine, who was the youngest of the three, having a wife and eight children depending upon him, was still too poor to follow their example. The Admiral's letters and his friends' replies have the same stamp of generous affection which seems to radiate from Keppel to all about him. Lee writes, "Will you make me a present of your picture, painted by Mr. Dance, who takes excellent likenesses, that I may keep it, and my family after me?" Keppel did better. He sat to Sir Joshua for a three-quarter length portrait, and had four repetitions of it painted, one of which he gave to Lee, one to Dunning, and one to Burke. The other hangs at Quiddenham. The portrait which he presented to Erskine was not completed till four years after this. The four portraits were finished by November, and on receiving his copy Burke writes, "I assure you, my dear sir, that though I possess the portraits of friends highly honoured by me and very dear to me on all accounts, yours stands alone, and I intend that it shall so continue, to mark the impression I have received of this most flattering mark of your friendship." This picture was preserved at Beaconsfield whilst Burke lived. His widow left it to Earl Fitzwilliam, and it still hangs at Milton. The above picture was the copy presented to Lee, who was himself painted by Reynolds in 1786, since which date the two portraits have always hung side by side, and have never been separated, and on that condition have been lent to the present Exhibition (see No. 97).

By SIR J. REYNOLDS, P.R.A.    Lent by The HON. F. B. MASSEY MAINWARING.

**99. ANNE, COUNTESS OF CHESTERFIELD (d. 1798).**

Daughter of the Rev. Robert Thistlethwayte, D.D., of Norman Court and Southwick Park, Hants, married in 1777, Philip 5th Earl of Chesterfield. Died October 20, 1798.

Full-length, life-size, seated to right, resting left arm on parapet, blue and white dress, gold embroidered scarf, powdered hair ; landscape background.  Canvas 86 × 61 in.

By T. GAINSBOROUGH, R.A.    Lent by The EARL OF CARNARVON.

**100. ADMIRAL EWARD BOSCAWEN (1711-1761).**

Younger son of the first Viscount Falmouth ; distinguished himself in the navy, especially at Porto Bello and Carthagena. Sailing for India in 1747 he conducted the siege of Pondicherry and recovered Madras : but the two great exploits of his life were the reduction of Louisburg in 1798, and the brilliant victory over the French fleet in Lagos Bay in 1759.

Half length, life-size, nearly facing, in naval uniform.  Canvas 30 × 24 in.

By SIR J. REYNOLDS, P.R.A.    Lent by JOHN LEVESON GOWER, ESQ.

**101. THOMAS PENN (1702-1775).**

Second son of William Penn, founder of Pennsylvania, and Hannah Callowhill, his second wife ; born at Stoke Poges ; was a joint proprietor of Pennsylvania, and as such was a feudal lord over 25,000,000 acres, nearly a quarter million of people, and the largest town in the American Colonies. He married, in 1751, Lady Juliana, fourth daughter of the 1st Earl of Pomfret (see No. 121).

Small full length, standing to right, in a room near a window ; drab coat and wig. Canvas 29 × 23 in.

This picture and No. 121, of Lady Juliana Penn, were painted in 1750 as a memorial of Thomas Penn's marriage. They descended to the Hon. Mrs. Stuart, and were presented by her in 1835 to Viscountess Northland, afterwards Countess of Ranfurly. The portrait of Thomas Penn has been engraved at least twice ; the upper part of the figure by C. Turner, probably to illustrate a publication of the Outinian Society, and the bust engraved in mezzotint.

By P. VAN DYK.    Lent by The EARL OF RANFURLY.

[NORTH GALLERY.] *Portraits.* 33

**102. THE HON. JOHN LEVESON GOWER (1740).**
   Admiral. Son of John, 1st Earl Gower and Lady Mary, daughter of Thomas, Earl of Thanet, appointed captain in the Navy in 1763 and admiral in 1787, was first captain of Lord Howe's ship at the relief of Gibraltar in 1782, and a Lord of the Admiralty 1783—1789. Married Frances, eldest daughter of Admiral Boscawen.
   Half-length, life-size, to right; in naval uniform. Canvas 30 × 24 in.
   By SIR J. REYNOLDS, P.R.A.          Lent by JOHN LEVESON GOWER, ESQ.

**103. HENRY ADDINGTON (AFTERWARDS 1ST VISCOUNT SIDMOUTH), SPEAKER (1755-1844).**
   Eldest son of Anthony Addington, M.D. Was educated in the same school as William Pitt, at whose recommendation he entered Parliament for Devizes in 1782; appointed Speaker 1789-1801; Chancellor of the Exchequer and First Lord of the Treasury in 1801, in succession to William Pitt, but resigning in 1804 was created Viscount Sidmouth. After Pitt's death, Lord Sidmouth formed a coalition ministry with Fox and Granville, which was broken up by the death of Fox. He was subsequently Home Secretary from 1812-1822. Being unpopular with the King he lived in retirement and died at the White Lodge, Richmond Park, of which he was deputy ranger.
   Full-length, life-size, to left, in Speaker's robes; his right hand rests on scroll partly opened, placed on table, on which are also a book, volume of the "Journals," and the mace, architectural background and view of Westminster Abbey. Canvas 93 × 64 in.
   This is one of the latest works by Copley, and was painted in 1814 after he had attained his 70th year.
   By J. S. COPLEY, R.A.          Lent by G. SOTHERAN ESTCOURT, ESQ.

**104. FREDERICK, 2ND EARL OF GUILDFORD, LORD NORTH, K.G. (1732-1792).**
   Statesman; better known as Lord North. Eldest son of Francis, 1st Earl, was elected Member of Parliament for Banbury in 1754, and having held several minor official offices, succeeded in 1767 Charles Townshend as Chancellor of the Exchequer and Leader of the House of Commons. He became Prime Minister in 1770. His administration continued throughout the American War, during which period he was incessantly assailed by the Opposition and threatened with impeachment. On his resignation of office in 1782, instead of instituting the long-threatened impeachment, a coalition was formed with the Whigs; but this heterogeneous administration only lasted a few months. He succeeded to the Earldom in 1790, and died two years afterwards. His correspondence with George III. was published in 1866.
   Three-quarter length, life-size, seated to left, in Chancellor's robes and ribbon of the Garter; arms resting on chair. Canvas 50 × 40 in.
   By N. DANCE, R.A.          Lent by The BODLEIAN LIBRARY, OXFORD.

D

34   Exhibition of the Royal House of Guelph.

**105.**  RIGHT HON. WILLIAM PITT, M.P. AS A BOY (1759-1806).

This great statesman was the youngest son of William Pitt the elder, Earl of Chatham. Born at Hayes in Kent, and being of delicate health, he was educated, first at home, and afterwards at Pembroke Hall, Cambridge. On coming of age, Pitt was returned to Parliament for Appleby, and at once proved himself, not only an orator but also a statesman. At the age of twenty-three he was appointed Chancellor of the Exchequer in Lord Shelburne's administration, but being displaced for a short period, he was in 1783 called upon to form an administration of his own, and he continued at the head of that administration for a period of seventeen years, viz. till 1801. Three years later he was recalled to power, but his health soon gave way amidst the toils and cares of his active life, and he died at Putney, January 23, 1806, and was buried in Westminster Abbey.

Full-length, life-size, reclining to right on a bank, his right arm resting on trunk of a tree, book in left, scarlet coat, white waistcoat and breeches, landscape background. Canvas 51 × 43 in.

Lent by The EARL OF CRAWFORD.

**106.**  RIGHT HON. EDMUND BURKE, M.P. (1729-1797).

Statesman, orator, and writer. Born in Dublin, entered the Middle Temple in 1753, where he applied himself more to general literature than to law. He projected in 1758 the *Annual Register*, and for some years wrote the whole of it. He entered Parliament in 1765 as Member for Wendover, was elected for Bristol in 1774, and Malton in 1787. He took a leading part in the debates, and especially distinguished himself by his speeches on the great American question, on Catholic Emancipation, economical reform, the affairs of India, and the prosecution of Warren Hastings. His speeches on the opening and conclusion of Hastings' impeachment were among the grandest efforts of his oratory. His views on the French Revolution occasioned a painful rupture with his old friend Fox. Died at Beaconsfield, July 8, 1797.

Half-length, life-size, head to left, brown coat, powdered hair; in his hand he holds a paper. Canvas 30 × 25 in.

Painted in 1792 and purchased in the same year by the Duke of Dorset, as appears by a label at the back. On the back is also written with a free brush, as if by the painter himself, "Opie Pinxit 1792. Ed. Burke, Esqre."

By J. OPIE, R.A.                    Lent by The LORD SACKVILLE.

**107.**  ALEXANDER, 10TH DUKE OF HAMILTON, K.G. (1767-1852).

Son of Archibald, 9th Duke, was educated at Christ Church, Oxford, sat in Parliament for Lancaster from 1802 to 1806, and in the latter year was sent as Ambassador to St. Petersburg, but recalled in 1807. He was summoned to the House of Lords in 1816 as Baron of Dutton, succeeded to the Dukedom in 1819, was elected a K.G. February 5, 1839, and was Lord High Steward of England at the coronation of Queen

Victoria. Died, August 18, 1852. He married, April 26, 1810, Susan, daughter of William Beckford, of Fonthill Gifford.

Half-length, life-size, to right, long hair, red coat, and white frill. Canvas 26½ × 21 in.

By SIR J. REYNOLDS, P.R.A. . Lent by the DUKE OF HAMILTON.

**108.** JOHN, 3RD EARL OF BUTE, K.G. (1713-1792).

Son of James, 2nd Earl, and Lady Elizabeth, dau. and co-heir of John, Duke of Argyll; succeeded his father in 1723, was made a K.T. in 1738, and Lord of the Bedchamber to Frederick, Prince of Wales, in 1750, and Groom of the Stole to George, Prince of Wales, in 1756. He was First Lord of the Treasury from May 1762 to April 1763, when he retired in a storm of unpopularity. Elected K.G. in 1762. He possessed an ardent taste for literature, and specially excelled in the science of botany. Married Mary, dau. of Edward Wortley Montagu.

Full-length, life-size, head to right, in robes of the Garter; hair powdered *en perruque*; in right hand plumed hat; his left holds up his cloak; architectural background and landscape. Canvas 94 × 58 in.

Painted in October, 1773.

By SIR J. REYNOLDS, P.R.A. Lent by The EARL OF WHARNCLIFFE.

**109.** JOHN, 4TH EARL OF BUTE AND 1ST MARQUESS (1744-1814).

Son of 3rd earl (see No. 108); entered Parliament for Bossoney in 1766; created Baron Cardiff in 1776; was appointed Envoy Extraordinary to Turin in 1779, and to Madrid in 1785: succeeded to the Earldom in 1794, and in February 1796 was created a Marquess. He again in 1795 went to Spain as ambassador, but returned the next year on the declaration of war. Married, first Charlotte Jane, dau. of Herbert, Viscount Windsor, and secondly Frances, dau. of Thomas Coutts.

Half-length, life-size, to left, head to right, in peer's robes, powdered hair *en perruque*; set in an oval; in background coat-of-arms and name. Canvas 30 × 21 in.

Painted in 1776, as stated on the picture.

By SIR J. REYNOLDS, P.R.A. Lent by The EARL OF WHARNCLIFFE.

**110.** RIGHT HON. GEORGE CANNING, M.P., WHEN YOUNG (1770-1827).

The eminent statesman, orator, and political writer. Born in London, was educated at Eton and Christ Church, Oxford, and entered at Lincoln's Inn, but soon abandoned law for politics. He sat in Parliament in 1793, and joining the ministerial party under Pitt, was appointed Under Secretary of State in 1796, Treasurer of the Navy in 1804, and Foreign Secretary in the Percival administration in 1807. In 1814 he went as Ambassador to Portugal, where he remained till after the Battle of Waterloo, and in 1816 was made President of the Board of Control. He was appointed in 1822 to succeed the

Marquess of Hastings as Governor-General of India, but on the eve of his departure, on account of the death of the Marquess of Londonderry, he was induced to accept the foreign seals, and in April, 1827, succeeded Lord Liverpool as Premier. His health, however, failed, and he died August 8 of the same year.

Half-length, life-size, facing, head to left, in Vandyck black dress slashed with white. Canvas oval 28 × 23 in.

This picture was painted just after Canning left Eton.

By T. GAINSBOROUGH, R.A.      Lent by The MARQUESS OF CLANRIKARDE.

**111.** ANNE LUTTRELL (MRS. HORTON), AFTERWARDS DUCHESS OF CUMBERLAND (d. 1803).

Full-length, life-size, facing, head to right, rich crimson robe over white embroidered petticoat, crimson ermine-lined mantle, powdered hair; her right elbow rests on pedestal of column, the finger of the hand touches her cheek; left hand holds her mantle; architectural background. Canvas 95 × 56 in.

By T. GAINSBOROUGH, R.A.      Lent by HER MAJESTY THE QUEEN
(Buckingham Palace).

**112.** MRS. SUMNER, *née* GAMBIER.

Bust, life-size, to right, in white dress, hair falling in curls on right shoulder. Canvas (oval) 20 × 16 in.

By LADY BARHAM.      Lent by T. LYON THURLOW, ESQ.

**113.** JOHN FREDERICK, 3RD DUKE OF DORSET, K.G. (1745-1799).

Nephew of Charles, 2nd Duke; represented Kent in Parliament, 1768-9, succeeded to the Dukedom, 1769, was Lord-Lieutenant, Vice-Admiral and Custos Rotulorum of the County of Kent, 1769-1797, Ambassador extraordinary to Paris, 1783-1784, elected a K.G., April, 1788, and was Lord Steward of the Household in 1789. Died, July 19, 1799. Wraxall (*Hist. Mem.*, ii, 472) says of him: "His person, if not handsome, was highly agreeable, the expression of his countenance noble and interesting; his manners soft, quiet, ingratiating, and formed for a court, destitute of all affectation but not deficient in dignity." He married Arabella Diana, daughter of Sir Charles Cope, Bart.

Full-length, life-size, facing, head to right, in peer's robes; his right-hand rests on table on which is placed a ducal coronet, sword, and ribbon of the Garter; his left is placed on his hip; books in the foreground; architectural background. Canvas 93 × 57 in.

Reynolds painted two portraits of the Duke of Dorset. The first, in April 1769, in which he is represented in a plain coat, white neckcloth, engraved by T. Hardy; the other the above picture, in July 1780; it is engraved by S. W. Reynolds.

By SIR J. REYNOLDS, P.R.A.      Lent by The LORD SACKVILLE.

NORTH GALLERY.]       *Portraits.*                    37

**114. RIGHT HON. WARREN HASTINGS (1733-1818).**

First Governor-General of India. Born at Daylesford, Worcestershire, went to India as a writer in 1750, was appointed second in Council at Madras in 1769, and became President of the Supreme Council of Bengal in 1772, and Governor-General of all British India in 1774. From this time began his remarkable administration, during which he successfully contended against a combination of enemies, and not only strengthened but also considerably increased the powers of the East India Company. He continued in office till 1785, but shortly after his return to England was impeached by the House of Commons for various acts of his government. After a trial lasting nine years he was acquitted on all charges; and he lived to see his plans for India publicly applauded.

Half-length, life size, facing in an oval; blue coat with scarf. Canvas 30 × 24 in.

By MORIER.                    Lent by The EARL OF LOUDOUN.

**115. WILLIAM BECKFORD (1759-1844).**

The author of *Vathek*. Son of Alderman Beckford, whose estates at Fonthill, Wiltshire, and large fortune, estimated at £100,000 a year, he inherited at the age of eleven. In 1777 he set out for the Continent with his tutor, where he spent much of the following years. In 1781 he wrote his celebrated romance of *Vathek*, an Arabian tale, in French, at a single sitting of three days and two nights, without "taking off his clothes the whole time." This was published at Lausanne in 1787; but it had been forestalled by an English translation in 1784 surreptitiously obtained. On taking up his residence in England in 1796, he settled at Fonthill, and devoted his time and money to rebuilding the Abbey, on which in the space of sixteen years he spent about £273,000, filling it with one of the finest libraries in England and with pictures and curiosities. In 1822 on account of pecuniary losses he was compelled to sell the Abbey and most of its rich and rare contents. He then took up his residence at Bath, where he died in 1844. Beckford was a man of great taste and knowledge. His collection of pictures embraced specimens of almost every painter of eminence of all ages and nations. His library was preserved intact till its sale in 1882.

Half-length, life-size, to left, black coat. Canvas 27 × 21 in.
Exhibited at the Royal Academy in 1782. Beckford sat for his portrait in February of that year.

By SIR J. REYNOLDS, P.R.A.            Lent by The DUKE OF HAMILTON.

**116. CHARLES WATSON WENTWORTH, 2ND MARQUESS OF ROCKINGHAM, K.G. (1730-1782).**

Statesman. Only son of the 1st Marquess, whom he succeeded in 1750; was elected K.G. in 1760, and became 1st Lord of the Treasury in succession to George Grenville in 1765. Though he held office on this occasion but one year, he was till his death the acknowledged leader of the liberal branch of the aristocracy. On the fall of Lord North's administration in March, 1782, Rockingham again became Prime Minister, but died suddenly in the following July.

Half-length, life-size, to left; in robes of the Garter, and collar. Canvas (oval) 27 × 24 in.

The Marquess of Rockingham sat to Reynolds in December 1766, and in June 1768. This portrait was probably painted on the first occasion.

By Sir J. Reynolds, P.R.A.  Lent by G. G. C. Wentworth-Fitzwilliam, Esq.

**117.** The Right Hon. William Pitt, M.P. (1759–1806).

Three-quarter length, life-size, to left, blue coat and wig, leaning against chair on which is thrown his Chancellor's robe; before him table with inkstand. Canvas 50 × 40 in.

Besides the above, which was painted in 1788, there are several other original portraits of Pitt by Gainsborough. Half-lengths are in the possession of Earl Stanhope at Chevening, and Earl Amherst at Montreal in Kent, and in the Fitzwilliam collection at Cambridge. Three-quarter lengths belong to the Duke of Richmond, the Earl of Normanton (painted for Sir William Young, a great friend of Pitt) and the Hon. Society of Lincoln's Inn.

By T. Gainsborough, R.A.  Lent by The Earl Bathurst.

**118.** Sir William Blackstone, LL.D. (1723–1780).

Legal writer and judge, and author of the well known *Commentaries on the Laws of England*. Born in Cheapside, the son of a silk-mercer, was educated at Charterhouse and Oxford, where he instituted a course of lectures on the English constitution and laws, and in 1758 was named first Vinerian Professor. After gaining great distinction as a lecturer, he was, in 1770, made a Justice of the Common Pleas, which office he held till his death.

Three-quarter length, life-size, standing facing, head to right, in Doctor's gown and wig, right hand rests on books on table, left on his hip. Above inscription. Canvas 50 × 40 in.

By T. Kettle.  Lent by The Bodleian Library, Oxford.

**119.** Henry Dundas, Viscount Melville (1740–1811).

Statesman. Son of Robert Dundas, Lord Arnistoun. Was educated at the University of Edinburgh; entered Parliament and was appointed Solicitor-General in 1773, and Lord Advocate in 1775. He was a warm adherent of Pitt, made Treasurer of the Navy in 1783, Secretary for the Home Department in 1791, which he exchanged in succession for the War and Colonial Offices. On the retirement of Pitt in 1801, he was raised to the

Peerage as Viscount Melville, and when Pitt returned to power he became First Lord of the Admiralty, and continued so till he was impeached in 1805 of high crimes and misdemeanours in his former office of Treasurer to the Navy. Acquitted, however, on all charges, he withdrew to Scotland, and never resumed office.

Full-length, life-size, head to right; in Chancellor's robes and wig; in right hand paper, left rests on his hip; on left, table with papers, &c. Canvas 99 × 62 in.

By G. ROMNEY.　　　　　　　　　Lent by ROBERT DUNDAS, ESQ., OF ARNISTON.

**120.** WILLIAM PITT, 1ST EARL OF CHATHAM (1708-1778).

Half-length, life-size, to left, red coat and wig. Canvas 24 × 17 in.

By W. HOARE.　　　　　　　　　Lent by The VISCOUNT COBHAM.

**121.** LADY JULIANA PENN (1729-1769).

Fourth daughter of Thomas, 4th Earl of Pomfret; married in August, 1751, Thomas Penn, one of the proprietors of Pennsylvania. Died March 1, 1769. (See No. 101).

Small full-length, in white dress, standing in a room. Canvas 29 × 23 in.

By P. VAN DYK.　　　　　　　　　Lent by The EARL OF RANFURLY.

**122.** RIGHT HON. CHARLES JAMES FOX, M.P. (1749-1806).

Statesman. Younger son of the 1st Lord Holland, was returned to Parliament for Midhurst at the age of nineteen, and held subordinate offices in Lord North's administration, from whom, however, he soon separated, and joining the opposition, harassed the Ministry throughout the American war. In the Ministry of Lord Rockingham, in the spring of 1782, Fox became Foreign Secretary; but resigning on the death of his chief, in the following July, formed, in 1783, his celebrated coalition with Lord North, resuming his former office of Foreign Secretary. The failure of the India Bill was fatal to the Ministry, and on Pitt assuming the reins of Government Fox remained out of office for over twenty-two years, consoling himself with the pursuits of scholarship and with delivering masterly speeches against his opponents. After the death of Pitt, in January, 1806, Fox again returned to office, but his health failing, he expired at Chiswick in the following September.

Half-length, life-size, in an oval, facing, head to left, dark red coat and waistcoat. Canvas 30 × 24 in.

By SIR J. REYNOLDS, P.R.A.　　　　　Lent by The PROVOST, ETON COLLEGE.

**123.** PHILIP STANHOPE, 5TH EARL OF CHESTERFIELD (1755-1815).

Cousin of the 4th Earl, from whom he received a number of letters which were recently published and edited by the late Earl of Carnarvon.

Full-length, life-size, seated to left, scarlet coat, buff breeches, top boots and wig, right hand caresses a dog, in left, hat and stick, landscape background. Canvas 86 × 61 in.

By T. GAINSBOROUGH, R.A.　　　　　Lent by The EARL OF CARNARVON.

**124.** JOHN JERVIS, 1ST EARL ST. VINCENT, K.B. (1734-1823).

Admiral. Son of Swynfen Jervis, Auditor of Greenwich Hospital; born at Meaford, Staffordshire; entered the navy at ten, and being appointed Post-Captain in 1760 commanded the *Foudroyant* in Keppel's memorable action off Ushant July 27, 1788. For his capture of the *Pégase* in 1782 he was made a K.B., was with Lord Howe at the relief of Gibraltar, took Guadaloupe, Martinique and St. Lucia in 1794; and on February 14, 1797, won his famous victory over the Spanish Fleet off Cape St. Vincent, for which he was created Earl St. Vincent, receiving also a pension of £3,000 a year. He was First Lord of the Admiralty from 1801-1804, was in command of the Channel Fleet and expedition to Portugal in 1806, and General of Marines in 1814. He held successively the posts of Admiral of the Blue 1793, of the White 1799, and of the Red 1803. In person he was "of short stature, his look was replete with intelligence, and he had an eagle's eye: his manners too were those of a highly polished gentleman."

Three-quarter length, life-size; facing, head to left, in naval uniform, ribbon and star of the Bath; upraised sword in right hand, left resting on a cannon. Canvas 55 × 46.

Presented to the Corporation of London by Mr. Alderman John Boydell in 1793.

By SIR W. BEECHEY, R.A.        Lent by THE CORPORATION OF THE CITY OF LONDON.

**125.** ADMIRAL EDWARD VERNON (1684-1757).

Born November 12, 1684, at Westminster; the son of a Secretary of State to King William. He entered the navy to the great reluctance of his parents, and was present at the battle in Vigo Bay in 1702, and in the engagement off Malaga in 1704. After much service under various commanders, he was made Vice-Admiral of the Blue in 1739, and sent to the West Indies, having declared in the House of Commons, in an attack on the Government with regard to the mode of carrying on the war against Spain, that Porto Bello might be reduced with six sail of the line. What he boasted he actually effected, and Porto Bello was captured November 22 of that year. His success was hailed with enthusiasm in England, but his popularity suffered by his failure on Carthagena in 1741, and being recalled he was employed in guarding the English coasts during the Rebellion of 1745. Soon afterwards, having acted in opposition to the Ministry, he was superseded, and even struck off the list of admirals.

Three-quarter length, life-size; to right, in red coat and wig; standing near a gun, his left hand rests on his sword, his right thrust into his coat: in background, naval engagement. Canvas, 49 × 41 in.

This picture was painted by Gainsborough during his residence at Ipswich. Philip Thicknesse, who was in that city about 1758, paid a visit to Gainsborough. He thus describes his introduction to the painter. "I immediately procured his address, visited Mr. Gainsborough, and told him I came to chide him for having imposed a shadow instead of a substance upon me. Mr. Gainsborough received me in his painting-room, in which stood several portraits, truly drawn, perfectly like, but stiffly painted, and worse coloured. Among them was the late Adm ral Vernon's, for it was not many years after he had taken Porto Bello, with six ships only; but when

I turned my eyes to his little landscapes and drawings, I was charmed; these were the works of fancy and gave him infinite delight."

By T. GAINSBOROUGH, R.A.  Lent by B. B. HUNTER RODWELL, Q.C.

**126.** ALEXANDER HOOD, 1ST VISCOUNT BRIDPORT, K.B. (1727–1814).

Admiral. Second son of the Rev. Samuel Hood, and younger brother of Samuel, Viscount Hood (see No. 128); was appointed Post-Captain in 1756, was Rear-Admiral under Lord Howe at the relief of Gibraltar in 1782, represented Bridgewater in Parliament in 1784, and was made a K.B. in 1788. He bore a part in Lord Howe's celebrated victory, June 1, 1794, and in the following year defeated a French squadron, capturing three sail of the line, and nobly distinguished himself on many other occasions during the war. He was successively Admiral of the Blue, 1794, of the White, 1795, and of the Red, 1805; was created Baron Bridport in Ireland, 1794, Baron Bridport of Cricket St. Thomas in Somerset, 1796, and advanced to a Viscountcy in 1801. Died at Bath May 3, 1814.

Three-quarter length, life-size, to left, head nearly facing, in naval uniform and Star of the Bath; right hand extended and pointing towards a naval engagement; left on hip. Canvas 50 × 40 in.

By L. F. ABBOTT.  Lent by The VISCOUNT HOOD.

**127.** TRIAL OF THE GOVERNOR OF THE FLEET.

Interior of a room, various personages seated round a table, others standing; the president of the court holds on the table an instrument of torture, and looks back at Bambridge, whilst a prisoner kneels in the foreground at the feet of a member of the court. Canvas 21 × 28 in.

This picture was given by Hogarth to Horace Walpole. It was painted when the House of Commons appointed a committee to inquire into the cruelties exercised on prisoners in the Fleet, to extort money from them. "The scene," Walpole says "is the committee, on the table are the instruments of torture, a prisoner in rags half starved appears before them; the poor man has a good countenance that adds to the interest. On the other hand is the inhuman gaoler. Villany, fear, and conscience are mixed in yellow and livid in the countenance, his lips are contracted by tremor, his face advances as eager to lie, his legs step back as thinking to make his escape; one hand is thrust precipitately into his bosom, the fingers of the other are catching uncertainly at his button-holes. If this was a portrait it is the most striking that ever was drawn; if it was not, it is still finer."

This portrait is that of Bambridge the Warden of the Fleet; and the sketch was taken in the beginning of the year 1729, when Bambridge and Huggins (his predecessor) were under examination. Both were declared "notoriously guilty of great breaches of trust, extortions, cruelties, and other high crimes and misdemeanours," and both were sent to Newgate. Bambridge was disqualified by Act of Parliament, and ended his life by suicide.

By W. HOGARTH.  Lent by The EARL OF CARLISLE.

**128.** SAMUEL, 1ST VISCOUNT HOOD, G.C.B (1724-1816).

Admiral. Son of the Rev. Samuel Hood and brother of Viscount Bridport (see No. 126); born at Butley, Somerset; entered the navy at the age of sixteen, captured the *Belliqueux* in 1757, and the *Bellona* in 1759, and was made a post-captain. In 1778 he was created a baronet, distinguished himself as rear-admiral in the famous defeat of De Grasse by Rodney, April 12, 1782, and for these services was rewarded with an Irish peerage. He sat in Parliament for Westminster, 1784-8 and 1790; was a lord of the admiralty in 1788, commanded the Mediterranean Fleet and took Toulon and Corsica 1793-4, and was created Viscount Hood of Great Britain in 1796, in which year also he became Governor of Greenwich Hospital. He subsequently was Admiral of the White and of the Blue, and was made a G.C.B. in 1815.

Three quarter-length, life-size, head to right, in naval uniform, in right hand cocked hat, left on his hip; behind is seen a ship. Canvas 50 × 40 in.

By B. WEST, P.R.A.                      Lent by The VISCOUNT HOOD.

**129.** GEORGE BRYDGES, LORD RODNEY (1718-1792).

Admiral. Son of Captain Rodney of the Royal Marines, became lieutenant in 1739, post-captain in 1742, and Commander of the Newfoundland Station in 1748. In 1759 he was made Rear-Admiral of the Blue, and in the same year destroyed the stores prepared at Havre de Grace for the invasion of England. For these and other services he was created a baronet in 1764, and went to Jamaica in 1771 as commander-in-chief. After a short retirement he was again called to active service, and being sent to relieve Gibraltar, defeated the French off Cape St. Vincent, Jan. 16, 1780. He subsequently served in the West Indies, and for his victory over Count de Grasse, April 12, 1782, off Dominica, by which he saved Jamaica, and ruined the naval power of France and Spain, he was raised to the peerage, and received a pension of £2,000 a year.

Full-length, life-size, to right, in naval uniform and wig, and ribbon of the Bath; his right hand rests on the fluke of an anchor, his left is placed on his chest; in the distance naval engagement. Canvas 92 × 58 in.

Painted after his celebrated victory over Count de Grasse, probably in 1784.

By SIR J. REYNOLDS, P.R.A.

Lent by HER MAJESTY THE QUEEN
(St. James's Palace).

**130.** ELIZABETH (GUNNING), DUCHESS OF HAMILTON AND OF ARGYLL (1734-1790).

Younger daughter of John Gunning of Castlecoote, county Roscommon, and sister of the Countess of Coventry (See No. 141), whom she equalled in beauty; married James, 6th Duke of Hamilton, February 14, 1752. Walpole to Sir Horace Mann, February 27, 1752, writes: "About a fortnight since, at an assembly at my Lord Chesterfield's, Duke Hamilton made violent love at one end of the room whilst he was playing at pharaoh at the other end . . . I own I was so little a professor of love that I thought all the parade looked ill for the poor girl . . . However, two nights afterwards, being left alone with her while her mother and sister were at Bedford House, he found himself so impatient that he sent for a parson. The doctor refused to perform the ceremony without license or ring ; the Duke swore he would send for the archbishop—at last they were married with a ring of the bed-curtain at half-an-hour after twelve at night at Mayfair Chapel." When the duchess was presented at court after her marriage, the noble mob clambered upon chairs to look at her. Her husband dying January 18, 1758, she married in March of the following year John Campbell, Marquess of Lorne, afterwards 5th Duke of Argyll. She still preserved her great beauty, and it is said that Queen Charlotte was jealous of the King's admiration of her. Her husband succeeded to the dukedom in 1770, and in 1776 she was created Baroness Hamilton of Hambledon. Wraxall says that "even in advanced life and with very decayed health she was remarkably beautiful, and seemed composed of a finer clay than the rest of her sex." Died in London, May 20, 1790.

Full-length, life-size, leaning on a sculptured pedestal, white dress, ermine mantle ; landscape background. Canvas 94 × 58 in.

Painted in January, 1759, and exhibited at the Society of Artists in 1760.

By SIR J. REYNOLDS, P.R.A.      Lent by The DUKE OF HAMILTON, K.T.

**131. JANE, DUCHESS OF GORDON (d. 1812), AND GEORGE, MARQUESS OF HUNTLY (1770–1836).**

Jane, daughter of Sir William Maxwell, Bart., married October 18, 1767, Alexander, 4th Duke of Gordon, died April 11, 1812. Her eldest son, George, Marquess of Huntly, born February 2, 1770, was a general officer, Colonel of the Scots Fusiliers. He was summoned to the House of Lords as Baron Gordon of Huntly; created a G.C.B. in 1820 ; appointed Lord High Constable of Scotland at the coronation of George IV., succeeded to the Dukedom June 17, 1827, and was Governor of Edinburgh Castle in 1827. Died May 28, 1836, without issue.

Three-quarter, life-size figures ; the Duchess is seated to left, her left elbow resting on a table, resting her head on her hand, white dress, and red scarf, her right hand holds a sketch; behind her stands her son leaning on the back of her chair, and looking down at the drawing which his mother is holding ; in right hand book. Canvas 50 × 40 in.

By Sir J. REYNOLDS, P.R.A.      Lent by SIR HERBERT MAXWELL, BART, M.P.

**132. HENRY, 10TH EARL OF PEMBROKE (1734–1794).**

General. Son of Henry, 9th Earl, was appointed a cornet of the "King's Own" in 1752, and gradually rose to the rank of General which he attained in 1792. He was aide-de-camp to George II. and a Lord of the Bedchamber to George III. before and after his accession. Married Lady Elizabeth Spencer, daughter of Charles, 2nd Duke of Marlborough.

Three-quarter length, life-size, to right, in military uniform ; right hand rests on hilt of his sword ; left holds cap ; battle-scene in the distance. Canvas 50 × 40. in. Painted probably in 1762. Lord Pembroke sat to Reynolds, with whom he was on special intimate terms, on frequent occasions from 1757 to 1783.

By SIR J. REYNOLDS, P.R.A.      Lent by The EARL OF PEMBROKE.

**133.** HORATIO, VISCOUNT NELSON (1758–1805).

The most glorious name in all our naval annals. Was the fourth son of the Rev. Edmund Nelson of Burnham Thorpe in Norfolk, entered the navy as midshipman in his twelfth year, under his uncle Captain Suckling of the *Raisonnable*. He attained the rank of post-captain in 1779. As it would be outside our limits to enumerate all Nelson's services, it must suffice to say that in 1798 he won over the French fleet in Aboukir Bay the famous victory of the Nile, for which he was created a baron; in 1801 he destroyed the Danish ships before Copenhagen, for which service he was advanced to a viscount; and on the 21st October, 1805, he encountered the French and Spanish fleets off Cape Trafalgar, in which engagement he received his death-wound by a musket ball from the *Redoubtable*. He was buried in St. Paul's, January 9, 1806. At the siege of Calvi in 1794 Nelson lost the sight of an eye, and at Teneriffe, in 1797, his left arm.

Three-quarter length, life-size, to right, in naval uniform; both hands rest on his sword; fort in the distance on which flies the British flag. Canvas 50 × 40 in.

This picture was given by the Admiral to Captain W. Locker and was placed by him between the portraits of Captains (afterwards Admirals) Sir Charles Montagu and Sir Charles Pole. It was purchased by the present owner of Captain Locker's son. The Admiral writes respecting it, "I hope when I come to town to see a fine trio in your room. If Rigaud has done the picture let me know when you next write, and I will send an order on my paymaster for it." On February 21, 1781, he again writes, "As to my picture it will not be the least like what I am now, that is certain. Tell Mr. Rigaud to add beauty to it, it will be much needed."

By J F. RIGAUD.                                    Lent by The EARL NELSON.

**134.** HORATIO, VISCOUNT NELSON (1758–1805).

Full-length, life-size, to left, in naval uniform, wearing ribbon and order of the Bath, &c.; left hand rests on rock, no right arm; naval engagement in the background. Canvas 92 × 58 in.

By J. HOPPNER, R.A.
　　　　　　　　　　　　　　　Lent by HER MAJESTY THE QUEEN
　　　　　　　　　　　　　　　　　　(St. James's Palace).

**135.** ARABELLA DIANA, DUCHESS OF DORSET (d. 1825).

Daughter and co-heir of Sir Charles Cope, Bart.; married 1st January 4, 1790, John Frederick, 3rd Duke of Dorset, by whom she had issue, George 4th Duke, and two daughters, and 2ndly, April 2, 1801, Charles, Earl Whitworth. Died at Knole, August, 1, 1825. The expenses of her funeral were estimated at over £2000.

Full-length, life-size, to left, white dress, and head-dress with feathers; left hand resting on her hip, walking in a landscape; dog running at her feet. Canvas 93 × 57 in.

By J. HOPPNER, R A.                                    Lent by The LORD SACKVILLE.

*Portraits.*

**136.** CAPTAIN BLIGH (1734–1817).

Navigator; commonly known as "bread-fruit Bligh." Accompanied Captain Cook on his second voyage in 1772–4, was present at the battle of Dogger Bank in 1781, and in 1787 was appointed to the command of the *Bounty*, and sent to convey bread-fruit plants from the South Seas to the West Indies. In a few days after leaving Otaheite his crew mutinied, and with eighteen of his men he was cast adrift in an open boat, in which with great skill he sailed a distance of 3618 miles, and eventually arrived safely in England. After various services Bligh was made Governor-General of New South Wales in 1805, but in less than two years his rigorous and arbitrary conduct led to his deprival of office. He returned to England, was made a rear-admiral in 1811, and vice-admiral in 1814.

Three-quarter length, seated, life-size, to left, in uniform, right arm resting on parapet, on which is his hat; landscape background. Canvas 50 × 40 in.

The name of a Mr. Bligh occurs among Reynolds's sitters for July, 1787.

By SIR J. REYNOLDS, P.R.A.　　　Lent by The HON. F. B. MASSEY MAINWARING.

**137.** LADY ELIZABETH SPENCER, COUNTESS OF PEMBROKE (d. 1831). AND HER SON GEORGE (AFTERWARDS 11TH EARL).

Daughter of Charles, 2nd Duke of Marlborough; married in 1756 Henry, 10th Earl of Pembroke (see No. 132), and by him had issue, one son, George, 11th Earl, and one daughter, Charlotte, who died young. She died April 30, 1831.

Three-quarter length figures, life-size; the Countess is seated to left, in pink dress, white veil covering her head and tied under her chin: her right arm is encircling her son, and with her left she holds his hand; the child, facing, leans against his mother's knee and holds a book in his right hand; architectural background. Canvas 50 × 40 in.

Painted in 1761. This portrait has been described as "one of the purest and sweetest that even Reynolds ever painted." The Countess was considered one of the most beautiful women of her time, and Walpole writing to Montagu, September 4, 1761, says of her, "Lady Pembroke alone at the head of the Countesses, was the picture of majestic modesty."

By SIR J. REYNOLDS, P.R.A.　　　Lent by The EARL OF PEMBROKE.

**138.** ADMIRAL SIR CHARLES HARDY, KNT. (1716–1780).

Son of Vice-Admiral Sir Charles Hardy; entered the navy as a volunteer in 1730, soon rose to distinction, and commanded in the war against Spain in 1741 and following years. In 1755 he was appointed governor of New York and was knighted; was second in command under Sir Edward Hawke during the blockade of Brest, and in the decisive battle of Quiberon; and continued in the same office till he was made Vice-Admiral in

1762. In 1770 he was advanced to be Admiral of the Blue, and was appointed Governor of Greenwich Hospital in 1771.

Three-quarter length, life-size, to left, in naval uniform; right hand resting on sword; ships in the distance.  Canvas 48 × 40 in.

By G. ROMNEY.  Lent by The LORDS OF THE ADMIRALTY
(Greenwich Hospital).

**139.** VICE-ADMIRAL SIR SAMUEL HOOD, BART., G.C.B. (1762–1814).

Youngest son of Samuel Hood, Kingsland, Dorset, and nephew of Viscounts Hood (see No. 128) and Bridport (see No. 126). Entered the navy at fourteen, was present in Admiral Rodney's action of April 12, 1782, and served in the Mediterranean under Lord Hood in the *Juno*, and distinguished himself at Toulon and Corsica, 1793–4. He commanded the *Zealous* at the Nile in 1798, reduced Tobago and Guiana in 1803, and in the engagement off Rochfort in 1806, in which he captured seven of the enemy's ships, he lost an arm. He was M.P. for Westminster in 1806, took part in the expedition against Copenhagen in 1807, created a baronet in 1809, and in the following year was appointed Commander-in-Chief in the East Indies, created a K.C.B. in 1812, a G.C.B. in 1813, and died at Madras in 1814.

Full-length, life-size, to left, in naval uniform; ribbon and Order of the Bath; hand rests on the fluke of an anchor; has lost right arm; naval battle in the distance. Canvas 94 × 58 in.

By J. HOPPNER, R.A.  Lent by The VISCOUNT HOOD.

**140.** FAMILY OF WILLIAM, 3RD DUKE OF DEVONSHIRE.

The children here portrayed are Lady Caroline Cavendish, god-child of George II., who was married to William, Lord Viscount Duncannon, and died in 1760; the eldest son William, who succeeded as 4th Duke (1720-1764); Lord George Cavendish, who was comptroller of the Royal Household, died 1794; and Lord Frederick Cavendish, who was aide-de-camp to George III., and attained the rank of Field-Marshal, died 1803.

Scene in the garden at Chiswick; the eldest daughter is seated in a swing; her eldest brother on her right leans against a tree, his left hand rests on a stick, his right is caressed by a dog; on her left one brother swings her, and the third, the youngest, runs towards her with outstretched arms. Canvas 39½ × 49½ in.

By W. HOGARTH.  Lent by The DUKE OF DEVONSHIRE, K.G.

**141.** MARIA GUNNING, COUNTESS OF COVENTRY (1733-1760).

Elder dau. of John Gunning, of Castle Coote, and Bridget, dau. of the 6th Viscount Mayo. She and her sister Elizabeth were pronounced "the handsomest women alive." It is said that one day when the sisters were going over Hampton Court, the housekeeper, wishing to show the company the rooms containing Kneller's pictures, or the Hampton

Court beauties, cried, "This way, ladies, for the beauties," and that on this the sisters flew into a passion and said they were come to see the palace and not to be shown as a sight. In March 1752, Maria married George William, 6th Earl of Coventry, whom Walpole describes as a pedant, but passionately attached to his beautiful young wife. So renowned were these sisters for their beauty and good fortune, that in Ireland the beggar women upon receiving alms exclaimed, " The luck of the Gunnings attend you." Walpole also tells us how the noble mob in the drawing-room clambered upon chairs and tables to look at the sisters; how seven hundred people in and about a Yorkshire inn sat up all night to see the Duchess of Hamilton get into her post-chaise in the morning, while a Worcester shoemaker made money by showing the shoe he was making for the Countess of Coventry. After her marriage people seemed never tired of running after the Countess of Coventry, and one Sunday in June 1759, when in company with the Countess of Waldegrave, she was so mobbed that the King, who took a good deal of notice of her, ordered that in future she should have a guard. The next Sunday she appeared accompanied with two sergeants of the guard in front, and twelve soldiers following her to keep off the admiring crowd. In the course of the winter of 1759 she was attacked by consumption, but lingered through the summer and died October 1, 1760.

Full-length, life-size, facing; gold brocade bodice and petticoat, over blue dress with white sleeves; right arm resting on pedestal of statue of Cupid; in left hand rose. Canvas 94 × 58 in.

By GAVIN HAMILTON.   Lent by The DUKE OF HAMILTON.

**142.   CUTHBERT COLLINGWOOD, 1ST LORD COLLINGWOOD (1748-1810).**

Admiral. Born at Newcastle-upon-Tyne; entered the navy at the age of 13; commanded *The Prince*, Admiral Bowyer's flag-ship in 1794, and the *Excellent* in the battle of St. Vincent in 1797. He was Vice-Admiral of the Blue, and second in command at the Nile, where he highly distinguished himself; and held the same post at the battle of Trafalgar, the chief responsibility devolving upon him on the death of Nelson. He was now advanced to the Vice-Admiral of the Red, confirmed in the command of the Mediterranean Fleet, and created a peer by the title of Baron Collingwood. Died off Minorca, March 7, 1810, and interred in St. Paul's Cathedral.

Three-quarter length, life-size, to right, in naval uniform, standing on a ship, telescope under right arm, left hand raised to his chin. Canvas 49 × 40 in.

Painted in 1806.

By H. HOWARD, R.A.   Lent by C. COLLINGWOOD DEANY, ESQ.

**143.   FRANCES WYNDHAM, COUNTESS ROMNEY (d. 1795).**

Daughter of Charles, 2nd Earl of Egremont, married August 30, 1776, Charles, 3rd Lord and 1st Earl Romney; died January 14, 1795.

Three-quarter length, life-size, to left; white dress, and grey scarf over shoulders; left hand extended, right holding scarf; landscape background. Canvas 55 × 44 in.

By SIR J. REYNOLDS, P.R.A.   Lent by The EARL OF CARNARVON.

**144.** HORATIO, ADMIRAL VISCOUNT NELSON (1758-1805).

Small full-length, to the left, in naval uniform and ribbon of the Bath; he is standing on the deck of his vessel; over chair on right is his cloak, behind him a gun, and in the background is seen naval engagement in distance; on a shield in the foreground is inscribed the name of the painter and the date 1799. His cocked hat is placed back on the forehead to avoid a wound on the right temple. Canvas 33 × 20 in.
The naval engagement in the background commemorates the taking of Fort St. Juan in Central America in 1780.

By L. GUZZARDI.                                    Lent by The EARL NELSON.

**145.** SIMON, 1ST EARL HARCOURT (1707-1777).

Grandson of the 1st Viscount, succeeded to the title in 1727, was present at Dettingen, and served in the Rebellion of 1745. He was created Viscount Harcourt of Nuneham-Courtenay and Earl Harcourt of Stanton Harcourt; constituted Governor to George Prince of Wales, in 1751, and in 1761 was sent as Ambasssdor-Extraordinary to Mecklenburg-Strelitz to demand Princess Charlotte in marriage. He went as Ambassador to France in 1768, and in the following year was appointed Lord-Lieutenant of Ireland. Died September 16, 1777. Walpole describes him as "civil and sheepish," and "though a little abashed, as never accustomed to speak in public, yet spoke with great grace and propriety."

Half-length, life-size, to left, head turned to right, in red dress, powdered hair *en perruque*; left hand thrust into his waistcoat. Canvas 34½ × 27½ in.

This picture was painted by Reynolds in 1755, it being recorded in his diary that Lord Harcourt was sitting to him in April of that year. A note appears in Lord Harcourt's accounts, "Paid Mr. Reynolds, the painter, for picture of myself and the boy, £26 5s."

By SIR J. REYNOLDS, P.R.A.                    Lent by E. W. HARCOURT, ESQ.

**146.** GEORGE, 1ST LORD LYTTELTON (1702-1773).

Statesman, poet, and historian. Eldest son of Sir Thomas Lyttelton, of Hagley, Worcestershire; sat in several Parliaments for Okehampton, and became a keen opponent of Sir Robert Walpole. This course of politics secured for him the favour of the Prince of Wales, and Lyttelton became his Private Secretary. In 1744 he was made a Lord of the Treasury, in 1756 Chancellor of the Exchequer, and in 1757 was advanced to the peerage. His principal works are, *Observations on the Conversion of St. Paul*, *Dialogues of the Dead*, and *A History of Henry II.*

Half-length, life-size, to right, in peer's robes and wig, holding scroll in right hand inscribed *George Lord Lyttelton, Aetatis suæ* 64, *anno. Dom.* 1773. Canvas 30 × 24 in.

By B. WEST, R.A.                                  Lent by The VISCOUNT COBHAM.

**147. SIR RICHARD ARKWRIGHT, KNT. (1732-1792).**

One of the principal inventors of machinery for textile manufactures. Born at Preston, in Lancashire, began life as a barber at Bolton, removed to Warrington, where he projected with Kay a machine for spinning cotton. In 1771 he erected works at Cromford, Derbyshire, and having patented various improvements in his machinery, ultimately established a great business, his fortune at his death in 1792 being valued at over half a million. In 1786 he was knighted by George III.

Full-length, life-size, seated, facing; brown coat, buff waistcoat, black breeches, and wig; his left hand rests on table on which is the spinning machine which he invented; his right on his leg. Canvas 95 × 59 in.

By J. WRIGHT, of Derby, A.R.A.        Lent by F. C. ARKWRIGHT, ESQ.

**148. MADAME GIOVANNA BACELLI (d. 1801).**

Celebrated dancer. Appeared in London at the Pantheon in 1779, and was most popular for some years. Walpole writes of her as dancing at Paris in 1788 with a blue bandeau on her head, having on it the motto of the Garter, she being then under the protection of the Duke of Dorset. She died in Sackville Street, Piccadilly, May 7, 1801, generally respected for her benevolence.

Half-length, life-size, to right, head turned to the spectator; yellow-dress, blue-mantle; head bound with vine-wreath; in right hand she holds a mask raised to her face; landscape background. Canvas 30 × 25 in.

This portrait was painted in 1782: Baccelli sat to Reynolds in June of that year.

By SIR J. REYNOLDS, P.R.A.        Lent by The LORD SACKVILLE.

**149. RICHARD BRINSLEY BUTLER SHERIDAN (1751-1816).**

Statesman, wit, and dramatist. Born in Dublin; the third son of Thomas Sheridan, the lexicographer; was educated at Harrow, and entered at the Middle Temple. In 1775 he brought out *The Rivals*, which was followed by the *Duenna*, and *School for Scandal*. In 1780 he entered Parliament for Stafford, and when the Rockingham Ministry came into power he was made an Under-Secretary, and in the Coalition Ministry Secretary to the Treasury. He attained great celebrity as an orator, especially during the Warren-Hastings trial. On the death of Pitt, Sheridan for a short period held the post of Treasurer of the Navy. Died in Savile Row, July 7, 1816, his constitution undermined by intemperance, and deeply involved in debt.

Half-length, life-size, seated to left; brown coat and wig; his left raised and grasping the end of his white cravat. Canvas 30 × 24 in.

Painted in 1788-89, this picture was exhibited in the Royal Academy of 1789, in which year Sir Joshua sent twelve pictures, which stood unapproached among the portrait painters. Walpole, in his catalogue, sets the following note against the picture: " Praise cannot overstate the merits of this portrait. It is not canvas and colour, it is animated nature." At the unaffected manner and character of the admired original, and on the picture of Lord Henry Fitzgerald, also hung this year, Walpole remarks, "This is Sir Joshua's second piece, and yields only to Mr. Sheridan's."

By SIR J. REYNOLDS, P.R.A.  Lent by HORACE N. PYM, ESQ.

**150. WILLIAM WINDHAM (1750-1810).**

Statesman. Entered Parliament for Norwich in 1783, took part in the impeachment of Warren Hastings, and in 1797 joined the Pitt administration as Secretary for War, but resigned in 1801, being opposed to the peace On the death of Pitt Windham again became Secretary for War in the "administration of All the Talents," which only lasted one year. Died June 4, 1810, from the effects of a fall, while exerting himself to save the library of Mr. North during a fire in Conduit Street. His diary, kept at the suggestion of Dr. Johnson, appeared in 1866.

Three-quarter length, life-size. standing to right in black coat and wig ; left arm raised and resting on some books in a cabinet, papers in left hand, on left table with ink-stand and papers. Canvas 50 × 40 in.
Exhibited at the Royal Academy in 1803.

By SIR T. LAWRENCE, P.R.A.  Lent by UNIVERSITY COLLEGE, OXFORD.

**151. LT.-COL. HON. ARTHUR WELLESLEY AFTERWARDS DUKE OF WELLINGTON (1769–1852).**

Fifth son of Garrett, 1st Earl of Mornington, and Anne, daughter of Arthur, 1st Viscount Dungannon : was educated at Eton and at Angiers in France ; received his first commission as Ensign in the 73rd Regiment of Foot, in 1787 ; was M.P. in the Irish Parliament for Trim ; appointed Colonel of the 33rd Regiment in 1796 ; went to India in 1797, and from this period he may be said to have fairly begun the splendid series of military exploits with which this great soldier astounded the world, and which added so much to the power and glory of the British Empire. The barest outline of them can only be given here. In September, 1803, he won the battle of Assaye ; returned to England in 1805 ; was appointed Commander-in-Chief of the British forces in the Peninsular war, 1808-1814, when ensued the most brilliant victories ever recorded, which terminated with his occupation of Paris, May 4, 1814. His patents of Viscount, Earl, and Marquess were read on the same day in the House of Lords, June 28, 1814. He won the victory of Waterloo, June 18, 1815, was Commander-in-Chief in 1827, First Lord of the Treasury in 1828 and 1834, again Commander-in-Chief in 1842, and died at Walmer Castle, September 14, 1852.

Three-quarter length, life-size, nearly facing, his arms folded ; black coat ; orders Golden Fleece, &c. Canvas 43 × 34 in.

By H. P. BRIGGS, R.A.  Lent by T. LYON THURLOW, ESQ.

NORTH GALLERY.]     *Portraits.*     51

**152.** MRS. POWYS, OF BERWICK, AND HER DAUGHTER ANNE CATHERINE, AFTERWARDS VISCOUNTESS FEILDING (1777).

Mrs. Powys was the wife of Thomas Jelf-Powys, of Berwick House, co. Salop. Her daughter Anne Catherine married, April 26, 1791, William, Viscount Feilding, son of Basil, 6th Earl of Denbigh, who died in his father's life-time, August 8, 1799. His widow survived him till January 1, 1852.

Full-length life-size figures; Mrs. Powys, facing, has her left arm round her daughter, who stands to left on a slab; her right hand is extended; the child, looking at her mother, raises its right hand towards its face; both dressed in white and pink; landscape background. Canvas 93 × 57.

Mrs. Powys and her daughter sat to Reynolds in June, 1777. In the painter's pricebook for 1779 we find the following entry—" Mrs. Powis for self and daughter, £112 13s. 6d."

By SIR J. REYNOLDS, P.R.A.     Lent by The EARL OF DENBIGH.

**153.** MARY, LADY HOLLAND (d. 1778).

Daughter of John Fitzpatrick, Earl of Upper Ossory. Married April 20, 1766, Stephen, 2nd Lord Holland, by whom she had issue—Henry, 3rd Lord Holland, and three daughters. Died October 4, 1778. Her character is thus described by her brother, Lord Ossory: "Lady Holland was the most amiable person that ever lived. She possessed the most perfect sweetness of manners, joined to an excellent understanding; the most elegant person; but, alas! too delicate a frame. Her temper was the sweetest I was ever acquainted with; her heart the tenderest and most sincere. She was the best wife that ever lived, and in the most trying situation that can be conceived, nothing could exceed her tenderness of attention to her children."

Half-length, life-size, facing; pink dress, long plaits of hair hanging over her shoulders; hands clasped, left arm resting on chair. Canvas 30 × 24 in.

Lady Mary Holland, sat to Reynolds in July, 1766, immediately after her marriage, and again in May, 1768, and February, 1769.

By SIR J. REYNOLDS, P.R.A.     Lent by The EARL OF ILCHESTER.

**154.** NAPOLEON I. (1769-1821).

Born at Ajaccio in Corsica, was a lieutenant in the army at the commencement of the revolution; assumed the title of Chief Consul of the Republic in 1799; was made First Consul in 1802, and consecrated Emperor 2nd Dec. 1804. Died at St. Helena, 5 May, 1821.

Half-length, life-size, to right; in uniform. Canvas 30 × 24 in.

By T. PHILLIPS, R.A.     Lent by HENRY IRVING, ESQ.

**155.** LADY ELIZABETH FOSTER, DUCHESS OF DEVONSHIRE (d. 1824).

Daughter of Frederick Augustus, 4th Earl of Bristol and Bishop of Derry, married 1st John Thomas Foster, and 2ndly, October 19, 1809, William, 5th Duke of Devonshire. After the decease of her husband in 1811, the Duchess resided much in Italy, chiefly at Rome, where she took great interest in the excavations carried on in that city between 1815-1819. These excavations were remarkable for the uncovering of the column of Phocas in 1816, an event commemorated by a series of medalets bearing the Duchess's bust.

Half-length, life-size, to right, white dress, blue sash, powdered hair; landscape background. Canvas 29 × 24½ in.

This portrait was painted by Reynolds in 1787, Lady Elizabeth Foster's name occurring amongst his sitters for April of that year. It was exhibited at the Royal Academy in the following year, at the same time as his *Infant Hercules*, which was painted for the Empress Catherine of Russia. Reynolds had no less than seventeen pictures at the Academy of that year—a remarkable sign of his unremitting vigour.

By SIR J. REYNOLDS, P.R.A.      Lent by The DUKE OF DEVONSHIRE, K.G.

**156.** ARTHUR, 1ST DUKE OF WELLINGTON, K.G., AS COL. OF THE 33RD FOOT.

Half-length, life-size, to left, in uniform of the 33rd Foot. Canvas 30 × 25 in.

By J. HOPPNER, R.A.      Lent by The DUKE OF WELLINGTON.

**157.** ARTHUR WELLESLEY, DUKE OF WELLINGTON, K.G. (1769-1852).

Full-length, life-size, facing, in a corridor; black coat, buff waistcoat, wearing orders of the Garter, Bath, and Golden Fleece; glove in left hand. Canvas 83 × 49 in.

By H. WEIGALL.      Lent by H. WEIGALL, ESQ.

**158.** THOMAS, 2ND LORD LYTTELTON (1744-1779).

Eldest son of 1st Lord (see No. 146). Was a young man of genius, but the reverse of his father in moral conduct, his days being passed in splendid misery and in the painful change of the most extravagant gaiety and the deepest despair. He filled the offices of Chief Justice in Eyre of his Majesty's forests north of the Tweed, and High Steward of Bewdley. Died under very mysterious circumstances, November 27, 1779. The writer in the *Quarterly Review*, December, 1851, endeavoured to prove that Lyttelton was Junius.

Half-length, life-size, to right, in judge's robes and wig, holding paper in right hand. Canvas 30 × 24 in.

After GAINSBOROUGH.      Lent by The VISCOUNT COBHAM.

[NORTH GALLERY.] *Portraits.* 53

**159.** THE HON. MRS. PETER BECKFORD AS "HYGIEIA."

Daughter of Colonel Julius Hering, and wife of Peter Beckford, Speaker of the House of Assembly at Jamaica, and brother of Alderman William Beckford.

Full-length, life-size, to left, standing before a lighted tripod and holding patera with vase, yellow dress, white scarf, hair powdered and surmounted by diadem; behind her an attendant pouring out a libation; architectural background. Canvas 94 × 58 in.

By SIR J. REYNOLDS, P.R.A. Lent by The DUKE OF HAMILTON.

**160.** MISS RIDGE.

Daughter of John Ridge, Alderman, a member of the Irish bar. Goldsmith, in his poem *Retaliation*, thus mentions him :—

"To make out the dinner, full certain I am
That Ridge is anchovy and Reynolds is lamb,
That Hickey's a capon, and by the same rule,
Magnanimous Goldsmith a gooseberry fool."

Half-length, life-size, seated facing; her left arm on table; white dress, blue ribbon in dress and hair. Canvas 30 × 24 in.

By SIR J. REYNOLDS, P.R.A. Lent by LIONEL DE ROTHSCHILD, ESQ.

**161.** FIELD MARSHAL LEBRECHT VON BLÜCHER (1742–1819).

Distinguished Prussian General whose intrepidity gained him the appellation of "Marshal Forward." Born at Rostock in Mecklenburg-Schwerin in 1742, entered the Swedish service, and being made prisoner by the Prussians, transferred his services to the enemy and rose to the rank of Captain, but being discontented received his discharge from Frederick the Great, who dismissed him with the remark that "he might go to the devil if he pleased." Being re-called by Frederick William, he commanded at Leystadt in 1794, and also at Jena, which battle decided for a time the Prussian Monarchy. In the European coalition against Napoleon in 1813, Blücher distinguished himself at Lützen and Leipsic, entered Paris with the allies in 1814, and commanded at Ligny in 1815, and by a desperate effort completed the defeat of the French at Waterloo. Died in Silesia, September 12, 1819.

Half-length, life-size, facing, head to left, in dark military uniform; orders on breast. Canvas 29 × 23 in.

Lent by The DUKE OF WELLINGTON.

**162.** GEORGIANA, DUCHESS OF DEVONSHIRE (1757–1806).

Half-length, life-size, to left, head nearly facing; black dress, white front, grey wig. Canvas 29 × 23 in.

The gash across the picture was made by George IV.

By G. ROMNEY. Lent by The DUCHESS OF ST. ALBANS.

**163.** EDWARD, LORD THURLOW (1732-1806).

Lord Chancellor. Son of the Rev. Thomas Thurlow, rector of Ashfield, Suffolk, where he was born; was educated at Canterbury and Caius College, Cambridge, and being called to the bar in 1754 his success was rapid and extraordinary. Having entered Parliament for Tamworth in 1768, he was appointed Solicitor-General in 1770, Attorney-General in 1771, and in 1778 became Lord Chancellor, being at the same time raised to the peerage as Baron Thurlow. He resigned the seals in April 1783, but resumed them on the dissolution of the Coalition Ministry of Lord North and Mr. Fox, and held them till 1792. Died at Brighton September 13, 1806. Lord Thurlow was a man of stern manners, of inflexible integrity, but as a judge did not stand very high. His dark complexion, stern and rugged features, and his bushy eyebrows, made him, as Fox said, "look wiser than any man ever was."

Three-quarter length, life-size, seated to left, in brown coat and wig; right hand rests on book placed on table; left on his leg. Canvas 50 x 40 in.

By T. PHILLIPS, R.A.            Lent by T. LYON THURLOW, ESQ.

**164.** LORD ROBERT KERR (d. 1746).

Second son of William, 3rd Marquess of Lothian, and younger brother of William, 4th Marquess. Received a commission in the 11th Dragoons, Lord Mark Kerr's, in 1739; was afterwards captain of the grenadier company of Barrell's Foot, and fell at Culloden, April 16, 1746. Standing at the head of his company when the rebels broke into the regiment, he received the foremost man on his spontoon, and was instantly killed with many wounds, being then in the bloom of his youth and extremely handsome.

Three-quarter length, life-size, to left, head facing, in uniform of Barrell's Foot; right hand resting on plumed helmet; left on his hip. Canvas 42 X 34 in.

By A. RAMSAY.            Lent by The MARQUESS OF LOTHIAN, K.T.

**165.** THE HON. AUGUSTUS JOHN HERVEY (CAPTAIN R.N.) AFTERWARDS 3RD EARL OF BRISTOL (1723-1799).

Grandson of John, 1st Earl; entered the Navy in 1744, appointed Post-Captain in 1747, Colonel of the Marines in 1775, and Commander-in-Chief in the Mediterranean in 1763. He was a Lord of the Admiralty in 1775, and in the same year succeeded his brother, George William, as 3rd Earl of Bristol. He was successively Rear-Admiral of the Blue, White, and Red. He married privately, in 1744, Miss Chudleigh, known afterwards as the Duchess of Kingston, from having contracted a bigamous marriage with the Duke of Kingston, for which she was tried and convicted.

Full-length, life-size, to left, standing on sea-shore; in naval uniform; resting against the fluke of an anchor, telescope in left hand, right on hip. Canvas 94 x 58.

By T. GAINSBOROUGH, R.A.            Lent by The MARQUESS OF BRISTOL.

NORTH GALLERY.] *Portraits.* 55

**166.** FRANCIS RAWDON, 1ST MARQUESS OF HASTINGS (1754–1826).

Eldest son of the Earl of Moira, distinguished himself in the American war, where he rose to the rank of Brigadier-General. On his return to England he was created Lord Rawdon in 1783, was appointed aide-de-camp to the King, and in 1790 assumed the name of Hastings, succeeding as Earl of Moira in 1793. He served under the Duke of York in Holland in 1794, was Master-General of the Ordnance in 1806, Governor-General of India from 1812-1821, and Commander-in-Chief of Malta in 1824. He was created Viscount Loudoun, Earl of Rawdon and Marquess of Hastings in 1816.

Half-length, life-size, facing, head to right, in military uniform. Canvas 30 × 24 in.

By SIR T. LAWRENCE, P.R.A.        Lent by The EARL OF LOUDOUN.

**167.** ELIZA ANNE LINLEY, MRS. SHERIDAN, AND HER BROTHER (1754-1792).

Daughter of Thomas Linley, the musical composer. Born in 1754; sang with her sister, afterwards Mrs. Tickell, at the concerts established by her father at Bath; married Richard Brinsley Sheridan in 1772 privately near Calais, whither she had travelled with the intention of entering a convent, and again in England, when her father's consent had been obtained. After her marriage she never sang in public. Died in 1792. She was an accomplished singer and remarkable for her beauty. Walpole writes of her, March 16, 1773: "I was not at the ball last night, and have only been to the opera, where I was infinitely struck with the Carrara, who is the prettiest creature upon earth. Mrs. Hartley I am to find still handsomer, and Miss Linley to be the superlative degree. The king admires the last, and ogles her as much as he dares to do in so holy a place as an oratorio, and at so devout a service as *Alexander's Feast.*"

Half-length figures; Miss Linley to left, head to right; in blue dress and white scarf, which she holds in both hands raised to her bosom; her brother in red jacket rests his head on her shoulder looking at the spectator, landscape background. Canvas 26½ × 23 in.

This picture was painted by Gainsborough during his residence at Bath and shortly before Miss Linley's marriage. Thicknesse tells the following anecdote: "After returning from a concert at Bath, where we had been charmed by Miss Linley's voice, I went home to supper with my friend (Gainsborough), who sent his servant for a bit of clay from the small beer barrel, with which he modelled and then coloured her head, and that too in a quarter of an hour, in such a manner that I protest it appeared to me even superior to his paintings. The next day I took a friend or two to his house to see it, but it was not to be seen, the servant had thrown it down from the mantel-piece and broken it. Mr. Leslie had in his possession an exquisite plaster cast of Miss Linley (from a clay model by Gainsborough) which shared the same fate. Gainsborough used now and then to model the faces of his friends in miniature, finding the material in the wax-candles before him."

By T. GAINSBOROUGH, R.A.        Lent by The LORD SACKVILLE.

**168.** CHARLES, 4TH DUKE OF RUTLAND, K.G. (1754-1787).

Son of John, Marquess of Granby (see No. 56); was M.P. for the University of Cambridge; succeeded to the dukedom on the death of his grandfather John, 3rd Duke, in 1779; elected K.G. 1782, and appointed Lord-Lieutenant of Ireland, 1784, in which office he died, October 24, 1787. Married Lady Mary Isabella, daughter of Charles, 4th Duke of Beaufort.

Half-length, life-size, to right, head to left, red cloak with fur trimming. Canvas (oval) 27½ × 22 in.

Painted in 1776. The following item appears in Reynolds's pocket-book for this year:—" Lord Granby given to Lord Lothian, Feb., £36 : 15 : 0." The Duke of Rutland was a great patron of the painter. In 1779 he bought " The Nativity," for which he paid £1,200—a price for an English picture at that time quite unexampled. Again in January, 1780, we find the painter visiting Belvoir and executing portraits of the Duchess and her two eldest children, the Marquess of Granby and Lady Elizabeth Manners; both pictures being afterwards burnt in 1816: and in 1786 Reynolds carries through for the Duke the purchase of the "Seven Sacraments" of Poussin, obtained from the Borrapudule Palace at Rome.

By SIR J. REYNOLDS, P.R.A.  Lent by The MARQUESS OF LOTHIAN, K.T.

**169.** GEORGE SIMON, VISCOUNT NUNEHAM, AFTERWARDS 2ND EARL HARCOURT AGED 17 (1736-1809).

Eldest son of the 1st Earl Harcourt. Was educated at Westminster; styled Viscount Nuneham in 1749; elected M.P. for St. Albans in 1761, and in the same year was Page of Honour to George III. at his Coronation. Succeeded as Earl Harcourt in 1777, and was appointed Master of the Horse to Queen Charlotte in 1790. Died without issue April 20, 1809. In his early days Lord Nuneham spent much time in foreign travels; in consequence his entrance into public life was marked by a decided preference for French manners and fashions, and his appearance so adapted to it as almost to disguise the exterior of an Englishman.

Half-length, life-size, to right, black dress; he holds in left hand a sketch. Canvas 34½ × 27½ in.

This picture was painted in 1753, or two years earlier than that of his father, the 1st Earl (see No. 145). There is no mention of it in Reynolds's diary. Lord Harcourt in his catalogue states that it cost £12 10s., and in praising the picture says "the transparent colouring of this head can scarcely be surpassed." The painter seems to have been on intimate terms with the Harcourt family, and Nuneham was one of his favourite visiting places. The 2nd Earl had a fine and cultivated taste in the arts, was an excellent etcher and a clever draughtsman. Walpole writes to him in the highest praise of his work.

By SIR J. REYNOLDS, P.R.A.  Lent by E. W. HARCOURT, ESQ.

NORTH GALLERY.]    *Portraits.*    57

**170. CHARLES PRATT, 1ST EARL OF CAMDEN (1714-1794).**

Lord Chancellor. 3rd son of Sir John Pratt, Chief Justice of the King's Bench ; was educated at Eton and King's College, Cambridge, rose to eminence at the bar, appointed Attorney-General to the Prince of Wales in 1755, Attorney-General in 1757, and Lord Chief Justice of the Common Pleas in 1762, when he was knighted. In this position he gained great popularity by discharging Wilkes in 1763. He was created Baron Camden in 1765, was Lord Chancellor for 1766-1770, Lord President of the Council in 1782, and again in 1784, and was advanced to an Earldom in 1786.

Three-quarter length, life-size, seated to left ; black gown, lace cravat, and ruffles. Canvas 50 × 40 in.

There are two other portraits of Earl Camden by Reynolds. One, painted in 1764-65 for the Common Council, in commemoration of the judgment in the matter of general warrants, is in the Guildhall ; the other, painted in 1767, now hangs at Bayham.

By SIR J. REYNOLDS, P.R.A.    Lent by The DUKE OF GRAFTON, K.G.

**171. WILLIAM CAVENDISH, 5TH DUKE OF DEVONSHIRE, K.G. (1748-1811).**

Son of the 4th Duke ; was Page of Honour to George III. at his coronation, succeeded as 5th Duke in 1764, was constituted Lord High Treasurer of Ireland in 1766, and created a K.G. in 1782. Died July 29, 1811. He married 1st Georgiana, daughter of John, 1st Earl Spencer, June 5, 1774 and 2ndly Elizabeth, daughter of Frederick, 42nd Earl of Bristol, October 19, 1809

Three-quarter length, life-size, to left, blue coat, red mantle, and perruque ; in right hand paper, left rests on marble-topped table. Canvas 53 × 38 in.
Painted at Rome.

By A. VON MARON.    Lent by The MARQUESS OF HARTINGTON, M.P.

**172. MRS. JOHN WILLIAMS (*née* CURRIE) AS "ST. CECILIA."**

Full-length, life-size ; seated to left ; head raised is looking up towards two cherubim ; white dress and gold girdle ; her right elbow rests on an organ, the hand being raised to the face ; in left scroll of music. Canvas 93 × 57 in.

The painter was very fond of this picture, and kept it in his studio, from whence it was taken shortly before his death by the father of the present owner. The picture was commenced about 1806, but it was several years before it was completed.

By SIR T. LAWRENCE, P.R.A.    Lent by COLONEL MORETON WHEATLEY.

**173. GENERAL SIR JOHN MOORE, K.C.B. (1761-1809).**

Eldest son of Dr. John Moore. Born at Glasgow ; obtained at the age of fifteen an ensigncy in the 51st Regiment, of which in 1790 he became Lieut.-Colonel and served with his corps in Corsica, where he was wounded in storming the Mazello fort at the siege of

Calvi. In 1796 he went to the West Indies as Brigadier-General to Sir Ralph Abercromby, and was appointed Governor of St. Lucia. On his return in 1797 he was employed in Ireland, took part in the expedition to Holland in 1799, and soon afterwards went to Egypt and was twice wounded. For his conduct in the campaign he was made a K.C.B. In 1808 he was appointed to the command in Spain, and fell by a cannon-shot under the walls of Corunna, January 16, 1809, after a skilful and arduous retreat before a very superior force. The House of Commons ordered a monument to be erected to him in St. Paul's Cathedral.

Half-length, life-size, facing, in military uniform. Canvas 30 × 24 in.

By SIR T. LAWRENCE; P.R.A. Lent by JOHN CARRICK MOORE, ESQ.

**174. ADMIRAL SIR GRAHAM MOORE, G.C.B. (1764–1843).**

Entered the navy at the age of thirteen, served in the West Indies under Lord Byron, and in the Mediterranean under Lord Howe, being present at the relief of Gibraltar. He was appointed Post-Captain in 1794, and being in command of the *Melampus* rendered signal service in the Channel during the long war with France. In 1815 he was made a K.C.B., promoted to the rank of Vice-Admiral in 1819 and sent to the Mediterranean, where he spent the usual period of command. In 1820 Moore was appointed a G.C.M.G., in 1836 a G.C.B., and in 1837 promoted to full Admiral. He retired from service in 1839, and died November 25, 1843, at Cobham, Surrey.

Half-length, life-size, facing, in naval uniform. Canvas 30 × 24 in.

By SIR T. LAWRENCE, P.R.A. Lent by JOHN CARRICK MOORE, ESQ.

**175. GEORGE AUGUSTUS ELIOT, LORD HEATHFIELD, K.B. (1718–1790).**

General. Youngest son of Sir Gilbert Eliot; studied at Leyden and at the military school of La Fère, Picardy; served in Germany, and was wounded at Dettingen; appointed in 1759 to raise the 1st Regiment of Light Horse, with which he served on the Continent with great reputation, and in 1775 Commander-in-Chief in Ireland, whence he returned soon afterwards and was made Governor of Gibraltar. That fortress he defended with consummate skill and courage when besieged by the French and Spaniards for a space of three years, from 1779-1783. On his return to England he was raised to the peerage under the title of Lord Heathfield, Baron Gibraltar, and made a K.B. Died in 1790 at Aix-la-Chapelle.

Three-quarter length, life-size; facing, head to left, in naval uniform and star of the Bath; in right hand key, which rests on left; on left, sextant; on right, mortar. Canvas 56 × 45 in.

The original of this picture, which represents Lord Heathfield at the age of nearly 70, was exhibited at the Royal Academy in 1788. It was painted for Mr. Alderman John Boydell, and is now in the National Gallery. Northcote describes Lord Heathfield as enlivening his sittings to Sir Joshua Reynolds with various narratives and droll anecdotes of the great Frederick and others. It has been engraved by Richard Earlom.

After SIR J. REYNOLDS, P.R.A. Lent by The CORPORATION OF THE CITY OF LONDON.

**176.** JOHN, 1ST EARL LIGONIER (1678-1770).

Distinguished general. Born of an ancient family; entered the army, and served through the Duke of Marlborough's campaigns with great distinction; was made a knight-banneret on the field at Dettingen in 1743; served with renown at Raucoux in 1746, and at Laffeldt in 1747, where he was taken prisoner. He was appointed Field-Marshal and Commander-in-Chief, and created an Irish peer by the title of Viscount Ligonier, and in 1763, advanced to the English peerage by the title of Baron Ligonier of Ripley, and in 1766, created Earl Ligonier. Died 1770, and was buried in Westminster Abbey.

Equestrian figure, under life-size, galloping to right, looking back, in military uniform and Order of the Bath; in right hand baton; in the background scene of the Battle of Dettingen. Canvas 56 × 60 in.

There is a replica of this picture in the National Gallery. It was painted in 1760, and exhibited in Spring Gardens in 1761 and following years. Lord Ligonier was in his eighty-second year when the picture was painted; it was necessary, therefore, for the painter to ante-date the features—a task of no small difficulty to one who represented nature as he saw it.

By SIR J. REYNOLDS, P.R.A.      Lent by The DUKE OF SUTHERLAND, K.G.

**177.** HESTER GRENVILLE, BARONESS AND COUNTESS CHATHAM (d. 1803).

The only daughter of Richard Grenville of Wootton, and Hester Temple created Countess of Temple; married October 16, 1754, William Pitt, afterwards 1st Earl of Chatham. She was created Baroness December 4, 1761, and became Countess in 1766 Died April 3, 1803.

Half-length, life-size, to right, white dress, blue scarf. Canvas 30 × 24 in.
Painted in 1750, and brought in 1848 from the collection at Stowe.

By T. HUDSON.      Lent by The EARL STANHOPE.

**178.** JOHN SCOTT, EARL OF ELDON (1751-1838).

Lord Chancellor. Born at Newcastle, the son of John Scott, coalfitter, and younger brother of Lord Stowell, was educated at University College, Oxford, where he took the Chancellor's prize, chose the bar as a profession, and in 1783, through the influence of Lord Thurlow, entered Parliament for the borough of Weobley, soon showing himself to be a clever legislator and a fluent speaker. He was appointed Solicitor-General, and knighted in 1788, Attorney General in 1793, and succeeded, in 1799, Sir James Eyre as Lord Chief Justice of the Common Pleas, being raised to his peerage as Baron Eldon of Eldon in Durham. In 1801 he was nominated Lord Chancellor, and but for a short period, from February, 1806, to April, 1807, retained the office till April, 1827. At the coronation of George IV., he was promoted to the dignities of Viscount Encombe and Earl of Eldon. Died in London, January 13, 1838. Sir Samuel Romilly declared in the House of

Commons that, "there never presided in the Court of Chancery, a man of more deep and various learning in his profession, and in anxiety to do justice that Court had never seen the equal of the Lord Chancellor."

Half-length, life-size, facing; black coat. Canvas 30 × 24 in.

Exhibited at the Royal Academy in 1825. It was engraved by G. T. Doo, R.A., in 1827, and by J. Porter in 1844 for the Lawrence work. Lawrence had executed a previous portrait of Eldon, as Chief-Justice of the Common Pleas. It was exhibited at the Royal Academy in 1800.

By SIR T. LAWRENCE, P.R.A.         Lent by the EARL OF ELDON.

**179.** DEATH OF ADMIRAL VISCOUNT NELSON, K.B., IN THE COCKPIT OF H.M.S. "VICTORY" OFF TRAFALGAR, OCTOBER 21, 1805.

Canvas 103 × 76 in.

After the Battle of Trafalgar Devis went out to meet the *Victory*, and made the sketch for this picture. It was engraved by W. Bromley in 1812, and was presented by the Right Hon. Lord Bexley to the Gallery of Greenwich Hospital in 1825.

By A. W. DEVIS.         Lent by The LORDS OF THE ADMIRALTY
(Greenwich Hospital).

**180.** CAPTAIN JAMES COOK, F.R.S. (1728–1779).

Celebrated navigator. Born at Marton, in Yorkshire, began his naval career in the merchant service, and obtained a warrant as master of the *Mercury*, in which ship he took part in the capture of Quebec. After various and arduous services he was raised to the rank of Lieutenant, and then commenced those series of voyages which have made his name so remarkable. His first voyage was in 1768, as commander of the *Endeavour*, in which he reached New Holland (Australia) in 1770. In his second voyage in 1772, with the *Resolution* and *Adventure*, he visited New Zealand, and in his third, again commanding the *Resolution*, and accompanied by the *Discovery*, he found the Sandwich Islands, where he was murdered by some of the natives of Owyhee, February 14, 1779. In 1775 Cook was elected a F.R.S., and was awarded the gold medal of the Royal Society for discoveries.

Three-quarter length, life-size, seated to left, head to right; in naval uniform, holding in hand a chart of the world. Canvas 50 × 40 in.

By N. DANCE, R.A.         Lent by The LORDS OF THE ADMIRALTY
(Greenwich Hospital).

**181.** EDWARD PELLEW, 1ST VISCOUNT EXMOUTH, G.C.B. (1757–1833).

Admiral. Born at Dover; entered the navy at the age of thirteen; appointed in 1793 Captain of *La Nymphe*, with which he captured the frigate *La Cleopatra* after a most determined and gallant action, and for which he was knighted. For his bravery and saving the crew of the *Dutton*, East Indiaman, in 1796 he was created a baronet, and afterwards distinguished himself in numerous engagements with the French. In 1810 he was advanced to the rank of Vice-Admiral of the Blue, blockaded Flushing in 1810, appointed Commander-in-Chief of the Mediterranean Fleet, and created Baron Exmouth in 1814, being raised to the rank of full Admiral. In 1815 took place his memorable bombardment of Algiers for which he received the thanks of Parliament and was created a Viscount, September 21, 1816. He was made a K.C.B. in 1815, and a G.C.B. in 1816; held the office of Commander-in-Chief of Gibraltar from 1817-21, and was successively Admiral of the White 1821, and of the Red 1830. In person he was "tall, full of strength and symmetry, and his personal activity and power were almost unrivalled."

Three-quarter length, life-size, facing, head to left; hands resting on sword; naval uniform; ribbon of the Bath and various orders. Canvas 50 × 40 in.

By W. OWEN, R.A.           Lent by The LORDS OF THE ADMIRALTY
(Greenwich Hospital).

**182. DOUGLAS, 8TH DUKE OF HAMILTON, DR. JOHN MOORE AND HIS SON JOHN (AFTERWARDS GENERAL) MOORE.**

The personages represented in this picture are Douglas, 8th Duke of Hamilton, died 1799, Dr. John Moore the eminent medical and miscellaneous writer (1729—1802), and his son John, the hero of Corunna (1761—1809), see No. 173. In 1772 the Duke of Hamilton set out on a lengthy tour on the Continent, accompanied by Dr. Moore as medical attendant and travelling tutor. They spent five years in visiting some of the most interesting parts of Europe. In company with them was John, Dr. Moore's eldest son. This picture was painted as a memorial of their visit to Rome, which took place in 1773, young Moore being then twelve years old.

Life-size figures; in the centre stands the Duke in red coat, buff waistcoat and breeches, black hat and cloak; he leans with his left hand on a pedestal; on his right is seated Dr. Moore, leaning right elbow on his chair and holding stick in his hand, his left hand extended; on the doctor's left is young Moore, his head raised and his left arm leaning on pedestal; in the foreground is a mastiff, in the background view of Rome. Canvas 70 × 56 in.

By GAVIN HAMILTON.           Lent by The EARL OF CARLISLE.

**183. RICHARD COLLEY, MARQUESS WELLESLEY, K.G. (1760-1842).**

Distinguished statesman. Eldest son of Garrett, 1st Earl of Mornington; born in Grafton Street, Dublin; succeeded as 2nd Earl of Mornington in the peerage of Ireland in 1781; created Baron Wellesley and Governor-General of India in 1797, where his administration was the most brilliant on record. Created Marquess Wellesley in 1799. He went as ambassador to Madrid in 1809; was Foreign Secretary in the administrations of the Duke of Portland and Spencer Perceval, and appointed Lord-Lieutenant of Ireland from 1821-1828, and again from 1833-4. Died at Knightsbridge, September 23, 1842. His youngest brother was Arthur, Duke of Wellington.

Half-length, life-size, to left; olive-green coat, and wig; orders on breast. Canvas 30 × 25 in.

By J. HOPPNER, R.A.            Lent by The DUKE OF WELLINGTON.

**184.** RIGHT HON. SPENCER PERCEVAL, M.P. (1762-1812).

Statesman. Second son of the 2nd Earl of Egmont; was educated at Harrow and Trinity College, Cambridge, and having applied himself to the study of the law, entered Parliament in 1796 as member for Northampton, and in 1801 was appointed Solicitor-General, and next year Attorney-General. On the change of administration in 1809, Perceval was appointed First Lord of the Treasury and Chancellor of the Exchequer, which offices he still held when he was assassinated by Bellingham in the lobby of the House of Commons, May 11, 1812.

Half-length, life-size, seated to left, black coat; paper in left hand. Canvas 29 × 24 in.

This picture was painted for Lord Sidmouth. It bore the inscription, "G. F. Joseph, R.A., pinxit 1812," and was marked "a posthumous portrait."

By G. F. JOSEPH, R.A.            Lent by H. SPENCER WALPOLE, ESQ.

# SOUTH GALLERY.

## ARTS, LETTERS, AND SCIENCE.

**185.** JAMES NORTHCOTE, R.A. (1746–1831).

The son of a watchmaker; born at Plymouth; conceived an irresistible inclination for the fine arts; and was recommended to Sir Joshua Reynolds, in whose studio he assiduously worked for over five years. After this apprenticeship he studied for three years in Rome, and returning to England, 1780, set up as an historical and portrait painter. He was elected an A.R.A. in 1786, and a full member in the following year. Died July 13, 1831. Northcote gained a considerable reputation, not only as a painter, but also an author. His chief publications were, *Memoirs of Sir Joshua Reynolds*, *One Hundred Fables*, and the *Life of Titian*.

Small half-length, facing, looking to left; black coat. Panel 8 × 7 in.

By SIR D. WILKIE, R.A.            Lent by G. P. BOYCE, ESQ.

**186.** CHARLES MATHEWS (1776–1835).

Comedian. Born in London; was educated at Merchant Taylors' School, and apprenticed to his father, a bookseller. To the horror of his parents, who were "Methodists," he took to the stage, his first appearance as a professional comedian being at the Theatre Royal, Dublin, in 1794; and in London at the Haymarket Theatre in 1803, as Jabal in *The Jew*. Among the characters in which he most excelled were Mawworm, Sir Fretful Plagiary, Morbleu, Monsieur Mallet, Dick Cyper, and Multiple in the *Actor of All Work*. In 1818 he abandoned the regular drama and commenced a species of entertainments in the form of a monologue, under the name of *Mr. Mathews at Home*. He twice visited America. Died at Plymouth, June 28, 1835.

Small half-length, to right; black coat. Canvas, 9½ × 7½ in.

By J. J. MASQUERIER.        Lent by The BARONESS BURDETT-COUTTS.

## 187. BENJAMIN FRANKLIN (1706-1790).

Philosopher, politician, and philanthropist. Born at Boston, New England, January 6, 1706, the son of a tallow chandler, worked for some years as a journeyman printer, and about 1728 established himself as a bookseller in Philadelphia, where, in 1732, he first published his *Poor Richard's Almanack*. He devoted himself to scientific investigations, establishing the identity of lightning and electricity, and on his appearance in England, in 1757, as agent for Pennsylvania, received the degree of Doctor of Laws at St. Andrew's, Edinburgh and Oxford. He took an active part in the contest between the mother country and her colonies, and as Commissioner for the United States signed the Treaty of Independence at Paris in 1783. He was made Governor of Pennsylvania in 1785, and died April 17, 1790, his countrymen marking their loss by a public mourning for two months.

Small half-length, to left, at a table reading from manuscript in left hand; right hand raised to the chin; blue coat and wig. Canvas 19 × 15 in.

This picture has been more than once engraved. It belonged to Charles, Earl Stanhope. By his will, dated 1805, he bequeathed it to Mr. Deane Walker, who, on retiring from his active avocations as a man of science in 1860, restored it to its place at Chevening.

By D. MARTIN.   Lent by The EARL STANHOPE.

## 188. LUKE HANSARD (1752-1828).

Printer. Born at Norwich, where he served his apprenticeship, came to London, and was employed in the office of Hughs, printer to the House of Commons, whom he joined in partnership, and ultimately succeeded in the entire business.

Three-quarter length, life-size, to left; black coat; in right hand a pen, with which he is writing at a table; in his left a paper. Canvas 36 × 28 in.

By W. LANE.   Lent by The STATIONERS' COMPANY.

## 189. SIR JOSEPH BANKS, BART., K.B. (1743-1820).

Zealous naturalist. The son of William Banks, of Revesby Abbey, was educated at Harrow, Eton, and Christchurch, Oxford; made a voyage in 1763 to Newfoundland and Labrador collecting plants, and in 1768, in company with Solander went with Cook round the world in the capacity of naturalist. In 1772 he visited the Hebrides and Iceland, whence he brought back a rich treasure of natural history specimens. In 1778 he received the Order of the Bath, was elected President of the Royal Society, an office which he held for forty-two years, and in 1781 was made a baronet. His valuable collection of specimens in natural history, as also his library, were bequeathed by him to the British Museum.

Three-quarter length, life-size, seated at a desk. in the act of reading a paper which he holds in his right hand; dark blue coat, ribbon and star of the Bath; on table below the mace of the Royal Society, inkstand, &c. Canvas 56 × 34 in.

By T. PHILLIPS, R.A.   Lent by The ROYAL SOCIETY.

SOUTH GALLERY.] *Portraits.* 65

**190.** WILLIAM WORDSWORTH (1770–1850).

Poet. Born at Cockermouth, Cumberland ; educated at St. John's College, Cambridge ; travelled in France during the period of the Revolution, and in 1808 settled at Allanbank, whence he removed in 1813 to Rydal, having as his near neighbours Coleridge and Southey, in conjunction with whom were issued the *Lyrical Ballads.* Under the patronage of Lord Lonsdale he held the appointment of Distributor of Stamps for the county of Westmoreland, which brought him in £500 a year. His great philosophical poem, the *Excursion*, was published in 1814, *The White Doe of Rylstone* in 1815, and *Peter Bell* in 1819. In 1843 he succeeded Southey as Poet Laureate.

Three-quarter length, life-size, seated under a rock, facing, head to left ; crimson-lined cloak ; left hand rests on papers, right on his knees ; landscape background. Canvas 64 × 52 in.

Painted at Rydal Mount for St. John's College, about 1831.

By H. W. PICKERSGILL, R.A.      Lent by ST. JOHN'S COLLEGE, CAMBRIDGE.

**191.** "A NEW WAY TO PAY OLD DEBTS," WITH EDMUND KEAN AS "SIR GILES OVERREACH," AND OTHERS.

The picture illustrates the last scene of the play in which Sir Giles Overreach is represented as drawing his sword upon his daughter. Beginning from the left the figures are : Oxberry, senr., as Marrall ; Munden as Justice Greedy ; Penley as Allworth ; Mrs. Odger as "Margaret"; Mrs. Knight as "Lady Allwork" ; Harley as "Wellborn" ; Hughes as "Order" ; Powell as "Welldo"; Kean as "Sir Giles Overreach"; Atwood as "Tapwell"; and Bass as "Furnace"; the kneeling figure is not a portrait, but is introduced to complete the composition. The heads of the painter Clint and the engraver Lupton are seen in the background on the left. Canvas 62 × 92.

This play by Massinger was revived at Drury Lane, January 12, 1816, and Kean produced a tremendous effect upon the town by his performance of "Sir Giles Overreach." He kept close to the character, and indulged himself in few or none of his freaks or relaxations of manner. His performance was vigorous, true, uniform, and complete. It threw the ladies in the side boxes into hysterics ; Lord Byron had a convulsive fit ; and one veteran actress was so overpowered by the last dying speech that she absolutely fainted upon the stage.

This picture was painted in 1820. Clint having been so successful in his engraving of the Kemble picture by Harlow, was induced by Welch to paint a companion subject to it. He chose for his composition Massinger's play, in which Kean was then drawing all the town.

By G. CLINT.      Lent by The COMMITTEE OF THE GARRICK CLUB.

**192.** JOSEPH NOLLEKENS, R.A. (1737–1823).

Sculptor. Son of John Francis Nollekens, a native of Antwerp ; born in London, became a pupil of Scheemakers, went to Italy and studied under Ciavetti. While at Rome he

F

gained a gold medal from the Academy of Painting, Sculpture and Architecture. Returning to England in 1770, he was elected a member of the Royal Academy, executed many works of great beauty, and amassed a fortune of £200,000. His best-known works are the monument of Mrs. Howard of Corby Castle, the statue of Pitt, at Cambridge, and the bust of Fox at Holland House.

Small three-quarter length, facing, leaning against block and holding hammer and chisel; black coat and trousers, and grey waistcoat. Canvas 20 × 15½ in.

By G. HARLOW.  Lent by The BARONESS BURDETT-COUTTS.

**193.** LADY ELIZABETH FOSTER, AFTERWARDS DUCHESS OF DEVONSHIRE (d. 1824).

Small bust to left; white dress, curling hair. Water Colour (oval) 9¼ × 8 in.

Lent by the DUKE OF DEVONSHIRE, K.G.

**194.** MRS. CHARLES MATHEWS.

Small half-length, facing; red dress lined with blue; long hair. Canvas 11 × 9½ in.

By J. J. MASQUERIER.  Lent by The BARONESS BURDETT-COUTTS.

**195.** WILLIAM STRAHAN, M.P. (1715-1785).

Eminent printer, and founder of the house of Messrs. Strahan and Co. Born at Edinburgh, whence, having acquired a knowledge of his profession, he removed to London, and in 1770 purchased a share of the patent office of King's printer. In 1775 he became member for the borough of Malmesbury, having for his colleague Charles James Fox; and in the next Parliament he had a seat for Wootton Basset. Died in 1785.

Half-length, life-size, seated to left; red coat and wig; book in right hand, left rests on his chair. Canvas 36 × 28 in.
Painted probably in 1783. The price paid for it, according to Sir Joshua's notebook was £38 15s.

By SIR J. REYNOLDS P.R.A.  Lent by MRS. ARTHUR LEMON.

**196.** RICHARD WATSON, BISHOP OF LLANDAFF (1737-1816).

Born at Heversham near Kendal; was educated there and at Trinity College, Cambridge; appointed Professor of Chemistry in 1764, and succeeded to that of Divinity in 1771. In 1776 he printed *An Apology for Christianity*, addressed to Gibbon, and in 1782 was advanced to the See of Llandaff, with permission to hold the Archdeaconry of Ely. He published many occasional tracts and writings, amongst which was his *Address to the People of England,* urging them to make large sacrifices to repel the French. He also wrote *An Apology for the Bible* in answer to Paine's *Age of Reason.*

Three-quarter length, life-size, head facing, standing to right at a table in a laboratory; on the table are a chemical furnace, books, &c. Canvas 50 × 40 in.

Sir Joshua Reynolds records in his Diary that "Mr. Professor Watson" sat for the picture October 6, 1769. He was then Professor of Chemistry at Cambridge.

By SIR J. REYNOLDS, P.R.A.            Lent by C. KNIGHT WATSON, ESQ.

**197. MATTHEW PRIOR (1664–1721).**

Poet, statesman, and diplomatist. Was educated at Westminster School, and attracting the notice of the Earl of Dorset, was sent by him to St. John's College, Cambridge. In 1687, Prior, in conjunction with Charles Montagu, afterwards Earl of Halifax, published *The City Mouse and the Country Mouse,* intended to ridicule Dryden's *Hind and Panther.* In 1691 he was appointed Secretary to the English Embassy at the Hague, in 1697 was Secretary to the Embassy at the Treaty of Ryswick, was afterwards Under-Secretary of State, and succeeded Locke at the Board of Trade. After the accession of Anne, Prior joined the Tories, was employed to negotiate the Treaty of Utrecht, and was sent as Ambassador to France. On his return he was threatened with an impeachment, which however, did not take place. He died September 18, 1721, and was buried in Westminster Abbey. It is as a poet that Prior is best remembered.

Half-length, life-size, head to right; red gown, large black cap with blue ribbon. Canvas 30 × 24 in.

This picture was formerly in the collection of Edward Harley, Earl of Oxford.

By SIR G. KNELLER.            Lent by The STATIONERS' COMPANY.

**198. EDWARD GIBBON (1737–1794).**

The celebrated historian of the *Decline and Fall of the Roman Empire.* Born at Putney, educated at home till the age of fifteen, then at Magdalen College, Oxford; became a convert to the Roman Catholic religion in 1753, but returned to Protestantism, and ended in being a sceptic. He studied at Lausanne, published an essay on the *Study of Literature,* in 1761, was Captain of the Hampshire Militia; in 1763 visited France and Italy, and in October 1764, while he "sat musing amidst the ruins of the Capitol," projected his *History of the Roman Empire,* the first volume of which appeared in 1776, the second and third volumes in 1781, and the three remaining volumes in June 1787, during his residence at Lausanne. He represented Liskeard in Parliament in 1774, and was appointed by Lord North a Commissioner for Trade and Plantations. Died in London, January 15, 1794, having come to England on a visit to Lord Sheffield.

Half-length, life-size, facing, head to left; in scarlet coat, and hair *en perruque.* Canvas 30 × 24.

                                       Lent by The EARL OF SHEFFIELD.

### 199. SIR JOHN VANBRUGH, KNT. (1666–1726).

Dramatist and architect. Descended from a Flemish family, his father being Comptroller of the Treasury-Chamber under Charles II. He brought out in 1697 his comedy of *The Relapse*, which was followed the next year by the *Provoked Wife* and *Æsop*. *The Confederacy*, written for Betterton and Congreve on their erecting a theatre in the Haymarket, was one of the most witty but most licentious of his productions. As an architect Vanbrugh gained distinction by the erection of Castle Howard and Blenheim Palace. Knighted in 1714, he was soon after made Comptroller of the royal works and Surveyor of Greenwich Hospital.

Half-length, life-size, in brown coat and wig; around neck gold chain, to which is suspended an Order; right hand resting on ledge holds a pair of compasses. Canvas 36 × 27 in.

By SIR G. KNELLER.   Lent by R. B. BAKER, ESQ.

### 200. RICHARD BRINSLEY SHERIDAN (1751–1681).

Half-length, life-size, to left; green coat with fur collar, and wig. Canvas 30 × 24 in.

By RAMBERG.   Lent by MRS. F. SHAW.

### 201. WILLIAM ROBERTSON (1721–1793).

Historian. Born at Borthwick, in Midlothian; was educated at Dalkeith and Edinburgh, and in 1743 was presented to the living of Glasmuir. He took up arms for the Government in the rebellion of 1745; was appointed Chaplain of Stirling Castle, and one of his Majesty's chaplains in 1762. He was made Principal of the University of Edinburgh in 1763, and held that office till his death. In 1764 the office of historiographer of Scotland was revived in his favour. His principal works are the *History of Charles V.* and the *History of America*—the last published in 1777.

Three-quarter length, life-size; seated to right at a table, on which are a mace and various books; his arms rest on the chair; in wig and gown. Canvas 48 × 38 in.

By SIR H. RAEBURN, R.A.   Lent by The UNIVERSITY OF EDINBURGH.

### 202. THOMAS CHATTERTON (1752–1770).

Poet. Born at Bristol, the son of the Master of the Free School there; was articled to an attorney in 1767, and in the following year, when the new bridge at Bristol was completed, communicated to Farley's newspaper " A Description of the Friars passing over the Old Bridge," pretended to be taken from an ancient manuscript. This forgery attracted considerable notice, and emboldened by its success, Chatterton imparted to his friends several papers declared by him to have been discovered in an old chest in Redclyffe Church. He also wrote to Horace Walpole, offering him notes about painters who had lived at Bristol, accompanying his letter with some verses, which he asserted

SOUTH GALLERY.]             *Portraits.*                                   69

were written in the 14th century. Walpole, with the aid of his friends Gray and Mason, detected the verses as forgeries. In 1769 Chatterton came to London in full confidence of rising by his talents, but though he was successful in obtaining literary work for magazines, he became despondent, and committed suicide by taking poison in Brook Street, Holborn, May 25, 1770.

Small bust, to right, in profile ; red coat, white collar ; long hair. Canvas 14½ × 12½ in.

This portrait, which represents Chatterton at the age of twelve, was given by his sister, Mrs. Newton, to Southey. It was purchased at the Southey sale by Miss Fenwick, and was given by her to Wordsworth with a reversion to Henry Taylor.

Lent by HARRY TAYLOR, ESQ.

**203.   EDWARD MOORE (1712-1757).**

Poet and dramatist. Son of a dissenting minister at Abingdon, Berkshire ; was bred a linen-draper in London, which he quitted for the profession of literature. In 1744 he published his *Fables for the Female Sex* which procured him many friends, among them being Lord Lyttelton, whom he complimented in a piece entitled *The Trial of Selim*. After two ineffectual attempts at dramatic composition in the comedies of the *Foundling* and *Gil Blas*, he succeeded greatly in the tragedy of *The Gamester*. He next became editor of *The World* in which he was assisted by Lords Lyttelton, Chesterfield and Bath, Horace Walpole, Richard Owen Cambridge and Soame Jenyns. Died February 28, 1757.

Small half-length, to left ; black coat, red waistcoat, embroidered in gold. Canvas (oval) 7 × 5½ in.

By T. WORLIDGE.                                      Lent by DR. EDWARD HAMILTON.

**204.   ALEXANDER POPE (1688-1744).**

The celebrated poet. Born in Lombard Street, where his father had been a successful linen-draper ; was educated at Twyford, near Winchester, whence, having lampooned his master, he was removed to Hyde Park Corner, and afterwards to Binfield, where he studied according to his own bent. He was only sixteen when he produced his *Pastorals*, which procured him the friendship of the most eminent wits of the time. His *Essay on Criticism* was published in 1711, the *Rape of the Lock* in 1714, the translation of Homer's *Iliad* in 1715-20, the *Odyssey* in 1725, the *Dunciad* in 1729, and the *Essay on Man* in 1734. From the proceeds of his *Iliad* he purchased a villa at Twickenham, which he greatly embellished and where he ever afterwards resided. Died there, May 30, 1744. His parents were Roman Catholics, and to their religion he consistently adhered through life.

Half-length, life-size, seated facing, right arm on book ; right hand supporting his head ; green gown and red cap. Canvas 28 × 23 in.

This picture is described in Lord Harcourt's *Catalogue* as "the best portrait of him and one of the best works of that master." At the back of the picture was transcribed (until the picture was re-lined by Rutley), the following letter to Simon, Lord Harcourt :—" August 22, 1723. MY LORD,—It is a satisfaction to me to tell your Lordship that I shall not be in any way disappointed of the honour you intend me, of filling a place in your library with my picture. I came to town yesterday, and got admission to Sir Godfrey Kneller, who assured me the original was done for your Lordship; and that you, and no man but you, should have it. I saw the picture there afterwards, and was told by his man that you had sent and put a seal upon it. Give me leave, my Lord, with great sincerity, to thank you for so obliging a thought, as thus to make me a sharer in the memory, as I was in the love, of a person who was justly the dearest object to you in the world; and thus to be authorized by you to be called his friend, after both of us shall be dust. I am ever with all good wishes to your Lordship and your family (in which, too, I must do my mother the justice to join her), my Lord Your most obliged and most faithful servant, A. POPE." In 1792 the picture was sent to London in order that a copy might be made of it for Lord Onslow. (See *Harcourt Papers*, Vol. III., p. 238.)

By SIR G. KNELLER.   Lent by E. W. HARCOURT, ESQ.

**205. SAMUEL JOHNSON, LL.D. (1709-1784).**

One of the most eminent literary characters of the last century, the son of a bookseller. Born at Lichfield, September 18, 1709; was educated at Lichfield and Stourbridge Grammar Schools, and at Pembroke College, Oxford. An academy which he started near Lichfield proving unsuccessful, he came to London in 1735, in company with his pupil David Garrick, and soon found literary work. He published his poem of *London*, a satire, in 1738, *Life of Savage*, in 1744, *The Vanity of Human Wishes* in 1749, and after more than seven years' labour, his *Dictionary of the English Language* in 1755; these were followed at a later date by *Rasselas, The Idler, Lives of the Poets*, &c. In 1762 he received a pension from George III., in 1765 the degree of LL.D. from Dublin, and M.A. from Oxford in 1755. Died December 13, 1784, and was buried in Westminster Abbey. "Johnson, in appearance, was in all respects massive. His exterior was unwieldy, his manners were not polished, but he had a tender heart."

Half-length, life-size, to right; brown gown, hands raised in act of declamation; books on shelf in background. Canvas 30 × 25 in.

This picture was exhibited at the Royal Academy in 1770, where it hung side by side with those of Goldsmith (see No. 24) and Colman. It was not the first portrait by Reynolds of his friend, as Johnson had already sat to him in 1757, 1761, 1763, and 1767. Again in 1777 Reynolds paints another portrait of Johnson in which he is represented holding a book close to his eyes. Johnson remonstrated against such a record of his near-sightedness, and said to Mrs. Thrale, "Reynolds may paint himself as deaf as he chooses, but I will not be *Blinking Sam*." Two years later, October 15, 1778, Johnson writes in his diary to Mrs. Thrale, "I have sat twice to Sir Joshua and he seems to like his own performance. He has projected another in which I am to be busy, but we can think on it at leisure." And again (October 31) "Sir Joshua has finished my picture and it seems to please everybody; but I shall wait to see how it pleases you."

By SIR J. REYNOLDS, P.R.A.   Lent by The LORD SACKVILLE.

**206. Thomas Gray (1716–1771).**

Poet and Scholar. Son of a money-scrivener, born in Cornhill, London, was educated at Peterhouse, Cambridge, and entered at the Inner Temple. He accompanied Horace Walpole on his travels abroad in 1739, but they parted and Gray returned home in 1741. He then settled at Cambridge, and published his *Ode on a Distant Prospect of Eton College*, 1747; *Elegy written in a Country Churchyard*, in 1752. He migrated to Pembroke Hall in 1756, declined the Poet-Laureateship in 1757, and was appointed Professor of Modern History in 1768. His *Progress of Poesy* and *The Bard* were both printed at Walpole's Strawberry Hill Press in 1757. He died in 1771, and was buried beside his mother at Stoke Poges.

Half-length, life size, to left, brown coat and wig. Canvas 30 × 24 in.

Lent by PEMBROKE COLLEGE, CAMBRIDGE.

**207. Rev. Lawrence Sterne (1713–1768).**

A descendant of Richard Sterne, Archbishop of York. Born at Clonmel, in Ireland; was educated at Halifax and Jesus College, Cambridge. Taking holy orders he obtained the living of Sutton with a prebendary stall in York Cathedral, and later on the rectory of Stillington and the curacy of Coxwold. Died in London, March 18, 1768. His literary works, the principal of which are *Tristram Shandy* and the *Sentimental Journey*, exhibit many pathetic and humorous scenes, but they often abound in the grossest indelicacies. When *Tristram Shandy* appeared, Walpole says, "Nothing was more talked of, and nothing more admired. The man's head, a little turned before, is now topsy-turvy with his success."

Three-quarter length, life-size, seated to left, blue gown and wig; resting head in right hand; writing table with papers. Canvas 50 × 40 in.

Sterne sat for this portrait in March, 1760. He had then produced the first and second volumes only of *Tristram Shandy*. The portrait was painted for Lord Ossory, then passed to Lord Holland, and then to the Marquess of Lansdowne, by whom it was purchased on the death of Lord Holland in 1840 for 500 guineas. Sterne, in writing to a friend who wished for his portrait, said, "You must mention the business to Reynolds yourself; for I will tell you why I cannot. He has already painted a very excellent portrait of me, which, when I went to pay him for, he desired me to accept as a tribute (to use his own elegant and flattering expression) that his heart wished to pay to my genius. That man's way of thinking and manners are at least equal to his pencil." In character Sterne was a "fellow of infinite jest, of most excellent fancy," and in this portrait, with all its expression of intellect and humour, the painter has given the true character of his sitter. Nor is the position of the figure less characteristic than the expression of the face. It is easy, but it has not the easiness of health. Sterne props himself up. His wig too was subject to odd chances from the humour that was uppermost with its wearer. When by mistake he had thrown a fair sheet of manuscript into the fire instead of the foul one, he tells us that he snatched off his wig "and threw it perpendicularly with all imaginable violence to the top of the room." While he was sitting to Reynolds, this same wig had contrived to get itself a little on one side; and the painter, with his readiness in taking advantage of accident to which we owe so many of the delightful novelties in his works, painted it so, for he must have known that a mitre would not sit long, bishop-fashion, on the head before him. (See Leslie, *Life*, &c., *of Sir Joshua Reynolds*.

By SIR J. REYNOLDS, P.R.A.    Lent by The MARQUESS OF LANSDOWNE.

**208.** JOSEPH ADDISON (1672-1719).

Poet, statesman, and essayist. Son of Lancelot Addison, Dean of Lichfield, born at Milston, in Wiltshire, was educated at Charterhouse and Oxford. Under the patronage of Lord Somers he travelled in Italy, commemorated the victory of Blenheim in a poem called " The Campaign "; in 1709 was appointed secretary to the Marquess of Wharton in Ireland, and in the same year being elected member for Malmesbury, held the seat to the end of his life. At this period, in connexion with Steele and Swift, he began his famous writings in *The Tatler*, *Spectator*, and *Guardian*. His tragedy of *Cato* appeared in 1713. On the accession of George I. he was appointed one of the principal Secretaries of State. Died at Holland House, June 17, 1719, and was buried in Westminster Abbey.

Half-length, life-size, to right, head facing, blue coat and wig ; right hand rests on his hip. Canvas 36 × 27 in.

By SIR G. KNELLER.    Lent by R. B. BAKER, ESQ.

**209.** JOHN GAY (1688-1732).

Poet and dramatist. Born at Barnstaple, Devonshire; began life as a silk mercer, but soon devoted himself to literature, and obtained the friendship of Pope and Swift, to the former of whom he dedicated his *Rural Sports* in 1711. He was secretary to the Duchess of Monmouth, and attended the Earl of Clarendon to Hanover in 1714. At the suggestion of Swift he composed the *Beggar's Opera*, and his well-known *Fables* were in 1726 written for the instruction of William, Duke of Cumberland. Gay died in Burlington Gardens at the residence of his patrons, the Duke and Duchess of Queensberry, and was buried in Westminster Abbey. Pope wrote the inscription on his monument.

Three-quarter length, life-size, seated to right, head nearly facing, loose white cloak with blue lining, and red cap band with blue ; right arm rests on table, left hand on knee ; dog in the foreground. Canvas 48 × 39 in.

Lent by The EARL OF LOUDOUN.

**210.** ROBERT SOUTHEY (1774-1843).

Poet. Son of a linendraper at Bristol ; was educated at Westminster and Balliol College, Oxford, where his talents attracted notice. Having abandoned his intention of taking orders, he travelled for some time in Spain and Portugal, and made his first appearance in the literary world as author of the epic poems *Joan of Arc* and *Wat Tyler*.

SOUTH GALLERY.] *Portraits.* 73

In 1803 he settled at Keswick, with his friends Coleridge and Wordsworth as neighbours, and there commenced a long career of literary labour. He published *The Curse of Kehama* in 1810, and *Roderick* in 1814, having in the previous year been appointed Poet-Laureate. He achieved great popularity through his biographies of Nelson, Wesley, Cowper, and Chatterton ; and having suffered long from the effects of overwork he died, March 21, 1843. His *Common-place Book* was published after his death.

Half-length, life-size, seated to right ; open black furred coat, holding book in his hands ; badge as Poet Laureate. Canvas 36 × 28 in.

By T. PHILLIPS, R.A. Lent by JOHN MURRAY, ESQ.

**211.** OLIVER GOLDSMITH (1728-1774).

This eminent poet, essayist, historian, and dramatist, born at Pallas in the county of Longford, Ireland, November 29, 1728, was educated at Trinity College, Dublin, led for some years a wandering life upon the Continent, and returned to England in 1756. He commenced his literary career in circumstances of great poverty, wrote at first obscurely for periodicals of the day, but his admirable poem *The Traveller*, published in 1765, introduced him to the notice of the most distinguished literary characters of the time. Two works of the highest merit followed, the *Vicar of Wakefield* in 1766, and the *Deserted Village* in 1770. His fame was further enhanced by his two comedies, *The Good-Natured Man* and *She Stoops to Conquer*. He died of a fever at his lodgings in the Temple in 1774.

Half-length, life-size, to left ; black coat, brown mantle with fur ; in left hand book. Canvas 30 × 25 in.

Goldsmith appears to have first made the acquaintance of Reynolds in 1762, and from that time till his death there existed the warmest affection between these two great men. This portrait was painted by Reynolds in 1766, but was not exhibited at the Academy till 1770, when it appeared side by side with that of Johnson (No. 205). Of this picture Leslie, *Life, &c., of Sir Joshua Reynolds*, says, "I have seen nothing on canvas more touching. It recalls all that is known of the sufferings of this tenderest and warmest of hearts. In that thoughtful, patient face, the traces of a life of endurance, and the consciousness of being misunderstood and undervalued are as unmistakeable as the benevolence that is meditating how to amuse and make better a world by which it was considered a vulgar face, and which had treated the owner of it so scurvily. Sir Joshua meant to paint the author of the *Vicar of Wakefield* and of the *Deserted Village*, and not the *Goldy* who was laughed at by Boswell and Hawkins and quizzed by Burke."

The portrait must have been an object of special attraction, as on May 26, just before the exhibition closed, appeared *The Deserted Village* with a dedication to Sir Joshua.

By SIR J. REYNOLDS, P.R.A. Lent by The LORD SACKVILLE.

**212.** PERCY BYSSHE SHELLEY (1792-1822).

Eminent poet. Son of Sir Timothy Shelley, born at Field Place, Horsham, Sussex, was educated at Eton, where at the age of fifteen he published two novels, *Justrozzi* and

*The Rosicrucian.* Went to Oxford, but was expelled for his small pamphlet entitled *The Necessity of Atheism.* Married in 1811 Harriet Westbrook, but separated from her in 1813. Having formed an acquaintance with Mary, daughter of John Godwin and Mary Wollstonecroft, he travelled with her on the Continent, married her on the death of his wife, and finally permanently resided in Italy, where he lived in friendship with Byron, Keats, and Leigh Hunt. In 1822, on returning from a visit to Byron at Pisa, he was drowned in an open boat in the Gulf of Lerici. His chief poetical works are *Queen Mab*, *The Revolt of Islam*, *Prometheus Unbound*, and *Cenci*.

Half-length, under life-size, facing, blue coat and large white open collar, his right arm on table and holding pen. Canvas 24 × 19 in.
Painted in Rome in 1818, and done from life at one sitting.

By MISS AMELIA CURRAN.  Lent by LADY SHELLEY.

### 213. GEORGE GORDON NOEL, 6TH LORD BYRON (1788–1824).

The Poet. Son of Captain John Byron and Catherine Gordon of Gight, born in Holles Street, London, January 22, 1788. Succeeded his great-uncle William, Lord Byron, in 1798, and was educated at Harrow and Trinity College, Cambridge. In 1815 he married the daughter of Sir Ralph Noel Milbank, but this union proved singularly infelicitous. A separation took place, and Byron retired to the Continent never to revisit his native country. He resided chiefly in Italy, but in 1823 was attracted to Greece to aid in the struggle for independence with his influence and his money. In the following year whilst at Missolonghi, he caught a severe cold, from the effects of which he died on April 19. His remains were brought to England, and were buried in the church of Hucknall, near Newstead. Lord Byron's writings are so well known and so recent, as not to require notice here.

Half-length, life-size, to left, in profile, his left arm placed on table and supporting his head; red coat and black cloak. Canvas 36 × 30 in.

By R. WESTALL, R.A.  Lent by The BARONESS BURDETT-COUTTS.

### 214. THOMAS CAMPBELL (1777–1844).

Poet. Son of a Scottish merchant, was born and educated at Glasgow, acted as private tutor in Edinburgh, and in 1799 published his *Pleasures of Hope*, which founded his fame. After travelling for a time on the Continent he wrote *The Exile of Erin*, *Hohenlinden*, and *Ye Mariners of England*, some of the noblest lyrics of modern times. Having settled in London, in 1803 he wrote *The Battle of the Baltic*, *Lord Ullin's Daughter*, *Specimens of British Poets*, with biographical and critical notices, and edited the *New Monthly* and *Metropolitan Magazines*, &c. He interested himself much in the foundation of the University of London, took an active part in the cause of Greece, and was twice Rector of the University of Glasgow. He died at Boulogne June 15, 1844, and was buried in Westminster Abbey.

Half-length, life-size, to left, head nearly facing; black coat, right arm resting on chair. Canvas 36 × 28 in.

By T. PHILLIPS, R.A.  Lent by JOHN MURRAY, ESQ.

## 215. SIR WALTER SCOTT, BART. (1771–1832).

Poet and novelist. Born at Edinburgh, the son of a Writer to the Signet, was educated at the High School in that city, and was called to the Bar in 1791. He produced in 1805 *The Lay of the Last Minstrel*, which was followed by *Marmion* in 1808, and *The Lady of the Lake* in 1809. *Waverley*, the first of the famous series of novels bearing that title, was issued in 1814. These were published anonymously, and it was not until 1827 that the authorship was publicly admitted. He was created a baronet by George IV. at Holyrood in 1822, and died at Abbotsford, worn out by his incessant exertions to retrieve his fortunes, having by the failure of his publishers in 1826 incurred an obligation to the amount of £100,000. He was buried at Dryburgh Abbey.

Half-length, life-size, facing, head to left, black coat, grey waistcoat. Canvas 30 × 24 in.

By SIR H. RAEBURN.   Lent by The BARONESS BURDETT-COUTTS.

## 216. THE REV. W. MUIR MASON (1725–1797).

Divine and Poet. Born at Hull, was educated at St. John's College, Cambridge, and became Fellow of Pembroke College in 1747, was rector of Aston, Yorkshire, chaplain to George II., and Canon of York. He was opposed to the American War, was the friend and biographer of Gray, and author of *Caractacus* and *Elfrida*, tragedies, of odes, and occasional poems. He possessed some skill as a painter and musician.

Half-length, life-size, to left ; brown coat ; scroll in left hand. Canvas 30 × 25 in.

Painted in 1775, Mason being then in his fiftieth year. This picture was given to Mr. Stonhewer, and bequeathed by him to Pembroke College, according to Mason's request.

By SIR J. REYNOLDS, P.R.A.   Lent by PEMBROKE COLLEGE, CAMBRIDGE.

## 217. SIR ISAAC NEWTON, KNT. (1642–1726).

Philosopher. Born at Woolsthorpe, Lincolnshire ; was educated at Grantham and Trinity College, Cambridge, where he studied mathematics with great diligence, and in 1664 made the discovery of the nature of light and colours. He succeeded Dr. Barrow as Lucasian Professor of Mathematics in 1669, and brought forward his discoveries in optics in his lectures, 1669–1671. In 1672 he was elected a F.R.S., represented Cambridge University in Parliament from 1689–90, and in 1699 was appointed Master of the Mint, in which capacity he effected many improvements in the coinage. He was chosen President of the Royal Society in 1703, and in 1705 received the honour of knighthood. His *Principia* was first published in 1687, but his *Observations on the Prophecies* did not appear till after his death. He died at Kensington at the age of eighty-four, having retained his faculties to the last ; and, after lying in state in the Jerusalem Chamber, he was buried in Westminster Abbey, where a monument was erected to him, which was executed by Rysbrack.

Three-quarter length, life-size, seated to right, head turned to left ; in light brown robe; right hand rests on table, left on his chest. Inscribed " Isaacus Newtonus, Aetatis 69, 1710. R. Bentleius, Coll. Mag." Canvas 50 × 40. Painted for Dr. Bentley, and given by him to the College.

By SIR J. THORNHILL.            Lent by TRINITY COLLEGE, CAMBRIDGE.

**218. SIR RICHARD STEELE, KNT. (1671–1729).**

Essayist and dramatic writer. Born at Dublin, his father being secretary to the Duke of Ormond; was educated at Charterhouse and Merton College, Oxford, and obtained an ensigncy in the Guards. While in that service he wrote the *Christian Hero*, which was followed by his first comedy in 1702 entitled *Grief à la Mode*. In 1709 he began the *Tatler* under the name of " Isaac Bickerstaff," aided by Addison, in laying down which he commenced the *Spectator*, which was succeeded by the *Guardian*. In 1713 Steele entered Parliament for Stockbridge, but was soon after expelled for writing the *Englishman and the Crisis*. At the accession of George I. he was made surveyor of the royal stables, governor of the King's company of comedians, and knighted. For his play of the *Conscious Lovers* the King gave him £500. Died at Llangunnor, Caermarthenshire.

Half-length, life-size, to right, head facing, brown loose coat and wig; right arm rests on pedestal. Canvas 36 × 27 in.

By SIR G. KNELLER.            Lent by R. B. BAKER, ESQ.

**219. SAMUEL RICHARDSON (1689–1761).**

Novelist. Born in Derbyshire, was apprenticed to a London printer named Wilde, and having set up for himself in business, was by the interest of Speaker Onslow employed in printing the Journals of the House of Commons. A flourishing business as a publisher afforded him opportunities for the publication of his own works. *Pamela* appeared in 1740, was followed by *Clarissa Harlowe*, and *The History of Sir Charles Grandison*, his last great work, in 1753. Richardson was pious and benevolent, but immensely vain, and lived surrounded by a circle of affectionate and flattering friends, mostly ladies.

Three-quarter length, life-size, to left; brown coat and wig; his right hand inserted in his coat; in left a book. Canvas 50 × 40 in.

By J. HIGHMORE.            Lent by The STATIONERS' COMPANY.

**220. WILLIAM COWPER (1731–1800).**

One of the most popular of English poets. Born at Berkhampstead, Herts, the son of the rector of the place; educated at Market Street, Herts, and at Westminster; was articled to a solicitor, took up his residence in the Temple, and being called to the Bar in 1754 was appointed a clerk in the House of Lords, but resigned owing to his extreme nervousness, which developed into insanity, a malady which occasionally returned. In 1782 he published a volume of poems; *The Task* in 1784, and in 1791 a translation of the *Iliad* and *Odyssey* of Homer. Becoming acquainted with Mrs. Unwin he resided chiefly with her till her death in 1796. He died April 25, 1800. His life and his admirable letters were published by William Hayley in 1803.

Half-length, life-size, to right, black coat, red cap. Canvas 30 × 24½ in.

This picture was presented by Romney to his friend, William Hayley, of Felpham, Sussex, and was brought from thence with the portrait of Anna Seward. (See No. 231.)

By G. ROMNEY. Lent by W. PERCIVAL BOXALL, ESQ.

**221. HENRY FIELDING, 1707–1754.**

Novelist. Born at Sharpham Park, Somersetshire; was educated at Eton and Leyden, and upon his return from thence began to write for the stage. His first piece was *Love in Several Masques*, which was well received, as also his comedy of *The Temple Bear*. After his marriage to Miss Craddock he was entered at the bar, but continued to write, and produced a number of political tracts; but his genius appeared to most advantage in his novels of *Joseph Andrews, Tom Jones, and Amelia*.

Half-length, life-size, seated to right, brown coat and wig, reading a book which he holds with both hands. Canvas 29 × 24 in.

Lent by The HON. GERALD PONSONBY.

**222. JOHN KEATS (1795–1821).**

Poet. Born in London, was apprenticed to a surgeon, but becoming acquainted with Leigh Hunt and other literary celebrities, and incited by their praises published a volume of poems. These were followed in 1817 by *Endymion*, a poetical romance, and in 1820 by *Lamia* and other poems. The severe criticisms which these poems met with in the *Quarterly Review* produced an injurious effect on the health of Keats, and in consequence he was recommended to try the climate of Rome, where he arrived in November, 1820, accompanied by his friend Severn the artist. He died at Rome, February 27, following.

Small half-length, to right, seated at a table, in grey coat; his right hand rests on an open book before him; his left hand supports his head. Panel 11¼ × 9 in.

A posthumous portrait painted by Joseph Severn at Rome in 1832.

By J. SEVERN. Lent by G. P. BOYCE, ESQ.

**223. CHARLES LAMB (1775–1834).**

Essayist and poet. Born in London; was educated at Christ's Hospital, and about 1789 obtained a situation as clerk in the India House, where he continued till 1825. Died at Edmonton, December 27, 1834. His first literary adventure was a small volume of poems (1797), written conjointly with Coleridge and Lloyd. This was followed by *John Woodvil*, a tragedy (1802); but Lamb's fame rests mainly on his prose works, especially his charming *Essays of Elia*.

Small half-length, facing, dark coat, hand on book, and holding pen. Canvas 14 × 11 in.

Lent by RIGHT HON. SIR CHARLES WENTWORTH DILKE, BART.

## 224. RICHARD BENTLEY, D.D. (1662-1742).

Eminent scholar and critic. Born at Wakefield, Yorks., was educated at St. John's College, Cambridge, and first showed the great power of his mind in 1692, when he was appointed first "Boyle Lecturer." Soon after broke out his quarrel with Boyle, the main result of which was his famous *Dissertations on the Epistles of Phalaris*. In 1700, he was made Master of Trinity College, Cambridge, and Archdeacon of Ely. Working hard as a scholar and effecting improvements in his college, he became involved in many quarrels and litigations with the college seniors, and after obtaining the Regius Professorship of Divinity was degraded and deprived by the senate. After years of litigation the sentence was annulled. His writings are very numerous, including editions of *Terence, Homer, Phædros*, Milton's *Paradise Lost*, &c. "In person he was tall, graceful, and well proportioned, his countenance comely and fresh, and his conversation cheerful, discreet, and very instructive."

Three-quarter length, life-size, facing, head to left, in gown, right hand rests on book placed on a table. Inscribed "Æt. 48. 1710." Canvas 50 × 40 in.

Lent by TRINITY COLLEGE, CAMBRIDGE.

## 225. REV. GEORGE CRABBE (1754-1832).

Poet. Born at Aldborough, Suffolk. Was brought up to the medical profession, but abandoned it for literature. He came to London in 1770, obtained the friendship of Burke, who took him into his house, examined all his compositions, and signifying his approval of *The Library* and *The Village*, assisted in their publication. Crabbe in 1781 took priest's orders, was soon after appointed Chaplain to the Duke of Rutland, and having held several benefices, died as rector of Trowbridge, Wiltshire. His other principal poems are *The Newspaper, The Parish Register, Tales of the Hall*, &c.

Half-length, life-size, seated, full face, hands clasped; black coat, landscape background, signed "T. P., 1820." Canvas 36 × 28 in.

By T. PHILLIPS, R.A.                      Lent by JOHN MURRAY, ESQ.

## 226. WILLIAM CONGREVE (1669-1728).

Dramatic writer and poet. Born at Bardsay Grange near Leeds; educated at Trinity College, Dublin; entered the Middle Temple, and published in 1693 his first play, *The Old Bachelor*, under the patronage of Dryden; *The Mourning Bride* in 1697, and *The Way of the World* in 1700. He held several government sinecures, and at his death left £30,000 to the Duchess of Marlborough. He was a handsome man, of polished address, and reputed the greatest wit of his time. He was buried in Westminster Abbey.

Half-length, life-size, to right; brown coat and wig; right hand pointing before him. Canvas 36 × 27 in.

By SIR G. KNELLER.                      Lent by R. B. BAKER, ESQ.

SOUTH GALLERY.] *Portraits.* 79

**227.** SAMUEL TAYLOR COLERIDGE (1772-1834).

Critic, poet, and metaphysician. Born at Ottery St. Mary in Devonshire, was educated at Christ's Hospital, where Charles Lamb was a pupil at the same time, and at Jesus College, Cambridge. At Bristol he associated with Southey, Burnet, and Lovell, to found a pansocratic community in America, but the scheme failed through want of funds. In 1794, with the aid of a Bristol bookseller, Coleridge was first enabled to publish a volume of poems, the commencement of an eminent literary career. The *Ancient Mariner* and the first part of *Christabel* were written in 1797, and his tragedy, *Remorse*, was also composed about this period. Later on he resided at the Lakes with Southey and Wordsworth as his neighbours. After the publication of the *Lyrical Ballads*, the three were known as the "Lake Poets." Coleridge afterwards became connected with the *Morning Post*, and died at Highgate, July 25, 1834.

Half-length, life-size, to left; black coat, in right hand snuff-box. Canvas 35 × 27½ in.

By T. PHILLIPS, R.A.   Lent by JOHN MURRAY, ESQ.

**228.** SAMUEL ROGERS (1762-1855).

Poet. Author of *The Pleasures of Memory, Human Life,* and *Italy.* Born at Stoke Newington, the son of a banker, received a careful education, and being introduced into the banking house, remained a partner through life. He formed a valuable collection of works of art, and was familiar with almost every distinguished contemporary author, orator, and artist, and many works were dedicated to him as memorials of friendship or admiration.

Half-length, life-size, to left, red coat; left hand raised to chin. Canvas 29 × 23 in.

By J. HOPPNER, R.A.   Lent by The EARL OF ILCHESTER.

**229.** JONATHAN SWIFT, D.D., DEAN OF ST. PATRICK'S (1667-1745).

Born in Dublin. Educated at Kilkenny and Trinity College, Dublin; became secretary to Sir William Temple, and in 1704 published the *Tale of a Tub.* Having joined the Tory party, he wrote many political pamphlets on their side, Harley and St. John being his principal friends. He is stated to have privately married in 1716 Esther Johnson, "Stella". He was appointed Dean of St. Patrick's in 1713, and published in 1724 the *Draper's Letters*, and in 1727 *Gulliver's Travels.* During the latter years of his life, his mind was clouded in consequence of an affection of the brain.

Half-length, life-size, to right, in Doctor's robes and wig. Canvas 29½ × 24 in.

By C. JERVAS.   Lent by The BODLEIAN LIBRARY, OXFORD.

**230.** WILLIAM GODWIN (1756-1836).

Novelist and miscellaneous writer. Son of a dissenting minister; born at Wisbech, entered on his profession as a preacher, but abandoned it for literature in 1783. His treatise on *Political Justice*, advocating the principles of the French Revolution, published in 1793, created a sensation, and was followed by the remarkable novel *Caleb Williams*. In 1797 he married Mary Wolstonecraft, who died the same year, and having remarried in 1801, opened a bookseller's shop in Skinner Street. After Lord Grey's accession to office Godwin was appointed Yeoman Usher to the Exchequer. Besides the above he wrote several novels, *St. Leon, Fleetwood, Mandeville*, tragedies, essays, &c., and some schoolbooks under the name of Edwin Baldwin.

Half-length, full face, brown coat. Canvas 30 × 25 in.

By SIR T. LAWRENCE, P.R.A.    Lent by THE LADY SHELLEY.

### 231. ANNA SEWARD (1747-1809).

Daughter of the Rev. Thomas Seward ; born at Eyam, Derbyshire ; wrote elegiac poems on Major André and Captain Cook, published in 1782 her poetical romance *Louisa*, a collection of sonnets in 1799, and a *Life of Darwin* in 1804. She resided chiefly at Lichfield, where her father had a canonry. Her miscellaneous works were edited by Sir Walter Scott in 1810, and her letters, which she left to Constable, were published in 1811.

Half-length, life-size, to left, head to right, white dress, black scarf, powdered hair ; sky background. Canvas 28 × 22½ in.

In the *Letters* of Anne Seward, published in 1811, are several mentions of this picture, which was painted by Romney at the suggestion of William Hayley, of Felpham, as a present to her father, to whom she was deeply attached. She thus writes from Lichfield, June 1, 1788: "We wish to express our gratitude for your having persuaded Romney to gratify my father, by his possessing, ere he dies, the promised treasure. It arrived last night ; rich, adorned, and invaluable, by the Romneyan powers, the most masterly portrait. . . . I placed it by my father's bedside at seven this morning. He wept with joy when I undrew the curtain, wanted to kiss it, and has talked of and looked at it all day." This letter was addressed to Mr. Hayley, and in it mention is made of young Cary (afterwards the translator of Dante), whose son some twenty years ago saw the picture, and at once recognized the portrait as that of his godmother, Anne Seward, and well remembered it in his childhood at Mr. Hayley's at Felpham.

By G. ROMNEY.    Lent by W. PERCIVAL BOXALL, ESQ.

### 232. JAMES HENRY LEIGH HUNT (1784-1859).

Poet and essayist. Son of Isaac Hunt, an American settled in London ; born at Southgate, and educated at Christ's Hospital. He commenced his literary career, soon after leaving school, as a theatrical critic, and founded in 1808, with his brother, the *Examiner*, for the purpose of promoting Liberal opinions and Parliamentary reform. He was prosecuted for his articles, and condemned to two years' imprisonment and a fine of £500, but on his release still continued to write in the same tone. In 1821 he went to Italy, where he spent some years in friendship with Byron and Shelley. His chief works were *The Story of Rimini; Wit and Humour; The Old Court Suburb; Men, Women, an Books*, &c. In 1847 he received a Government pension of £200, and died at Putney i 1859.

Three-quarter length, life-size, seated to left, face turned to the spectator, black coat; open book in left hand. Canvas 42 × 34 in.

By S. LAURENCE. Lent by MISS LAURENCE.
(The daughter of the artist.)

### 233. JOHN FAWCETT (1768-1837).

Actor. Son of an actor. Born in London; was engaged in the York Company, where he married Mrs. Mills, who died in 1797; appeared in London at Covent Garden in 1791 as Cubit in *He would be a Soldier;* and a few years later made a great hit as Dr. Pangloss. His characters were not very numerous, but were highly finished delineations, particularly Autolycus, Touchstone and other Shakespearian parts. He retired from the stage 1830, and died at his house near Botley, Hants, March 13, 1837.

Half-length, life-size, to left; in black coat and hat. Canvas (oval) 30 × 24 in.

By SIR M. A. SHEE, P.R.A. Lent by HENRY IRVING, ESQ.

### 234. MRS. ELIZABETH BILLINGTON (1768-1818).

The most celebrated English female singer of her time. Daughter of Carl Weichsel, a good musician born in London; exhibited her musical talents at an early age, and married when only sixteen John Billington, one of the band at Drury Lane. She appeared at Covent Garden in 1786 as Rosetta in Arne's *Love in a Village*, and from thenceforward was a leading vocalist both at home and abroad. Her husband dying in 1796, she married soon afterwards M. de Felissent, a French adventurer. Died at her estate of Artier, near Venice, August 25, 1818.

Three-quarter length, life-size, seated to left, white dress; left hand on her lap holds end of her scarf. Canvas 35 × 27 in.

By J. HOPPNER, R.A. Lent by H. L. BISCHOFFSHEIM, ESQ.

### 235. SAMUEL FOOTE (1720-1777).

Actor and dramatist. Born at Truro, was educated there and at Worcester College, Oxford, studied law at the Temple, but took to the stage, combining acting with dramatic writing. In 1747 he commenced at the Haymarket portraits of characters in which he alone appeared on the stage. At various times he wrote upwards of twenty plays. In 1765 he broke his leg and had it amputated, but acted with a cork leg. After a life of great vicissitudes and irregularity, he died at Dover, October 21, 1777, on his way to France, and was buried in Westminster Abbey. His conversational wit was considered unrivalled. Foote married Mary, sister of Sir Horace Mann; and Horace Walpole in a letter, December 26, 1743, says, "I knew your new brother-in-law at school; but have not seen him since. But your sister was in love, consequently must be happy to have him. Yet I own I cannot much felicitate anybody that marries for love. It is bad enough to marry, but to marry where one loves, ten times worse."

Three-quarter length, life-size, facing, head raised to left; leaning on a stick, arms crossed; white coat, yellow-flowered waistcoat and wig. Canvas 50 × 40 in.

By SIR J. REYNOLDS, P.R.A.      Lent by The LORD SACKVILLE.

### 236. KITTY FISHER (d. 1771).

The daughter of a German staymaker; was a celebrated beauty of her time, and remarkable for her wit. She married, in 1766, Mr. Norris, a Kentish gentleman and died about September, 1771. There are seven portraits of her by Sir Joshua Reynolds: she first sat to him in 1759.

Three-quarter length, seated, facing, head to left; white dress; hands folded on her knee; landscape background. Canvas 50 × 40 in.

By F. COTES, R.A.      Lent by CHARLES BUTLER, ESQ.

### 237. WILLIAM HOGARTH (1697–1764).

Eminent painter. Born in St. Bartholomew's, London; was the son of a schoolmaster from Westmoreland. At an early age he was apprenticed to Ellis Gamble, a silversmith, by whom he was employed in engraving arms and cyphers upon pieces of plate. He soon, however, displayed a genius for painting, and the first piece which he executed was one of the Wanstead Assembly. He was the first artist who conceived and executed the idea of representing a series of adventures on canvas, in which the fortune of one character was conducted from the cradle to the grave. He met, moreover, with considerable success as a portrait-painter. The *Harlot's Progress* was painted in 1734, and the *Rake's Progress* appeared in the following year. The *Marriage à la Mode*, a series of pictures now in the National Gallery, was published by engravings in 1745. He married Jane, only daughter of Sir James Thornhill, by whom he had no issue. About 1757 he succeeded his brother-in-law, Thornhill, as King's serjeant-painter. One of his latest works was his famous caricature of Wilkes.

Half-length, life-size, to left, head facing; brown coat and red cap; in an oval. Canvas 30 × 24 in.

By HIMSELF.      Lent by The HON. MRS. MAXWELL-SCOTT.

### 238. WILLIAM WHITEHEAD (1715–1788).

Poet. The son of a baker, born at Cambridge, was educated at Winchester and Clare Hall, and succeeded in 1757 Colley Cibber as poet-laureate, which post he held till his death, April 14, 1788. He wrote the tragedies of *The Roman Father*, and *Creusa*, the comedy of *The School for Lovers*; a farce, *Trip to Scotland*, and several miscellaneous pieces. His writings are now almost forgotten.

Half-length, life-size, to right, in brown coat and brown wig; badge of the Poet-Laureate. Canvas oval 29 × 24 in.

The artist appears to have been a long time painting this picture. Its progress is mentioned in several letters from Whitehead to Lord Nuneham, extending from June 20, 1758, to September 16, 1760. (See *Harcourt Papers*, Vol. III., p. 251.)

By R. WILSON.                Lent by E. W. HARCOURT, ESQ.

**239. PORTRAIT OF A LADY, AN ACTRESS.**

Half-length, life-size, facing; black dress, white stomacher, and high white cap; powdered hair. Canvas 30 × 25 in.

By J. HOPPNER, R.A. ?          Lent by G. P. BOYCE, ESQ.

**240. JAMES QUIN (1693-1766).**

Actor. Son of a barrister of Irish family; born in King Street, Covent Garden; he received his education in Dublin, where he went on the stage in 1714; next appeared at Drury Lane, where Booth and Cibber were acting, and played with success in tragedy and comedy, but especially as Falstaff. In 1741 he returned to Dublin for a short time, but again appeared in London, performing in 1746 with Garrick at Covent Garden in the *Fair Penitent*. Soon afterwards he retired to Bath, only once more appearing in 1749, as Coriolanus in Thomson's posthumous tragedy. Quin was a noted *bon vivant* and wit; and was employed to instruct George III. in elocution. When he heard how well the King delivered his first speech, he exclaimed, "I taught the boy." Died at Bath. Garrick wrote the epitaph for his monument in Westminster Abbey.

Head, life-size, to left; wig; unfinished. Canvas 25½ × 20 in.

By T. GAINSBOROUGH, R.A.      Lent by HER MAJESTY THE QUEEN
(Buckingham Palace).

**241. LADY HAMILTON (1761 ?-1815).**

Born in humble life; the daughter of Henry Lyon of Nesse, in the parish of Great Neston, Cheshire; christened Amy, but after various changes finally adopted the name of Emma; was for a time a servant-girl at Hawarden, came to London in 1777, and was exhibited by Dr. Graham, a noted quack, as the Goddess Hygeia; but her beauty and the exquisite grace of her figure caused her to become a favourite sitter to artists, Romney being specially devoted to her. In 1791 she was married to Sir William Hamilton, and on her arrival at Naples obtained great influence with the court there, and was the object of Lord Nelson's passionate attachment. She died in comparative neglect near Calais. Romney alone is said to have painted twenty-three portraits of her;

G 2

and she also sat to Reynolds, Hoppner, and Lawrence in England, and to numerous artists in Italy.

Half-length, life-size, to left, head facing, leaning on a table, her head resting on her crossed hands, white dress and scarf tied round her head. Canvas 23 × 19½ in.

This is the first portrait done by Romney of Lady Hamilton. He was on a visit to Ickwell Bury to paint the then Mrs. Harvey's portrait, saw the beautiful girl, who was a servant in the house, and was so struck with her, that he at once asked for permission to make this likeness.

By G. ROMNEY.   Lent by MRS. HARVEY, of Ickwell Bury.

**242. RICHARD COSWAY, R.A. (1741–1821).**

Miniature painter. Born at Tiverton; studied in London under Hudson, the former instructor of Sir Joshua Reynolds; soon became a fashionable artist, and is specially known by his miniatures and tinted pencil drawings. He was elected a Royal Academician in 1771.

Small three-quarter length, to right, black coat and wig, in left hand, palette and brushes. Canvas 17 × 15 in.

By HIMSELF.   Lent by The VISCOUNT POWERSCOURT, K.P.

**243. SIR JOSHUA REYNOLDS, P.R.A. (1723–1792).**

The greatest of English portrait-painters. Born at Plympton in Devon, was placed under Hudson, with whom he studied for two years. In 1749 he made the acquaintance of Captain Keppel, in whose ship he went to the Mediterranean and visited Italy, where he stayed, studying the old masters till 1753, and on his return became the leading portrait painter of his day. He was the first President of the Royal Academy, founded in 1768, and in that capacity delivered his well-known discourses. He continued to exercise his profession in full vigour till 1790, when his eyesight suddenly failed. Died at his house in Leicester Fields, and was buried in St. Paul's. He was the intimate friend of Burke, Goldsmith and Johnson, and other eminent men, and in conjunction with the last established "The Club" which still exists.

Head to left. Canvas 14 × 12 in.

Lent by HORACE N. PYM, ESQ.

**244. SIR GODFREY KNELLER, BART. (1646–1723).**

Portrait-painter. Born at Lübeck; studied painting under various masters; visited Italy in 1672, and coming to London in 1675 was appointed portrait-painter to Charles II., and subsequently held the same office under James II., William III., Anne, and George I. He was made a baronet in 1715, and died October 27, 1723, having amassed a large fortune. Kneller painted the Beauties at Hampton Court for William III., also the portraits of the forty-eight members of the Kit-Cat Club, of ten Sovereigns, including

Louis XIV., Peter the Great, and Charles VI. of Spain, and almost every notable person in England in his time.

    Small half-length, to right, head turned to left, brown coat, puce mantle, and wig; right hand rests on table; left holds his mantle; building in the background. Canvas 17½ × 14 in.

    This portrait was presented by the painter to Jacob Tonson. It belongs to the "Kitcat" series; but it differs from the other portraits in being smaller in size, a mark of deference shown by the painter who was not a member of the club but only their acknowledged artist.

By SIR G. KNELLER.                              Lent by R. B. BAKER, ESQ.

**245.** MRS. SIDDONS AS "THE TRAGIC MUSE" (1774–1831).

    Celebrated actress. Daughter of Roger Kemble, the manager of an itinerant company; was born at Brecon in South Wales; commenced her theatrical career as a vocalist; and in her eighteenth year married Mr. Siddons, a young actor. In 1775 she appeared in London as Portia in *The Merchant of Venice*, when Garrick was the Shylock, but she did not display much genius. Time, with study and practice, matured her powers, and when she re-appeared at Drury Lane in 1782, as Isabella in the *Fatal Marriage*, her success was complete, and from that time forward her theatrical career was one continued triumph. Her principal characters were Lady Macbeth, Constance in *King John*, Queen Catherine and Lady Randolph in Horne's tragedy of *Douglas*. She retired from the stage in 1812, and died in London in 1831. Besides Reynolds, there are portraits of Mrs. Siddons by Gainsborough, Sir Thomas Lawrence, and Sir William Beechy.

    Full length, life-size, seated on a throne that appears to be raised above the clouds, in an attitude of inspired ecstasy; brown dress with white sleeves; massive fine necklace. Behind her in the shadowy background stand two mutes, the one holding the bowl, the other the dagger, the insignia of tragedy. Canvas 94 × 58 in.

    Though Reynolds' pocket-book for 1783 is lost, the sittings which Mrs. Siddons gave for this picture began during the autumn of 1783, and continued into the spring of 1784, in which year it was exhibited at the Royal Academy. In the quality of colour, the stateliness of the action and the loftiness of the expression, the picture ranks amongst the finest of this master. It has been supposed that the conception of this work was suggested by Michael Angelo's Isaiah. Mrs. Siddons, however, told Mr. Phillips " that it was the production of pure accident. Sir Joshua had begun the head and figure in a different view; but while he was occupied in the preparation of some colour she changed her position to look at a picture hanging on the wall of the room. When he again looked at her, and saw the action she had assumed, he requested her not to move; and thus arose the beautiful and expressive figure we now see in the picture." According to Mrs. Jameson, Mrs. Siddons used to describe Sir Joshua as taking her by the hand, and leading her up to his platform with the words " Ascend your undisputed throne, bestow on me some idea of the Tragic Muse." " On which," she said, " I walked up the steps and seated myself in the attitude in which the Tragic Muse now appears." Another charming anecdote is related of this picture. Sir Joshua had painted his name in the gold border of the drapery. Mrs. Siddons on examining the picture near, perceived it, and made the remark to Sir

Joshua. He replied, with a sort of poetical courtesy, " I could not lose the honour this opportunity afforded me of going down to posterity on the hem of your garment."

By SIR J. REYNOLDS, P.R.A.     Lent by The DUKE OF WESTMINSTER, K.G.

**246.   MRS. ELIZABETH HARTLEY AS " ELFRIDA " (1751–1824).**

Actress; first appeared at Bath about 1771, and became very popular as a tragic actress. Her extreme beauty and the truth and nature of her acting attracted universal admiration, and secured her the first place in her profession till the appearance of Mrs. Siddons. She left the stage in 1780, and died at Woolwich February 2, 1824. The play of *Elfrida* was specially written for her by Mason, and was one of his most successful characters. She was a favourite subject of Sir Joshua Reynolds, and appears in a number of his pictures as Jane Shore, Bacchante, &c.

Bust, life-size, to right, red dress, brown scarf over head and shoulders. Canvas 21 × 18 in.

By SIR J. REYNOLDS, P.R.A.     Lent by The DUKE OF WESTMINSTER, K.G.

**247.   DAVID GARRICK (1716–1779).**

" The greatest of English actors." Born at Hereford, February 28, 1716, was educated at Lichfield under Dr. Johnson, with whom, in 1736, he set out for London, where both arrived with only a few pence in their pockets. Garrick adopted the stage as a profession, and in 1741 made his *début* at Ipswich, in the tragedy of *Oroonoko*. In the same year he appeared for the first time on the London stage at the Goodman's Fields Theatre, as Richard III. Pope thus wrote of him to Lord Orrery, " That young man never had his equal as an actor, and never will have a rival." In 1742 the crowds that gathered to see him in Dublin were so great as to produce an epidemic, called in jest " the Garrick fever." In 1747 he became joint-patentee of Drury Lane, and sole patentee in 1773. The powers of Garrick were universal. He excelled equally in the sublimest tragedy, the most refined comedy, or the broadest farce; and the parts in which he attained the greatest celebrity, Macbeth and Abel Drugger, were the very opposite in character. He died January 20, 1779, and was buried in Westminster Abbey.

Half-length, life-size, to left, brown coat and cloak. Canvas 30 × 20 in.

Painted in 1768. Kitely, the principal character in Jonson's *Every Man in his Humour*, was acted by Garrick in 1751 and 1766. There is a repetition of this picture in the possession of Mr. Louis Huth from the collection of the late General C. R. Fox, to whom it was bequeathed by Henry Lord Holland. The great power of portraiture is well illustrated in this and other likenesses of Garrick by Reynolds. Whilst Garrick was sitting for this picture Northcote overheard him telling the painter, with great glee, how he had bothered an indifferent painter to whom he was sitting by perpetual changes of expression and contortions of feature, till the artist dashed down the pencils in despair.

By SIR J. REYNOLDS, P.R.A.     Lent by HER MAJESTY THE QUEEN
                                                (Windsor).

SOUTH GALLERY.]        *Portraits.*                    87

**248.** MRS. MARY ROBINSON (1758-1800).

Actress. Daughter of Captain Darby of Bristol, married when only fifteen, an attorney named Robinson, who caused her to go on the stage to relieve his necessities. She obtained success as Juliet and Imogen, and as Perdita, in the *Winter's Tale*, attracted the notice of the Prince of Wales, who sent Mrs. Robinson his portrait set in diamonds; one side was inscribed *Je ne change qu'en mourant*, and on the other "Unalterable to Perdita through life." An intimacy ensued which lasted two years. Being deprived of the use of her limbs by a rheumatic fever, she retired to Englefield Green, and died there in December, 1800. Her writings consist of novels, poems, and *Memoirs of her own Life*, which were published by her daughter.

Half-length, life-size, towards left, black dress, white stomacher, large black hat with feathers, black band round neck, hair powdered; red curtain and landscape background. Canvas 29 × 24 in.

This picture was painted in 1782, one year after Mrs. Robinson had left the stage, and had even lost the affections of the Prince for some months. She was, however, still in the flower of her youth and loveliness. Sir Joshua painted at least two portraits of her, and probably used her as a model in some of his fancy pictures, for she sat to him very assiduously throughout this year.

By SIR J. REYNOLDS, P.R.A.        Lent by The DUCHESS OF ST. ALBANS.

**249.** MATTHEW PRIOR (1664-1721).

Half-length, life-size, to left, head to right, grey coat and black cap. Canvas (oval) 29½ × 24¼ in.

This picture was a present from the poet to Lord Chancellor Harcourt.

By M. DAHL.                       Lent by E. W. HARCOURT, ESQ.

**250.** MRS. MARY ROBINSON (1758-1800 ?).

Three-quarter length, life-size, seated facing, head to left, resting on left hand, the right on her lap; white dress, red sash; landscape background. Canvas 29 × 24 in.

Lent by The HON. F. B. MASSEY MAINWARING.

**251.** LADY MARY WORTLEY MONTAGU (1690?-1762).

Daughter of Evelyn Pierpoint, 1st Duke of Kingston. Received a classical education under Bishop Burnet; married in 1712 Edward Wortley Montagu and, four years later, upon her husband being appointed ambassador to the Porte, accompanied him to the East, and during his residence in the Levant wrote the well-known *Letters* which form one of the most delightful books in our language. In 1718 she returned to England, and settled at Twickenham, where she renewed her acquaintance with Addison and Pope, but the friendship of the latter, owing to political as well as personal differences, was afterwards converted into hatred. In 1739 Lady Mary went to Italy for her health, and did not revisit England till 1761. She died the following year, August 21, 1762. During her residence at Constantinople, she was enabled to confer on Europe a benefit of the greatest consequence; namely, inoculation for the small-pox, which was at that time universal in Turkey. She had so much faith in its safety that she tried it first on her own son.

Three-quarter length, life-size, "in Turkish costume"; in the background is the city of Constantinople and Pera. Canvas 48 × 37 in.

"This picture was a gift from Lady Mary to her godson, the Rev. and Hon. Mr. Molesworth, late of James Street, Westminster, and Vicar of Northfleet, in Kent, at whose death it was purchased for the Duke of Bedford, and sold with the rest of His Grace's cabinet pictures at the great sale at Bloomsbury House, &c. (sd.) T. Nicholls."

By J. RICHARDSON.       Lent by The EARL OF WHARNCLIFFE.

**252. GARRICK AND HIS WIFE.**

Three-quarter lengths, life-size; Garrick seated at a table resting his cheek on his right hand which holds a pen, his left hand extended; his wife bends over him, and is about to take the pen from his hand. She wears a yellow dress. On table, paper inscribed the "Prologue Taste." Canvas 50 × 40.

It appears that Mr. Garrick was dissatisfied with this picture, and that some dispute arose between him and the painter, who struck his pencil across the face, and damaged it. The picture was unpaid for at the time of Hogarth's death. His widow then sent it home to Mr. Garrick without any demand. In 1823 it was sold at the sale of Mrs. Garrick's effects to the late Edward Hawke Locker, one of the Commissioners of Greenwich Hospital, for £75 11s. 0d.; this gentleman, however, relinquished it to George IV., who added it to the collection at Windsor.

By WILLIAM HOGARTH.      Lent by HER MAJESTY THE QUEEN
                      (Windsor).

**253. HORACE WALPOLE, 4TH EARL OF ORFORD, F.R.S. (1717-1797).**

Third and youngest son of Sir Robert Walpole, the Prime Minister; was educated at Eton and King's College, Cambridge. After completing his education Walpole travelled on the Continent for two years in company with the poet Gray; but the friends quarrelled, and Walpole returned to England in 1741. He immediately took his seat for Callington, which he exchanged for Castle Rising in 1744, and for King's Lynn in 1754. In 1768 he retired from public business, and giving up his time exclusively to literature and the fine arts, settled at Twickenham in a cottage, which soon grew into the mansion so well known as "Strawberry Hill," and which became a depository of objects of every kind of artistic, historic, or literary value. He succeeded in 1791 to the earldom on the death of his nephew George, but never took his seat in the House of Lords. His literary works comprise *Anecdotes of Painting in England*, compiled from notes of the engraver Vertue; *Royal and Noble Authors*, published in 1758; the popular romance *The Castle of Otranto*, 1764; *Memoirs of the Last Ten Years of George II.*, &c. Walpole is perhaps most generally admired for his epistolary correspondence. Sir Walter Scott called him "the best letter-writer in the English language."

Half-length, life-size, to left, in puce coat and wig; left arm resting on table, hand holding book. Canvas 35 × 27½ in.

By W. HOGARTH.        Lent by H. SPENCER WALPOLE, ESQ.

**254.** HARRIET MELLON, AFTERWARDS DUCHESS OF ST. ALBAN'S (1775–1837).

Actress. Daughter of Matthew Mellon the actor, followed her father's profession, for which she developed a great taste at a very early age, and made her *début* at Drury Lane as Lydia Languish in 1795 under the patronage of Sheridan. In 1814 she married Thomas Coutts the banker, on whose death in 1822 she became the sole mistress of one of the most colossal fortunes in England. In 1827 she was married to William, Duke of St. Alban's, and dying in 1837 bequeathed her property to Miss Angela Burdett (daughter of Sir Francis Burdett), who took the name of Coutts, and has since been raised to the peerage by the title of the Baroness Burdett-Coutts.

Half-length, life-size, to left, looking up, right hand raised; red dress. Canvas 30 × 24 in.

By SIR W. BEECHEY, R.A.    Lent by The BARONESS BURDETT-COUTTS.

**255.** COLLEY CIBBER (1671–1757).

Poet and dramatist. Son of Caius Gabriel Cibber. Born in London, educated at Grantham, and entered the army, but soon quitted it for the stage. In 1695 he brought out a play called *Love's Last Shift*, the principal character in which he performed himself, and from that time his reputation in comedy was unrivalled. *The Careless Husband* followed next, and then came *The Nonjuror*, which procured him a pension and the post of poet-laureate. Cibber incurred the ill-will of Pope, who made him the hero of *The Dunciad*, for which Cibber attacked him in a very spirited remonstrance. He quitted the stage in 1730, and died in 1757. His plays have been published in five volumes. His *Apology for his own Life* is one of the most amusing biographies in the English language.

Three-quarter length, life-size, facing, brown coat, lace ruffles; his left arm rests on a pedestal. Canvas 45 × 33 in.

            Lent by W. PERCIVAL BOXALL, ESQ.

**256.** MRS. HANNAH PRITCHARD AS "HERMIONE" (1711–1768).

Actress. Her maiden name was Vaughan. Made her appearance in one of Fielding's pieces at the little theatre in the Haymarket; acted subsequently in Goodman's Fields, and in 1733, when Mr. Highmore took the Haymarket, he engaged Mrs. Pritchard, who made her *début* as Belona in a play called *The Mother-in-Law*. She performed with like success both in tragedy and comedy. She took leave of the stage in the spring of

1768, and died in August of the same year. Davies praises "her genteel person, attractive countenance, her expressive yet simple manner"; and Lord Harcourt, in comparing her with Mrs. Siddons, on the latter's first appearance, writes : "To say that Mrs. Siddons in one word is supreme to Mrs. Pritchard in Lady Macbeth would be talking nonsense, because I don't think it is possible."

Half-length, life-size, in an oval, wearing white dress and veil, and diadem. Canvas 26½ × 21 in.

By J. PINE.  Lent by E. W. HARCOURT, ESQ.

**257. JOHN BANNISTER (1760–1836).**

Comedian. Born at Deptford, son of Charles Bannister, actor and vocalist. Having early obtained the notice of Garrick, he made his *début* at the Haymarket in 1778. At first he aspired to tragedy, but his talents lay in the other direction, and the parts he most excelled in were those of Sylvester, Daggerwood, Lingo, Trudge, Bobadil, Dr. Pangloss, &c. In 1802-3 he was acting manager at Drury Lane, and in 1815 retired from the stage. Died in Gower Street, November 7, 1836. Horace Walpole calls him " his favourite."

'Bust, life-size, to right, grey coat, hair powdered. Canvas 20 × 16 in.

By SIR J. REYNOLDS, P.R.A.  Lent by MRS. T. HUTCHINSON LEE.

**258. LADY HAMILTON (1761?–1815).**

Bust, life-size, to left, head looking upwards. Sketch, 22 × 17 in.

By G. ROMNEY.  Lent by The EARL OF WEMYSS.

**259. FRANCES BURNEY, MADAME D'ARBLAY (1752–1840).**

Poetess and novelist. 2nd dau. of Dr. Charles Burney (see No. 269), born at Lynn Regis ; published her first novel, *Evelina*, in 1778, which, being praised by Dr. Johnson, at once made her popular. Her second novel, *Cecilia*, appeared in 1782. In 1786 she was appointed Keeper of the Robes and Reader to Queen Charlotte ; in 1793 she married M. D'Arblay, a French emigrant artillery officer, and in 1795 had her tragedy of *Edwy and Elgiva* performed at Drury Lane. She afterwards wrote two novels, *Camilla* and *The Wanderer*, *Memoirs of Dr. Burney*, and, surviving her husband twenty-two years, died at Bath, January 6, 1840.

Half-length, life-size, seated to left, white dress, black scarf and large white hat with puce ribbons, powdered hair. Canvas 34½ × 24 in.

This portrait was engraved as a frontispiece to Madame D'Arblay's works. The painter (1766–1848) was her cousin : he executed a few good portraits, but is best known by his book-illustrations. He, like his cousin, was a friend of Sir Joshua Reynolds.

By E. BURNEY.  Lent by The REV. HENRY BURNEY.

SOUTH GALLERY.]  *Portraits.*  91

**260.** ALLAN RAMSAY (1713-1784).

Portrait painter. Son of Allan Ramsay, the author of *The Gentle Shepherd*, born at Edinburgh, studied in Italy, founded in Edinburgh in 1754 the "Select Society," and soon after settling in London was through the interest of Lord Bute named first painter to George III. in 1767. He visited Rome several times, was frequently at Johnson's parties, and was the author of some political and other papers, published under the title of *Investigator*. Died at Dover, when returning from his last journey to Rome.

Half-length, life-size, to right, brown coat and cap.  Canvas 30 × 24 in.

By W. AIKMAN.   Lent by SIR GEORGE D. CLERK, BART.

**261.** SIR JOHN HAWKINS, KNT. (1819-1789).

Historian of music and miscellaneous writer; born in London, practised as a solicitor with reputation for some years, and at the same time devoted himself to general literature. A taste for music led him to become a member of the Academy of Ancient Music, and in 1742 he became a member of Johnson's Literary Club. Having in 1753 married Miss Sidney Storer, who brought with her a large fortune, he relinquished his profession and became an active magistrate for Middlesex. He was knighted in 1772. His principal work is *A General History of the Science and Practice of Music*, five volumes, published in 1776, and which had occupied him sixteen years.

Half length to right; red coat; wearing a wig; seated in a library, holding a book in right hand. Canvas, 30 × 24.

Lent by The UNIVERSITY OF OXFORD.

**262.** BENJAMIN WEST, P.R.A. (1738-1820).

Eminent painter. Born at Springfield, Pennsylvania, showed his talent for drawing when a child, and was taught by some Indians how to prepare a few colours, supplying himself with hair pencils from his mother's cat, studied at Philadelphia, and afterwards in 1760, visited Rome. He came to England in 1763, received the patronage of George III., and was one of the first members of the Royal Academy, of which he became President on the death of Reynolds in 1792. He produced a great number of historical works, amongst which are the *Death of General Wolfe*, and the *Battle of La Hogue*. Died in Newman Street, March 4, 1820, and was buried in St. Paul's.

Three-quarter length, life-size; seated to left at a table, on which his left hand rests; on table papers and books; right arm on elbow of chair; black coat; in the background is a torso. Canvas 40 × 52 in.

By HIMSELF.   Lent by The ROYAL ACADEMY.

**263.** JAMES THOMSON (1700-1748).

The celebrated author of *The Seasons*. Born at Ednam, Roxburghshire, was educated at Jedburgh and Edinburgh with a view to entering holy orders, but relinquished that intention and took to literature. He came to London and in 1726 published his poem,

*Winter;* those of *Summer, Spring,* and *Autumn* appearing at intervals till 1730. He travelled in Italy with the son of Lord Chancellor Talbot, and on his return was made Secretary of the Briefs, and later on Surveyor of the Leeward Islands. His tragedy of *Tancred and Sigismunda* was produced in 1745; his latest poem was the *Castle of Indolence.*

 Half-length, life-size, to right, head facing, brown coat and blue cap. Canvas 30 × 24 in.

By W. AIKMAN.         Lent by The VISCOUNT COBHAM.

**264. JOHN MACMURRAY, OR MURRAY (1754–1793).**

 Lieutenant, Royal Marines, and afterwards founder of the publishing house. Father of Lord Byron's publisher.

 Half-length, life-size, to right; red coat, wearing a wig, book in right hand. Canvas 30 × 24 in.

              Lent by JOHN MURRAY, ESQ.

**265. SIR HANS SLOANE, BART. F.R.S. (1660–1752).**

 Physician and collector of natural history. Born at Killileagh in Ireland; went to Jamaica as physician to the Duke of Albemarle, whence he returned with a rich store of plants; chosen Secretary of the Royal Society in 1693, and attended Queen Anne in her last illness. He was created a baronet in 1716, appointed Physician-General of the Army, and President of the College of Physicians in 1719. He succeeded Sir Isaac Newton in the Chair of the Royal Society in 1727. His collections formed the foundation of the British Museum.

 Half-length, life-size, to left, head nearly facing, in brown coat and wig. Canvas 30 × 25 in.

By SIR G. KNELLER.        Lent by The ROYAL SOCIETY.

**266. JOHN CONSTABLE, R.A. (1776–1837).**

 Landscape painter. Born at East Bergholt, in Suffolk, the son of a wealthy miller; admitted a student of the Royal Academy in 1799, and first exhibited there in 1802. He soon gained distinction as one of the foremost landscape painters; was elected an A.R.A. in 1819, and a full Academician in 1829. Died April 1, 1837, in Charlotte Street, Fitzroy Square.

 Half-length, life-size, seated facing, black coat; in right hand book. Canvas 30 × 24½ in.

By R. REINAGLE, R.A.    Lent by W. CUTHBERT QUILTER, ESQ., M.P.

## 267. WILLIAM CROFT, MUS. DOC. (1657-1727).

Musician educated under Doctor Blow; was composer to the Chapel Royal and organist of Westminster Abbey. Created Musical Doctor of Oxford.

Half-length, life-size, to left, in robes of Mus. Doc., and wig. Canvas 29 × 24 in.

By T. MURRAY.   Lent by The UNIVERSITY OF OXFORD.

## 268. CHARLES DIBDIN (1748-1814).

Dramatist and Song-writer. Born at Southampton, was educated at Winchester, which he left at 16, and brought out an opera by himself called *The Shepherd's Artifice*. This was followed by *Lionel and Clarissa* and *The Padlock*, in which cast he performed Mungo. He built the circus now known as the Surrey Theatre, and later on a small theatre in Leicester Fields, which he named the "Sans Souci," where he continued his entertainments with success. During the war he wrote a number of legal and nautical songs, for which Pitt granted him a pension of £200 a year. This was withdrawn at Pitt's death, and being reduced to poverty he became a bankrupt.

Half length facing, dark blue coat, yellow waistcoat, gray wig. Canvas 30 in. × 24 in.

Lent by The CORPORATION OF SOUTHAMPTON.

## 269. DR. CHARLES BURNEY, F.R.S. (1726-1814).

Musician and composer. Father of Fanny Burney (Madame D'Arblay) (see No. 259), born at Shrewsbury, studied under Dr. Arne, resided at Lynn as organist for nine years, returned to London in 1760, and in 1769 received the honorary degree of Mus. Doc. at Oxford. In 1770 and 1772 he visited the Continent to collect material for his *History of Music*, which was published 1776-1789. He was elected an F.R.S. in 1773. He composed the music for several dramas, concertos, &c., and was acquainted with almost every distinguished personage in literature and art of his time, being on intimate terms with Johnson and Reynolds.

Half-length, life-size, to left, head facing, in wig and robes of Mus. Doc.; in right hand scroll of music. Canvas 30 × 25.

A similar picture is in the possession of the Ven. Archdeacon Burney: it was painted in 1781 and exhibited at the Royal Academy in that year. It was begun when both painter and sitter were the guests of the Thrales. It was engraved in stipple by Bartolozzi for the Doctor's *History of Music*. When Sir Joshua began his work he delighted in it, and prophesied (as he often did as he was sitting down to a new canvas) that it would be his best work. This frequent conviction shows with how much spirit Sir Joshua set about each successive picture. Walpole in his *Catalogue* for 1781, noted it as "excellent," and Sir Thomas Lawrence considered it one of the greatest works of Sir Joshua.

By SIR J. REYNOLDS, P.R.A.   Lent by The UNIVERSITY OF OXFORD.

## 270. GEORGE ROMNEY AND HIS FATHER.

Painter. Son of John Romney, cabinet-maker; born at Dalton-le-Furness, studied under Steele at Kendal, came to London in 1762, where he quickly rose to fame as a portrait-painter, dividing the patronage of the fashionable world with his rivals Reynolds and Gainsborough. Lord Thurlow declared that the whole town was divided into two—the Romney and the Reynolds factions, adding "and I am of the Romney faction." Visited Italy in 1773, and on his return resided in Cavendish Square, and later on at Hampstead. Died at Dalton, having fallen into a state of hopeless imbecility.

Half-lengths, life-size, to right; both figures enveloped in one plaid; his father, who is blind, holds a staff; in background moonlight sky. Canvas 30 × 26 in.

By GEORGE ROMNEY. Lent by The EARL OF WARWICK.

## 271. THOMAS GAINSBOROUGH, R.A. (1727–1788).

Eminent painter. Born at Sudbury, Suffolk, came to London at the age of fifteen, and studied under Gravelot and Hayman. He settled at Ipswich in 1745, removed to Bath, and returned to London in 1774, taking up his residence in Schomberg House, Pall Mall. He soon rose to the highest reputation as a portrait painter, was the friend and rival of Reynolds, and an original member of the Royal Academy. Died August 2, 1788. "Whether in landscape, pastoral, or in portraiture, Gainsborough drew his inspiration entirely for his subject and tinged it with his own sentiment. So he became the father of modern landscape, and in his portraits he was scarcely less original, painting his ladies or gentlemen in a manner entirely pure and unaffected, yet with such spirit, grace, and dignity as nature had endowed them with."

Half-length, life-size, to right, in green coat, white tie. Canvas 30 × 24 in.
Purchased from the Gainsborough family in 1840.

By HIMSELF. Lent by MRS. WILLIAM SHARPE.

## 272. GEORGE FREDERICK HANDEL (1684–1759).

The great musical composer. Son of an eminent physician at Hallé in Saxony, showed at a very early age a great propensity for music, in which he was encouraged by the then reigning Duke, and at the age of nine composed a Church service for voices and instruments. In 1704 he brought out his first opera, *Almira*, and having spent some time in travelling in Germany and Italy, came to London in 1710, where he met with a flattering reception from Queen Anne. His early compositions were for Italian operas, and he was assisted by George I. in establishing the Italian Opera in the Haymarket. This undertaking having failed, Handel turned his attention to sacred music, and composed his sublime oratorios, *Israel in Egypt* in 1738, the *Messiah* in 1741, and *Judas Maccabæus* in 1746. He composed sixteen English oratorios in all, *Jephtha*, the last, being produced in 1751. In 1750 he lost his sight, and gradually declined in health from that time till his death. He was buried with great pomp in Westminster Abbey.

Three-quarter length, life-size, seated to right; red coat and cap; his left arm rests on a harpsichord, hand supporting his head; in right, pen; before him on a circular table is a sheet of music upon which he is engaged; high green chair. Canvas 50×40 in.

This picture was left by Handel to Thomas Harris, brother of the great-great-grandfather of the present owner, together with half his manuscripts containing all his operas now in the library at Heron Court. Handel left the other half containing his oratorios to the then Lord Shaftesbury.

By P. MERCIER.                   Lent by The EARL OF MALMESBURY.

**273.** THOMAS MOORE (1779–1852).

This great master of lyrical poetry was born at Dublin, entered at Trinity College, and afterwards at the Middle Temple, London; but all his tastes and talents were directed to poetry and other branches of learning. His *Anacreon* appeared in 1801; but it is perhaps on his Irish melodies and *Lalla Rookh* that his fame mainly rests. In 1827 he published the *Life of Sheridan*, and in 1830 the *Life of Byron*, of whom he had been an intimate friend. At the time of his death he was engaged on a history of Ireland.

Three-quarter length, life-size, seated to left at a table, on which he rests left arm, and on which are placed papers; right hand holding eye-glass; brown coat. Canvas 35 × 27 in.

By SIR MARTIN SHEE, P.R.A.          Lent by The EARL OF ILCHESTER.

**274.** JACOB TONSON (d. 1736).

Son of a barber-surgeon in Holborn. Was apprenticed to a bookseller named Thomas Bassch, and in 1677 commenced business on his own account. At first he made but little progress in his trade, but in 1688 he purchased the copyright of Milton's *Paradise Lost*, which quickly proved a financial success. It was at Tonson's suggestion that Dryden undertook to translate Virgil's *Aeneid* and *Georgics*, for each work of which the author received £50. On the formation of the Kit-Cat club Tonson became its secretary, and held that office during its entire existence. His appointment to the office of stationer, bookseller, and printer to Queen Anne and to George I., was a source of great profit to him. In 1720 he retired from business and resided at Barn Elms, Hertfordshire, where he died about eighty years of age.

Half-length, life-size, seated to right, head turned to left; in green loose coat and red cap; he holds in right hand a book inscribed "Milton's *Paradise Lost*." Canvas 36 × 27 in.

The Kit-Cat Club was instituted about 1700, and its members included the principal noblemen and gentlemen who were opposed to the arbitrary measures of James II., and had contrived to bring about the Revolution. Their ostensible object was the encouragement of literature and the fine arts, but the end that they laboured most assiduously to accomplish was the promotion of loyalty to the House of Hanover. The Club derived its name from having met for some time in the house of Christopher Cat, a pastrycook. Malone says that the pies which he made were called "Kit-Cats."

The Club was dissolved about 1720, Jacob Tonson having acted as its secretary during the whole period of its existence. Previous to its dissolution each member presented to Tonson his portrait (half-length figure), painted a uniform size by Sir Godfrey Kneller, who added his own, smaller than the rest in size. The portraits, forty-eight in number, were hung in a room at Tonson's house at Barn Elms. At his death they passed to his nephew Jacob, and from him to his brother Richard, who removed them to his residence at Water Oakley, near Windsor. At Richard's death the pictures were inherited by the eldest daughter of the second Jacob, who had married Alderman Baker, father of Sir William Baker, M.P. for Hertfordshire, and ancestor of the present owner.

By SIR G. KNELLER. Lent by R. B. BAKER, ESQ.

**275.** FRANCIS JOSEPH HAYDN (1732–1809).

German musical composer. Born at Rohrau, a small town near Vienna; was received at an early age into the choir of the cathedral at Vienna; but on the breaking of his voice was dismissed, and entered the service of Prince Esterhazy, whose chapel-master he continued to be till the end of his life. He came to England in 1791 to attend the Handel Commemoration, and received the degree of Mus.Doc. from the University of Oxford. He returned to Vienna in the following year, but again visited England in 1794. It was after this visit that he composed his *chef-d'œuvre*, the *Creation*.

Three-quarter length, life-size, seated to right; dark red coat and wig; left hand rests on a book or manuscript placed on a table in front of him; in right pen. Canvas 35 × 28 in.

Probably painted when the musician was in England for the second time in 1793, and when he was at the height of his reputation. It was painted for George III.

By J. HOPPNER, R.A. Lent by HER MAJESTY THE QUEEN
(Hampton Court).

**276.** SIR JOSHUA REYNOLDS, P.R.A. (1723–1792).

Half-length, life-size, to right, red dress, black cap; left hand holding lappet of coat. Canvas 30 × 24 in.

It is known that Reynolds painted no less than eighteen portraits of himself. One of the earliest of the series is now in the National Portrait Gallery, painted when he was about seventeen years of age, and in the act of shading his eyes with his left hand, while holding a palette by the handle in his right. This picture was produced before Reynolds went to Italy, and in its style it approaches his earlier portraits.

By HIMSELF. Lent by The HON. F. B. MASSEY MAINWARING.

**277.** MARTIN FOLKES, P.R.S. (1690–1754).

Scholar and antiquary. Born in Great Queen Street, was educated at Saumur and Clare College, Cambridge, elected a Fellow of the Royal Society at the age of twenty-three.

of which he became President in 1741, and President of the Society of Antiquaries in 1750. He was a large contributor to the *Philosophical Transactions* and published *A Table of English Gold Coins.*

Half-length, life-size, to left, brown coat and wig; right hand raised in act of declamation. Canvas 29 × 24 in.

Painted in 1741, and engraved by Hogarth.

By W. HOGARTH. Lent by The ROYAL SOCIETY.

**278. JOHN HOPPNER, R.A. (1758-1810).**

Painter. Born in Whitechapel of German parentage; was a choir-boy in one of the royal chapels; entered the Academy as a student in 1775, and obtained a medal for his scene of *King Lear.* He became an associate in 1793, and full academician in 1795. Through the patronage of the Prince of Wales, he was a very fashionable portrait-painter, and for many years was a rival of Sir Thomas Lawrence.

Half-length, life-size, to right; brown coat. Canvas 30 × 24 in.

By HIMSELF. Lent by The ROYAL ACADEMY.

**279. GEORGE FREDERICK HANDEL (1684-1759).**

Three-quarter length, life-size, seated, head to right, grey gold-embroidered coat, red dress, and wig, his left hand resting on table holds a partition of music, his right rests on his leg. Canvas 50 × 40 in.

By T. HUDSON. Lent by The BODLEIAN LIBRARY, OXFORD.

**280. ANTONIO CANOVA (1747-1822).**

Italian sculptor. Born at Possagno in the Venetian territory, studied under Toretto, and in 1779 was called to Rome. He visited Germany in 1798, France in 1802, 1809, and again in 1815 as papal ambassador for the restoration to Italy of the ancient works of art which had been carried off by the French. On this occasion he crossed over to England to see the Elgin marbles. Died at Venice, 1822.

Half-length, life-size, seated to left, in red furred gown. Canvas 36 × 28½ in.

Lent by The DUKE OF DEVONSHIRE, K.G.

**281. WILLIAM AIKMAN (1682-1731).**

Painter. A native of Cairnay, in Forfarshire; studied law, but his inclination for painting led him to change his profession. He went to Italy in 1707, visited Turkey, and on his return to Scotland in 1712, met with great encouragement as a portrait painter. He came to London in 1723, where he successfully practised his art till his death in 1731.

He lived on intimate terms with Kneller, whose style of portraiture he imitated, Allan Ramsay, Thomson, and others.

Half-length, life-size, to right, nearly full-face; grey coat and wig; in an oval. Canvas 30 × 24 in.

By HIMSELF.                                  Lent by SIR GEORGE D. CLERK, BART.

**282.** JOHN FLAXMAN, R.A. (1755–1826).

Eminent Designer and Sculptor. Born at York, the son of a moulder of figures, but when only a few months old was brought by his father to London and resided in the neighbourhood of Covent Garden. As a child he was continually amusing himself with modelling in wax and plaster on a small scale. At fifteen he gained his first prize at the Society of Arts, became a student of the Royal Academy, and within twelve months was awarded its silver medal. He first supported himself by working for Wedgwood and others, but in 1787 went to Rome and whilst there produced his well-known outlines from Homer and Dante, engraved by Piroli in 1793. He was elected an Associate of the Royal Academy in 1797, a full member in 1808 and its Professor of Sculpture in 1810. Of the numerous statues which he executed those of Lord Mansfield in Westminster Abbey, of Nelson, Howe, Kemble and Sir Joshua Reynolds in St. Paul's are the best known.

Half-length, life-size, to left, head nearly facing; black coat. Canvas 30 × 24 in.

By W. DERBY.                                Lent by The BARONESS BURDETT-COUTTS.

**283.** JOSIAH WEDGWOOD, F.R.S. (1730–1805).

An ingenious improver of the English pottery manufacture. Was a member of a family of potters at Burslem, and at an early age showed considerable skill in the production of ornament and coloured pottery. He established himself in his native place in 1759, and soon became widely known by his Queen's ware, black basalt ware, cameos, &c. To extend his works he founded the village of Etruria in 1766, and engaged Flaxman, the sculptor, as a designer. He succeeded in imitating the Portland vase in 1790. Died at Etruria, January 3, 1805. Wedgwood was a Fellow of the Royal Society, and of the Society of Antiquaries.

Half-length, life-size, to left: red coat and wig. Canvas 30 × 24 in.

By SIR J. REYNOLDS, P.R.A.                  Lent by The EARL OF CRAWFORD.

**284.** GEORGE MORLAND (1764–1804).

Painter. The son of an indifferent artist who employed him in such works as would obtain a ready sale, till at length, tired of this drudgery, he set up for himself. Unfortunately, from the manner in which he had been bred, he contracted irregular habits, so that most of his pictures were painted under circumstances of distress. He fell a

SOUTH GALLERY.]    *Portraits.*

victim to intemperance, October 29, 1804 ; his wife, who was of a similar disposition, dying a few days after. His subjects were landscapes, views on the sea-coast, stables, farmyards and animals, executed with admirable spirit and accuracy.

Half-length, life-size, facing, blue coat, white waistcoat, black hat ; his left arm thrown over a chair ; his right rests on table, on which is a glass and a bottle. Canvas 29 × 24 in.

This portrait of himself was presented to the lady whom he wished to marry, but the habit he indulged in, as testified by the glass at his side, caused her to refuse him. At her death it was sold, and came into the possession of the present owner.

By HIMSELF.    Lent by W. PERCIVAL BOXALL, ESQ.

**285.** SIR DAVID WILKIE, R.A. (1785–1841).

Painter. Born at Cults in Fifeshire ; studied at the Academy at Edinburgh under Graham ; came to London in 1805, and in the following year exhibited at the Royal Academy *The Village Politicians*, which was painted for the Earl of Mansfield. This picture laid the foundation of his fame, and became the first of a splendid series, perhaps unequalled in one branch of art. In 1830 Wilkie was appointed Painter in Ordinary to William IV., and in 1836 was knighted. In 1840 he went to the East, painted the portrait of the Sultan at Constantinople, but died off Gibraltar on his way home, and was buried at sea.

Half-length, life-size, to left, head nearly facing, brown coat. Canvas 30 × 25 in. Painted in 1840, the year previous to the artist's death, and just before his departure on his journey to the East.

By HIMSELF.    Lent by COLONEL DAVID WILKIE.

**286.** THOMAS GIRTIN (1775–1802).

Painter. Was a pupil of Edward Dayes, a founder of the English School of painting in water-colours, and a friend of Turner, next to whom in point of merit he is generally classed. He exhibited at the Royal Academy from 1795 to 1801, many of his pictures representing views of London, the Lake District, and Devonshire. A special exhibition of his works was held at the Burlington Fine Arts Club in 1875.

Half-length, life-size, to right, head to left, seated at a table, black coat ; in right hand drawing-pen, in left sketch-book. Canvas 30 × 25 in.

This picture was painted in 1800 and was exhibited at the Royal Academy in 1820, and also at the Burlington Fine Arts Club in 1875, together with the collection of Girtin's works.

By J. OPIE, R.A.    Lent by D. H. GIRTIN, ESQ.

**287.** MRS. JORDAN (1762–1816).

Actress. Her real name was Dorothea Bland ; born at Waterford ; appeared on the stage in 1777, afterwards at Leeds, and in 1785 at Drury Lane, when she assumed the name of Mrs. Jordan. She was a most bewitching and delightful actress. Her connection with the Duke of Clarence, afterwards William IV., is well known; it began in 1790 and lasted till 1811. She died at St. Cloud July 5, 1816, having left England for the purpose of avoiding creditors, her debts being the consequence of bills given by her to relieve a near relation.

Half-length, life-size, facing, head to left; white dress and black girdle, in which is stuck a sprig of orange blossom. Canvas 29 × 24 in.

By G. RAMSAY.                                    Lent by GENERAL MACKENZIE.

**288.** SIR THOMAS LAWRENCE, P.R.A. (1769–1830).

Portrait-painter. Born at Bristol; the son of an innkeeper; began at the age of ten to take crayon portraits, and soon established himself at Bath, where he met with great success. In 1787 he entered the Royal Academy as a student, was elected an Associate in 1791, succeeded Sir Joshua Reynolds as principal Painter-in-Ordinary to George III. in 1792, and became a full Academician in 1794. At the peace of 1814 Lawrence was commissioned by the King to paint the portraits of the allied Sovereigns, their ministers, &c.; was knighted in 1815, and in 1820 succeeded West as President of the Academy. Died in Russell Square, January 7, 1830, and was buried in St. Paul's Cathedral.

Half-length, life-size, nearly facing; black coat. *Unfinished.* Canvas 36 × 27 in.

This picture was sold at the Artist's sale, in 1831, to the Earl of Chesterfield for £493 10s., from whom it was acquired by the Royal Academy. It was engraved by S. Cousins, R.A., in 1830, by G. T. Doo, R.A., in 1877, and by William Giller for the Lawrence work.

By HIMSELF.                                      Lent by The ROYAL ACADEMY.

**289.** ANGELICA MARIA CATHERINA KAUFFMANN, R.A. (1740–1807).

Painter of ornamental and classical subjects and portraiture. Born in the village of Schwartzenburg in the Bregenzer Wald; showed at an early age a taste for drawing, and studied painting in Italy. In 1765 she established herself in England under the patronage of Queen Charlotte and many of the nobility. She was nominated one of the original members of the Royal Academy in 1769. In 1782 she married Antonio Zucchi, a Venetian painter, with whom she retired to Rome, where she died at the age of sixty-seven.

Half-length, life-size, to left, head nearly facing, in white dress, and blue shawl over right shoulder; holding brushes and pallet. Canvas 30 × 24 in.

By HERSELF.                                      Lent by The REV. J. E. WALDY.

**290.** THE KEMBLE FAMILY IN "HENRY VIII."

Interior of hall representing trial of Queen Catherine, wife of Henry VIII. Mrs. Siddons is in the character of Catherine, Stephen Kemble as Henry VIII. Charles Kemble as the youth in the centre, and J. P. Kemble as Cardinal Wolsey. Miss Stephens, as waiting-woman, stands behind Charles Knyvett as Cardinal

SOUTH GALLERY.]  *Portraits.*  101

Campeggio. The handsome face seen furthest on the right is that of Conway. The artist himself is to be found in the furthest left-hand corner. Canvas 63 × 85 in.

This picture was painted for Welch, the professor of music. Its popularity was very great, and the print, which was engraved from it in mezzotint by George Clint, had an extensive sale both in England and on the Continent. Knowles, in his life of Fuseli, says: "In the year 1817 Fuseli sat at my request to Harlow for his portrait. I attended Fuseli at each sitting, and during the progress of the portrait, Harlow commenced and finished his last and most esteemed work, *The Trial of Queen Catherine*, in which he introduced many portraits, especially those of the Kemble family. At the suggestion of Fuseli, Harlow made many alterations in the picture, re-arranging the position of several of the figures, and changing the foreground. When these improvements were made, Fuseli then said : ' So far you have done well ; but now you have not introduced a back figure to throw the eye of the spectator into the picture :' and then pointed out by what means he might improve it in this particular. Accordingly Harlow introduced the two boys who are taking up the cushion ; that which shows the back is altogether done by Fuseli." According to Knowles Fuseli afterwards attempted to get Harlow to improve the drawing of the arms of Queen Catherine, but without much effect.

By G. H. HARLOW.  Lent by MRS. MORRISON.

**291.** PEG WOFFINGTON AS " PENELOPE " (1720-1760).

Comic actress. Born in Dublin ; her father kept a huckster's shop ; was brought up to the stage by Madame Violante, a rope-dancer ; appeared first in Dublin, and in 1738 at Covent Garden as " Sir Harry Wildair," where her beauty and liveliness won admiration. In 1742 she returned to Dublin with Garrick for a short time, but again resumed her position at Covent Garden, where she continued to be a special favourite till her retirement in 1757, on account of a stroke of paralysis. Her early life had been a very free one, but she now became simple in her attire and manners, and was noted for her numerous benevolent and charitable actions.

Three-quarter length, life-size, to left ; blue and white dress, coronet on her head from which falls a veil ; her hands crossed on her bosom ; in background lighted urn. Canvas 36 × 28 in.

By SIR J. REYNOLDS, P.R.A.  Lent by The LORD SACKVILLE.

**292.** LADY HAMILTON (1761 ?–1815).

Bust, facing, life-size, slight drapery. Sketch 23  19.

By G. ROMNEY.  Lent by The EARL OF WEMYSS.

**293.** SIR FRANCIS BURDETT, BART., M.P. (1770-1844).

Politician. Educated at Westminster School and Oxford, and succeeded to the baronetcy on the death of his grandfather, Sir Robert Burdett, in 1797. Entering Parliament, he speedily attained high distinction as an orator in the foremost Opposition ranks. In 1807 he was returned for Westminster, and represented that constituency for over thirty years. In 1810 he was imprisoned for breach of privilege, and after his release distinguished himself by his speeches against the suspension of the Habeas Corpus Act, and in favour of Parliamentary Reform and Catholic Emancipation. At the general election he declined to stand for Westminster, and was returned for North Wilts, transferring his influence to the side of the Conservatives. Died January 23, 1844. He married in 1793 Sophia, youngest daughter of Thomas Coutts the banker. She died in the same month as her husband.

Three-quarter length, life-size, to left, in black coat ; in right hand scroll, left rests on papers placed on table. Canvas 55 × 44 in.

By Sir M. Shee, P.R.A.      Lent by The Baroness Burdett-Coutts.

**294.** William Crotch (1775–1847).

Musical composer. Born at Norwich, the son of a carpenter; at a very early age showed great talent for music, and was appointed in 1786 assistant to Dr. Randall, professor of music and organist at Trinity and King's College, Cambridge. He removed to Oxford in 1788, became professor of music in 1797, and took the degree of Mus.Doc. in 1799. He became head of the Royal Academy of Music in 1822, and died at Taunton in 1847. His compositions, both vocal and instrumental, are numerous.

Full-length, life-size, seated to right, light brown jacket and trousers, large white collar ; he is writing in a book which rests on arm of chair, and is held by his left hand. Canvas 50 × 40 in.

By Sir W. Beechey, R.A.      Lent by The Royal Academy of Music (London).

# THE BALCONY.

## PORTRAITS.

**295.** WILLIAM BOYCE (1710–1779).

Musical composer; born in London, the son of a cabinet-maker, was a chorister at St. Paul's, and in 1736 became composer to the Chapels Royal, and in 1758 organist. He received the degree of Mus.Doc. from the University of Cambridge in 1749. His works consist chiefly of anthems, but he also published a magnificent collection of *Cathedral Music of the English Masters.* He died in 1779, and was buried in St. Paul's Cathedral.

Full-length, life-size, standing to left, in grey coat and wig; in right hand he holds a book inscribed "Solomon; a Serenata," before him an organ. Canvas 88 × 53 in.

By T. HUDSON.     Lent by The UNIVERSITY OF OXFORD.

**296.** DAVID GARRICK, WHEN YOUNG (1716–1779).

Half-length, slightly under life-size, to right; blue coat and wig; right hand pointing. Pastel 22 × 18½ in.

By MISS READ.     Lent by The DUKE OF DEVONSHIRE, K.G.

**296A.** MRS. GARRICK, WHEN YOUNG (1724–1822).

Half-length, life-size, to left; grey dress, blue bodice, cap tied under the chin by blue ribbon. Pastel 22 × 18½ in.

By MISS READ.     Lent by The DUKE OF DEVONSHIRE, K.G.

**297.** WILLIAM WYNDHAM, LORD GRENVILLE (1759–1834).

Half-length, life-size, to left, blue coat and wig, in right hand, book. Canvas 32 × 27 in

Lent by The PROVOST, ETON COLLEGE.

**298. JANE MAXWELL, DUCHESS OF GORDON (d. 1812).**

Half-length, life-size, facing, head to left, white dress embroidered in gold, high collar, puffed sleeves, wears a miniature suspended by a chain. Canvas 30 × 24 in.

Painted in 1774-5, and exhibited at the Royal Academy in 1775.

By SIR J. REYNOLDS, P.R.A.      Lent by THE DUKE OF RICHMOND AND GORDON, K.G.

**299. JOHN, LORD HERVEY (1696–1743).**

Eldest son of John, 1st Earl of Bristol; distinguished himself as an orator in both Houses of Parliament, was raised to the Peerage in 1733 as Lord Hervey of Tekworth, appointed Lord Privy Seal in 1740, and in the same year nominated one of the Lords Justices during the absence of the King. He suffered from epilepsy, on account of which he subjected himself to a strict diet of asses' milk and flour-biscuits, and is said to have used paint for his complexion. In consequence he was ridiculed by Pope as "Lord Fanny"; and in the *Satirist*, under "Sporus," he is described as "that mere white curd of asses' milk," and "that painted child of dirt that stinks and sings." Yet Princess Charlotte is said to have been in love with him, and he married the beautiful Mary Lepel.

Full-length life, seated, facing, drab coat, gray wig, holds on his knee the purse of the Privy Seal. To left hat and gloves on table. Canvas 72 × 54 in.

Painted by VAN LOO.      Lent by THE MARQUIS OF BRISTOL.

**300. JOSEPH ADDISON (1672–1719).**

Half-length, life-size, to right; in painted oval; black coat, white cravat, and long wig. Canvas 30 × 25 in.

This picture belonged to Addison's daughter, by whom it was presented to the Rev. T. W. Addison, the rector of Worthington, and grandfather of the present owner.

By SIR G. KNELLER.      Lent by W. ADDISON, ESQ.

**301. HENRY KIRKE WHITE (1785–1806).**

Poet. Born at Nottingham, was first placed with a stocking-weaver, then removed to an attorney's office, where, imbued with an ardent desire for learning, he devoted his spare moments to the study of the classics. Through the generosity of Wilberforce he was admitted a student of St. John's College, Cambridge, where he applied himself to his studies with such unremitting labour that his constitution broke down, and he died October 19, 1806. His poems, letters, and fragments, were edited by Southey.

Half-length, life-size, to left, in black coat, landscape background. Canvas 30 × 24½ in.

By J. HOPPNER, R.A.      Lent by THE CORPORATION OF NOTTINGHAM.

**302. WILLIAM COWPER (1731–1800).**

Half-length, life-size, to left, looking upwards; black cloak and grey waistcoat, white cap; his left-hand thrust in his waistcoat. Canvas 30 × 24 in.

By L. F. ABBOTT.      Lent by J. P. BOYCE, ESQ.

**303. EDWARD GIBBON (1737–1794).**

Half-length, life-size, to left, head turned to right; in puce coat, white waistcoat and wig. Canvas 29½ × 25½ in. Presented to Balliol College by Henry Willett, Esq.

By G. ROMNEY.      Lent by BALLIOL COLLEGE, OXFORD.

**304. GEORGE WILLIAM, 6TH EARL OF COVENTRY (AND HIS WIFE, MARIA GUNNING) (1722–1809).**

Son of William, 5th Earl: was appointed Lord-Lieutenant and Custos Rotulorum of the County of Worcester in 1751; succeeded to the Earldom in 1751, became Lord of the Bedchamber to George II., and was continued in that Office by George III. Married, first, Maria, daughter of John Gunning, and secondly, Barbara, daughter of John, Lord St. John of Bletsoe.

Small, full-lengths, standing facing, in a garden. On the right is the Earl in blue coat embroidered in gold, white gold-embroidered waistcoat and blue breeches: his right hand rests on hip, his left points to building in background; on the left, Lady Coventry in white dress and hat leans on the pediment of a vase; between them a dog. Canvas 29 × 48 in.

By W. HOGARTH.      Lent by The EARL OF COVENTRY.

**305. THE REV. LAURENCE STERNE (1713–1768).**

Half-length, seated, nearly facing, right elbow on table and right hand supporting his head, in gown and wig. Canvas 30 × 25 in.

This picture was given by Sterne to Edward Stanley, Esq., and bequeathed by him to his son-in-law, James Whatman, Esq., of Vinters, Maidstone. (See No. 207.)

By SIR J. REYNOLDS, P.R.A.      Lent by MRS. WHATMAN.

**306. JOHN FANE, 10TH EARL OF WESTMORELAND, K.G. (1759–1841).**

Eldest son of John, 9th Earl; was educated at Charterhouse and Emmanuel College, Cambridge, where he made the acquaintance of William Pitt; succeeded to the earldom at the age of 15; was appointed Paymaster-General in 1789, and Lord-Lieutenant of Ireland in 1790, and Lord Privy Seal in 1798, which last office he retained till 1827. He was elected a K.G. in 1793. For many years before his death he retired from politics, and during the last year or two of his life was quite blind.

Half-length, life-size, to right, in brown coat, tan gloves, hair powdered, right arm resting on rock; landscape background. Canvas 36 × 28 in.

By SIR T. LAWRENCE, P.R.A.   Lent by The RIGHT HON. SIR SPENCER PONSONBY FANE, K.C.B.

**307.** HORATIO, VISCOUNT NELSON (1758–1805).

Small three-quarter length, facing head to left; naval uniform; Star of the Bath; left hand resting on sword. Canvas 16½ × 13½.

Lent by W. S. GREEN, ESQ.

**308.** EVA MARIA VIOLETTE, MRS GARRICK (1724–1822).

The reputed daughter of a Viennese citizen named Veigel; came to London in 1746, was engaged as a dancer at the Haymarket, and became the guest of the Earl and Countess of Burlington. On her marriage with Garrick, June 22, 1749, the Earl of Burlington is said to have settled on her £6,000. This marriage embroiled Garrick with many of the leading actresses, more than one of whom had regarded him as in some shape pledged to her. Died in 1822.

Small full length, facing, dancing, arms extended; white gold embroidered dress. Canvas 13½ × 11½ in.

Edward Moore wrote a poem on the marriage, entitled, *Envy and Fortune; A Tale*: in which are the following lines on this lady:—

"I'll show you a sight that you'll fancy uncommon:
Wit, Beauty, and Goodness all met in a woman;
A heart to no folly or mischief inclined,
A Body all Grace and all sweetness a Mind."

By W. HOGARTH.   Lent by DR. EDWARD HAMILTON.

**309.** HENRY FREDERICK, DUKE OF CUMBERLAND (1745–1790).

Fourth son of Frederick, Prince of Wales, and Princess Augusta of Saxe-Gotha, created Duke of Cumberland 1766, married Anne Luttrell, Mrs. Horton, dau. of Simon Luttrell, afterwards Earl of Carhampton; died without issue 1790, and was buried in Westminster Abbey. This marriage so incensed George III. that he procured the passing of the Royal Marriage Act, which forbids any of the royal family marrying without the consent of the Sovereign.

Bust to left, life-size; unfinished. Canvas 54 × 40.

By T. GAINSBOROUGH, R.A.   Lent by HER MAJESTY THE QUEEN (Windsor).

### 310. "THE MIDNIGHT MODERN CONVERSATION," OR "THE PUNCH BOWL."

Interior of a room; various persons seated at a round table, on which is a large bowl of punch; many intoxicated, one in the foreground having fallen on the floor. Canvas 29 × 35 in.

This picture was painted by Hogarth in 1734. In point of chronology its proper place lies between the two *Progresses* — *The Harlot's Progress* and *The Rake's Progress*. Ireland said that most of the figures in the picture were portraits. This is not unlikely, but only two have been identified with any certainty. Sir John Hawkins identified the rosy-gilled parson who presides over the capacious bowl of punch as Orator Henley, but Mrs. Piozzi as the Rev. Cornelius Ford, a cousin of Dr. Johnson, who described him as a "man of great parts, very profligate, but I never heard he was impious." The figure on his left, seated at the table, is Counsellor Kettleby, a vociferous bar-orator, remarkable, though an utter barrister, for wearing a full-bottomed wig, which he is here drawn with, as also for a horrible squint. There are several repetitions of this picture; one is at the Earl of Egremont's at Petworth. It was engraved by Hogarth in 1734; by Riepenhausen in 1786, under the title of "Société Nocturne, nommée communement Côterie de Débauche en Ponche"; and by the French engraver Creite, who added beneath his print the following lines:—

"Si pour éclater sa joye, un François chante,
Si les Italiens se plaisent aux concerts,
Si l'Allemand chérit la Table et les Desserts,
L'Anglois s'entient au Ponche, et la Pipe l'enchante."

Walpole says that this was the first work that showed Hogarth's command of character. It is the plate of all others that has been most generally popular on the Continent, particularly in Germany, where copies of it have been multiplied *ad infinitum*.

By W. HOGARTH. Lent by MRS. MORRISON.

### 311. THOMAS COUTTS (1735-1822).

Banker. Fourth son of Lord Provost John Coutts, of Edinburgh; founded with his brother James the banking house of Coutts & Co., of which, in 1778, he became sole partner. He was banker to George III., and to a large number of the aristocracy. He was a gentleman of wide accomplishments, and very charitable. Died February 24, 1822. Married Harriet Mellon, the actress.

Half-length, life-size, to left, head nearly facing; black coat. Canvas 30 × 24 in.

By SIR W. BEECHEY, R.A. Lent by The BARONESS BURDETT-COUTTS.

### 312. JOHN GAY (1688-1732).

Bust, life-size, to left, in blue gown and cap. Canvas 22 × 17 in.

By W. AIKMAN. Lent by The LORD SCARSDALE.

**313. JAMES BOSWELL (1740–1795).**

The biographer of Johnson. Born at Edinburgh, the son of Alexander, Lord Auchinleck, studied law at Edinburgh and Glasgow, came to London, and on May 16, 1763, was introduced to Dr. Johnson, with whom he soon formed a close friendship. In 1773, they together visited the Hebrides, an account of which was afterwards published by Boswell in 1785. Having settled in London in 1782, Boswell was called to the English Bar, but did not succeed in getting any practice. His *Life of Johnson* appeared in 1790, five years after his friend's death, and met with an immense success. He was also the author of various political and professional pamphlets; and wrote the life of Paoli, whose acquaintance he had made in Italy in 1763. Died in Great Portland Street, May 19, 1795.

Half-length, life-size, to left, black coat and wig; red curtain and landscape in background. Canvas 30 × 24 in.

This picture is a repetition of that in the National Gallery which came from the collection of Sir Robert Peel. In 1785 Boswell was very anxious to have his portrait painted by Reynolds, but being very short of money wrote the following very characteristic letter to the painter: "The debts which I contracted in my father's lifetime will not be cleared off by me for some years, I therefore think it unconscientious to indulge myself in any expensive article of elegant luxury. But in the meantime you may die, or I may die, and I should regret very much that there should not be at Auchinleck my portrait painted by Sir Joshua Reynolds, with whom I have the felicity of living in social intimacy. I have a proposal to make to you. I am for certain to be called to the English bar next February. Will you now do my picture? and the price shall be paid out of the first fees which I receive as a barrister at Westminster Hall. Or, if that fund should fail, it shall be paid at any rate five years hence by myself or my representatives. (Signed) James Boswell." This letter was endorsed by Sir Joshua, "I agree to the above conditions." This picture was painted, but there is no proof that it was ever paid for, as Boswell's attempts at the bar were a failure.

By SIR J. REYNOLDS, P.R.A.      Lent by PHILIP NORMAN, ESQ.

**314. HORACE WALPOLE, 4TH EARL OF ORFORD (1717–1797).**

Half-length, life-size, to right, head to left, in red furred coat and black hat under which is a white domino. Pastel 24 × 19 in.

This portrait is said to have been a present from Walpole to Kitty Clive. He was fond of her society and gave her a house on his Strawberry Hill estate, called Little Strawberry Hill.

By ROSALBA CARRIERA.      Lent by H. SPENCER WALPOLE, ESQ.

**315. FOOTE AND HAYES IN THE CHARACTERS OF "MAJOR STURGEON" AND "SIR JACOB JOLLUP" IN THE FARCE OF "THE MAYOR OF GARRATT."**

Interior of a room: Foote as "Major Sturgeon," in militia uniform, holds stick in right hand; on his right stands Hayes as "Sir Jacob Jollup," in drab gold embroidered coat, breeches, and wig; his hands on his sides. Canvas 40 × 50 in.

A comedy, in two acts, by Foote, performed at the Haymarket Theatre in 1763. "In this very humorous and entertaining piece the character of Major Sturgeon, a City militia officer, is highly wrought up, and was most inimitably performed by Foote."

By J. ZOFFANY, R.A.                                  Lent by The EARL OF CARLISLE.

**316. DAVID GARRICK AS "ABEL DRUGGER," BURTON AS "SUBTLE," AND JOHN PALMER AS "FACE," IN THE "ALCHEMIST," ACT II. SC. 6.**

Interior of a room: the figure to right holding a pipe is Garrick as "Abel Drugger"; in the centre is Palmer as "Face"; and on the left Burton as "Subtle." Near an open window on the left is a table, on which are placed a globe, bottles, &c. On a shelf in the background other properties of an alchemist. Canvas 41 × 39 in.

The *Alchemist*, by Ben Jonson, was played by Garrick, March 21, 1743, and repeated on several occasions till April, 1776. Garrick as "Abel Drugger," the Tobacco Boy, was a wonderful delineation of character. "The moment he came upon the stage," says Davis, "he discovered such awkward simplicity and his looks so happily bespoke the ignorant, selfish, and abashed tobacco merchant, that it was a contest not easily to be decided whether the bursts of laughter or applause were the loudest." This picture was exhibited at the Royal Academy in 1770. Sir Joshua Reynolds had bought it in the room and agreed to give 100 guineas for it. Lord Carlisle half-an-hour afterwards offered Reynolds twenty to part with it, which he generously refused, resigning his intended purchase to the lord and the emolument to his brother artist.

By J. ZOFFANY, R.A.                                  Lent by The EARL OF CARLISLE.

**317. FOOTE AND WATSON IN THE CHARACTERS OF "THE PRESIDENT" AND "DR. LAST" IN THE "DEVIL UPON TWO STICKS."**

Interior of a room; on the right is Foote as "The President," in black clothes, scarlet cloak, and wig; right arm raised; left holding stick over his shoulders; on left facing him is Watson as "Dr. Last," in green coat and red waistcoat; in right hand he holds a pair of shoes; in left his hat; in background table and chair. Canvas 40 × 50 in.

This comedy, by Foote, was acted at the Haymarket Theatre in 1768. It was one of Foote's most successful performances. The active part taken by Sir William Browne, President of the College of Physicians, in the contest with the Licentiates, occasioned his being introduced by Foote in this comedy. Upon Foote's exact representation of him, with his identical wig and coat, tall figure, and glass stiffly applied to his eye, Sir William sent him a card complimenting the actor in having so happily represented him; but as he had forgotten his muff, he had sent him his own. Watson as "Dr. Last, by trade a doctor, and by profession a maker of shoes," acted his part with such simplicity, that Northcote said, "it was impossible from looking at him, for any-one to say he was acting. You would suppose they had gone out and found the actual character they wanted and brought him upon the stage."

By J. ZOFFANY, R.A.       Lent by The EARL OF CARLISLE.

**318.  RIGHT HON. EDMUND BURKE, M.P. (1729-1797).**

Half-length, to left, brown coat, grey wig.   Canvas 29 × 24.
By SIR JOSHUA REYNOLDS, P.R.A.       Lent by The VENERABLE ARCHDEACON BURNEY.

**319.  JOHN OPIE (1761-1807).**

Painter. Born at St. Agnes, Cornwall; the son of a house carpenter who wished to bring him up in his own business, but coming under the notice of Dr. Wolcot, "Peter Pindar," his taste for painting was encouraged, and he received many commissions as a portrait painter. In 1780 he visited London, where he acquired celebrity by his pictures in the Royal Academy, and by those which he painted for the Boydell and Macklin galleries. He was elected an A.R.A. in 1786, and R.A. in the following year. In 1804 he delivered four lectures which have been published. Died in 1807, and was buried in St. Paul's Cathedral.

Bust, to left, life-size.   Canvas 23 × 19½ in.
By HIMSELF.       Lent by W. PERCIVAL BOXALL, ESQ.

**320.  CAPTAIN THOMAS CORAM (1668-1751).**

Philanthropist. Born at Lyme Regis, Dorset, was a captain in the merchant service; planned many philanthropic schemes, particularly in connection with the Colonies of North America. Horace Walpole said of him that he knew more about the American Colonies than any other man living. In 1739 he established the Foundling Hospital, and by this and other benevolent actions he so impoverished himself that at the close of his life a sub-scription was entered into for his support and an annuity provided for him. He died March 29, 1751, and was buried in the Foundling Chapel.

Half-length, life-size, seated at a table and folding a letter with both hands; grey coat, gold-embroidered vest, and wig; ink-bottle, sealing-wax, and taper on table. Canvas 35 × 27½ in.

This is a fine portrait of a remarkable man. In the Foundling Hospital hangs the other portrait of Coram by Hogarth—a full-length. Of this one Hogarth wrote, "The portrait which I painted with most pleasure, and in which I particularly wished to excel, was that of *Captain Coram* for the Foundling Hospital; and if I am so wretched an artist as my enemies assert, it is somewhat strange that this, which was one of the first I painted the size of life, should stand the test of twenty years' competition, and be generally thought the best portrait in the place, notwithstanding the first painters in the kingdom exerted all their talents to vie with it."

By W. HOGARTH.       Lent by The DUKE OF SUTHERLAND, K.G.

**321. JOHN WILKES (1727-1797), JOHN GLYNN (1722-1779), AND JOHN HORNE TOOKE (1736-1812).**

The three principal characters connected with the *North Briton* riots. Wilkes, as publisher of the paper, was the chief actor. Glynn, whose practice at the Bar and knowledge of law was scarcely equalled by any one of his time, took the lead in the cases connected with Wilkes. He acted for him in his application for a writ of *habeas corpus* in May 1763, and also in the trial which took place in 1764 on the re-publication of the *North Briton*. Horne Tooke, though in orders, was an ardent friend of Wilkes, and not only supported his pretensions and pledged his credit for his expenses, but declared "that in a cause so holy and so just he would dye his black coat red."

Small figures; seated at a table on which are papers; in the centre is Wilkes in his alderman's gown; on his right is Glynn, and on his left Horne Tooke, both in black gowns and wigs. Canvas 21 × 30 in.

By HOUSTON.   Lent by The BARONESS BURDETT-COUTTS.

**322. RICHARD COWLEY, MARQUESS WELLESLEY, K.G. (1760-1842).**

Eldest son of Garrett, 1st Earl of Mornington; succeeded as 2nd Earl of Mornington in 1781; was appointed Governor-General of India in 1797; created Baron Wellesley in 1797, and Marquess Wellesley in 1799. Was Lord-Lieutenant of Ireland in 1821 and again in 1833.

Three-quarter length, life-size, seated to left, black coat, grey waistcoat, and wig: both hands thrust into his waistcoat. Canvas 31 × 27 in.

Lent by The PROVOST OF ETON COLLEGE.

**323. LADY MARY WORTLEY MONTAGU AND HER HUSBAND, EDWARD WORTLEY MONTAGU.**

Small full-length figures, seated at a table; in Turkish costume; he on left holds book in right hand and rests left on the table; and she on right rests right arm on the table. Canvas 29 × 24 in.

By J. HIGHMORE.   [Lent by T. HUMPHRY WARD, ESQ.

**324. EDMUND KEAN (1787-1833).**

Study for the figure in the large picture, *A New Way to Pay Old Debts*. (See No. 191.) Canvas 30 × 24 in.

By G. CLINT.   Lent by HENRY IRVING, ESQ.

**325. WILLIAM IV. (1830-1837.)**

Life-size bust, to right, in garter robes, unfinished. Canvas 42 × 36 in.
By SIR DAVID WILKIE.          Lent by THE LORD DE L'ISLE and DUDLEY.

**326. SIR RALPH ABERCROMBY, K.C.B. (1734-1801).**

General. Entered the army in 1756, served in Germany and Ireland for above twenty years, and from 1783-1793 lived in retirement. He then took part in the disastrous campaign in Holland ; received the Order of the Bath in 1795: was appointed Commander-in-Chief of the forces in the West Indies, and to the chief command in Ireland in 1798. His most splendid achievement was the conduct of the expedition to Egypt in 1801, and his landing at Aboukir Bay, on which occasion he was mortally wounded. He was buried in St. Paul's Cathedral.

Half-length, life-size, facing, head to left, in military uniform and Star of the Bath. Canvas 30 × 24 in.
By J. HOPPNER, R.A.          Lent by JOHN CARRICK MOORE, ESQ.

**327. JOHN HOWARD (1726-1790).**

Philanthropist. Born at Hackney ; the son of a London tradesman, but inheriting a competent fortune, settled at Carlington, near Bedford. Being made High Sheriff of Bedfordshire in 1773, he began to examine into the state of the prisons, travelled through France and Germany with the same benevolent object, and in 1777 published his great work on prisons, which he dedicated to the House of Commons. The result was the passing of two Acts for the better regulation of prison discipline. He next turned his attention to the lazarettos in Europe, an account of which he published in 1789. Having visited the East in 1790, with a view of ascertaining the nature of the plague then raging, he died of fever at Cherson. A monument was erected to his memory in St. Paul's Cathedral.

Half-length, life-size, to left, brown coat and wig ; background, red curtains, &c. Canvas 30 × 24 in.
By H. BURCH.          Lent by JOHN HARLEY, ESQ.

**328. SIR ISAAC NEWTON, KNT. (1642-1726).**

Philosopher. Born at Woolsthorpe, Lincolnshire ; he was educated at Grantham and Trinity College, Cambridge, where he studied mathematics with great diligence, and in 1664 made the discovery of the nature of light and colours. He succeeded Dr. Barrow as Lucasian Professor of Mathematics in 1669, and brought forward his discoveries in optics in his lectures, 1669-1671. In 1672 he was elected a F.R.S., represented Cambridge University in Parliament from 1689-90, and in 1699 was appointed Master of the Mint, in which capacity he effected many improvements in the coinage. He was chosen President of the Royal Society in 1703, and in 1705 received the honour of knighthood. His *Principia* was first published in 1687, but his *Observations on the Prophecies* did not appear till after his death. He died at Kensington at the age of eighty-four, having retained his faculties to the last ; and, after lying in state in the Jerusalem Chamber, he was buried in Westminster Abbey, where a monument was erected to him, which was executed by Rysbrack.

Half-length, life-size, to right ; brown cloak, white necktie, long hair. Canvas 29½ × 24½ in.

Lent by ALFRED MORRISON, ESQ.

**329. DAVID GARRICK (1716-1779).**

Half-length, life-size, seated to left, head facing ; brown coat and wig ; hands crossed, resting on paper inscribed *Prologue*, placed on green table, with inkstand, books, &c. Canvas 30 × 25 in.

There is a replica of this picture in the possession of Archdeacon Burney, from the Thrale collection, painted in 1776, and exhibited in that year at the Royal Academy. This picture was purchased by the Duke of Dorset in 1778. Garrick was now in his sixtieth year, worn by gout and fretted by the cabals and jealousies which distracted the little world at Drury Lane. But in his picture he looks still full of life and vigour. "It is an admirable example of that 'momentary' quality which Northcote was accustomed to praise as distinctive of Sir Joshua's pictures."

By SIR J. REYNOLDS, P.R.A.   Lent by The LORD SACKVILLE.

**330. HORATIO, 1ST LORD WALPOLE (1678-1757).**

Diplomatist. Second son of Robert Walpole of Houghton, and younger brother of Sir Robert Walpole, the eminent statesman ; accompanied General Stanhope to Barcelona as Private Secretary in 1705 ; went with Lord Townshend to the Hague in 1709 to assist at the Congress of Getruydenberg, and was Secretary of the Treasury on the appointment of his brother as Prime Minister in 1715. In 1723 he commenced his embassy at Paris, where he resided till 1727, and from 1733-40 was sent as Plenipotentiary to the States-General, during which period he carried on a correspondence with Queen Caroline. For these and other important services he was created in 1756 a Peer of England under the title of Lord Walpole of Wolterton in Norfolk.

Three-quarter length, life-size, seated at a table to right, in grey coat and wig, in right hand pen, his left arm rests on table. Canvas 50 × 40 in.

By J. B. VAN LOO.   Lent by H. SPENCER WALPOLE, ESQ.

**331. RICHARD PORSON (1759-1808).**

Classical Scholar. Born at East Euston, Norfolk, was educated at Eton and Trinity College, Cambridge, where he was appointed Professor of Greek in 1795. He was afterwards Librarian of the London Institution, and author of *Adversaria, Notes and Emendations to the Greek Poets, etc.* Died in London, 1808.

Three-quarter length, life-size, seated to left, in black gown ; left arm resting on table, papers in his hand. Canvas 50 × 40 in.

Lent by TRINITY COLLEGE, CAMBRIDGE.

**332.** MARGARET GEORGIANA, COUNTESS SPENCER (1737–1814), AND HER DAUGHTER GEORGIANA, AFTERWARDS DUCHESS OF DEVONSHIRE (1757–1806).

The Countess Spencer was the daughter of the Right Hon. Stephen Poyntz of Midgham, Berks; she married in 1755 John Spencer, created a Viscount in 1761, an Earl in 1765. Her daughter Georgiana was the first wife of William, 5th Duke of Devonshire, in 1774. Both mother and daughter were celebrated for their beauty and accomplishments, the latter also for the interest she took in politics. She was the author of a poem, *The Passage of Mount St. Gothard.*

Small figures; the Countess, three-quarter length, near a table on which stands her child, whom she clasps round the legs; the child has its left hand on her mother's shoulder, her right resting against her bosom; near the child also on the table is a dog with right paw raised. Canvas 22 × 20 in.

Painted in September, 1761, and engraved by James Watson, 1771, and C. Corbutt.

By SIR J. REYNOLDS, P.R.A.        Lent by The EARL OF CARLISLE.

**333.** MRS. FITZHERBERT (1756–1837).

Half-length, life-size, to left, white dress with black band on sleeve, powdered hair. Canvas (Oval) 33½ × 26 in.

Painted either in 1786 or 1788. The Prince of Wales and Mrs. Fitzherbert were often together at the painter's studio.

By SIR J. REYNOLDS, P.R.A.        Lent by THE EARL OF PORTARLINGTON.

**334.** JOHN SCOTT, EARL OF ELDON (1751–1838).

Three-quarter length, life-size, seated full face, in Lord Chancellor's robes and wig; holding Purse of the Great Seal in right hand. Canvas 50 × 40 in.

By W. OWEN, R.A.        Lent by UNIVERSITY COLLEGE, OXFORD.

**335.** FIELD-MARSHAL GENERAL HENRY SEYMOUR CONWAY (1720–1795).

Second son of Francis Seymour, 1st Baron Conway; served with reputation in Germany during the Seven Years' War, and held command in the British force under Prince Ferdinand of Brunswick in 1761. He sat in the Irish and English House of Commons, and in 1765 became joint Secretary of State with the Duke of Grafton, but resigned in 1768. In 1782 he was appointed Commander-in-Chief of the Forces. General Conway wrote several poetic pieces, a comedy called *False Appearances*, and also political tracts. He was a friend of Horace Walpole.

Three-quarter length, life-size, to left; head facing; in military uniform, and wig; his right hand rests on paper on table, left holds letter; on the table globe, inkstand, etc. Canvas 56 × 46 in.

This picture, which was formerly in the possession of General Conway's daughter, the Hon. Anne Seymour Damer, is a copy of the portrait painted by Reynolds at the request of the citizens of New York as an acknowledgment of their gratitude to the General for his exertions against the Stamp Act, in 1772. The original picture hangs in the Town Hall of that city.

By G. BERWICK. Lent by MRS. CAMPBELL JOHNSTON.

**336. GEORGIANA SPENCER, DUCHESS OF DEVONSHIRE (1774-1806).**

Three-quarter length, life-size, to right, white dress, blue scarf, right arm resting on pedestal; both hands hold ends of scarf; architectural background. Canvas 53 × 38 in.

This is a copy by Rising of the picture at Althorp, by Gainsborough.

By RISING. Lent by The MARQUESS OF HARTINGTON, M.P.

**337. WILLIAM AUGUSTUS, DUKE OF CUMBERLAND (1721-1765).**

Small full-length equestrian figure, to left, in uniform. Canvas 62 × 58 in.

Lent by W. HERBERT EVANS, ESQ.

**338. ELIZABETH HOWARD, DUCHESS OF RUTLAND (d. 1825).**

Daughter of Frederick, 5th Earl of Carlisle, K.G., married April 22, 1799, John Henry 5th Duke of Rutland. Died November 28, 1825.

Three-quarter length, life-size, seated to left; grey dress, blue ribbon in her hair; left arm rests on a parapet; landscape background. Canvas 50 × 40 in.

By J. HOPPNER, R.A. Lent by The EARL OF CARLISLE.

**339. CHARLES LENNOX, 3RD DUKE OF RICHMOND, K.G. (1735-1806).**

Succeeded his father, Charles, 2nd Duke, in 1750, entered the army and distinguished himself at Minden. He became a colonel in 1758, and subsequently rose through the intermediate gradations to the rank of field-marshal. At the accession of George III. he was appointed a Lord of the Bedchamber, Ambassador to France in 1765, Principal Secretary of the Southern Division in 1766, and elected a K.G. in 1782. In politics he was a strong Whig, opposed the Government in its policy during the American War, and was in favour of annual parliaments, and universal suffrage. He was also a patron of literature and the fine arts.

Three-quarter length, life-size, facing, in military uniform, ribbon and star of the Garter; left hand on sword; battle-scene in background. Canvas 50 × 40 in.

By T. GAINSBOROUGH, R.A. Lent by The DUKE OF RICHMOND AND GORDON, K.G.

**340. WILLIAM SCOTT, LORD STOWELL (1745-1836).**

Eminent lawyer and judge. Born at Heworth, co. Durham; the son of a coalfitter, and elder brother of Lord Chancellor Eldon; was educated at Newcastle Grammar School and Oxford, and was called to the Bar in 1780. Having become a member of the Literary Club, he was on terms of close friendship with Dr. Johnson, and accompanied him on his journey to the Hebrides as far as Edinburgh. His superior powers led to numerous appointments, among which may be named those of Judge of the Consistory Courts in 1788, when he was knighted, Advocate-General, Master of the Faculties in 1790, and Judge of the High Court of Admiralty in 1798. He was elected Member for the University of Oxford in 1801, and retained this seat till his elevation to the peerage in 1821. He retired from the Court of Admiralty in 1828.

Three-quarter length, life-size, seated to left, in robes and wig; on left, table with inkstand. Canvas 50 × 40 in.

By J. HOPPNER, R.A.                 Lent by UNIVERSITY COLLEGE, OXFORD.

**341. GEORGE, VISCOUNT KEITH (1747-1823).**

Admiral. Fourth son of Charles, 10th Lord Elphinstone; entered the Navy at an early age, and obtained the rank of Post-Captain in 1775. He served with distinction during the American War, assisted at the reduction of Toulon in 1793, and in 1795 commanded the Fleet destined for the capture of the Cape of Good Hope. He was raised to the Irish Peerage by the title of Baron Keith in 1797, commanded in 1798 in the Mediterranean under Earl St. Vincent, and especially distinguished himself in the landing at Aboukir in 1801. For these services he was created a Baron of the United Kingdom. He was afterwards successively Commander-in-Chief in the North Sea and of the Channel Fleet, was raised to the dignity of a Viscount in 1814, and effected the capture of Napoleon after Waterloo.

Three-quarter length, life-size, to left, in robes, collar, &c., of the Bath; his right hand holds up his cloak, his left grasps his sword; hair grey. Canvas 50 × 40 in.

By T. PHILLIPS, R.A.             Lent by HER MAJESTY THE QUEEN
                                                      (Hampton Court).

**342. RIGHT HON. JOHN HOOKHAM FRERE, M.P. (1769-1846).**

Born in London, was educated at Eton, where began his friendship with Canning, whom he assisted in the *Microcosm*, and afterwards in the *Anti-Jacobin;* was a Fellow of Caius College, Cambridge, and in 1796 was returned to Parliament for West Looe. He succeeded Canning in 1799 as Under-Secretary for Foreign Affairs, and was subsequently despatched as Ambassador to Portugal, Spain, and Prussia, and afterwards resided at Malta, where he occupied himself with literary pursuits. Died there January 7, 1846.

Three-quarter length, life-size, to left, wrapped in a black cloak; sky background. Canvas 50 × 40. in.

Exhibited at the Royal Academy in 1806, and engraved by W. W. Burney. It is considered one of Hoppner's best works. Cunningham mentions it in his selections of the principal works of this painter.

By J. HOPPNER, R.A.                      Lent by JOHN TUDOR FRERE, ESQ.

### 343. EDWARD WORTLEY MONTAGU (1713–1776).

Son of Lady Mary Wortley Montagu (see No. 251). Was placed at Westminster School, from whence he ran away three times. In 1747 he was elected into Parliament, and in 1751 went to Paris, where, says Walpole, "after a variety of adventures he was imprisoned for cheating and robbing a Jew." In 1759 he published his *Reflections on Ancient Republics*. After the death of his mother, he went to Italy, where he turned Catholic. He then travelled in Arabia and Egypt, and became a Muhammedan. Died at Padua.

Three-quarter length, life-size, in Turkish costume; in right hand mace; left on his hip; battle-scene in the background. Canvas 56½ × 43 in.

Painted at Venice in 1774, where the painter met Montagu, who was living there in the manners, habit, and magnificence of a Turk. Romney conceived a sudden affection for the picturesque personage; drew an admirable head of him in his Eastern garb; and willing to show all respect to the city where he sojourned, coloured and finished it in the style of the great Venetian masters with a success which surprised many. It is one of his finest men's portraits.

By G. ROMNEY.                      Lent by The EARL OF WHARNCLIFFE.

### 344. BYNG, 1ST VISCOUNT TORRINGTON, K.B. (1663–1733).

Admiral. Born at Wrotham in Kent; entered the navy in 1678, served in the fleet sent to oppose the Prince of Orange, but went over to his party, commanded in the battle off Beachy Head 1690, and afterwards was in the Mediterranean under Admirals Rooke and Russell. He served under Sir Cloudesley Shovel as rear-admiral, commanded in the attack on Gibraltar in 1704, and distinguished himself at Malaga, for which service he was knighted. In 1706 he went to succour Barcelona, and took part in the capture of Alicant. At the accession of George I. he was created a baronet, won the victory over the Spaniards at Cape Passaro in 1718, and two years later was raised to the peerage as Viscount Torrington. At the time of his death, January 17, 1733, he was First Lord of the Admiralty.

Small full-length, to left, in peer's robes; the right hand rests on table, on which is a coronet, left holds his robe; sea with ships in the background. Inscribed with name and date 1731. Canvas 30 × 23 in.

                                       Lent by The EARL OF STRAFFORD.

### 345. THE MISSES WESTON.

They were the daughters of Thomas Weston, who died August 12, 1729. He was a particular friend of Addison, and wrote one or more of the papers which go under the name of the *Spectator*. He is said to have been possessed of an income of £5,000 a year. The portraits of his daughter must have been painted early in Hogarth's career.

 Group of four figures, life-size, half-length. The figure on the extreme right holds a paroquet; while one of her sisters is placing a scarf around her shoulders, and another is holding a bowl, the fourth sister holds a book. Canvas 40 × 50 in.

By W. HOGARTH.       Lent by HORACE A. HELYAR, ESQ.

**346.** STEPHEN FOX-STRANGWAYS, 1ST EARL OF ILCHESTER (1704–1776).

 Eldest son of Sir Stephen Fox, statesman: represented Shaftesbury in 1726, and in the two succeeding years; was Joint-Secretary of the Treasury from 1739-1741, in which latter year he was created Baron Ilchester and Strangways, and Baron Ilchester and Stavordale in 1747, and in 1756 advanced to the dignity of Earl of Ilchester. In 1747, he was constituted a Comptroller of Army Accounts, and confirmed in that office by George III., who also admitted him to the Privy Council, April 22, 1763. Married Elizabeth, daughter of Thomas Strangways-Horner, by whom he had three sons and six daughters.

 Three-quarter length, life-size, to left; brown coat and black hat; gun in left hand, and dead bird in right. Canvas 49 × 39 in.

            Lent by The EARL OF ILCHESTER.

**347.** GEORGE PARKER, 2ND EARL OF MACCLESFIELD, P.R.S. (1697–1714).

 Only son of Thomas, 1st Earl, whom he succeeded in 1732, was one of the originators and the introducer of the Bill for the Reformation of the Calendar, and President of the Royal Society 1752-1764, to the Journal of which Society he contributed many papers.

 Three-quarter length, life-size, seated to right, in peer's robes and wig, holds document in right hand. Canvas 50 × 40 in.

By T. HUDSON, R.A.       Lent by The ROYAL SOCIETY.

**348.** SIR ROBERT WALPOLE, 1ST EARL OF ORFORD, K.G. (1676–1745).

 Three-quarter length, life-size, to right, head turned to left, in Chancellor's robes, ribbon, George, and star of the Garter, and wig; in right hand papers, left rests on table, on which is placed the purse of the Great Seal. Canvas 50 × 40 in.

            Lent by The EARL OF CHICHESTER.

**349.** WILLIAM, 5TH DUKE OF DEVONSHIRE, K.G. (1748–1811).

 Three-quarter length, life-size, seated to right, in Vandyck costume, crimson slashed coat, lace collar; in left hand hat, right rests on chair; powdered hair *en perruque;* architectural background. Canvas 50 × 40 in.

 The Duke of Devonshire sat to Reynolds on several occasions, viz. in October, 1766; January, 1767; and May, 1782. This picture was probably painted in 1766, in which year various members of the Rockingham Administration successively took their seats in Reynolds's chair. The names which occur are those of Lord Albemarle and Sir Charles Saunders, the Dukes of Portland and Devonshire, Lord Hardwicke, General Conway, Mr. Burke, and Lord Rockingham himself.

By SIR J. REYNOLDS, P.R.A.    Lent by The HON. F. B. MASSEY MAINWARING.

### 50. WILLIAM PITT, 1ST EARL AMHERST (1773–1857).

Son of Lieut.-General William Amherst; succeeded to the barony on the death of Jeffrey, first Lord Amherst; was appointed in 1816 Ambassador Extraordinary to the Emperor of China, but refusing to submit to the humiliating ceremonies of the Court, his mission was rendered fruitless. On his return journey he was wrecked off the island of Pulo Leat, from whence he proceeded to Batavia, and finally reached England, having visited Napoleon I. at St. Helena. Subsequently he was appointed Governor-General of India, and for his services there was in 1826 created Earl Amherst and Viscount Holmesdale. Died at Knowle House, Kent, March 15, 1857.

Three-quarter length, life-size, head to right, in peer's robes; his right hand holds and rests on papers on table, his left on his hip; landscape background. Canvas 56 × 44 in.

Lent by CHRIST CHURCH, OXFORD.

### 5.. ADMIRAL ADAM DUNCAN, 1ST VISCOUNT DUNCAN, K.C.B. (1731–1804).

Admiral. Second son of Alexander Duncan of Lundie, Perthshire; entered the navy in 1746 was Post-Captain in 1761, took part in the reduction of Havanna in August 1762, and had a full share in Rodney's victory over the Spaniards off St. Vincent in 1780, and in the relief of Gibraltar. He was made Rear-Admiral in 1787; had command in the North Seas in 1795, and gained at Camperdown June 11, 1797, the great victory over the Dutch in wich De Winter, the Dutch Admiral and eight ships were taken. Upon this he received the tanks of Parliament, and was created a viscount with a pension of £3,000 a year to himself, and the two next heirs of the peerage.

Three-quarter length, life-size; to left, head facing, in naval uniform; ribbon and star of the Bath; with right hand he points to naval engagement in the distance; le rests on sword. Canvas 55 × 46 in.

Presented to the Corporation of London by Mr. Alderman John Boydell in 1793.

By J. HOPPNER, R.A.    Lent by The CORPORATION OF THE CITY OF LONDON.

### 52. THE RT. HON. WILLIAM PITT (1759–1806).

Three-quarter length, life-size, to left; blue coat and wig; leaning against chair, on whh is thrown his Chancellor's robe; before him table with inkstand. Canvas 50 40 in.

By T. GAINSBOROUGH, R.A.    Lent by The DUKE OF RICHMOND AND GORDON, K.G.

**353.** WILLIAM COWPER (1731-1800).

Three-quarter length, life-size, seated to left at a desk; blue coat, yellow waistcoat and breeches; his left hand rests on book placed on desk; right on his knee holding pen. Canvas 50 × 40 in.

It was on this portrait that he wrote his sonnet to Romney, which begins:

> "Romney, expert infallibly to trace
> On chart or canvas, not the form alone
> And semblance, but, however faintly shown
> The mind's impression too on every face."
>
> See Cowper's *Poems*, Ed. 1815, Vol. III. p. 297.

By G. ROMNEY.    Lent by ST. R. VAUGHAN JOHNSON, ESQ.

**354.** MRS. SARAH SIDDONS (1755-1831).

Full-length, life-size, to left; black gown, white scarf around her head; she holds mask in left hand, and dagger in right; behind pedestal on which is seated a cupid, landscape background. Canvas 93 × 56 in.

By SIR J. REYNOLDS, P.R.A.    Lent by the EARL OF WARWICK

## MINIATURES, RELICS, AND PLATE.

### CASE A—West Gallery.

*MINIATURES*
*LENT BY HER MAJESTY THE QUEEN.*

**355.** GEORGE III., 1760-1820.
   By J. P. FISCHER.

**356.** VICTORIA MARIA LOUISA, DUCHESS OF KENT, 1786-1861.
   By SIR W. ROSS.

**357.** SIR FRANCIS CHANTREY, R.A., sculptor, 1782-1841.
   By A. ROBERTSON.

**358.** SOPHIA, ELECTRESS OF HANOVER, 1630-1714.

**359.** CHARLOTTE, PRINCESS OF WALES, Queen of Würtemberg, 1766-1828.

**360.** WILLIAM IV. AS DUKE OF CLARENCE, 1765-1837.
   By J. MEYER.

**361.** PRINCESS SOPHIA, daughter of George III., 1777-1848.
   By R. COSWAY, R.A.

**362.** WILLIAM IV. AS DUKE OF CLARENCE, 1765-1837.
   By R. COSWAY, R.A.

**363.** EDWARD, DUKE OF KENT, 1767-1820.
   By A. ROBERTSON.

**364.** QUEEN CHARLOTTE, wife of George III., 1744-1818.
By OZIAS HUMPHREY, R.A.

**365.** QUEEN CAROLINE, wife of George II., 1682-1737.

**366.** FREDERICK, DUKE OF YORK, K.G., 1763-1827.
By J. MEYER, K.G.

**367.** MARIA, DUCHESS OF GLOUCESTER, 1737-1808.
By OZIAS HUMPHREY, R.A.

**368.** PRINCESS MARY, daughter of George III., Duchess of Gloucester, 1776-1857.
By R. COSWAY, R.A.

**369.** PRINCESS AMELIA, daughter of George III., 1783-1810.

**370.** AUGUSTUS FREDERICK, DUKE OF SUSSEX, K.G., 1773-1843.
By R. COSWAY, R.A.

**371.** CHARLOTTE, PRINCESS OF WALES, daughter of George IV., 1796-1817.
By COLLINS, after DAWE.

*LENT BY H.R.H. THE PRINCE OF WALES.*

**372.** WILLIAM HENRY, 1ST DUKE OF GLOUCESTER, 1743-1805.

**373.** WILLIAM IV. AS DUKE OF CLARENCE, 1765-1837.
By R. COSWAY, R.A.

**374.** GEORGE III., 1760-1820.
After GAINSBOROUGH.

WEST GALLERY.]   *Miniatures, Relics, and Plate.*

**375.** KITTY FISHER.
Lent by H.R.H. the PRINCESS LOUISE
(Marchioness of Lorne).

**376.** QUEEN CHARLOTTE, 1744-1818. A present from the Queen to Elizabeth, Countess Harcourt, wife of George Simon, 2nd Earl.
Lent by E. W. HARCOURT, ESQ.

### *LENT BY H.R.H. THE DUKE OF CAMBRIDGE.*

**377.** IVORY CARD-CASE, with miniature of Princess Mary, daughter of George III.

**378.** PRINCESS AMELIA.

**379.** IVORY PATCH-BOX, with miniature of Princess Augusta.

**380.** PRINCESS MARY, daughter of George III.

**381.** THE LATE DUKE OF CAMBRIDGE.

**382.** QUEEN CHARLOTTE, d. 1818.

**383.** GEORGE IV., 1820-1830.

**384.** THE DUKE OF SUSSEX, 1773-1843.

**385.** THE PRINCESS ROYAL.

**386.** WILLIAM, 1ST DUKE OF GLOUCESTER.

**387.** WILLIAM IV., 1830-1837.

**388.** PORTRAIT OF A LADY.

**389.** PORTRAIT OF A LADY.

**390.** GEORGE IV.

**391.** QUEEN CHARLOTTE, d. 1818.

392. PRINCESS SOPHIA, d. 1857.

393. QUEEN CHARLOTTE.

394. PRINCESS ELIZABETH, d. 1840.

395. PRINCESS AMELIA, d. 1810.

396. PORTRAIT OF A BABY.

## *LENT BY THE EARL WALDEGRAVE.*

397. MARIA WALPOLE, COUNTESS WALDEGRAVE, DUCHESS OF GLOUCESTER, 1737-1807. As a child.

398. WILLIAM FREDERICK, 2ND DUKE OF GLOUCESTER, 1776-1834.

399. WILLIAM HENRY, 1ST DUKE OF GLOUCESTER, 1743-1805.

400. WILLIAM FREDERICK, 2ND DUKE OF GLOUCESTER, 1776-1834.

401. MARIA WALPOLE, COUNTESS WALDEGRAVE, DUCHESS OF GLOUCESTER, 1737-1807.

402. WILLIAM FREDERICK, 2ND DUKE OF GLOUCESTER, 1776-1834.

403. GEORGE III., 1760-1820.

404. MARIA WALPOLE, DUCHESS OF GLOUCESTER.

405. MARIE ANTOINETTE, wife of Louis XVI. of France, 1755-1793.

406. PRINCESS SOPHIA, daughter of George III., 1777-1848.

407. THE DAUPHIN, son of Louis XVI. and Marie Antoinette.

WEST GALLERY.] *Miniatures, Relics, and Plate.* 125

**408.** GEORGE IV. AS PRINCE OF WALES, 1762-1830.
            Lent by MRS. MOSS COCKLE.

**409.** EDWARD AUGUSTUS, DUK OF KENT, father of Queen Victoria, 1767-1820.
            Lent by MRS. MOSS COCKLE

**410.** MRS. FITZHERBERT, 1756-1837.
            Lent by MRS. MOSS COCKLE.

**411.** FRAME I.
 1. THE PRINCE OF WALES, elder brother of George III., who died early.
 2. WILHELMINA, PRINCESS OF ORANGE.
 3. WILLIAM, DUKE OF CUMBERLAND, 1721-1765.
 4. PORTRAIT OF A GENTLEMAN.
 5. LOUIS XVIII. OF FRANCE.
 6. VOLPONI, favourite dog of the Duke and Duchess of Gloucester.
           Lent by The EARL WALDEGRAVE.

*MINIATURES AND RELICS WHICH BELONGED TO MRS. FITZ-HERBERT, LENT BY THE EARL OF PORTARLINGTON.*

**412.** GEORGE IV. AS PRINCE OF WALES, 1762-1830. *Unfinished.*
  By R. COSWAY, R.A.

**413.** PRINCESS CAROLINE OF WÜRTEMBURG. *Unfinished.*
  By R. COSWAY, R.A.

**414.** WILLIAM IV., 1830-1837. *Unfinished.*
  By R. COSWAY, R.A.

**415.** GEORGE IV. AS PRINCE OF WALES, 1762-1830.
  By W. GRIMALDI.

**416.** GEORGE IV. AS PRINCE OF WALES, 1762-1830.
  By W. GRIMALDI.

**417.** LADY CAROLINE DAMER.

418. GENERAL SIR CHARLES STUART.

419. MARIA WALPOLE, COUNTESS WALDEGRAVE, DUCHESS OF GLOUCESTER, 1737-1807

420. ALEXANDER I. OF RUSSIA, dated 1814.

421. MRS. FITZHERBERT, 1756-1837; with her hair.

422. GEORGE IV. AS PRINCE OF WALES, 1762-1830; with his hair.

423. MRS. FITZHERBERT, 1756-1837.
    By R. COSWAY, R.A.

424. GEORGE IV. AS PRINCE OF WALES, 1762-1830.
    By R. COSWAY, R.A.

425. WEDDING-RINGS OF MRS. FITZHERBERT AND THE PRINCE OF WALES.

426. CAMEO ONYX OF GEORGE IV. AS PRINCE OF WALES.

427. GEORGE IV. AS PRINCE OF WALES, 1762-1830.
    By R. COSWAY, R.A.

428. EYE OF MRS. FITZHERBERT.
    By R. COSWAY, R.A.

429. EYE OF GEORGE IV. AS PRINCE OF WALES.
    By R. COSWAY, R.A.

430. LADY HORATIA SEYMOUR.
    By R. COSWAY, R.A.

431. TITIAN'S DAUGHTER.

432. BONBONNIÈRE OF MOSS AGATE.

433. MARIA WALPOLE, COUNTESS WALDEGRAVE AND DUCHESS OF GLOUCESTER 1737-1807.

WEST GALLERY.]  *Miniatures, Relics, and Plate.*  127

434. FRAME, WITH HAIR OF NELSON, WELLINGTON, AND NAPOLEON I., given by themselves to Mrs. Fitzherbert.

35. TWO GOLD RINGS WITH CAMEOS.

436. THE HON. MRS. DAWSON DAMER, sculptor (1748–1828).

437. MRS. FITZHERBERT'S ROSARY.

438. TULIP-SHAPED BONBONNIÈRE, enamelled and ornamented with pearls.

439. SCENT-BOTTLE.

440. CORAL AND BELLS WHICH BELONGED TO GEORGE IV.

441. ETUI CASE OF SATIN, with enamelled fittings.

442. QUIZZING GLASS.

443. GILT FILIGREE SCENT-BOTTLE.

444. SEAL AND HAIR CHAIN WHICH BELONGED TO FREDERICK, DUKE OF YORK.

445. SNUFF-BOX OF FELSPAR.

JOHN, 1ST EARL OF PORTARLINGTON, 1744-1798.

447. NAPOLEON I. (1769–1821).

448. THOMAS WORLIDGE, as Rembrandt, Miniature Painter.
By HIMSELF.

449. THE HON. MRS. DAWSON DAMER, sculptor (1748-1828).
By COSWAY.

450. GENERAL WEBB. Enamel; signed " C. F. Zincke *fecit*. 1715."
Lent by The LATE SIR WILLIAM DRAKE.

451. ELIZABETH LINLEY, MRS. SHERIDAN, 1754?-1792. Painted shortly after her marriage; on ivory; signed "S.C. 1773."
By SAMUEL COLLINS.   Lent by The LATE SIR WILLIAM DRAKE.

452. PRINCESS SOPHIA, daughter of George III., 1777-1848; in gold locket.
By R. COSWAY, R.A.   Lent by The LATE SIR WILLIAM DRAKE.

453. MRS. SARAH SIDDONS, Actress, 1755-1831. On ivory; signed "H. H. 1784."
By HORACE HONE, R.A.   Lent by The LATE SIR WILLIAM DRAKE.

454. KITTY FISHER, celebrated beauty, d. 1771.
Lent by The LATE SIR WILLIAM DRAKE.

455. FRAME II.
1. WILLIAM FREDERICK, 2ND DUKE OF GLOUCESTER, 1776-1834.
By DAY.
2. WILLIAM HENRY, 1ST DUKE OF GLOUCESTER, 1743-1805.
3. WILLIAM FREDERICK, 2ND DUKE OF GLOUCESTER (1776-1834).
By The DUCHESSE DE BOURBON, 1787.
4. MARIA WALPOLE, COUNTESS WALDEGRAVE, DUCHESS OF GLOUCESTER, 1737-1807.
5. WILLIAM FREDERICK, 2ND DUKE OF GLOUCESTER (1776-1834).
6. WILLIAM FREDERICK, 2ND DUKE OF GLOUCESTER (1776-1834).
Lent by The EARL WALDEGRAVE.

## CASE B—West Gallery.

*RELICS.*

456. CHRISTENING ROBE OF PRINCESS AMELIA, youngest daughter of George III.
Lent by MISS BUZZARD.

457. GERMAN ALMANACK, bound in silver, which belonged to George III.
Lent by MISS BUZZARD.

458. PAIR OF WHITE EMBROIDERED SILK SHOES, of the last century.
Lent by J. E. COLLINGWOOD, ESQ.

**459.** PAIR OF BLUE SHOES, embroidered silk, with buckles, of the last century.
Lent by J. E. COLLINGWOOD, ESQ.

**460.** RIBBON worn at the Thanksgiving for the recovery of George III. in 1789.
Lent by MISS HILL.

**461.** LARGE SILVER SALVER, designed by Hogarth and presented to Sir Robert Walpole by the Corporation of the City of London, upon his being presented with the freedom of the City. From the Strawberry Hill collection.
Lent by The EARL OF ORFORD.

**462.** WHITE SILK BAG, used by Queen Charlotte, wife of George III.
Lent by MRS. W. FOLLEN BISHOP.

**463.** BAG, embroidered with beads by Princess Sophia, daughter of George III.
Lent by MRS. W. FOLLEN BISHOP.

**464.** A SILK-EMBROIDERED WAISTCOAT, *temp.* George II.
Lent by MRS. HARVEY, of Ickwell-Bury.

## CASE C—West Gallery.

### ROYAL RELICS.

**465.** SETTING OF THE CROWN OF GEORGE IV.
Lent by W. A. TYSSEN AMHERST, ESQ., M.P.

**466.** BIBLE, upon which George III. took his Coronation Oath.
Lent by W. A. TYSSEN AMHERST, ESQ., M.P.

**467.** SILVER-GILT SEAL, with bust of Frederick, Duke of York.
Lent by The HON. GERALD PONSONBY.

**468.** GOLD SNUFF-BOX, which belonged to George IV.
Lent by T. LYON THURLOW, ESQ.

**469.** QUEEN CHARLOTTE'S SEAL, on the bezel her favourite dog "Muff"; the handle also is a model of the dog.
Lent by A. W. S. GWYN, ESQ.

K

470. A GLASS GOBLET, commemorating the coronation of George IV.
On the bowl is engraved a figure of the Champion of England holding up the gauntlet, and the device G. R.
IV.
1821.
            Lent by S. J. NICHOLL, ESQ.

470*. A GLASS GOBLET, engraved on the bowl with the device of a crown with wreaths and G. R. IIII., and dated "July 19th, 1821."
            Lent by S. J. NICHOLL, ESQ.

471. MEMORIAL RING OF PRINCESS AMELIA.
            Lent by MISS LEWIS.

472. SMALL GOLD RING containing hair of George II.
            Lent by COUNT KIELMANSEGG.

473. GOLD SNUFF-BOX, with miniature by Cosway, and lock of hair of Princess Amelia, daughter of George III., given by her to the Hon. General Fitzroy.
            Lent by The HON. MRS. WILLIAM LOWTHER.

474. A GOLD ENAMELLED BADGE, to be worn as a pendant, made in commemoration of the recovery of George III. It bears the inscription "Regi amato reduci, vivat G. R. III. Mart: X. MDCCLXXXIX."
            Lent by The HON. GERALD PONSONBY.

475. GOLD SNUFF-BOX, enamelled, in shape of the British Lion, which belonged to Queen Charlotte.
            Lent by HENRY WEIGALL, ESQ.

476. CAMEO PENDANT, with head of George IV. and the motto "Honneur au Roi George 4th." The word "Fidelité" is enamelled on the back.
            Lent by The HON. GERALD PONSONBY.

477. A SET OF CHESSMEN, in coloured Ivory, representing Hanoverian Soldiers, &c.; time of George II. These are said to have been presented by the late King of Hanover to the Elector of Cassel.
            Lent by H. T. PFUNGST, ESQ.

478. GOLD AND TORTOISESHELL WORKBOX used by Queen Adelaide.
            Lent by JOHN CLELAND, ESQ., of Stormont.

WEST GALLERY.] *Miniatures, Relics, and Plate.*

**479.** IVORY FAN painted with flowers.
Lent by A. W. S. GWYN, ESQ.

**480.** AN IVORY CARD CASE, which belonged to Queen Caroline.
Lent by MISS EMILY COLE.

**481.** FAN, of ivory and mother-of-pearl, which belonged to Queen Charlotte.
Lent by A. W. S. GWYN, ESQ.

**482.** SNUFF-BOX, with portraits of George III. and Queen Charlotte.
Lent by HENRY HUCKS GIBBS, ESQ.

**483.** FAN with Ivory handle, painted with pastoral subjects.
Lent by A. W. S. GWYN, ESQ.

**484.** IVORY FAN which belonged to Queen Charlotte.
Lent by A. W. S. GWYN, ESQ.

**485.** WALKING-STICK, with gold mounts, presented by George IV. when Regent to Sir William Knighton.
Lent by J. ASHBY STERRY, ESQ.

**486.** GOLD-HEADED WALKING-STICK which belonged to William IV., presented by the King to Captain Grantham, and by him to the present owner.
Lent by W. H. WING, ESQ.

**487.** GOLD SNUFF-BOX, given by George IV. to Sir Walter Scott.
Lent by The HON. MRS. MAXWELL-SCOTT.

**488.** GOLD BUST OF GEORGE IV., ornamented with a diamond decoration.
Lent by MRS. MOSS COCKLE.

**489.** LAMBETH PLATE, with portrait of George I., and inscribed G.R.
Lent by JOHN EVANS, ESQ., P.S.A.

**490.** LAMBETH PLATE, inscribed "God Save King George, 1715."
Lent by JOHN EVANS, ESQ., P.S.A.

491. ALBUM, with miniature of Queen Adelaide on the outside, and containing a pencil drawing by the Queen of John, 4th Earl of Mayo.

This album was presented by Queen Adelaide to Arabella, Countess of Mayo, who was her lady-in-waiting.
*Lent by* The EARL OF MAYO.

492. GOLD AND TORTOISESHELL SNUFF-BOX, with bust of George IV. as Prince of Wales, to whom it formerly belonged.
*Lent by* CHARLES A. JONES, ESQ.

493. SARDONYX PENDANT, with heads of George III. and Queen Charlotte.
*Lent by* W. R. HARCOURT GWYN, ESQ.

494. CARVING KNIFE AND FORK with silver-gilt handles, used at the coronation of George IV.
*Lent by* The EARL OF DENBIGH.

495. MOURNING RING OF GEORGE III.
*Lent by* JOHN EVANS, ESQ., P.S.A.

496. BLOODSTONE CAMEO LOCKET OF WILLIAM, DUKE OF CUMBERLAND (1721-1765).
*Lent by* JOHN EVANS, ESQ., P.S.A.

497. ONYX CAMEO RING, with portrait of George I.
*Lent by* JOHN EVANS, ESQ., P.S.A.

498. SMALL SACHET worked by Queen Adelaide.
*Lent by* G. MILNER-GIBSON-CULLUM, ESQ.

499. A LEATHER LETTER BAG, which belonged to George III. It is stamped "Hanover," and bears a shield with the royal monogram, supporters, and crest.

This bag was presented by George III. to his daughter Charlotte, Queen of Würtemberg, who gave it to the Duchess of Beaufort, and was given by her to the grandmother of the exhibitor, the late Mrs. Gould of Amberd.
*Lent by* The REV. F. NUTCOMBE OXENHAM.

500. BLUE SILK BAG, ornamented with *fleurs-de-lis*, which belonged to Queen Charlotte.
*Lent by* W. R. HARCOURT GWYN, ESQ.

[WEST GALLERY.] *Miniatures, Relics, and Plate.*

**501.** THE DUCHESS OF YORK'S SHOE.
   Lent by W. R. HARCOURT GWYN, ESQ.

**502.** IVORY FAN which belonged to Queen Caroline.
   Lent by MRS. E. HAMILTON GELL.

**503.** SCENT-BOTTLE which belonged to George IV.
   Lent by JOHN CLELAND, ESQ., of Stormont.

**504.** SNUFF-BOX, which belonged to George IV.
   Lent by JOHN CLELAND, ESQ., of Stormont.

**505.** TORTOISE-SHELL FAN, which belonged to Queen Charlotte.
   Lent by W. R. HARCOURT GWYN, ESQ.

**506.** GOLD AND MOTHER-OF-PEARL FAN, which belonged to Queen Charlotte.
   Lent by W. R. HARCOURT GWYN, ESQ.

**507.** IVORY AND GOLD FAN, which belonged to Queen Charlotte.
   Lent by W. R. HARCOURT GWYN, ESQ.

**508.** CALENDAR (Rider's British Merlin, 1762) given by George III. to Queen Charlotte, Feb. 17, 1762.
   Lent by DR. EDWARD HAMILTON.

**509.** A ROSEWOOD AND BLUE SILK FAN, which belonged to Queen Charlotte, Consort of George IV., and presented by her to the grandmother of the present owner.
   Lent by CHARLES A. JONES, ESQ.

**510.** PIECE OF THE CORONATION CANOPY OF GEORGE III.
   Lent by HENRY H. P. COTTON, ESQ.

**511.** SNUFF-BOX, with medallion of George III.
   Lent by HENRY H. P. COTTON, ESQ.

**512.** RICHLY ENGRAVED STEEL KEY, with pierced monogram of George III.
   Lent by HENRY WHITE, ESQ.

**513.** CRYSTAL AND GOLD LOCKET, with hair of Princess Charlotte.
   Lent by CHARLES A. JONES, ESQ.

514. SHOULDERED WINE-GLASS of a Whig Club, *temp.* George I., bearing in relief on the sides, "GOD SAVE KING GEORGE," and on each shoulder a crown.
Lent by ALBERT HARTSHORNE, ESQ.

515. CHINA CUP, the last used by Queen Caroline, wife of George II.
It was given by Mrs. Ainger, whose mother was dresser to Queen Caroline, to Miss Popplewell, and by her to her god-daughter, mother of the present owner.
Lent by S. CHISENHALE MARSH, ESQ.

516. TWO GOLD SNUFF-BOXES, presented to Richard, 5th Viscount Powerscourt, by King George IV. on his visit to Ireland in 1821.
Lent by The VISCOUNT POWERSCOURT, K.P.

517. GOLD WATCH, which belonged to William IV. Given by him to his son, Lord Frederick Fitzclarence.
Lent by The EARL OF RANFURLY.

518. WAX MEDALLION OF GEORGE IV.
Lent by CHARLES A. JONES, ESQ.

519. SILVER ETUI which belonged to Queen Charlotte, wife of George III.
Lent by MRS. EDWARD F. WAYNE.

519a. PINCUSHION in silver filigree, which belonged to Queen Charlotte, wife of George III.
Lent by MRS. EDWARD F. WAYNE.

520. A FIGURE OF GEORGE III., modelled in terra-cotta and coloured. "Published May 8, 1820, by F. Hardenberg, 19, Mount Street, London."
Lent by CHARLES DAVIS, ESQ.

## CASE D—West Gallery.

### *MINIATURES.*

**521.** PRINCESS SOPHIA DOROTHEA, Electress of Hanover, as mother of George I. 1630-1714.
Lent by MISS HOLTBY.

**522.** GEORGE, PRINCE OF WALES, on vellum.
Lent by MISS HOLTBY.

**523.** DUCHESS OF BRUNSWICK, daughter of Frederick, Prince of Wales.
Lent by MISS HOLTBY.

**524.** PRINCESS ANNE, wife of William IV. of Orange, d. 1759.
Lent by MISS HOLTBY.

**525.** PRINCESS AMELIA, daughter of George III., 1783-1810.
Lent by MISS HOLTBY.

**526.** PRINCESS AUGUSTA SOPHIA, daughter of George III.
Lent by MISS HOLTBY.

**527.** PRINCESS ROYAL, daughter of George III.
Lent by MISS HOLTBY.

**528.** PRINCESS ELIZABETH, daughter of George III.
Lent by MISS HOLTBY.

**529.** PRINCESS MARY, daughter of George III.
Lent by MISS HOLTBY.

**530.** PRINCESS SOPHIA, daughter of George III.
Lent by MISS HOLTBY.

**531.** PRINCESS AMELIA, daughter of George III.
Lent by MISS HOLTBY.

**532.** MRS. FITZHERBERT, 1756-1837.
Lent by MISS HOLTBY.

**533.** QUEEN CHARLOTTE, wife of George III., 1744-1818.
Lent by MISS HOLTBY.

**534.** GEORGE III., 1760-1820.
Lent by MISS HOLTBY.

**535.** GEORGE IV. WHEN PRINCE OF WALES, 1762-1830.
Lent by MISS HOLTBY.

**536.** ELIZABETH GUNNING, DUCHESS OF HAMILTON, d. 1790.
By B. DENNER. Lent by The RIGHT HON. SIR C. WENTWORTH DILKE, BART.

**537.** JOSEPH ADDISON, Statesman and man of letters, 1672-1719. From Lady Morgan's Collection.
Lent by The RIGHT HON. SIR C. WENTWORTH DILKE, BART.

**538.** MARIA GUNNING, COUNTESS OF COVENTRY, 1733-1760.
By B. DENNER.
Lent by The RIGHT HON. SIR C. WENTWORTH DILKE, BART.

**539.** SIR ROBERT WALPOLE, 1ST EARL OF ORFORD, Statesman, 1676-1745.
Lent by The EARL OF ORFORD.

**540.** HORATIO, 1ST LORD WALPOLE, Diplomatist, 1678-1757.
Lent by The EARL OF ORFORD.

**541.** MARY LOMBARD, LADY WALPOLE, wife of Horatio, 1st Lord.
Lent by The EARL OF ORFORD.

**542.** CATHARINE II. OF RUSSIA, 1729-1796. Presented by her to Horatio, 1st Lord Orford.
Lent by The EARL OF ORFORD.

**543.** JOHN CHURCHILL, 1ST DUKE OF MARLBOROUGH, K.G., 1650-1722.
Lent by C. E. LEES, ESQ.

**544.** RICHARD TICKELL, Poet, &c., d. 1793.
By T. GAINSBOROUGH, R.A.
Lent by C. E. LEES, ESQ.

**545.** MARY LINLEY, MRS. TICKELL, Vocalist.
By T. GAINSBOROUGH, R.A.
Lent by C. E. LEES, ESQ.

**546.** SIR WALTER SCOTT, BART., Poet and Novelist, aged five years, 1771-1832.
Lent by The HON. MRS. MAXWELL-SCOTT.

**547.** LADY CHARLOTTE SCOTT, wife of Sir Walter Scott.
Lent by The HON. MRS. MAXWELL-SCOTT.

**548.** SIR WALTER SCOTT, BART.
Lent by The HON. MRS. MAXWELL-SCOTT.

WEST GALLERY.] *Miniatures, Relics, and Plate.* 137

**549.** GEORGE I., 1714-1727. Oil.
               Lent by The REV. JAMES BECK.

**550.** EMANUEL SCROPE, 2ND VISCOUNT HOWE, d. 1735.
               Lent by COUNT KIELMANSEGG.

**551.** GEORGE III., 1760-1820. On satin.
               Lent by The EARL OF MAYO.

**552.** QUEEN CHARLOTTE, 1744-1818. On satin.
               Lent by The EARL OF MAYO.

**553.** WILLIAM HOGARTH, Painter, 1697-1754.
  By HIMSELF.     Lent by G. MILNER-GIBSON-CULLUM, ESQ.

**554.** NAPOLEON I., 1769-1821.
               Lent by The EARL OF ILCHESTER.

**555.** ROBESPIERRE, with inscription on back, in handwriting of C. J. Fox, "Un Scélérat, un lâche, et un fou."
               Lent by The EARL OF ILCHESTER.

**556.** SIR ROBERT WALPOLE, 1ST EARL OF ORFORD, K.G., 1676-1745.
  By C. F. ZINCKE.     Lent by The EARL OF DERBY, K.G.

**557.** JOHN LAW OF LAURISTON, Financial projector, 1671-1729.
  By COATER.      Lent by The EARL OF DERBY, K.G.

**558.** DOROTHY BLAND, MRS. JORDAN, Actress, 1762-1815.
               Lent by COLONEL H. MALET.

**559.** GEORGE III., 1760-1820.]
  By H. BONE, R.A.     Lent by W. W. ASTON, ESQ.

**560.** QUEEN CHARLOTTE, 1744-1818, Queen of George III. Presented by the Queen to Sir Thomas Neale.
  By H. BONE, R.A.     Lent by W. W. ASTON, ESQ.

**561.** LADY ATTENDANT ON PRINCESS CHARLOTTE. Enamel.
  By C. MUSS.      Lent by W. W. ASTON, ESQ.

**562.** GEORGIANA, COUNTESS COWPER, wife of William, 2nd Earl.
By N. HONE, R.A.   Lent by W. W. ASTON, ESQ.

**563.** JAMES GIBBS, Architect, 1674-1754. Enamel.
By C. F. ZINCKE.   Lent by W. W. ASTON, ESQ.

**564.** JOHN, 1ST DUKE OF MARLBOROUGH, 1650-1722. Enamel.
By C. F. ZINCKE. *Signed*, " C. F. Z." in monogram.
Lent by W. W. ASTON, ESQ.

**565.** ANN HILL, COUNTESS OF MORNINGTON, mother of Arthur, 1st Duke of Wellington, d. 1831.
By A. PLIMER.   Lent by W. W. ASTON, Esq.

**566.** GEORGE III., 1760-1820. Painted between the years 1776-1788, and presented to the artist by the King.
By GEORGE ENGLEHEART. Lent by J. GARDNER D. ENGLEHEART, ESQ., C.B.

**567.** GEORGE ENGLEHEART, Painter, 1752-1829. Painted in 1814.
By J. C. D. ENGLEHEART.
Lent by J. GARDNER D. ENGLEHEART, ESQ., C.B.

**568.** FREDERICK AUGUSTUS, DUKE OF YORK, 1763-1827. This miniature belonged to the Princess Amelia, his sister.
Lent by The HON. MRS. WILLIAM LOWTHER.

**569.** PRINCESS SOPHIA, daughter of George III., 1777-1848. This miniature belonged to the Princess Amelia, her sister.
Lent by The HON. MRS. WILLIAM LOWTHER.

**570.** JAMES, 1ST EARL OF LONSDALE, d. 1802.
Lent by The HON. MRS. WILLIAM LOWTHER.

**571.** MRS. LANE FOX.
Lent by The HON. MRS. WILLIAM LOWTHER.

**572.** ELIZABETH GUNNING, DUCHESS OF HAMILTON AND ARGYLL, 1734-1790. Inscribed on back with her name and the initials P. C.
Lent by The DUKE OF HAMILTON, K.T.

WEST GALLERY.]  *Miniatures, Relics, and Plate.*  139

**573.** SIR WILLIAM HAMILTON, K.B., Ambassador, 1730-1815.
   Lent by The DUKE OF HAMILTON, K.T.

**574.** RICHARD SUMNER.
   By LADY BARHAM. Lent by MISS SUMNER.

**575.** MRS. CORNISH (*née* Mary Gambier).
   By R. EASTON, R.A. Lent by MISS SUMNER.

**576.** MR. MONTGOMERIE.
   Lent by MISS SUMNER.

**577.** GEORGE MONTGOMERIE, 1712-1766.
   Lent by MISS SUMNER.

**578.** JOHN, 10TH EARL OF WESTMORELAND AND COSWAY.
   Lent by The RIGHT HON. SIR SPENCER PONSONBY-FANE, K.C.B.

**579.** ADMIRAL SIR CHARLES SAUNDERS, K.B.
   Lent by The RIGHT HON. SIR SPENCER PONSONBY-FANE, K.C.B.

**580.** WILLIAM COWPER, Poet, 1731-1800; with his autograph.  From Lady Morgan's Collection.
   Lent by The RIGHT HON. SIR C. WENTWORTH DILKE, BART.

**581.** PORTRAIT OF A GENTLEMAN.
   Lent by J. E. COLLINGWOOD, ESQ.

**582.** MARQUESS CORNWALLIS.
   Lent by J. E. COLLINGWOOD, ESQ.

**583.** QUEEN ADELAIDE, 1792-1849.
   By LEE. Lent by The EARL OF MAYO.

**584.** GEORGE I., 1714-1727.
   Lent by JOHN EVANS, ESQ., P.S.A.

**585.** JAMES DRUMMOND, OF CONCRAIG, Commissary-General at Paris 1818-1821.
   By BERTRAND. Lent by CAPTAIN TELFER, R.E.

**586.** CECILIA A. DRUMMOND, wife of the above.  Enamel.
   By MORTEAUX. Lent by CAPTAIN TELFER, R.N.

587. RICHARD BRINSLEY SHERIDAN, Statesman and Dramatist, 1751-1816.
By T. GAINSBOROUGH, R.A.     Lent by C. E. LEES, ESQ.

588. JOSEPH ADDISON, Statesman and Man of Letters, 1672-1719. From the Strawberry Hill Collection.
By C. F. ZINCKE.     Lent by C. E. LEES, ESQ.

589. SIR ISAAC NEWTON, Philosopher, &c., 1642-1727.
Lent by HENRY H. P. COTTON, ESQ.

590. MRS. FITZHERBERT, 1756-1837.     Lent by MRS. LE FANU.

591. LADY C. MORANT.     Lent by MRS. LE FANU.

592. A LADY.     Lent by MRS. LE FANU.

593. THE HON. DENIS BROWNE, 1763-1828.     Lent by MRS. LE FANU.

594. JOHN ABERNETHY, M.D., 1764-1831.     Lent by MRS. LE FANU.

595. LADY HESTER STANHOPE, 1766-1829.     Lent by MRS. LE FANU.

596. TIPPOO SAHIB.     Lent by MRS. LE FANU.

597. WILLIAM WILBERFORCE, M.P., Philanthropist, 1759-1833.
Lent by MRS. LE FANU.

598. LADY SARAH BUNBURY.     Lent by MISS A. T. SELBY LOWNDES.

599. BOY WITH BIRD'S NEST.
By HORACE WALPOLE.     Lent by THE DUCHESS OF ST. ALBANS.

600. THREE DRAWINGS OF PITT, ELDON, AND THURLOW.
By SAYERS.     Lent by T. LYON THURLOW, ESQ.

601. SIR FRANCIS CHANTREY, R.A., Sculptor, 1782-1841. Enamel.
By H. BONE, R.A.     Lent by The BARONESS BURDETT-COUTTS.

WEST GALLERY.] *Miniatures, Relics, and Plate.*

**602.** WAX PORTRAIT OF A LADY UNKNOWN.
Lent by ISAAC FALCKE, ESQ.
**603.** WAX PORTRAIT OF DR. SAMUEL JOHNSON.
Lent by ISAAC FALCKE, ESQ.
**604.** MODEL OF JOHN FLAXMAN.
By HIMSELF.
Lent by ISAAC FALCKE, ESQ.
**605.** WAX PORTRAIT OF GEORGE III.
Lent by ISAAC FALCKE, ESQ.
**606.** WAX CAST OF SIR JOSHUA REYNOLDS.
By MOUNTSTEPHEN.
Lent by The EARL OF ILCHESTER.
**607.** WAX CAST OF THE HON. EDWARD BURKE.
Lent by The EARL OF ILCHESTER.
**608.** IVORY MEDALLION OF GEORGE I.
Lent by The COUNT KIELMANSEGG.
**609.** WAX PORTRAIT OF LORD CHARLES TOWNSHEND.
Lent by ISAAC FALCKE, ESQ.
**610.** WAX PORTRAIT OF EARL GRANVILLE.
Lent by ISAAC FALCKE, ESQ.
**611.** WAX PORTRAIT OF QUEEN CHARLOTTE.
Lent by ISAAC FALCKE, ESQ.
**612.** WAX PORTRAIT OF GEORGE III.
By FLAXMAN.
Lent by ISAAC FALCKE, ESQ.
**613.** WAX PORTRAIT OF GENTLEMAN UNKNOWN.
Lent by ISAAC FALCKE, ESQ.
**614.** WAX PORTRAIT OF GEORGE II.
Lent by The REV. F. R. ELLIS.
**615.** WAX PORTRAIT OF FREDERICK, PRINCE OF WALES.
Lent by The REV. F. R. ELLIS.
**616.** WAX PORTRAIT OF THE PRINCESS OF WALES.
Lent by The REV. F. R. ELLIS.
**617.** PORTRAIT IN OIL OF DEFOE.
Lent by The BARONESS BURDETT-COUTTS.

**618.** THOMAS PHILLIPS, R.A., painter, 1770-1845. Enamel.
By H. BONE, R.A. Lent by ISAAC FALCKE, ESQ.

**619.** WILLIAM WINDHAM, 1750-1810.
Lent by MRS. DALTON.

**620.** LORD BYRON.
By GIOFFOI. Lent by TRINITY COLLEGE, CAMBRIDGE.

**621.** MARTIN FOLKES, born 1690, died 1754.
Lent by G. MILNER-GIBSON-CULLUM, ESQ.

**622.** JOHN FANE, 11TH EARL OF WESTMORELAND, General, 1784-1859. Enamel.
By H. BONE, R.A. Lent by ISAAC FALCKE, ESQ.

**623.** TWO IVORY MEDALLIONS OF GEORGE III. AND QUEEN CHARLOTTE.
Lent by H. SALUSBURY MILMAN, ESQ.

**624.** CHARLES HEATH, engraver, 1784-1848. Enamel.
By H. BONE, R.A. Lent by ISAAC FALCKE, ESQ.

**625.** JOHN KEATS, 1795-1821.
By J. SEVERN. Lent by The RT. HON. SIR CHARLES W. DILKE, BART.

**626.** WILLIAM HENRY, LORD LYTTELTON, d. 1808. Enamel.
By H. BONE, R.A. Lent by ISAAC FALCKE, ESQ.

**627.** MRS. HENRY TIGHE.
By ROBERTSON. Lent by The RT. HON. SIR CHARLES W. DILKE, BART.

**628.** JOHN KEATS, 1795-1821. Painted at Rome from life.
By J. SEVERN. Lent by The RT. HON. SIR CHARLES W. DILKE, BART.

**629.** MRS. RAOW. Enamel.
By H. BONE, R.A. Lent by ISAAC FALCKE, ESQ.

**630.** GEORGE I., as a child.
Lent by JOHN JACKSON, ESQ.

**631.** JOHN KEATS, 1795-1821. Copied by Severn immediately after Keats's death.
By J. SEVERN. Lent by The RT. HON. SIR CHARLES W. DILKE, BART.

WEST GALLERY.] *Miniatures, Relics, and Plate.* 143

## CASE E—West Gallery.

*RELICS AND SNUFF-BOXES, WATCHES, BADGES, ETC., LENT BY H.R.H. THE PRINCE OF WALES.*

**632.** SILVER WATCH, which belonged to William III. with his arms on the dial. Maker, *Peter Garon,* London.

**633.** GOLD WATCH, with the Prince of Wales's plumes and motto, and around the additional inscription PRO PRINCIPE SEMPER. Maker, *John Weller,* London.

**634.** GOLD RING, with miniature of George III.

**635.** GOLD BADGE, for suspension round the neck, with the Prince of Wales's plumes and motto of the Garter. On back, ICH DIEN.

**636.** GOLD SCARF PIN, with miniature of George III.

**637.** SARDONYX CAMEO, with portrait of George III. Mounted as a brooch.

**638.** A GOLD ENAMELLED BADGE to be worn as a pendant, made in commemoration of the recovery of George III. and worn on his visit to St. Paul's Cathedral. It bears the inscription, "Regi amato reduci, vivat G. R. III. March X. MDCCLXXIX."

**638a.** INVALID DRINKING CUP, in silver, belonging to George IV.

**638b.** A LETTER-WEIGHT, with a bust of George IV. upon it.

*BONBONNIÈRES, SNUFF-BOXES, AND OTHER OBJECTS, LENT BY H.R.H. THE DUKE OF CAMBRIDGE, K.G.*

**639.** COLLAR, RIBBAND, CROSS, and STAR OF THE ORDER OF THE GUELPHS OF HANOVER.

**640.** STAR OF THE ORDER OF THE GUELPHS, which belonged to H.R.H. the late Duke of Cambridge.

**641.** LOUIS XV. BONBONNIÈRE OF GOLD REPOUSSÉE AND ENGRAVED AGATE.

642. LOUIS XVI. OVAL MOTHER-OF-PEARL BONBONNIÈRE.

643. LOUIS XV. OBLONG MOTHER-OF-PEARL BONBONNIÈRE.

644. LOUIS XVI. SHELL-SHAPED BONBONNIÈRE, enamelled with designs.

645. LOUIS XV. GLASS BONBONNIÈRE, decorated with "repoussée à jour" work.

646. DRESDEN BONBONNIÈRE, decorated with views.

647. AMETHYST BONBONNIÈRE, surmounted with dog, formerly belonged to George IV.

648. GEORGE III. BLOODSTONE BONBONNIÈRE, with gold chased lid, on which is a Bacchanalian subject.

649. LOUIS XIV. MARBLE BONBONNIÈRE, mounted with gold and richly chased.

650. GEORGE II. ONYX BONBONNIÈRE, mounted with gold and richly chased.

651. GEORGE II. BONBONNIÈRE, with cornelian panels.

652. GEORGE II. OBLONG AGATE BONBONNIÈRE, the top decorated with gold repoussée.

653. GEORGE II. BLOODSTONE BONBONNIÈRE, mounted in gold and chased.

654. GEORGE II. SMALL BONBONNIÈRE, enamel.

655. GEORGE II. AGATE BONBONNIÈRE, decorated with gold repoussée work.

656. GEORGE II. AGATE BONBONNIÈRE, with rose.

657. GEORGE III. AGATE BONBONNIÈRE, mounted in gold.

658. GEORGE III. ROUND GOLD BONBONNIÈRE, mounted in gold.

659. GEORGE III. BONBONNIÈRE, with moss-agate.

660. GEORGE III. ROCK CRYSTAL BASKET-SHAPED BONBONNIÈRE.

661. GEORGE III. AMBER BONBONNIÈRE.

662. GOLD OBLONG CHASED SNUFF-BOX, with repoussée lid, subject "Cleopatra."

663. GOLD "EMAILLE EN PLEIN" BOX, with pastoral subjects by Guiraud of Paris, *temp.* Louis XV.

664. OVAL GOLD SNUFF-BOX, with six enamelled panels of classical design, *temp.* Louis XVI.

665. GOLD SNUFF-BOX, ornamented with enamelled subjects of dogs and birds.

666. BLOODSTONE SNUFF-BOX, with dog on cover, with diamond eyes and teeth and cornelian tongue, *temp.* George III.

667. LOUIS XV. ETUI, of chased gold and coloured panels.

668. LOUIS XV. GOLD CHASED ETUI.

669. GEORGE II. ETUI, of repoussée work with inscription, "*Rien n'est trop bon pour ce qu'on aime.*"

670. LOUIS XV. VINAIGRETTE.

671. GOLD SCENT-BOTTLE, enamelled with flowers.

672. SMALL GOLD THIMBLE-CASE inscribed, *J'aime mon choix*, *temp.* George II.

673. REPOUSSÉE GOLD CROSS, *temp.* George III.

674. REPOUSSÉE GOLD CROSS, *temp.* George III.

675. SMALL GOLD SEAL, with amethyst head.

676. SMALL GOLD SEAL, with negro's head.

677. GOLD FILIGREE LOCKET, with portraits.

678. LAPIS-LAZULI NEEDLE-CASE, set with rubies.

679. SMALL GOLD BROOCH, *temp.* George III.

680. GOLD NEEDLE CASE, *temp.* George III.

681. JADE SCENT-BOTTLE, mounted in gold, *temp.* George III.

682. ROYAL SEAL, with topaz handle.

683. GOLD PENCIL-CASE, with royal seal.

684. LOUIS XV. VINAIGRETTE.

685. GEORGE III. PLUM GOLD VINAIGRETTE, with mosaic.

686. GEORGE III. GOLD CHASED VINAIGRETTE, with mosaic.

687. GEORGE III. BLOODSTONE VINAIGRETTE, decorated with cameo.

688. GEORGE III. BLOODSTONE VINAIGRETTE, mounted with classical head.

689. SILVER NUTMEG-GRATER, which belonged to William IV. Hall mark.
Lent by The COUNTESS OF MUNSTER.

690. SILVER BASIN, given by Queen Adelaide to William IV.
Lent by The COUNTESS OF MUNSTER.

691. SILVER PAP-BOAT of William IV.
Lent by The COUNTESS OF MUNSTER.

692. GRAND CROSS, BADGE AND STARS OF THE ORDER OF THE GUELPHS OF HANOVER, which belonged to William IV.
Lent by The COUNTESS OF MUNSTER.

693. GOLD SNUFF-BOX, with cornelian top, presented to the Right Hon. Sir John Hookham Frere.
Lent by JOHN TUDOR FRERE, ESQ.

694. GOLD SNUFF-BOX, with bloodstone top and bottom, presented to the Right Hon. Sir John Hookham Frere.
Lent by JOHN TUDOR FRERE, ESQ.

695. SILVER SNUFF-BOX, niello with subjects, presented to the Right Hon. Sir John Hookham Frere.
            Lent by JOHN TUDOR FRERE, ESQ.

696. SNUFF-BOX, lapis-lazuli, with gold corners and mounts, presented to the Right Hon. Sir John Hookham Frere.
            Lent by JOHN TUDOR FRERE, ESQ.

697. GOLD SNUFF-BOX, engine-turned and engraved, presented to the Right Hon. Sir John Hookham Frere.
            Lent by JOHN TUDOR FRERE, ESQ.

698. RED GOLD SNUFF-BOX, plain, presented to the Right Hon. Sir John Hookham Frere.
            Lent by JOHN TUDOR FRERE, ESQ.

699. GOLD POCKET SNUFF-BOX, chased and engraved, presented to the Right Hon. Sir John Hookham Frere.
            Lent by JOHN TUDOR FRERE, ESQ.

700. GOLD SNUFF-BOX, incised with mythological subject, "Thetis and Vulcan," presented to the Right Hon. Sir John Hookham Frere.
            Lent by JOHN TUDOR FRERE, ESQ.

701. GOLD ENAMELLED SNUFF-BOX, with portrait on lid, presented to the Right Hon. Sir John Hookham Frere.
            Lent by JOHN TUDOR FRERE, ESQ.

## CASE F—West Gallery.

### MINIATURES.

### LENT BY THE EARL OF CARLISLE.

702. MARGARET LEVESON GOWER, COUNTESS OF CARLISLE, d. 182;.
  By J. MEYER.

703. ISABELLA BYRON, 2nd wife of the 4th Earl of Carlisle.

704. DUCHESS OF DEVONSHIRE.

**705.** GEORGE FREDERICK HANDEL, Musician, 1684–1759.
  By WILLIAM HOGARTH.

**706.** CAROLINE, LADY CAWDOR, daughter of Frederick, 5th Earl of Carlisle, and wife of John, 1st Lord Cawdor. When young.

**707.** THOMAS MOORE, Poet, 1779–1852.

**708.** FREDERICK, 6TH EARL OF CARLISLE, 1748–1825.

**709.** LADY CAWDOR.

**710.** GEORGIANA SPENCER, DUCHESS OF DEVONSHIRE, 1757–1806.

**711.** GEORGIANA SPENCER, DUCHESS OF DEVONSHIRE, AND CHILD, 1757–1806.

**712.** GEORGIANA SPENCER, DUCHESS OF DEVONSHIRE, 1757–1806.

**713.** LADY CHARLOTTE SPENCER.

**714.** GEORGE, LORD MORPETH.

**715.** FREDERICK, 5TH EARL OF CARLISLE, 1748–1825.

**716.** CHARLES III., DUKE OF QUEENSBERRY, 1698-1778.

**717.** ALEXANDER POPE, Poet, 1688–1744. Enamel.

**718.** THE DUKE OF DEVONSHIRE.

**719.** HENRY, 4TH EARL OF CARLISLE, K.G., 1699–1758.

**720.** DAVID GARRICK, Actor, 1716–1779.

---

**721.** PRINCESS CHARLOTTE OF WALES, daughter of George IV., 1796–1817.
  By G. STUART.       Lent by The LORD WILLOUGHBY DE ERESBY.

**722.** LADY SOPHIA HEATHCOTE.
  By R. COSWAY, R.A.       Lent by The LORD WILLOUGHBY DE ERESBY.

WEST GALLERY.] *Miniatures, Relics, and Plate.* 149

**723.** ADMIRAL VISCOUNT KEITH, 1747–1823.
By R. COSWAY, R.A. Lent by The LORD WILLOUGHBY DE ERESBY.

**724.** SARAH, COUNTESS OF JERSEY.
Lent by The LORD WILLOUGHBY DE ERESBY,

**725.** PETER ROBERT, 2ND LORD GWYDYR, afterwards 19th Baron Willoughby de Eresby, 1782–1865.
By R. COSWAY, R.A. Lent by The LORD WILLOUGHBY DE ERESBY.

**726.** LADY WILLOUGHBY DE ERESBY.
Lent by The LORD WILLOUGHBY DE ERESBY.

**727.** SAMUEL JOHNSON, LL.D., 1709–1784.
By S. SHELLEY. Lent by J. L. G. MOWATT, ESQ.

**728.** LADY FOLEY.
Lent by The LORD WILLOUGHBY DE ERESBY.

**729.** THE ANCASTER BOX in a frame comprising :—

LADY WILLOUGHBY DE ERESBY and LADY GEORGIANA CHARLOTTE BERTIE, MARCHIONESS OF CHOLMONDELEY, d. 1838.
By R. COSWAY, R.A. Lent by The LORD WILLOUGHBY DE ERESBY.

MARY PANTON, DUCHESS OF ANCASTER, wife of 3rd Duke.
By R. COSWAY, R.A. Lent by The LORD WILLOUGHBY DE ERESBY.

ROBERT BERTIE, 4TH DUKE OF ANCASTER, 1756–1779.
By R. COSWAY, R.A. Lent by The LORD WILLOUGHBY DE ERESBY.

LORD GWYDYR.
By R. COSWAY, R.A. Lent by The LORD WILLOUGHBY DE ERESBY.

**730.** LADY SOPHIA HEATHCOTE.
Lent by The LORD WILLOUGHBY DE ERESBY.

**731.** SIR GILBERT HEATHCOTE.
Lent by The LORD WILLOUGHBY DE ERESBY.

**732.** LORD GWYDYR, set in brilliants on tooth-pick case.
By R. COSWAY, R.A. Lent by The LORD WILLOUGHBY DE ERESBY.

733. ELIZABETH, wife of Sir Gilbert Heathcote.
By R. COSWAY, R.A.   Lent by The LORD WILLOUGHBY DE ERESBY.

734. LADY CATHERINE MEADE, 2nd daughter of John, 1st Earl of Clanwilliam, and wife of Richard, 4th Viscount Powerscourt, d. 1793.
Lent by The VISCOUNT POWERSCOURT, K.P.

735. ROBERT, VISCOUNT CASTLEREAGH, 2ND MARQUESS OF LONDONDERRY, K.G., Eminent Statesman, 1769-1822.
Lent by The VISCOUNT POWERSCOURT, K.P.

736. GEORGE IV. AS PRINCE REGENT, 1762-1830.
By R. COSWAY, R.A.   Lent by The HON. GERALD PONSONBY.

### LENT BY THE EARL OF WHARNCLIFFE.

737. JOHN, 1ST MARQUESS OF BUTE, 1744-1814.
By N. HONE, R.A.

738. MARY ISABELLA, DUCHESS OF RUTLAND, d. 1831.
By H. HONE.

739. ELIZABETH FARREN, COUNTESS OF DERBY, 1759-1829.
By R. COSWAY, R.A.

740. RICHARD BRINSLEY SHERIDAN, Statesman, &c., 1751-1816. Dated 1785.
By L. SICARDY.

741. MRS. DANIELL.
By R. COSWAY, R.A.

742. MRS. ROBINSON, AS "PERDITA," 1758-1800.
By R. COSWAY, R.A.

743. LADY MARY WORTLEY MONTAGU, IN TURKISH COSTUME, 1690-1762.

744. MRS. FITZHERBERT, 1756-1837.
By R. COSWAY, R.A.

745. MRS. WHITMORE.
By R. COSWAY, R.A.

WEST GALLERY.]   *Miniatures, Relics, and Plate.*   151

746. LADY HAMILTON, 1761-1815.
     UNKNOWN.

747. LADY ELIZABETH FOSTER, DUCHESS OF DEVONSHIRE, d. 1824.
     By R. COSWAY, R.A.

748. JAMES, 1ST LORD WHARNCLIFFE, 1776-1845.
     By J. HOLMES.

749. EDWARD WORTLEY MONTAGU, 1713-1776.
     UNKNOWN.

750. GEORGIANA, DUCHESS OF DEVONSHIRE, 1757-1806.
     By R. COSWAY, R.A.

751. MRS. ABINGTON, Actress, 1737-1815.
     UNKNOWN.

752. LADY ELIZABETH FOSTER, DUCHESS OF DEVONSHIRE, d. 1824.
     By R. COSWAY, R.A.                    Lent by H. DRAKE, ESQ.

753. LADY HARCOURT.
     By R. COSWAY, R.A.                    Lent by H. DRAKE, ESQ.

754. WILLIAM BECKFORD, Author, &c., 1760-1844.
     By N. PLIMER.                         Lent by H. DRAKE, ESQ.

755. MRS. FITZHERBERT, 1756-1837.
     By R. COSWAY, R.A.                    Lent by H. DRAKE, ESQ.

*LENT BY THE DUKE OF DEVONSHIRE, K.G.*

756. WILLIAM, 4TH DUKE OF DEVONSHIRE, K.G., 1720-1764.

757. WILLIAM, 5TH DUKE OF DEVONSHIRE, K.G., 1748-1811.

758. GEORGE JOHN, 2ND EARL SPENCER, 1758-1834.

759. ELIZABETH FOSTER, DUCHESS OF DEVONSHIRE, d. 1824.

760. PORTRAIT OF A LADY WITH VIOLET SCARF. *Signed* "S. 1786."

761. QUEEN CAROLINE, wife of George II., 1682-1737. Enamel.
By L. CARSTAIRS.

762. GEORGIANA SPENCER, DUCHESS OF DEVONSHIRE, 1757-1806.
By R. COSWAY.

763. THE SAME.

764. THE SAME.

765. ELIZABETH (FOSTER), DUCHESS OF DEVONSHIRE, d. 1824.

766. PORTRAIT OF A GENTLEMAN IN BLUE COAT.

767. WILLIAM, 5TH DUKE OF DEVONSHIRE, K.G., 1748-1811. Enamel.
By HENRY BONE, R.A. *Signed* " H. B."

768. PORTRAIT OF A LADY, WITH DOVES.

769. PORTRAIT OF A GENTLEMAN IN GREEN COAT AND WIG.

770. PRINCESS AUGUSTA, wife of Frederick, Prince of Wales.

771. FREDERICK THE GREAT, KING OF PRUSSIA, 1740-1786. In square locket.

772. RICHARD BOYLE, 3RD EARL OF BURLINGTON, 1695-1753.

773. FRANCIS, 5TH DUKE OF BEDFORD, 1765-1802.
By W. GRIMALDI.

774. GEORGE II., 1727-1760.                     Lent by The EARL STANHOPE.

775. GEORGE IV. WHEN PRINCE OF WALES, 1762-1830. Formerly belonged to Mrs. Fitzherbert.
By R. COSWAY, R.A.              Lent by BASIL FITZHERBERT, ESQ.

WEST GALLERY.] *Miniatures, Relics, and Plate.* 153

776. MRS. FITZHERBERT, 1756-1837. Formerly belonged to Mrs. Fitzherbert.
By SARAH MEE. Lent by BASIL FITZHERBERT, ESQ.

777. FRAME CONTAINING MINIATURES OF—
   1. THE HON. CAROLINE FOX.
   2. RT. HON. CHARLES JAMES FOX, M.P., 1749-1806.
   3. THE HON. T. PELHAM, d. 1781.
   4. GEORGIANA SPENCER, DUCHESS OF DEVONSHIRE, wife of William, 5th Duke, 1757-1806.
   5. HENRIETTA SPENCER, COUNTESS OF BESSBOROUGH, wife of Frederick, 3rd Earl, d. 1821.
   6. AUGUSTUS FREDERICK, DUKE OF SUSSEX, K.G., 1773-1843.
   7. LORD HENRY SPENCER.
   8. LADY ELIZABETH FOSTER, afterwards Duchess of Devonshire, 1759-1824.
   9. STEPHEN FOX, 2ND LORD HOLLAND.
   10. HENRY FOX, 1ST LORD HOLLAND, Statesman, 1705-1774.
   11. THOMAS, EARL WYCOMBE.
Lent by The EARL OF ILCHESTER.

778. A SERIES OF MINIATURES of Princess Charlotte, 1796-1817, representing her at various ages.
By MISS CHARLOTTE JONES. Lent by SIR LAWRENCE JONES, BART.

## CASE G—West Gallery.

*PLATE.*

779. SILVER EPERGNE, which belonged to George II.
    Lent by SAMUEL MONTAGU, ESQ., M.P.

780. A PAIR OF SILVER SALT-CELLARS of pierced work. Hall mark 1768.
    Lent by HUBERT DYNES ELLIS, ESQ.

781. A PAIR OF SILVER SALT-CELLARS of pierced work. Hall mark 1772.
    Lent by HUBERT DYNES ELLIS, ESQ.

782. TWELVE SILVER-GILT SPOONS. London mark.
    Lent by COLONEL FOLLETT.

783. SILVER CAUDLE CUP WITH COVER, STAND AND SPOON. London mark for 1738.
    Lent by The VISCOUNT MIDLETON.

784. PAIR OF SILVER DRINKING CUPS. London mark for 1829.
    Lent by COLONEL FOLLETT.

785. SILVER TEA-POT. Hall mark.
    Lent by JOHN JACKSON, ESQ.

786. SILVER SAUCE PAN. London mark for 1787.
    Lent by COLONEL FOLLETT.

787. THREE SILVER PUNCH LADLES. London marks for 1718, 1727, and 1723.
    Lent by COLONEL FOLLETT.

788. TWO SILVER SUGAR-SPOONS. London Hall mark 1716-1717.
    Lent by MRS. H. A. GRUEBER.

789. FOUR SILVER SALT CELLARS, pierced and ornamented with flowers. London Hall mark for 1792. Maker's initials, I. G.
    Lent by MRS. H. A. GRUEBER.

790. A SILVER SALVER of pierced work, with vine-pattern border. Hall mark 1771.
    Lent by HUBERT DYNES ELLIS, ESQ.

WEST GALLERY.]  *Miniatures, Relics, and Plate.*  155

791. A PAIR OF OBLONG SILVER BASKETS of pierced work with bevelled ends, and with the king's head duty mark; in case.  Hall marks 1784 and 1785.
Lent by HUBERT DYNES ELLIS, ESQ.

792. SILVER CUP with harp-shaped handles.  Dublin mark for 1720.
Lent by COLONEL FOLLETT.

793. SILVER TANKARD.  London mark for 1744.
Lent by COLONEL FOLLETT.

794. SILVER PATEN.  York mark.
Lent by COLONEL FOLLETT.

795. SILVER TEA-KETTLE AND STAND.  London mark for 1720.
Lent by COLONEL FOLLETT.

796. A FINELY-CHASED TEA-CADDY SET, with two Tea-holders and covered Sugar-Basin on ball and claw feet.  By Newton.  London mark for 1736.
Lent by WILFRED CRIPPS, ESQ., C.B.

797. A SILVER COMMUNION-SERVICE SPOON, used to remove flies, &c., from the sacred wine.  Hall mark 1722.
Lent by HUBERT DYNES ELLIS, ESQ.

798. A SILVER CAKE-BASKET of pierced work.  By William Plummer.  Hall mark 1772.
Lent by HUBERT DYNES ELLIS, ESQ.

799. SILVER SUGAR-BASKET.  Hall mark.
Lent by JOHN JACKSON, ESQ.

800. SILVER TEA-POT.  London mark for 1746.
Lent by COLONEL FOLLETT.

801. A PLAIN BALUSTER-STEM SILVER CANDLESTICK with hexagonal base.  Hall mark 1717.
Lent by HUBERT DYNES ELLIS, ESQ.

802. A FLUTED TEA-CANISTER with open-work foot.  Hall mark 1762.
Lent by HUBERT DYNES ELLIS, ESQ.

803. SILVER TANKARD.  Newcastle mark for 1784.
Lent by COLONEL FOLLETT.

**804.** SILVER TWO-HANDLED CUP. London mark for 1720.
Lent by COLONEL FOLLETT.

**805.** A PLAIN TWO-HANDLED SILVER PORRINGER of the pattern which superseded the Queen Anne pattern. Hall mark 1728.
Lent by HUBERT DYNES ELLIS, ESQ.

**806.** TALL OCTAGONAL COFFEE-POT. By Bodington. London mark for 1715.
Lent by WILFRID CRIPPS, ESQ., C.B.

**807.** A PAIR OF TEA-CADDIES. By Newton. London mark for 1736.
Lent by WILFRED CRIPPS, ESQ.

**808.** SILVER BEAKER JUG. London mark for 1748.
Lent by COLONEL FOLLETT.

**809.** SILVER COFFEE-POT. London mark for 1745.
Lent by COLONEL FOLLETT.

**810.** SILVER SUGAR-BASIN, part of a wedding gift from the Princesses Augusta and Mary, daughters of George III. to the grandmother of the present owner.
Lent by CHARLES A. JONES, ESQ.

**811.** SILVER SPOONS. London mark for 1756-1759.
Lent by COLONEL FOLLETT.

**812.** TWO SILVER CASTORS. London mark for 1732.
Lent by COLONEL FOLLETT.

**813.** SILVER NUTMEG-GRATER. London mark for 1715.
Lent by COLONEL FOLLETT.

**814.** PAIR OF SILVER SNUFFERS. London mark for 1815.
Lent by COLONEL FOLLETT.

**815.** OPEN WORK SILVER CAKE-BASKET (the Walpole Basket). Hall-mark 1731 (Paul de Lamerie).
Lent by MRS. DENT OF SUDELEY.

**816.** A SILVER BEER-JUG. Hall mark.
Lent by MISS REID.

**817.** SILVER CUP. London mark for 1774.
Lent by COLONEL FOLLETT.

WEST GALLERY.] *Miniatures, Relics, and Plate.*

**818.** PIERCED AND REPOUSSÉE SILVER CAKE BASKET, Hall marked 1775 (T. Daniell).
Lent by MRS. DENT OF SUDELEY.

**819.** THREE SILVER NUTMEG-GRATERS. Hall mark.
Lent by JOHN JACKSON, ESQ.

**820.** A PIERCED SILVER SUGAR-BASIN with glass liner. Hall mark 1783.
Lent by HUBERT DYNES ELLIS, ESQ.

**821.** SILVER TEA-POT TRAY. Hall mark.
Lent by JOHN JACKSON, ESQ.

**822.** SILVER CREAM JUG. Hall mark.
Lent by JOHN JACKSON, ESQ.

**823.** A PAIR OF TALL SILVER CORINTHIAN-COLUMN CANDLESTICKS with removable nozzles, at this period first introduced. Hall mark 1758.
Lent by HUBERT DYNES ELLIS, ESQ.

**824.** A PAIR OF PLAIN BALUSTER-STEM SILVER CANDLESTICKS, with octagonal bases and sockets, bevelled and counter-bevelled. Hall mark 1716.
Lent by HUBERT DYNES ELLIS, ESQ.

**825.** A PAIR OF PLAIN BALUSTER-STEM CANDLESTICKS with square bases, the corners cut off and rounded in. By Paul de Lamerie. Hall mark 1723.
Lent by HUBERT DYNES ELLIS, ESQ.

**826.** OLD IRISH SILVER-GILT BOWL, *temp.* George II.
Lent by MRS. HAROLD HARDY.

**827.** SILVER CENTRE-PIECE, designed by Flaxman for George III. Hall mark.
Lent by JOHN JACKSON, ESQ.

**828.** A TWO-HANDLED SILVER PORRINGER of the Queen Anne pattern, with a cable band above and spiral flutings below : this form went out of fashion about the end of the reign of George I. Hall mark 1725.
Lent by HUBERT DYNES ELLIS, ESQ.

## Case H—North Gallery.

### RELICS.

**829.** A LARGE PUNCH GLASS, with stem and foot. The bowl is inscribed by engraving with the name of "NELSON," below which is an anchor between laurel branches, vine and grapes, ears of barley, hop spray, and the initials of the owner, "F. M. N.," in a shield, with the date (1806) of Nelson's funeral. Of these "Nelson funeral glasses" few are known to exist.
*Lent by* MISS FORTNUM.

**830.** PATCH BOX OF BILSTON ENAMEL, with inscription—"United to be Happy."
*Lent by* J. E. COLLINGWOOD, ESQ.

**831.** PATCH BOX OF BILSTON ENAMEL, with inscription—"Be Just before you are Generous."
*Lent by* J. E. COLLINGWOOD, ESQ.

**832.** PATCH BOX OF BILSTON ENAMEL, with design of a Hen and Chicken.
*Lent by* J. E. COLLINGWOOD, ESQ.

**833.** GOLD SNUFF-BOX, containing a Miniature of Mary (Lepel), Lady Hervey, and a Cameo of John, Lord Hervey.
*Lent by* THE MARQUESS OF BRISTOL.

**834.** SERJEANT'S RING OF SIR WILLIAM BLACKSTONE (1728-1780).
*Lent by* JOHN EVANS, ESQ., P.S.A.

**835.** MOURNING RING OF THE HON. SPENCER PERCEVAL (1762-1812).
*Lent by* JOHN EVANS, ESQ., P.S.A.

**836.** NELSON MEMORIAL GOBLET in glass. Engraved on one side, "IN MEMORY OF LORD NELSON, JANUARY 9, 1806," and on the other a representation of the funeral car.
*Lent by* ALBERT HARTSHORNE, ESQ.

**837.** GOLD SNUFF-BOX, taken at Manilla in 1762 by Admiral Sir Samuel Cornish.
*Lent by* MISS SUMNER.

NORTH GALLERY.] *Miniatures, Relics, and Plate.*

**838.** NELSON MEMORIAL GOBLET in glass. Engraved with representation of the funeral car. This goblet came direct to the present owner from Mrs. Kilwick, whose husband was an officer on board the *Victory* at the time of Nelson's death.
Lent by MISS HARTSHORNE.

**839.** TWO SILVER NUTMEG-GRATERS.
Lent by J. E. COLLINGWOOD, ESQ.

**840.** SILVER NUTMEG-GRATER: egg-shaped.
Lent by J. E. COLLINGWOOD, ESQ.

**841.** ROBERT BURNS'S TUMBLER, with the following verses cut by him with a diamond on the sides.

" Ye be welcome, Willie Stewart,
Ye be welcome, Willie Stewart;
There's no a flower that comes in May
That's half sae welcome's thou art.
Come, camper high, express your joy,
The bowl ye maun renew it;
The tappit hen, gae, fetch her ben,
To welcome Willie Stewart.

May foes be strong and friends be slack,
May he ilk action rue it;
May woman on him turn her back,
Would wrong thee, Willie Stewart."
Lent by The HON. MRS. MAXWELL SCOTT.

**842.** BUTTON (Wedgewood plaque set in copper), which belonged to Lord George Gordon.
Lent by JOHN HIPKINS, ESQ.

**843.** GOLD LOCKET containing a lock of hair of the Duke of Wellington, which he sent to his mother from the Peninsula in 1813.
Lent by HENRY WEIGALL, ESQ.

**844.** GOLD WATCH, given by "Horace Walpole to his esteemed friend David Garrick."
Lent by The EARL OF ORFORD.

**845.** MEDALLION containing Sir Isaac Newton's hair.
Lent by G. MILNER-GIBSON-CULLUM, ESQ., F.S.A.

**846.** SCALE FOR WEIGHING GUINEAS, of the last century.
Lent by J. E. COLLINGWOOD, ESQ.

## Exhibition of the Royal House of Guelph.

**847.** TIN SNUFF-BOX, with Portrait.
           Lent by MISS LEWIS.

**848.** STATUETTE OF NAPOLEON I. in wood.
           Lent by S. LYON THURLOW, ESQ.

**849.** SNUFF-BOX, with bust of Napoleon I.
           Lent by HENRY H. P. COTTON, ESQ.

**850.** COMPASS, from Moscow, which belonged to Napoleon I.
           Lent by HENRY H. P. COTTON, ESQ.

**851.** MEDALLION OF GEORGE IV., 1820-1830, in bronze.
           Lent by The DUKE OF DEVONSHIRE, K.G.

**852.** SNUFF-BOX, with painting of the "Hell Fire Club," Dublin.

The "Hell Fire Club" was a club which existed in Dublin before the Union, and which met at a house on the hill above Rathfernham, near Dublin. It held orgies there in imitation of a similar institution in England called "The Monks of Medmenham Abbey," near Great Marlow on the Thames, and itself sometimes designated as the "Hell Fire Club." Wilkes was a member of the latter.

There is a large picture of the Dublin "Hell Fire Club" in the National Gallery of Ireland, painted by Slaughter, with portraits of Lord Bantry, Colonel Ponsonby, Colonel Clements, Mr. Luttrell, and Colonel St. George, grouped round a table on which are bottles and glasses. This picture formerly belonged to Sir Charles Domville, was purchased by Mr. Wardell, of Dublin, and presented to the National Gallery of Ireland.
           Lent by The VISCOUNT POWERSCOURT, K.P.

**853.** SILVER-GILT VINAIGRETTE.
           Lent by Mrs. HAROLD HARDY.

**854.** WHITE SATIN SHOE which was worn by Georgiana, Duchess of Devonshire, when a child.
           Lent by the DUKE OF DEVONSHIRE, K.G.

**855.** TWO WOODEN SNUFF-BOXES, with portraits of Elizabeth Gunning, Duchess of Hamilton, and her sister Maria, Countess of Coventry.
           Lent by The RIGHT HON. SIR C. WENTWORTH DILKE, BART.

**856.** PART OF THE SILVER-GILT NÉCESSAIRE OF THE EMPEROR NAPOLEON I., consisting of a small tray, powder and soap-boxes, and dressing-table candlestick, taken from his carriage at Waterloo, and sold by the soldiers to the Rev. Sir Thomas Gery

NORTH GALLERY.] *Miniatures, Relics, and Plate.*

Cullum, Bart., of Hardwick House, Bury St. Edmunds. The nécessaire was made for Napoleon in August, 1806, by the well-known goldsmith Brennais. It accompanied him in all his campaigns, including that of Russia, and his exile to Elba, and was finally lost at the Battle of Waterloo. Sir Thomas Cullum requested Brennais to attest its authenticity, which was accordingly done on the back of the tray, and accompanying these relics is Brennais' account presented to the Emperor for the same. To these is added one of twenty-four knives taken at the same time, and all of which were also purchased by Sir Thomas Cullum.

Lent by G. MILNER-GIBSON-CULLUM, ESQ., F.S.A.

857. BLOTTING-BOOK, taken from the carriage of Napoleon I. at Waterloo.
Lent by The HON. MRS. MAXWELL-SCOTT.

858. GOLD TIE-CLASP, taken from the carriage of Napoleon I. at Waterloo.
Lent by The HON. MRS. MAXWELL-SCOTT.

859. LOCK OF HAIR OF NAPOLEON I., with writing.
Lent by HENRY H. P. COTTON, ESQ.

860. GLASS used by Napoleon I. during the Battle of Waterloo.

It was given to the present owner by Mrs. Molke, whose father was in Napoleon's tent when he came in and drank out of it. He brought it away as a relic.
Lent by S. CHISENHALE MARSH, ESQ.

861. TRAVELLING CLOCK, from Napoleon's carriage at Waterloo.
Lent by HENRY H. P. COTTON, ESQ.

862. SEALS OF SIR PETER RUSSELL, afterwards 1st Lord Gwydyr.
Lent by The LORD WILLOUGHBY DE ERESBY.

863. MAZER, which belonged to Robert Burns.
Lent by The REV. F. G. LEE, D.D.

864. JASPER MEDALLION, set in gold, with portrait of Richard, Earl Howe, K.G. Admiral, 1725-1799.
Lent by COUNT KIELMANSEGG.

864a. PATTERN FIVE-POUND PIECE OF GEORGE III., 1820.
Lent by The VISCOUNT DILLON.

M

**864*b*.** Pattern Two-Pound Piece of George III., 1820.
<br>Lent by The Viscount Dillon.

**865.** Impression of the Great Seal of England, 1818-1821.
<br>Lent by Captain Telfer, R.N.

**866.** Box containing miniatures of Sir Andrew Barnard and his wife, Lady Anne (Lindsay) of Balcarres, the authoress of *Auld Robin Gray*.
<br>Lent by The Earl of Crawford.

**867.** Gold Snuff-box, with miniature of Mrs. Montgomerie by R. Cosway, R.A.
<br>Lent by Miss Sumner.

**868.** Silver-gilt Clasp of Sword-belt, with the royal arms in enamel, worn by the 4th Duke of Ancaster.
<br>Lent by The Lord Willoughby de Eresby.

**869.** Gold Watch, the case embossed with representation of the "Judgment of Solomon."
<br>Lent by J. E. Collingwood, Esq.

**870.** Ivory Patch-Box, and examples of patches as used early in the last century.
<br>Lent by W. Johnston Stuart, Esq.

**871.** Brooch with classical design.
<br>By Angelica Kauffmann, R.A.   Lent by W. Johnston Stuart, Esq.

**872.** Bronze-Gilt Ticket of Admission to New Park, Richmond. The Princess Amelia, daughter of George III., was Ranger when this ticket was issued.
<br>Lent by Henry Spencer Walpole, Esq.

**873.** Star of Legion of Honour, containing a lock of hair of Napoleon I.
<br>Lent by The Lord Willoughby de Eresby.

**874.** Bracelet, with portrait of Admiral Lord Howe, K.G., 1725-1797.
<br>Lent by Miss Holtby.

**875.** Gold Watch, with French piqué work, presented by the Duke of York to Mrs. Clarke.
<br>Lent by W. Johnson Stuart, Esq.

**876.** Mary Bruce, wife of Dugald Stuart, Lord of Session.
<br>By C. F. Zincke.   Lent by W. Johnston Stuart, Esq.

**877.** Locket, with hair of John Keats, 1796-1820; cut from his head after death.
<br>Lent by The Right Hon. Sir C. Wentworth Dilke, Bart.

## Miniatures, Relics, and Plate.

**878.** BADGE OF THE PITT CLUB.
*Lent by* H. DRAKE, ESQ.

**879.** GOLD ENAMELLED WATCH.
*Lent by* J. E. COLLINGWOOD, ESQ.

**880.** CASE CONTAINING MODELS OF THE PITT, ORLOFF, AND PIGOT DIAMONDS.
*Lent by* J. E. COLLINGWOOD, ESQ.

**881.** FIVE FANS, three large and two small, of ivory and silk, of the last century.
*Lent by* J. E. COLLINGWOOD, ESQ.

**882.** A POLITICAL FAN (*circa* 1746). With a coloured print representing the Duke of Cumberland on horseback with Highlanders making their submission to him.
*Lent by* S. J. NICHOLLS, ESQ.

**883.** FAN, which belonged to Mrs. Jordan, the actress (1762–1816).
*Lent by* G. MILNER-GIBSON-CULLUM, ESQ., F.S.A.

**884.** LADY'S RIDING-WHIP, of the last century.
*Lent by* MISS LEWIS.

**885.** SWORD, with cut-steel hilts, which belonged to the late Colonel Wildman, of Newstead Abbey, Notts, and presented to him by Augustus, Duke of Sussex.
*Lent by the* CORPORATION OF NOTTINGHAM.

**886.** BEAU BRUMMEL'S SWORD.
The hilt and guard of cut and polished steel set with Wedgwood medallions and balls; the sheath is covered with parchment and mounted in polished steel. Date *circa* 1790.
*Lent by the* CORPORATION OF NOTTINGHAM.

**887.** SCRAPER OF IVORY, which belonged to Georgiana, Duchess of Devonshire, and given to her by the servants on her birthday.
*Lent by* JOHN CLELAND, ESQ., of Stormont.

**888.** COFFEE CUP AND SAUCER, of Capo di Monte porcelain, the cup painted with a portrait of Nelson, whose name is inscribed in gold on the saucer. These must have been made at the time when Nelson was in the Bay of Naples with the fleet.
*Lent by* C. DRURY E. FORTNUM, ESQ., D.C.L.

**889.** SILVERED BASKET, used at the Coronation of George IV.
*Lent by* CHARLES A. JONES, ESQ.

890. SHAWL PIN, with Cameo in profile of the Duke of Wellington.
Lent by JOHN JACKSON, ESQ.

891. PORTFOLIO, embroidered leather, formerly belonging to Thomas Pelham, Duke of Newcastle, with his arms.
Lent by LIONEL CUST, ESQ.

892. MOURNING FAN, commemorating the death of Princess Charlotte.
Lent by MISS LEWIS.

893. JEWELLED FAN, with Portrait of the Marquess of Harcourt, who conducted to England Queen Charlotte, wife of George III.
Lent by MISS LEWIS.

894. BROOCH, oval-shaped, cornelian set in gold, worn by Napoleon I. in his shirt-frill on board the *Bellerophon* when bound for Plymouth Sound.

On leaving the vessel, 7th August, 1815, to be taken by the *Northumberland* to St. Helena, Napoleon gave souvenirs to most of the officers, and this brooch thus became the property of John William Ellis, father of the present owner, who died in 1850.
Lent by MRS. RUTTER.

## CASE I—North Gallery.

### A SERIES OF BATTERSEA ENAMELS LENT BY CHARLES STORR KENNEDY, ESQ.

These Enamels date from about the year 1750, when Sir Theodore Janssen (Lord Mayor of London in 1754) established a manufactory at York House, Battersea. Horace Walpole, in his catalogue of his collection, describes them as a "manufacture stamped with copper plates." The art was however not confined to transfer printing, as many well-known artists were employed in the work. On one of the étuis exhibited is a portrait of the wife of Brooks, who was at the head of the works from 1770-1780. The art was employed to produce candlesticks, snuff, toilet, or patchboxes, salt-cellars, watch cases, wine labels, tea caddies, &c.

895. PAIR OF CADDIES (oval).

896. CASKET, containing Two Caddies, in blue enamel.

897. PAIR OF SQUARE WHITE CADDIES.

898. SET OF THREE SQUARE BLUE CADDIES, in case.

899. SET OF THREE GREEN CADDIES, one square and two shaped.

900. INKSTAND, with ink-bottle and sand-sifter.

901. LARGE GREEN BOX, fitted as an inkstand.

902. LARGE BLUE AND PINK BOX, fitted as an inkstand.

903. SHAPED BOX, fitted as writing case, in blue enamel.

904. SQUARE TURQUOISE BOX, fitted as a writing-case.

905. PAIR OF TRANSFER-PAINTED PLAQUES OF GEORGE II. AND FREDERICK PRINCE OF WALES.

906. MASONIC BADGE, set in silver gilt, date 1757.

907. LARGE PLAQUE, with harvest scene.

908. PAIR OF PLAQUES, in metal-gilt frames. Boucher subjects.

909. PAIR OF TOILET-POTS, in pink, white, and gold.

910. DRINKING-CUP, painted in views and bouquets.

911. SET OF FIVE PINK PERFORATED CARD-TRAYS FOR PLAYING QUADRILLE.

912. KNIFE, in sheath of raised enamel, painted in flowers.

913. MUSTARD-POT, with helmet-shaped top and a pepper-castor in blue.

914. BONBONNIÈRE, formed as a shoe, in blue enamel.

915. BONBONNIÈRE, formed as a shoe, in pink enamel.

916. SCENT-BOTTLE, with miniature in pink enamel.

917. BONBONNIÈRE AND SCENT-BOTTLE combined, in pink enamel.

918. SCENT-BOTTLE, NEEDLE-CASE, AND THIMBLE combined, with motto, "Secret en Amour."

919. SCENT-BOTTLE, NEEDLE-CASE, AND THIMBLE combined, with motto, "Secret en Amitié."

920. SMALL ORANGE-COLOURED CASE FOR SCENT-BOTTLES, with portraits of Garrick and Mrs. Siddons.

921. CHATELAINE, with four plaques, shaped etui with fittings, basket and egg-shaped pendants.

922. CHATELAINE, pink enamel, with two plaques, etui, and two egg-shaped scent-cases.

923. SQUARE ETUI AND SCENT-CASE combined, with portrait of Lady Fenhoulet and another portrait.

924. PINK ETUI, painted with miniature and flowers.

925. BLUE ETUI, painted with miniature and flowers.

926. PURPLE ETUI, painted with miniature and flowers.

927. MAZARIN BLUE ETUI, painted with miniature and flowers.

928. PINK ETUI, painted with miniature of Mrs. Brooks, whose husband was director of the Battersea works.

929. BOX, painted with a tea-party and views, with miniature of lady inside.

930. DARK-BLUE BOX, painted with Watteau subjects; on lid miniature of a lady.

931. PINK BOX, with portrait of Frederick the Great, King of Prussia.

932. OBLONG BOX, with Watteau subject and views.

933. SHAPED BLUE BOX, with equestrian figures and a beggar.

NORTH GALLERY.] *Miniatures, Relics, and Plate.*

934. SQUARE BLUE BOX, with miniature of Oliver Cromwell.

935. SQUARE LAVENDER BOX, with views on lid and panels of flowers.

936. SQUARE TURQUOISE BOX, painted with views on top and sides.

937. OVAL PINK BOX, with views on lid and sides.

938. BOX OF CANARY YELLOW, painted with classical subjects.

939. SHAPED PINK BOX, painted with lady with mask and fishing scenes.

940. BONBONNIÈRE formed as head of Miss Gunning, afterwards the Duchess of Hamilton.

941. BONBONNIÈRE shaped as hen and chickens.

942. BONBONNIÈRE shaped as dog and cat fighting.

943. BONBONNIÈRE shaped as tiger devouring a negro.

944. BONBONNIÈRE shaped in the form of an apple.

945. BONBONNIÈRE shaped as a lemon.

946. BONBONNIÈRE formed as terrestrial globe.

## CASE J—North Gallery.

### *MINIATURES.*
### *LENT BY JEFFERY WHITEHEAD, ESQ.*

**947.** GEORGE, LORD BYRON, Poet, 1788-1824.
By ANDREW ROBERTSON.

**948.** VITTORIO, COUNT ALFIERI, 1749-1803, Italian Poet. On the back is written by Lord Byron "Alfieri, given to me by the Lady H. in 1813."

**949.** LADY CAROLINE MONTAGU-SCOTT, daughter of Henry, 3rd Duke of Buccleuch, married to Charles, Marquess of Queensberry.
By G. HAYTER. *Signed.*

**950.** LADY HARRIET MONTAGU-SCOTT, sister of the preceding, married to William, 6th Marquess of Lothian.
By G. HAYTER. *Signed.*

**951.** ROBERT SOUTHEY, Poet and Writer, 1774-1843.
By ANDREW ROBERTSON.

**952.** MISS FANNY KEMBLE (MRS. BUTLER), Actress and Authoress, 1809—living.
By C. HAYTER. *Signed.*

**953.** PRINCE EUGENE OF SAVOY, General, 1663-1736.
*Signed* C.T.

**954.** JOHN LAW of Lauriston, Financial Projector, 1671-1729. Enamel.
By G. EMRICH. *Signed.*

957. LOUIS XVI. OF FRANCE, 1774-1793.
By RICHAULT.

958. MARIE ANTOINETTE OF AUSTRIA, Queen of Louis XVI. of France, 1755-1793.

959. NAPOLEON I., when General Bonaparte, 1769-1821.
By J. B. ISABEY.

960. NAPOLEON I., 1769-1821. In Coronation robes.

961. EMPRESS JOSEPHINE, 1st wife of Napoleon I., 1763-1814.

962. EMPRESS MARIE LOUISE, daughter of Francis I. of Austria, 2nd wife of Napoleon I. 1791-1847.
By AGRICOLA.

963. NAPOLEON I., 1769-1821.
By J. PARENT. *Signed.*

964. FREDERICK II., "THE GREAT," KING OF PRUSSIA, 1712-1786.

965. HESTER JANE, 2nd wife of R. B. SHERIDAN.
By S. SHELLEY.

966. ELIZA FARREN, COUNTESS OF DERBY, Actress, 1759-1829.
By S. SHELLEY.

967. MRS. SIDDONS, Actress, 1755-1831.
By S. SHELLEY.

968. SAMUEL SHELLEY, Miniature Painter, 1750-1808.
By HIMSELF.

969. JOHN FITZGIBBON, EARL OF CLARE, Lord Chancellor of Ireland, 1749-1802.
By J. SMART, 1767. *Signed.*

970. SHOLTO CHARLES, EARL OF MORTON, 1732-1774, and KATHERINE, COUNTESS OF MORTON.
By J. SMART, 1769. *Signed.*

971. ADMIRAL SIR C. SAUNDERS, K.C.B.
   By J. SMART, 1778. *Signed.*

972. RIGHT HON. RICHARD BRINSLEY SHERIDAN, Dramatist and Statesman, 1751-1816.
   By J. SMART, 1785. *Signed.*

973. RIGHT HON. JOHN PHILPOT CURRAN, Advocate and Politician.
   By J. SMART, 1788. *Signed.*

974. CHARLES, 1ST MARQUESS CORNWALLIS, General and Governor-General of India, 1738-1805.
   By J. SMART, 1792. *Signed.* Painted in India.

975. ADMIRAL SIR EDWARD PELLEW, 1ST VISCOUNT EXMOUTH, 1757-1833.
   By J. SMART.

976. ANGELICA MARIA CATHERINE KAUFFMANN, R.A., Painter, 1740-1807.
   By HERSELF. *Signed.*

977. FRANCESCO BARTOLOZZI, R.A., Engraver, 1725-1815.

978. GEORGE I., 1714-1727.
   By J. A. ARLAUD.

979. SOPHIA DOROTHEA, Queen of George I., 1662-1726.

980. FREDERICK LEWIS, PRINCE OF WALES, eldest son of George II., 1707-1751.

981. GEORGE III., 1760-1820. Enamel.

982. QUEEN CHARLOTTE, Consort of George III., 1744-1818. Enamel.
   By H. BONE, R.A., 1801. *Signed.*

983. GEORGE IV. AS PRINCE OF WALES, 1762-1830.
   By R. COSWAY, R.A.

984. PRINCESS CHARLOTTE, daughter of George IV., 1796-1817.

985. ADOLPHUS FREDERICK, DUKE OF CAMBRIDGE, 1774-1850. Enamel.
   By H. BONE, R.A., after a miniature by Saunders, 1814. *Signed.*

986. GEORGE IV. AS PRINCE REGENT, 1762-1830.
By J. G. P. FISCHER. *Signed.*

987. FREDERICK, DUKE OF YORK AND ALBANY, 1763-1827.

988. EDWARD, DUKE OF KENT, father of Her Majesty Queen Victoria, 1767-1820.

989. QUEEN ADELAIDE, Consort of William IV., 1792-1849.
By S. RAVEN. *Signed.*

990. WILLIAM IV., 1830-1837. Enamel.
By H. BONE, R.A., 1831. *Signed.*

991. WILLIAM IV. AS DUKE OF CLARENCE, 1755-1837.
By A. ROBERTSON.

992. PRINCESS SOPHIA, daughter of George III., 1777-1848.

993. SIR JOSHUA REYNOLDS (?), P.R.A., 1723-1792.
By HIMSELF. On the back the initial " R " designed in floral mosaic.

994. SIR THOMAS LAWRENCE, P.R.A., 1769-1830.
By A. ROBERTSON.

995. JOSEPH ADDISON, Statesman and Essayist, 1672-1719.

996. ROBERT HARLEY, 1ST EARL OF OXFORD, Statesman, 1661-1724.

997. JOHN, 2ND DUKE OF ARGYLL, Commander and Ambassador, 1678-1743.

998. HAMLET WINSTANLEY, Painter and Engraver, 1700-1761. Oil.
By HIMSELF.

999. SIMON FRASER, LORD LOVAT, Scottish Chieftain, 1668-1747. Enamel.

1000. FRANCIS ATTERBURY, Bishop of Rochester, Jacobite, 1662-1733.

1001. WILLIAM PULTENEY, 1ST EARL OF BATH, Statesman, 1682-1764.

1002. REV. SAMUEL WESLEY, Poet, and father of John Wesley, 1662-1735.

1003. JOSEPH ADDISON, Statesman and Essayist, 1672-1719. Enamel.
By C. F. ZINCKE.

1004. JOHN, 1ST DUKE OF MARLBOROUGH, General and Statesman, 1650-1722. Enamel.
By C F. ZINCKE.

1005. CHARLES, 3RD EARL OF PETERBOROUGH, General and Statesman, 1658-1735. Enamel.

1006. SIR RICHARD HOARE, Lord Mayor of London during the Rebellion of 1745. Enamel.
By C. F. ZINCKE.

1007. SIR ROBERT WALPOLE, 1ST EARL OF ORFORD, K.G., Statesman, 1676-1745. Enamel.
By C. F. ZINCKE.

1008. JAMES BUTLER, DUKE OF ORMONDE, General, 1665-1745. Enamel.
By C. F. ZINCKE.

1009. HENRY ST. JOHN, VISCOUNT BOLINGBROKE, Statesman, 1678-1751. Enamel.
By C. F. ZINCKE.

1010. ADMIRAL EDWARD VERNON, 1684-1757. Enamel.
By C. F. ZINCKE.

1011. CHARLES SPENCER, 2ND DUKE OF MARLBOROUGH, 1706-1758. Enamel.

1012. MARIA GUNNING, COUNTESS OF COVENTRY, celebrated for her beauty, d. 1760. Enamel.
By G. SPENCER. *Signed.*

1013. RICHARD, 1ST EARL TEMPLE, Statesman, 1711-1779. Enamel.
By C. F. ZINCKE.

NORTH GALLERY.] *Miniatures, Relics, and Plate.* 173

**1016.** WILLIAM PITT, 1ST EARL OF CHATHAM, Statesman, 1708-1778. Enamel.

**1017.** CHARLES WATSON WENTWORTH, 2ND MARQUESS OF ROCKINGHAM, Prime Minister, 1730-1782. Enamel.
W. B., 1786. *Signed.*

**1018.** ELIZABETH CHUDLEIGH, DUCHESS OF KINGSTON, 1720-1788. Enamel.

**1019.** ELIZABETH GUNNING, DUCHESS OF HAMILTON AND ARGYLL, d. 1790. Enamel.

**1020.** JAMES BOSWELL, Biographer of Johnson, 1740-1795. Enamel.
By N. HONE, R.A., 1763. *Signed.*

**1021.** HORACE WALPOLE, 4TH EARL OF ORFORD, 1717-1797. Enamel.
By N. HONE, R.A., 1760. *Signed.*

**1022.** GEORGE BRIDGES, LORD RODNEY, Admiral, 1718-1792. Enamel.
By C. F. ZINCKE.

**1023.** CHARLES COMPTON, 9TH EARL AND 1ST MARQUESS OF NORTHAMPTON, 1760-1828. Enamel.
By C. F. ZINCKE.

**1024.** SIR JAMES LOWTHER, 1ST EARL OF LONSDALE, 1736-1802. Enamel.
By PERRACHE, 1789. *Signed.*

**1025.** THOMAS DAWSON, 1ST LORD DARTREY AND 1ST VISCOUNT CREMORNE, d. 1813. Enamel.
By J. H. HURTER, 1784. *Signed.*

**1026.** ANNE HILL, COUNTESS OF MORNINGTON, mother of Arthur, Duke of Wellington, d. 1831.
By H. EDRIDGE, R.A.

**1027.** ALEXANDER, 4TH DUKE OF GORDON, 1743-1827.
By W. GRIMALDI, 1805. *Signed.*

**1028.** GEORGIANA SPENCER, DUCHESS OF DEVONSHIRE, 1757-1806.
By A. PLIMER, 1785. *Signed.*

1029. MRS. GARRICK, JUN., wife of Garrick's nephew.
By R. COSWAY, R.A., 1795. *Signed.*

1030. MRS. MARY ROBINSON AS "PERDITA," Actress, 1758-1800.
By O. HUMPHRY, R.A.

1031. HARRIET MELLON, DUCHESS OF ST. ALBANS, d. 1837.

1032. QUEEN ADELAIDE, Consort of William IV., 1792-1849.
By H. EDRIDGE, A.R.A.

1033. MRS. SIDDONS, Actress, 1755-1831.
By R. COSWAY, R.A.

1034. MISS SIDDONS, daughter of the actress.
By R. COSWAY, R.A., 1800. *Signed.*

1035. SIR WILLIAM MUSGRAVE, BART.
By R. COSWAY, R.A., 1792.

1036. JOHN RUSSELL, 6TH DUKE OF BEDFORD, 1766-1839.
By S. COLLINS, 1786. *Signed.*

1037. JOHN HORNE TOOKE, M.P., Political Writer, &c., 1736-1812.
By S. COLLINS, 1786. *Signed.*

1038. GEORGE, 2ND MARQUESS TOWNSHEND, 1755-1811.
By S. COTES.

1039. RIGHT HON. SPENCER PERCEVAL, Prime Minister, 1762-1812.
By W. WOOD.

1040. EDWARD GIBBON, Historian, 1737-1794.

1041. REV. WILLIAM DODD, LL.D.(?), Popular Preacher and Writer, 1729-1777.

1042. CATHERINE CLIVE, Actress, 1711-1785.
By P. C. *Signed.*

NORTH GALLERY.] *Miniatures, Relics, and Plate.*

**1043.** EVA MARIA VIOLETTE, MRS. GARRICK, wife of David Garrick, 1724-1823.
By L. SULLIVAN, 1761. *Signed.*

**1044.** MRS. CATHERINE GORDON, BYRON, mother of Lord Byron, poet.
By H. BONE, R.A.

**1045.** GENERAL SIR HENRY CLINTON, commanded in America, d. 1795.
By R. COSWAY, R.A.

**1046.** GEORGE, 3RD LORD WALSINGHAM, 1776-1831.
By R. COSWAY, R.A.

**1047.** ROBERT, 1ST LORD CLIVE, Governor-General of India, 1725-1774.

**1048.** ISABELLA GORDON, COUNTESS OF CARLISLE, d. 1795.

**1049.** MRS. SIDDONS AND CHILD, 1755-1831.
By G. CHINNERY, R.H.A. *Signed.*

**1050.** DAVID GARRICK AS "KITELY" IN *Every Man in his Humour*, 1716-1779.
After REYNOLDS.

**1051.** DR. THOMAS AUGUSTINE ARNE, Musical Composer, 1710-1778.

**1052.** CHARLES KEMBLE, Actor, 1775-1854.

**1053.** DAVID GARRICK, Actor, 1716-1779.
By G. ENGLEHEART.

**1054.** MRS. SIDDONS, Actress, 1755-1831.
By W. HAMILTON, R.A.

**1055.** LADY CHARLOTTE MURRAY. Beethoven's monogram, set in brilliants, on the reverse.
By STOVELY, of Vienna. *Signed.*

**1056.** FREDERICK, LORD NORTH, 2ND EARL OF GUILDFORD (?) Statesman, 1732-1792.

**1057.** MISS DUNCAN, AFTERWARDS MRS. DAVIDSON, Actress.
By J. HARGREAVES, 1809.

**1058.** SIR DAVID BAIRD, BART., General, 1757-1829.
By A. ROBERTSON.

**1059.** ARTHUR WELLESLEY, 1ST DUKE OF WELLINGTON, 1769-1852. Enamel.
By H. BONE, R.A., after LAWRENCE. *Signed.*

**1060.** ARTHUR WELLESLEY, 1ST DUKE OF WELLINGTON, 1769-1852. Painted at Paris.
By J. B. ISABEY. *Signed.*

**1061.** GENERAL SIR JOHN MOORE, 1761-1809.
By F. FERRIÈRE. *Signed.*

**1062.** HORATIO, VISCOUNT NELSON, Admiral, 1758-1805. Enamel.
By H. BONE, R.A., after ABBOT, 1826. *Signed.*

**1063.** ROBERT, VISCOUNT CASTLEREAGH, 2ND MARQUESS OF LONDONDERRY, 1769-1822.

**1064.** ADAM DUNCAN, VISCOUNT DUNCAN, Admiral, 1731-1804.

**1065.** ROBERT BANKS JENKINSON, 2ND EARL OF LIVERPOOL, 1770-1828.

**1066.** CHARLES JAMES FOX, Statesman, 1749-1806.
By O. HUMPHRY (?), after SIR J. REYNOLDS.

**1067.** HENRIETTA, DUCHESS OF MARLBOROUGH, daughter of 1st Duke, d. 1733. Plumbago.
By T. FORSTER.

**1068.** LORD BYRON, Poet, 1788-1824. Given by himself to R. H. Hoppner, British Consul at Venice.

**1069.** LADY MARY WORTLEY MONTAGU, Authoress, 1690-1762.
By B. LENS, 1726. *Signed.*

**1070.** GEORGE WASHINGTON, American General, 1732-1799. Pastel.

**1071.** SAMUEL PROUT, Water-Colour Painter, 1783-1852.
By FISCHER.

## CASE K—North Gallery.

### MINIATURES.

### LENT BY J. LUMSDEN PROPERT, ESQ., M.D.

1072. ERNEST AUGUSTUS, DUKE OF BRUNSWICK LUNEBURG, father of George I., 1692-1698.

1073. GEORGIANA SPENCER, DUCHESS OF DEVONSHIRE, 1757-1806.
By H. BONE, R.A.

1074. CATHERINE, DUCHESS OF BUCKINGHAM, DAUGHTER OF JAMES II., AND HER SON.
By C. F. ZINCKE, 1726. *Signed.*

1075. MRS. SIDDONS, Actress, 1755-1831.
By HORACE HONE, 1790. *Signed.*

1076. JOHN KEMBLE, Actor, 1757-1823.
By HORACE HONE, 1790. *Signed.*

1077. CHARLES MORDAUNT, 3RD EARL OF PETERBOROUGH, 1658-1735.
By GONZALES.

1078. NAPOLEON I., 1769-1821, AND JOSEPHINE, 1763-1814.
By L. F. AUBREY. *Signed.*

1079. EMPRESSES JOSEPHINE AND MARIE LOUISE, wives of Napoleon I.
By J. B. ISABEY.

1080. ANTONIO CANOVA, Sculptor, 1775-1822.
By F. H. FÜGER.

1081. ROBERT BURNS, Poet, 1759-1796.

1082. PRINCESS ELIZABETH, daughter of George III., 1770-1829.
By J. SMART. *Signed.*

1083. ELIZABETH GUNNING, DUCHESS OF HAMILTON AND ARGYLL, 1734-1790.
By N. PLIMER.

1084. GEORGE IV., as an Infant, 1762-1830.
By R. COSWAY, R.A.

1085. GEORGE IV., as Regent, 1762-1830.
By R. COSWAY, R.A.

1086. ELEANOR, COUNTESS OF EGLINTON, wife of Hugh, 12th Earl.
By R. COSWAY, R.A.

1087. MARIA LINLEY (MRS. RICHARD TICKELL).
By R. COSWAY, R.A.

1088. JOHN KEMBLE, as Hamlet, 1757-1823.
By R. COSWAY, R.A.

1089. ELIZABETH MILBANKE, LADY MELBOURNE.
By R. COSWAY, R.A.

1090. RICHARD COSWAY, Miniature Painter, 1740-1821.
By HIMSELF.

1091. MRS. FITZHERBERT, 1756-1837.
By R. COSWAY, R.A.

1092. ELIZABETH, DUCHESS OF GORDON, 1774-1864.
By R. COSWAY, R.A.

1093. SIR E. PAGET.
By R. COSWAY, R.A.

1094. LADY E. PAGET.
By R. COSWAY, R.A.

1095. MR. MOFFATT.
By R. COSWAY, R.A. *Signed.*

1096. MRS. MOFFATT.
By R. COSWAY, R.A. *Signed.*

1097. MISS NEWCOME (LADY GARDINER).
By R. COSWAY, R.A.

1098. CHARLES JENKINSON, 1ST EARL OF LIVERPOOL, Statesman, 1727-1808.
By R. COSWAY, R.A.

1099. HON. ANNE DAWSON-DAMER, Artist, 1748-1828.
By R. COSWAY, R.A.

1100. LADY FOX STRANGWAYS.
By R. COSWAY, R.A.

1101. ELIZABETH, LADY HOLLAND, 1770-1845.
By R. COSWAY, R.A.

1102. MISS GUTHRIE.
By R. COSWAY, R.A.

1103. ELIZABETH, DUCHESS OF SUTHERLAND, 1765-1839.
By R. COSWAY, R.A.

1104. HENRY, 2ND EARL OF CARNARVON, 1772-1833.
By R. COSWAY, R.A.

1105. CHARLES MORDAUNT.
By R. COSWAY, R.A.

1106. GEORGE, 3RD LORD WALSINGHAM, 1776-1831.
By R. COSWAY, R.A.

1107. LADY HAMILTON, 1761-1815.
By N. PLIMER.

1108. REBECCA BOWLES, LADY NORTHWICK, wife of 1st Baron.
By N. PLIMER.

1109. ANNE HORATIA WALDEGRAVE, LADY HUGH SEYMOUR.
By N. PLIMER.

1110. ANNE, DAUGHTER OF JOHN RUSHOUT, 1ST LORD NORTHWICK, d. 1849.
By N. PLIMER.

1111. CATHERINE SHORTER, LADY WALPOLE, first wife of Sir Robert Walpole.
Lent by MRS. CAMPBELL JOHNSTON.

1112. JOHN, 2ND DUKE OF ARGYLL AND GREENWICH, Field-Marshal, 1678-1743.
By C. F. ZINCKE.   Lent by MRS. CAMPBELL JOHNSTON.

1113. JOHN, 2ND DUKE OF ARGYLL AND GREENWICH, Field-Marshal, 1678-1743.
Lent by MRS. CAMPBELL JOHNSTON.

1114. PEG WOFFINGTON, Actress, 1720-1760.
Lent by MRS. CAMPBELL JOHNSTON.

1115. CASE OF MINIATURES of George, 3rd Duke of Marlborough (d. 1758); his wife, Elizabeth, daughter of Thomas, Lord Trevor, and their Children.
Lent by The DUKE OF MARLBOROUGH.

1116. SIR ISAAC NEWTON, Philosopher, 1642-1727.
By D. E. LOS.   Lent by The MARQUESS OF BRISTOL.

1117. STEPHEN FOX, 1ST EARL OF ILCHESTER, 1704-1776.
Lent by The MARQUESS OF BRISTOL.

1118. HENRY FOX, 1ST LORD HOLLAND, Statesman, 1705-1774.
Lent by The MARQUESS OF BRISTOL.

1119. JOHN AUGUSTUS, LORD HERVEY, d. 1803.
By R. COSWAY, R.A.   Lent by The MARQUESS OF BRISTOL.

1120. MARY (LEPEL) LADY HERVEY, 1700-1768.
Lent by The MARQUESS OF BRISTOL.

1121. AUGUSTUS JOHN, 3RD EARL OF BRISTOL, 1724-1779.
By R. COSWAY, R.A.   Lent by The MARQUESS OF BRISTOL.

**1122.** GEORGE II., 1727-1760.
　　　　　　　　　　　　　　　　Lent by The MARQUESS OF BRISTOL.

**1123.** QUEEN CAROLINE, wife of George II., 1682-1737.
　　　　　　　　　　　　　　　　Lent by The MARQUESS OF BRISTOL.

**1124.** JOHN AUGUSTUS, Lord Hervey, d. 1803.
　　　By R. COSWAY, R.A.　　　Lent by The MARQUESS OF BRISTOL.

**1125.** QUEEN CAROLINE, wife of George II., 1682-1737.
　　　　　　　　　　　　　　　　Lent by The MARQUESS OF BRISTOL.

**1126.** PRINCESS AUGUSTA, daughter of George III., 1768-1840.
　　　By G. SPENCER.　　　Lent by The MARQUESS OF BRISTOL.

**1127.** PORTRAIT OF A GENTLEMAN.
　　　By R. COSWAY, R.A.　　　Lent by H. H. P. COTTON, ESQ.

**1128.** PORTRAIT OF A GENTLEMAN.
　　　By R. COSWAY, R.A.　　　Lent by H. H. P. COTTON, ESQ.


## *LENT BY THE EARL OF DARTREY.*

**1129.** THOMAS, 1ST LORD DARTREY AND VISCOUNT CREMORNE, d. 1813. Enamel.

**1130.** ANNE, VISCOUNTESS PRIMROSE, daughter of Drelincourt, Dean of Armagh. Enamel.
　　　By J. H. HURTER, 1785.

**1131.** QUEEN CHARLOTTE, 1744-1818. Enamel.
　　　By J. F. C. HURTER, after GAINSBOROUGH.

**1132.** LADY ANNE FERMOR. Enamel. Inscribed on back "Lady Anne Dawson."
　　　By J. F. C. HURTER, 1755.

**1133.** RICHARD, LORD ROKEBY, Archbishop of Armagh, 1709-1794. Enamel.
　　　By J. H. HURTER, after REYNOLDS.

1134. HON. RICHARD DAWSON, d. 1807. Enamel.
By J. H. HURTER, 1783.

1135. GEORGE III., 1760-1820. Enamel, dated 1781.
By J. H. HURTER.

1136. LADY ANNE FERMOR, wife of Thomas, 1st Lord Dartrey and Viscount Cremorne, d. 1769. Enamel.
By J. A. SEWE, 1754.

1137. PHILADELPHIA FREAME, LADY DARTREY, granddaughter of William Penn. Enamel.
By J. H. HURTER, 1780.

1138. THOMAS, 1ST LORD DARTREY AND VISCOUNT CREMORNE, d. 1813. Enamel.
By J. F. C. HURTER.

1139. JOSEPH ADDISON, Author, &c., 1672-1789. Enamel.
By C. F. ZINCKE.

1140. PHILADELPHIA FREAME, LADY DARTREY, granddaughter of William Penn. Enamel.
By H. SPICER.

1141. JOHN HENRY HURTER, Miniature painter. Born 1734. Enamel.
By HIMSELF, 1782.

1142. LADY ANNE WHALEY, daughter of John, Earl of Clanwilliam, d. 1826.

1143. "THE COALITION." Half-masks of Lord North and C. J. Fox. From Sayer's Caricatures. Enamel.

1144. RIGHT HON. WARREN HASTINGS, 1733-1818. An Unfinished Miniature on Ivory made on the Voyage to India.
By OZIAS HUMPHRY, R.A.   Lent by The REV. JAMES BECK.

1145. THE HON. MRS. TWISTLETON.
By SARAH MEE.   Lent by The REV. JAMES BECK.

1146. PORTRAIT OF A LADY. Dated 1786.
By A. PLIMER.   Lent by The REV. JAMES BECK.

**1147.** Ernest Augustus, Elector of Hanover, father of George I.
By Artaud.                    Lent by The Rev. James Beck.

**1148.** Portrait of a Lady.
By G. Chinnery. *Signed.*     Lent by The Rev. James Beck.

**1149.** Portrait of a Gentleman.
By G. Engleheart.             Lent by The Rev. James Beck.

**1150.** Richard Nash ("Beau Nash"), d. 1761. Oil.
                              Lent by The Rev. James Beck.

**1151.** Portrait of a Gentleman. Dated 1798.
By Mrs. Hill.                 Lent by The Rev. James Beck.

**1152.** Sir Francis Burdett, Bart., M.P., 1770-1844.
By R. Cosway, R.A.            Lent by The Baroness Burdett-Coutts.

**1153.** Harriet Mellon, Duchess of St. Albans, Actress, d. 1837.
By J. S. Stump.               Lent by The Baroness Burdett-Coutts.

**1154.** Sir Francis Burdett, Bart., M.P., 1770-1844.
By R. Cosway, R.A.            Lent by The Baroness Burdett-Coutts.

**1155.** Napoleon I., 1769-1821.
By J. B. Isabey.              Lent by The Baroness Burdett-Coutts.

**1156.** Sophia Coutts, Lady Burdett.
By R. Cosway, R.A.            Lent by The Baroness Burdett-Coutts.

**1157.** Susan Coutts, Countess of Guildford, and Frances Coutts, Marchioness of Bute.
                              Lent by The Baroness Burdett-Coutts.

**1158.** Arthur Wellesley, 1st Duke of Wellington, K.G., 1769-1852.
By R. Thorburn, A.R.A.        Lent by The Baroness Burdett-Coutts.

**1159.** Susan Coutts, Countess of Guildford, and Sophia Coutts, Lady Burdett.
                              Lent by The Baroness Burdett-Coutts.

**1160.** JAMES CRAGGS, SEN., M.P., Postmaster-General. Enamel.
Lent by The BARONESS BURDETT-COUTTS.

**1161.** MRS. RICHARD ELIOT, daughter of J. Craggs, Jun. Enamel.
Lent by The BARONESS BURDETT-COUTTS.

**1162.** JAMES CRAGGS, JUN., Statesman, 1686-1721. Enamel.
By C. F. ZINCKE. Lent by The BARONESS BURDETT-COUTTS.

**1163.** THOMAS COUTTS, Banker, 1735-1822. Dated 1816.
By J. S. STUMP. Lent by The BARONESS BURDETT-COUTTS.

**1164.** GEORGE FREDERICK HANDEL, Musician, 1684-1759. Enamel.
By C. F. ZINCKE. Lent by The BARONESS BURDETT-COUTTS.

**1165.** THE REV. JOHN WESLEY, 1703-1791. Enamel.
By W. GRIMALDI. Lent by The BARONESS BURDETT-COUTTS.

*LENT BY SIR JULIAN GOLDSMID, BART., M.P.*

**1166.** CAPTAIN J. WESLEY WRIGHT, R.N., 1769-1805.

**1167.** MRS. ROXBURGH.

**1168.** LADY CATHERINE POWLETT, DUCHESS OF CLEVELAND, d. 1807.

**1169.** ANN RUSHOUT, daughter of John, 1st Lord Northwick, d. 1849.
By N. PLIMER.

**1170.** PORTRAIT OF A LADY, unknown.

**1171.** PORTRAIT OF A LADY, unknown; hair and initials at back.

**1172.** ANN RUSHOUT, daughter of John, 1st Lord Northwick, d. 1849.

**1173.** MRS. MARY ROBINSON, 1758-1800.
By R. COSWAY, R.A.

NORTH GALLERY.] *Miniatures, Relics, and Plate.*

**1174.** ELIZABETH FITZCLARENCE, COUNTESS OF ERROL, d. 1836.
By R. COSWAY, R.A.

**1175.** LADY ELIZABETH CAMPBELL.
By R. COSWAY, R.A.

**1176.** PORTRAIT OF A LADY, unknown ; hair at back.

**1177.** PORTRAIT OF A GENTLEMAN, unknown ; hair at back.

**1178.** PORTRAIT OF A BOY.
By R. COSWAY, R.A.

**1179.** PORTRAIT OF A LADY, unknown ; hair at back.

---

**1180.** DR. CHARLES BURNEY, F.R.S., 1726-1815.
Lent by The VEN. ARCHDEACON BURNEY.

**1181.** ARTHUR, MARQUESS OF WELLINGTON, afterwards Duke, K.G., 1769-1852.
By T. HEAPHY, Sen.  Lent by HENRY WEIGALL, ESQ.

**1182.** CATHERINE HYDE, DUCHESS OF QUEENSBERRY, 1700-1777.
Lent by HENRY WEIGALL, ESQ.

**1183.** GEORGE IV., 1820-1830.
By R. COSWAY, R.A.  Lent by HENRY WEIGALL, ESQ.

**1184.** ANNE, wife of Colonel Sir Henry Fane, G.C.B.
By R. COSWAY, R.A.  Lent by HENRY WEIGALL, ESQ.

**1185.** MARIA ELEANOR FORBES, COUNTESS OF CLARENDON, d. 1844.
By R. COSWAY, R.A.  Lent by HENRY WEIGALL, ESQ.

**1186.** THE HON. COLONEL FANE, afterwards Sir Henry, G.C.B., 1778-1840, Commander-in-Chief in India.
By R. COSWAY, R.A.  Lent by HENRY WEIGALL, ESQ.

**1187.** SIR ARTHUR WELLESLEY, G.C.B., afterwards Duke of Wellington, 1769-1852.
By R. COSWAY, R.A.  Lent by HENRY WEIGALL, ESQ.

**1188.** CATHERINE ELIZABETH FORBES, COUNTESS OF MORNINGTON, 1760–1851.
By R. COSWAY, R.A.        Lent by HENRY WEIGALL, ESQ.

**1189.** THE HON. WILLIAM WELLESLEY, afterwards 3rd Earl of Mornington, d. 1845.
By R. COSWAY, R.A.        Lent by HENRY WEIGALL, ESQ.

**1190.** PRINCESS CHARLOTTE OF WALES, 1796-1817.
By STEWARD.        Lent by HENRY WEIGALL, ESQ.

**1191.** RICHARD, MARQUESS WELLESLEY, K.G., Governor-General of India, 1760-1842.
Lent by The DUKE OF LEEDS.

**1192.** ARTHUR, DUKE OF WELLINGTON, K.G., 1769-1852.
Lent by The DUKE OF LEEDS.

**1193.** ARTHUR, DUKE OF WELLINGTON, K.G., 1769-1852. Painted at Madrid in 1812.
By BAZIL.        Lent by ALFRED STOWE, ESQ.

**1194.** GEORGE IV. as Prince Regent, 1762-1830.
By R. COSWAY, R.A.        Lent by The HON. GERALD PONSONBY.

**1195.** GEORGE IV., 1820-1830, set in pearls.
By R. COSWAY, R.A.        Lent by EDWARD JOSEPH, ESQ.

**1196.** THE HON. MRS. PHIPPS, set in diamonds.
By R. COSWAY, R.A.        Lent by EDWARD JOSEPH, ESQ.

**1197.** RICHARD COSWAY, R.A., Miniature Painter, 1740-1821 ; set in diamonds. *Signed*.
By HIMSELF.        Lent by EDWARD JOSEPH, ESQ.

**1198.** RT. HON. WILLIAM PITT, Statesman, 1759-1806.
By A. PLIMER.        Lent by EDWARD JOSEPH, ESQ.

**1199.** ELIZABETH GUNNING, DUCHESS OF HAMILTON, d. 1790.
By R. COSWAY, R.A.        Lent by EDWARD JOSEPH, ESQ.

**1200.** QUEEN CHARLOTTE, 1744-1818 ; presented by the Queen to Caroline Willis with a service of plate in 1786.
Lent by EDWARD JOSEPH, ESQ.

## CASE L—North Gallery.

### RELICS OF NELSON AND WELLINGTON.

1201. GOLD PENCIL-CASE used by the Duke of Wellington during the Peninsular War and at Waterloo.
Lent by GERALD E. WELLESLEY, ESQ.

1202. THE DUKE OF WELLINGTON'S EYE-GLASSES.
Lent by HENRY WEIGALL, ESQ.

1203. THE DUKE OF WELLINGTON'S OWN WATERLOO MEDAL.
Lent by HENRY WEIGALL, ESQ.

1204. LOCK OF THE DUKE OF WELLINGTON'S HAIR, in silver box.
Lent by The HON. MRS. MAXWELL-SCOTT.

1205. RING FOR SNAFFLE AND BRIDLE of the Duke of Wellington's horse Copenhagen.
Lent by The BARONESS BURDETT-COUTTS.

1206. CRIMSON NETTING, made and presented by the ladies of Madrid to the Duke of Wellington for his horse Copenhagen.
Lent by The BARONESS BURDETT-COUTTS.

1207. PAIR OF PISTOLS carried by the Duke of Wellington during the Peninsular War.
Lent by The BARONESS BURDETT-COUTTS.

1208. TEA-POT used by the Duke of Wellington during his campaigns.
Lent by W. R. HARCOURT GWYN, ESQ.

1209. SWORD worn by the Duke of Wellington at Waterloo.
Lent by The DUKE OF WELLINGTON.

1210. FIELD-GLASS used by the Duke of Wellington at Waterloo.
Lent by The DUKE OF WELLINGTON.

1211. CLOAK worn by the Duke of Wellington at Waterloo.
Lent by The DUKE OF WELLINGTON.

1212. LOCK OF LORD NELSON'S HAIR, in silver box.
Lent by The HON. MRS. MAXWELL-SCOTT.

1213. LORD NELSON'S TELESCOPE.
Lent by The EARL NELSON.

1214. LORD NELSON'S WALKING STICK.
Lent by The EARL NELSON.

1215. WATCH, left by Lord Nelson to Captain William Locker.
Lent by The EARL NELSON.

1216. BOX with miniature, containing hair of Lord Nelson.
Lent by The EARL NELSON.

1217. MEDAL, commemorating the Battle of the Nile, 1st August, 1798, which belonged to Lord Nelson.
Lent by The EARL NELSON.

1218. A MODEL made from the wood of the mast of the *Victory*, showing all splices and injuries sustained at Trafalgar.
Lent by The EARL NELSON.

1219. GOLD RING with Cameo of Lord Nelson.
Lent by HENRY H. P. COTTON, ESQ.

1220. SASH, worn by General Wolfe at Quebec.
Lent by The OFFICERS OF THE 1ST LANCASHIRE FUSILIERS.

1221. SNUFF-BOX, tortoiseshell, mounted in silver, formerly belonging to General Wolfe.
Lent by The HON. MRS. FETHERSTONHAUGH.

1221a. LOCKS OF LADY HAMILTON'S HAIR, with writing.
Lent by ALFRED MORRISON, ESQ.

1221b. SEAL OF LORD NELSON.
Lent by The EARL NELSON.

## CASE M—North Gallery.

### HISTORICAL COLLECTION OF WATCHES, FROM THE 16th TO THE 19th CENTURY.

This series of Watches is exhibited to show the gradual development of the art of Watchmaking, specially as regards the 17th and 18th centuries. A few specimens of an earlier period have been introduced in order to illustrate the succession of the various forms. In the 16th century Watches were made in all imaginable shapes and sizes. In the form of Eggs, called Nuremberg Eggs—that city being the chief place of manufacture —of Crosses and Crucifixes, called Abbess's Watches, of a Death's Head, of Flowers, Shells, &c. During the early part of the 17th century nearly all these quaint and *bizarre* forms passed out of fashion, at which time watchmakers seem to have devoted their attention chiefly to the compact character of their work. The art of the goldsmith and the enameller however was still exercised in the manufacture of watches, and many designs in *repoussé* are of excellent workmanship and the enamelling and jewellery are of the highest order. Many watches of the last century were of base metal, these are known by the appellation of "Pinchbecks," the name being taken from the manufacturer, John Pinchbeck, a "toyman" who lived in the Strand.

## CASE N.—North Room.

### PLATE.

1222. LARGE SILVER CUP, presented to Lord Nelson by the Governor and Company of Merchants of England trading in the Levant Seas, in commemoration of the Battle of the Nile.

Round the rim of the cup are engraved the names of the French ships captured or destroyed in the battle.

It was left in the Admiral's will to his eldest sister, Mrs. Bolton, grandmother of the present owner.

*Lent by* The EARL NELSON.

1223. LARGE SHELL-SHAPED CAKE-BASKET, elaborately pierced, the handle formed by a female figure.
Lent by ASHER WERTHEIMER, ESQ.

1224. TWO SILVER TANKARDS from the Duke of Sussex's sale. German.
Lent by H. L. BISCHOFFSHEIM, ESQ.

1225. LOVING CUP.
Lent by the MASTER AND WARDEN OF THE SALTERS' COMPANY.

1226. PAIR OF SILVER CANDLE-STICKS (boys supporting the sockets), which formerly belonged to Thomas, 1st Earl of Mornington. Hall-mark.
Lent by H. WEIGALL, ESQ.

1227. PAIR OF SMALL SILVER CANDLE-STICKS, with monogram and crests of Wellesley Pole, Mornington, and the Duke of Wellington. Hall-mark.
Lent by H. WEIGALL, ESQ.

1228. SMALL SILVER WAITER, which formerly belonged to Thomas, 1st Earl of Clarendon, and afterwards to Richard, 2nd Earl of Mornington, with their crests. Hall-mark.
Lent by H. WEIGALL, ESQ.

1229. SILVER COFFEE-POT, which belonged to Thomas, 1st Earl of Clarendon, with his crest. Hall-mark.
Lent by H. WEIGALL, ESQ.

1230. TWO SILVER-GILT CHRISTENING SPOONS. London mark for 1739.
Lent by H. L. BISCHOFFSHEIM, ESQ.

1231. FOUR LARGE CANDELABRA, for two lights.
Lent by ASHER WERTHEIMER, ESQ.

1232. TWO LARGE SAUCE-BOATS, with griffin-shaped handles.
Lent by ASHER WERTHEIMER, ESQ.

1233. SILVER SOUP TUREEN, which formerly belonged to Richard, 2nd Earl of Mornington, and Arthur, 1st Duke of Wellington, with their crests. Hall-mark.
Lent by H. WEIGALL, ESQ.

1234. SILVER BREAD BASKET, presented to the 1st Lord Exmouth after the Battle of Algiers.
Lent by E. JOSEPH, ESQ.

*Miniatures, Relics, and Plate.*

**1235.** FOUR SMALL CIRCULAR SILVER SALT-CELLARS. Hall-mark 1731. By Paul de Lamerie. Lent by The LORD HOTHAM.

**1236.** A SILVER EPERGNE, with the Royal Arms. Hall-mark 1729. By P. Crespein.
Lent by The LORD HOTHAM.

**1237.** A LARGE TWO-HANDLED SILVER CUP AND COVER, chased. Hall-mark 1720. By Paul de Lamerie. Lent by The LORD HOTHAM.

**1238.** PAIR OF SILVER SALT-CELLARS, which formerly belonged to Richard, 2nd Earl of Mornington, with his crest. Hall-mark. Lent by H. WEIGALL, ESQ.

**1239.** PAIR OF SILVER SAUCE-BOATS, which formerly belonged to Arthur, 1st Duke of Wellington, with his crest. Hall-mark.
Lent by H. WEIGALL, ESQ.

**1240.** GOLD CHRISTENING CUP, presented by George II. to his godson George, 2nd Viscount Midleton, in 1732.
Lent by The VISCOUNT MIDLETON.

**1241.** GOLD CUP AND COVER, the gift of Thomas Roberts in 1795 to the Merchant Taylors' Company. London Hall-mark 1741.
Lent by The MASTER AND WARDENS OF THE MERCHANT TAYLORS' COMPANY.

**1242.** TWO LARGE SAUCE-BOATS, with stork handles. By Kandler.
Lent by ASHER WERTHEIMER, ESQ.

**1243.** SILVER BREAD-BASKET which belonged to Richard, 2nd Earl of Mornington.
Lent by H. WEIGALL, ESQ.

**1244.** SILVER WAITER, which belonged to Thomas, 1st Earl of Clarendon, and Richard, 2nd Earl of Mornington, with their crests. Hall-mark.
Lent by H. WEIGALL, ESQ.

**1245.** SILVER COFFEE POT.
Lent by The MASTER AND WARDENS OF THE SALTERS' COMPANY.

**1246.** FOUR SILVER-GILT 18TH CENTURY SPOONS.
Lent by MRS. GRUEBER.

## CASE O—South Gallery.

*RELICS OF POETS, DRAMATISTS, ARTISTS, ETC.*

**1247.** LORD BYRON'S SWORD-STICK.   Lent by MAJOR-GENERAL JOHN BYRON.

**1248.** SCENT-BOTTLE which belonged to Lord Byron.
Lent by MAJOR-GENERAL JOHN BYRON.

**1249.** WHITE NECKERCHIEF which belonged to Lord Byron, given by Fletcher, his valet to the present owner.
Lent by MAJOR-GENERAL JOHN BYRON.

**1250.** LOCKET, with hair of Lord Byron cut at Missolonghi.
Lent by MAJOR-GENERAL JOHN BYRON.

**1251.** LOCKET, with hair of Lord Byron at the age of eight years.
Lent by MAJOR-GENERAL JOHN BYRON.

**1252.** BYRON'S "POEMS ON VARIOUS OCCASIONS," published 1807. To the book is attached a letter from the poet's mother, dated Feb. 1807, in which she refers to her son's book.
Lent by MAJOR-GENERAL JOHN BYRON.

**1253.** SWORD worn by Lord Byron while in Greece. It was presented to Harrow School in 1837 by Byron Drury (son of the Rev. Henry Drury, Assistant-Master of Harrow School), godson of Lord Byron.
Lent by The HEAD MASTER OF HARROW SCHOOL.

**1254.** GOLD SNUFF-BOX, given by Lord Byron to Edmund Kean.
Lent by MRS. LOGIE.

**1255.** MRS. JOHNSON'S WEDDING RING, enamelled in memory of Dr. Johnson.
Lent by A. C. LOMAX, ESQ.

**1256.** DR. JOHNSON'S SILVER BIB-HOLDER.   Lent by A. C. LOMAX, ESQ.

SOUTH GALLERY.] *Miniatures, Relics, and Plate.*

**1257.** SMALL WATER-COLOUR PAINTING, representing the interior of a Club, various members standing about, some in conversation; amongst them the figures of Boswell and Dr. Johnson have been identified; the latter is standing at a table mixing a bowl of punch, into which he is squeezing a lemon; in the background is a table spread for supper.
Lent by J. E. COLLINGWOOD, ESQ.

**1258.** WALKING STICK OF DR. JOHNSON.
Lent by JAMES HENRY JOHNSON, ESQ.

**1259.** IVORY TABLET, which belonged to Dr. Johnson.
Lent by A. C. LOMAX, ESQ.

**1260.** BALL OF WORSTED, wound by William Cowper, the poet, for Mrs. Unwin.
Lent by The REV. W. COWPER JOHNSON, Jun.

**1261.** NETTING done by William Cowper, the poet.
Lent by The REV. W. COWPER JOHNSON, Jun.

**1262.** SEAL-RING WITH HEAD OF OMPHALE, given to William Cowper, the poet, by his cousin Theodora Cowper.
Lent by The REV. W. COWPER JOHNSON, Jun.

**1263.** POCKET BOOK, which belonged to John Keats, the poet.
Lent by The RIGHT HON. SIR C. WENTWORTH DILKE, BART.

**1264.** WALKING STICK OF DAVID GARRICK.
Lent by H. FOSTER, ESQ.

**1265.** GARRICK'S FAVOURITE SNUFF-BOX, with portrait of his brother Peter, painted at Lisbon.
Lent by FREDERICK HINCKLEY, ESQ.

**1266.** SILVER PEN, presented by Edmund Burke to Dr. Johnson on the completion of the *Dictionary*.
Lent by FREDERICK HINCKLEY, ESQ.

**1267.** PORTRAIT OF DR. YOUNG, Author of *Night Thoughts*.
Lent by The REV. F. G. LEE, D.D.

**1267a.** THE WATCH which belonged to William Cowper, the poet.
Lent by The REV. W. COWPER JOHNSON.

**1267b.** CAP worn by Cowper when writing.
Lent by The REV. W. COWPER JOHNSON.

O

**1268.** DRAWING OF JOHN KEATS.
By W. HILTON, R.A.
Lent by RIGHT HON. SIR CHARLES WENTWORTH DILKE, BART.

**1269.** THE ORIGINAL DESIGNS FOR THE ODYSSEY OF HOMER.
By JOHN FLAXMAN. Lent by ISAAC FALCKE, ESQ.

## CASE P—Central Hall.

*WEDGWOOD CHINA, LENT BY FELIX JOSEPH, ESQ.*

**1270.** VASE, blue and white jasper, oviform, serpent handles, "Sacrifice to Cupid," and Pedestal, square, female figures in relief and festoons.

**1271.** VASE, oviform, with serpent handles, "Venus and Car," swans and cupids in clouds, and Pedestal, square, blue jasper, white figures in medallions, festoons of flowers.

**1272.** VASE AND COVER, blue and white, ornaments of leaves, foliage and friezes of classical figures upon the upper bands, and Pedestal, square, with griffin's head and ram's heads, at the angles, females in relief.

**1273.** VASE AND PEDESTAL, light blue and white; vase decorated with rams' heads, garlands of flowers, and figures in medallions; pedestal with rams' heads and griffins at corners, and four female figures.

**1274.** VASE, black and white jasper, Bacchanalian triumph, Bacchus, Ariadne, Silenus, and attendants; borders of leaves and scrolls, pedestal to match.

**1275.** JUGS, pair, blue and white, representing Wine and Water. The one representing wine is surrounded by festoons of vine leaves, with rams' head, masks in front, and white figure of a satyr clasping his arms round the neck of vase. The water jug represents water similarly treated with festoons of water leaves and masks in front of a dolphin, with white figure of a merman clasping neck of jug.

1276. HOMERIC VASE AND COVER, green ground, with white subjects in high relief round the vase, the handles formed of two serpents holding an egg in their mouths, the cover surmounted by a white Pegasus in blue clouds. This vase is one of Josiah Wedgwood's finest productions. From Lord Tweedmouth's collection.

1277. VASE AND COVER, blue and white, decorated with scroll ornament; on each side is a medallion, in the centre of one is a portrait of George IV., when Prince of Wales, surmounted with a crown and Prince of Wales's feathers; in the centre of the other is a figure of Plenty, surmounted with a double cornucopia; on the cover is a seated figure of Britannia; the vase rests upon a base and is supported by the Lion and the Unicorn.

1278. THE PORTLAND OR BARBERINI VASE.

The "Purnell-Tite" copy of the Portland vase, in the British Museum, made by Josiah Wedgwood at Etruria, Staffordshire, about 1790. This vase, No. 29 of the original fifty copies, was purchased in 1830 from a descendant of the Wedgwood family, by Mr. Purnell B. Purnell, of Stanscombe Park, Gloucestershire, and afterwards in 1872 by the late Sir William Tite. At the sale of Sir William Tite's effects in 1888, it was purchased by Mr. Asher Wertheimer. The modellers were three years making the necessary models, and Wedgwood made many experiments and trials for the "body" (or paste) of the vase, which was finally completed in bluish-black jasper and reliefs in white. The reliefs were most carefully undercut and polished after firing.

1279. PORTLAND VASE.

This is one of the original trial copies made by Josiah Wedgwood, from which the celebrated series of fifty subscription copies was produced. The other vase in this case is one of the fifty.

1280. OPERA GLASS, Wedgwood ware, steel, very highly finished, blue and white Wedgwood case, classical subject (formerly belonged to Queen Charlotte).

## CASE Q—Central Hall.

*CUPS AND SAUCERS AND OTHER OBJECTS IN WEDGWOOD WARE, LENT BY ISAAC FALCKE, ESQ.*

1281. CUP AND SAUCER, blue ground, white classical figures.

1282. CUP AND SAUCER, blue ground, subjects after Lady Diana Beauclerk.

1283. CUP AND SAUCER, green ground, Cupids, &c.

1284. SMALL CUP, blue and white, cross-barred ornament.

1285. TWO CUPS AND SAUCERS, pink ground, white scroll ornaments, and signs of the Zodiac.

1286. CUP AND SAUCER, white ground, green ivy-leaf ornament, and pink medallions.

1287. CREAM JUG AND COVER, green ivy-leaf ornaments, and pink medallions.

1288. TWO CUPS AND SAUCERS, black ground, white scroll ornaments, and signs of the Zodiac.

1289. TWO CUPS AND SAUCERS, blue ground, white scroll ornaments, and signs of the Zodiac.

1290. TWO CUPS AND SAUCERS, blue ground, white rams' heads, &c.

1291. CUP AND SAUCER, black ground, ivy-leaf ornaments in white.

1292. CUP AND SAUCER, blue ground, Cupids in white.

1293. MUG, green ground, domestic subject in white.

1294. CUP AND SAUCER, green ground, classical subjects in white.

1295. MUG, green ground, ivy swags, and black medallions.

1296. CUP AND SAUCER, blue ground, classical subjects in white.

1297. INKSTAND, pink ground, Cupids and children in white.

## CASE R—Central Hall.

*SPECIMENS OF PORCELAIN SERVICES MADE FOR MEMBERS OF THE ROYAL FAMILY, LENT BY C. WENTWORTH WASS, ESQ.*

1298. SALOPIAN PLATE, with arms of William V., Prince of Orange, grandson of George II. of England, elected K.G. 1752.

1299. WORCESTER PLATE, from service made for the Duke of Clarence (William IV.), with emblematical figure of Hope with an anchor, 1792.

1300. WORCESTER PLATE, from service made for George IV., with crown, monogram, and motto in centre, 1821.

1301. WORCESTER PLATE, from dinner service made for William IV. The centre is richly emblazoned with the Royal arms and supporters, surrounded with six jewelled medallions, representing the insignia of the Orders of Knighthood. Made for the King on his accession in 1830.

1302. ROCKINGHAM PLATE, from dessert service made for William IV. Royal arms and supporters in centre, with turquoise and richly gilt border of acorns and oak-leaves. The service cost £5,000. Made for the King on his accession in 1830.

1303. ROCKINGHAM PLATE, made for William IV. The centre is emblazoned with the Royal arms and supporters, with medallions of landscape and flowers, and emblems of England, Scotland, and Ireland. This plate is unique, being the only one made for the King's inspection on his accession in 1830.

1304. ROCKINGHAM PLATE, made for William IV. The centre is richly emblazoned with the Royal arms and supporters, with medallions of acorns and oak-leaves, richly gilt compartments. This plate is unique, being the only one made for the King's inspection on his accession in 1830.

1305. LOWESTOFT CUP AND SAUCER, enamelled with the Royal arms. From service presented by George III. to his daughter, the Princess Elizabeth, on her marriage with the Margrave of Hesse.

**1306.** CAPO DI MONTE CUP AND SAUCER, from service presented to George III. by Frederick, King of the Two Sicilies, in 1787.

**1307.** WORCESTER COFFEE-CUP AND SAUCER, from service made for George IV., emblazoned with the Royal arms and supporters, 1824.

**1308.** WORCESTER TEA-CUP AND SAUCER, of the same service.

**1309.** WORCESTER CUP AND SAUCER, from service made for the Duke of Cumberland, with coronet and motto, richly decorated.

**1310.** WORCESTER CUP AND SAUCER, from service made for Lord Nelson in 1802, with baron's coronet and Order of San Josef in panels, with decorations in Oriental style.

## WATCHES OF THE EIGHTEENTH AND NINETEENTH CENTURIES, LENT BY GEORGE CARR GLYN, ESQ.

**1311.** SILVER WATCH, with engraved silver dial. Maker, *De Charmes, London*. Beginning of the 18th cent.

**1312.** DOUBLE CASED WATCH, outer case blue enamel. Maker, *C. Thomson, London*. Middle of the 18th cent.

**1313.** DOUBLE CASED WATCH, with embossed case. Maker, *C. Clay, London*. Middle of the 18th cent.

**1314.** SILVER WATCH, with embossed case, enamel face. Maker, *Tarts, London*.

**1315.** SILVER WATCH, with embossed case, enamel face. 18th cent.

**1316.** SILVER WATCH, with [tortoiseshell case, inlaid with silver; silver dial. Maker, *Windmills, London*.

**1317.** GOLD REPEATER WATCH, black leather case; gold dial. Maker, *Thomas Tompson London*.

1318. SILVER ALARM WATCH, engraved and perforated case; silver dial.

1319. PINCHBECK WATCH, shagreen case. Maker, *T. Montagu, London.*

1320. PINCHBECK REPEATER WATCH, with tortoiseshell case. Maker, *Van der Maaten, Amsterdam.*

1321. SHAGREEN WATCH, studded with gold. Maker, *Inwood, London.*

1322. PINCHBECK WATCH, embossed case. Maker, *Delabene, London.*

1323. SILVER WATCH, embossed case. Maker, *Dillington, London.*

1324. SILVER ALARM WATCH, engraved and perforated cases. Maker, *J. Tornique, London.*

1325. SILVER WATCH, chased and enamelled dial.

1326. SILVER WATCH, embossed case. Maker, *Miller, London.*

1327. SILVER WATCH, embossed case by *Cochin.* Maker, *Wilton, London.*

1328. SILVER WATCH, embossed case, with enamel medallion. Maker, *J. Wilter, London.*

1329. SILVER WATCH, embossed case by *Maweis.* Maker, *Harry Potter, London.*

1330. SILVER WATCH, embossed case by *Cochin.* Maker, *Ch. Cabrier, London.*

1331. SILVER WATCH, shagreen case. Maker, *Jas. Turlis, Windsor.*

1332. SILVER ALARM WATCH, pierced case. Maker, *Rowisalt, Archalt.*

1333. SILVER WATCH, embossed case. Maker, *J. Wilder, London.*

1334. SILVER REPEATER WATCH. Maker, *Brequet, Paris.*

1335. SILVER WATCH, engraved silver dial. Maker, *Adrian de Bayhyn, Amsterdam.*

1336. SILVER CLOCK AND ALARM WATCH, engraved and perforated case. Maker, *J. Bayes, London.*

1337. SILVER WATCH, engraved silver dial. Maker, *Markham, London.*

1338. SILVER WATCH, engraved silver dial. Maker, *W. Bertram, London.*

1339. SILVER WATCH, outer case black leather, studded with silver. Engraved silver dial. Maker, *O. Herman, Coupar.*

1340. TREBLE CASED WATCH, embossed. Maker, *Williamson, London.*

1341. SILVER WATCH, engraved and enamelled dial. Maker, *Kornelly, Paris.*

1342. SILVER WATCH, embossed case. Maker, *Seamore, London.*

1343. PINCHBECK WATCH, tortoiseshell case studded with gold. Maker, *W. Bramley, Andover.*

1344. SILVER WATCH, engraved silver dial. Maker, *J. Whitfield, London.*

1345. SILVER WATCH, outer case engraved. Maker, *Rigaud, London.*

1346. SMALL FRENCH MOVEMENT WATCH, enamelled case in shape of mandoline.

1347. SILVER CLOCK WATCH, pierced silver cases. Maker, *Ed. East, London.*

1348. SILVER-GILT WATCH, case tortoiseshell. Maker, *Warren, Canterbury.*

1349. PURPLE ENAMEL WATCH.

1350. PINCHBECK WATCH WITH CHATELAINE. Enamel medallion on back, surrounded by marquisates. Makers, *Jean Fagy & Fils.*

1351. GOLD WATCH, in shape of shell.

1352. GOLD WATCH, engraved case. Maker, *Hamlet, London.*

1353. WATCH MOVEMENT, in enamelled case in shape of a ball. Maker, *Michael Lemann, Vienna.*

1354. SINGLE CASED WATCH, gold engraved dial. Maker, *Sam Dryer, London.*

CENTRAL HALL.] *China and Relics.*

**1355.** SILVER WATCH, engraved case. Makers, *Isaac Soret & fils.*

**1356.** SILVER WATCH, black leather case, studded with silver. Maker, *Nathaniel Barrow, London.*

**1357.** PINCHBECK WATCH, engraved and enamelled dial. Maker, *Gaudron, Paris.*

**1358.** GOLD WATCH, enamelled and engraved case, surrounded with pearls: gold dial Maker, *L. Duchène & fils.*

**1359.** GOLD WATCH, black leather case, studded with gold: blue enamel dial.

**1360.** GOLD WATCH, green enamelled and engraved case, dial surrounded by diamonds Maker, *Bordier, Geneva.*

**1361.** GOLD WATCH, with agate case, mounted in diamonds. Maker, *J. Hubert, London.*

**1361a.** COLLECTION OF 18 BATTERSEA ENAMEL PATCH BOXES.
Lent by MRS. BOLTON.

**1362.** A GOLD WATCH, ornamented with wreath and crown in diamonds.
Lent by MISS REID.

**1363.** A SMALL BLUE ENAMELLED GOLD WATCH, with leaves on the back.
Lent by MISS REID.

**1364.** A BLUE ENAMELLED GOLD WATCH, with two female figures and a ship with sail painted on the back.
Lent by MISS REID.

**1365.** A BLUE ENAMELLED GOLD REPEATER, set with pearls and diamonds.
Lent by MISS REID.

**1366.** GOLD WATCH, set with pearls, with engine-turned enamelled back.
Lent by MRS. GODFREY CLARK.

**1367.** GOLD ENAMELLED WATCH, set with pearls.
Lent by MRS. GODFREY CLARK.

**1368.** GOLD WATCH, set with turquoise.
Lent by MRS. GODFREY CLARK.

**1369.** PLAIN GOLD WATCH, taken by Lord Macartney on his Embassy to China, 1792.
Lent by MRS. GODFREY CLARK.

**1370.** MINIATURE OF LADY MARY WORTLEY MONTAGU.
Lent by MRS. GODFREY CLARK.

**1371.** MINIATURE OF THE MARCHIONESS OF BUTE.
Lent by MRS. GODFREY CLARK.

**1372.** MINIATURE OF THE COUNTESS OF PORTARLINGTON.
Lent by MRS. GODFREY CLARK.

## CASE T—Central Hall.

*FAN-LEAVES AND FANS, LENT BY LADY CHARLOTTE SCHREIBER.*

### UNMOUNTED FAN-LEAVES.

**1373.** ATTACK ON CARTHAGENA by Admiral Vernon, 1741.

**1374.** VAUXHALL.

**1375.** ARTHUR, DUKE OF WELLINGTON, his Victories, 1815.

**1376.** RODNEY'S VICTORIES, 1782.

**1377.** MARRIAGE OF ANNE, PRINCESS OF WALES, DAUGHTER OF GEORGE II., WITH WILLIAM IV., PRINCE OF ORANGE, 1734.

**1378.** THE TRIAL OF WARREN HASTINGS, 1788.

**1379.** PORTO BELLO, taken by Admiral Vernon, 1739.

**1380.** THE SENTIMENTAL JOURNEY, 1796.

1381. ROYAL CONCERT, 1781.

1382. DRURY LANE THEATRE, 1794.

1383. THE ROYAL FAMILY OF ENGLAND, 1795.

1384. BARTHOLOMEW FAIR.

1385. LAMENT FOR THE DEATH OF FREDERICK, PRINCE OF WALES, 1751.

1386. CORONATION BANQUET OF GEORGE II., 1727.

1387. SIR ROBERT WALPOLE'S EXCISE BILL, 1733.

1388. RANELAGH.

1389. THE HARLOT'S PROGRESS, after Hogarth.

1390. RT. HON. CHARLES JAMES FOX, Statesman, 1749-1806.

1391. GEORGE IV. AS PRINCE OF WALES, AND PRINCESS CAROLINE, 1795.

1392. JUBILEE OF GEORGE III., 1810.

1393. ST. JAMES'S PARK, 1741.

1394. CORONATION BANQUET.

1395. SENTIMENTAL JOURNEY.

## MOUNTED FANS.

1396. RECOVERY OF GEORGE III., 1789.

1397. GEORGE III. AND QUEEN CHARLOTTE.

1398. GEORGE IV. AS PRINCE OF WALES, AND PRINCESS CAROLINE, 1795.

1399. JUBILEE FAN.

1400. JUBILEE FAN.

1401. NELSON AND VICTORY, 1799.

1402. A DANCE FAN, 1793.

403. THE OPERA HOUSE, 1797.

1404. FREDERICA, DUCHESS OF YORK, 1791.

1405. A CHURCH FAN, 1796.

1406. THE KING'S THEATRE, 1788.

1407. A CHAPEL FAN, 1796.

1408. WEDDING FAN.

1409. TRIAL OF WARREN HASTINGS.

1410.

1411.

1412.

1413.

1414.

## CASE U—Central Hall.

*HISTORICAL ENGLISH CHINA, LENT BY HENRY WILLETT, ESQ.*

1415. GEORGE I. Bust. Whealdon ware.

1416. SOPHIA, WIFE OF GEORGE I. Whealdon ware.

1417. MEMORIAL ON DEATH OF QUEEN CAROLINE. Plate 1738.

1418. GEORGE II. Bust. Chelsea ware.

1419. GEORGE III. WHEN PRINCE OF WALES. Chelsea.

1420. GEORGE III. Plate. King and Child.

1421. GEORGE III. Statuette Bust.

1422. GEORGE III. Battersea Wedding Snuff-box.

1423. GEORGE III. Jug (Hadfield shot at the King).

1424. GEORGE III. Statuette in his own costume.

1425. QUEEN CHARLOTTE. Worcester Vase with portrait

1426. GEORGE IV. Plaque.

1427. QUEEN CAROLINE. Plaque.

1428. QUEEN CAROLINE. Plate.

1429. QUEEN CAROLINE. Mug.

1430. QUEEN CAROLINE. Mug.

1431. QUEEN CAROLINE. Mug.

1432. QUEEN CAROLINE, WITH PORTRAIT OF PRINCE LEOPOLD AND PRINCESS CHARLOTTE.

1433. WILLIAM IV. Sitting on sofa. Derby.

1434. WILLIAM IV. Bottle. Lambeth.

1435. QUEEN ADELAIDE. Bust. Derby.

1436. DUKE OF KENT. Plate.

1437. DUKE OF CUMBERLAND. Bust. Whealdon ware.

1438. LORD BROUGHAM. Bust.

1439. DUKE OF YORK. Equestrian portrait. Plate.

1440. ADMIRAL BOSCAWEN. Mug.

1441. GENERAL CONWAY. Statuette. Chelsea.

1442. LORD CORNWALLIS. Teapot.

1443. PETERLOO MASSACRE. Mug.

1444. KITTY CLIVE. Statuette. Chelsea.

1445. ADMIRAL VERNON. Teapot, with figure of Vernon, and ship. Burfield.

1446. ADMIRAL NELSON. Bust.

1447. MODEL OF BATTLE OF TRAFALGAR. Mug.

1448. BATTLE OF TRAFALGAR. Names of ships. Mug.

1449. BATTLE OF THE NILE. Mug.

1450. ADMIRAL NELSON. "England expects every man to do his duty." Mug.

1451. LORD HOWE. Victory, 1st June. Mug.

1452. LORD HOWE. Mug with portrait.

1453. ADMIRAL DUNCAN. Mug.

1454. GENERAL WOLFE. Statuette. Bow China.

1455. MARQUESS OF GRANBY. Statuette. Bow China.

1456. ADMIRAL RODNEY. Mug. Coloured Bust.

1457. GEORGE WASHINGTON. Statuette.

1458. NAPOLEON. Bust.

1459. ADMIRAL KEPPEL. Statuette. Derby.

1460. DUKE OF WELLINGTON. Bust.

1461. CUP OF THE BEEFSTEAK CLUB.

1462. DUKE OF BRIDGWATER. Bust.

### CASE V—Central Hall.

1463. HANDEL. Bust. Staffordshire.

1464. POPE. Bust. Staffordshire.

1465. PRIOR. Bust. Turner's Ware.

1466. SCHOOLMISTRESS AND CHILDREN. Group.

1467. COSTUME OF THE REGENCY. Two figures grouped.

1468. COSTUME OF THE REGENCY. Single figure.

1469. COSTUME OF THE REGENCY. Single figure.

1470. MARRIAGE AT GRETNA GREEN. Plaque.

1471. HEART-IN-HAND. Sign of Fleet Marriage.

1472. BECKFORD. Nicholas Wood.

1473. JOHN WILKES. Statuette.

1474. TOM PAYNE. Portrait on Mug.

1475. BELLINGHAM PORTRAIT. Mug.

1476. WOODWARD, THE ACTOR. Chelsea.

1477. HANNAH MORE. Statuette. Derby Biscuit.

1478. WILLIAM WILBERFORCE. Statuette. Derby Biscuit.

1479. STATUETTE OF PILLION, showing method of riding. Whealdon ware.

1480. LORD ANSON. Worcester Mug.

1481. DEATH OF PERCEVAL. Mug.

1482. GENERAL WOLFE. Jug.

1483. SIR SIDNEY SMITH. Mug.

1484. CUP OF LIVERPOOL MERCHANTS WITH FLAGS.

1485. KEAN AS "RICHARD III." Staffordshire.

1486. WILLIAM PITT. Statuette. Derby Biscuit.

1487. CHARLES JAMES FOX. Statuette. Derby Biscuit.

1488. FIRST RAILWAY JOURNEY. Mug.

1489. ADMIRAL VERNON. British Glory. Carved basin.

*ELEVEN LIVERPOOL TRANSFER TILES, AS FOLLOWS:—*

1490. MRS. LEWIS as "Hippolitus."

1491. MRS. LESINGHAM as "Ophelia."

1492. MRS. YATES as "Lady Townley."

1493. MISS P. HOPKINS as "Lavinia."

1494. MR. WOODWARD as "Razor."

1495. MRS. YATES as "Jane Shore."

1496. Mrs. Barry as "Athenais."

1497. Mrs. Hartley as "Imoinda."

1498. Mrs. Abington as "Estafinia."

1499. Mrs. Lewis as "Douglas."

1500. Mr. Macklin as "Shylock."

## CASE W—Central Hall.

### CHINA.

1501. Vase and Cover, Chelsea Porcelain, painted with Chinese figures and flowers on gold ground, and bands of "claret" colour; scroll handles; English, late Eighteenth Century.
Lent by R. C. Naylor.

1502. Pair of Crown Derby Pot-Pourri Vases on Tripod Base, with ornaments in form of ram's horns, very richly gilt.
Lent by J. H. Fitzhenry, Esq.

1503. Chessmen, after designs by Flaxman.
Lent by Isaac Falcke, Esq.

1504. Six Plates in cream-coloured ware.
Lent by Isaac Falcke, Esq.

1505. Tea-Pot, Sugar Basin, and Cream Jug, of Wedgwood ware (*Rosso Antiquo*), mounted in silver.
Formerly belonged to Queen Adelaide.
Lent by Isaac Falcke, Esq.

1506. Pair of Chelsea Plates.
Lent by Isaac Falcke, Esq.

1507. Two Cream-ware Wedgwood Plates.
Lent by Isaac Falcke, Esq.

1508. Vase of Unglazed Yellow Wedgwood Ware.
Lent by Isaac Falcke, Esq.

P

**1510.** VASE OF ETRUSCAN WARE.
By WEDGWOOD.
Lent by ISAAC FALCKE, ESQ.

**1511.** WILKES'S TEAPOT.
Lent by T. ASHBY STERRY, ESQ.

**1512.** FOUR PIECES OF A BLUE JASPER TEA SERVICE, consisting of a tea-pot, basin, saucer, and milk-jug, with scroll decoration and borders in white relief with the monogram of G. E. Made by Josiah Wedgwood.
Lent by W. JOHNSTON STUART.

**1514.** SAUCE BOAT AND TWO PLATES OF WEDGWOOD WARE.
Lent by G. WHITWORTH WALLIS, ESQ.

**1515.** FOUR PLAYING CARDS, style of Hogarth.
Lent by ISAAC FALCKE, ESQ.

**1516.** PACK OF PLAYING CARDS, with musical compositions.
Lent by ISAAC FALCKE, ESQ.

**1517.** PACK OF PLAYING CARDS, in commemoration of the South Sea Bubble.
Lent by ISAAC FALCKE, ESQ.

**1518.** PACK OF PLAYING CARDS, with representations of the Kings and Queens of England to George III.
Lent by ISAAC FALCKE, ESQ.

**1519.** PACK OF PLAYING CARDS, humorous subjects, dated 1780.
By COWELL.
Lent by ISAAC FALCKE, ESQ.

**1520.** PACK OF PLAYING CARDS.
By OLIVETTE.
Lent by ISAAC FALCKE, ESQ.

**1521.** PACK OF PLAYING CARDS, with emblematical subjects, 1775.
By S. HOOPER.
Lent by ISAAC FALCKE, ESQ.

## THE SCREEN (Central Hall).

*TABLETS BY WEDGWOOD IN JASPER WARE, LENT BY ISAAC FALCKE, ESQ.*

1522. ENDYMION AND DOG ON MOUNT PATMOS, green ground, white figures.

1523. THE TRIFORM GODDESS, LUNA, DIANA, AND HECATE, with boar's head.

1524. PRIAM BEGGING FOR THE BODY OF HECTOR FROM ACHILLES, green ground, white figures.

1525. ACHILLES WITH THE DAUGHTER OF LYCOMEDES, black ground, white figures.

1526. MERCURY UNITING THE HANDS OF ENGLAND AND FRANCE, in china and blue-ball clay. Original model signed by Flaxman.

1527. PEACE PREVENTING MARS FROM OPENING THE GATES OF THE TEMPLE OF JANUS, in china and blue-ball clay. Original model signed by Flaxman.

1528. THE APOTHEOSIS OF HOMER, blue ground, white figures.

1529. AESCULAPIUS AND HYGEIA, blue ground, white figures.

1530. THREE WARRIORS AND A HORSE, blue ground, white figures.

1531. PORTRAIT OF BENJAMIN FRANKLIN, blue and white jasper.

1532. PORTRAIT OF HOMER, blue and white, trial piece.

1533. PORTRAIT OF DR. JOSEPH PRIESTLEY, lapis-lazuli ground, trial piece.

1534. JOHN FLAXMAN.

1535. MRS. FLAXMAN.

1536. TWO PARTS OF THE BORDER OF A SALVER, in bronze; made by George IV.; designed by Thomas Stothard.

**1537.** BRISTOL CUP AND SAUCER, made by Richard Champion, the proprietor, and presented to the wife of Edmund Burke, with coat of arms of Burke and his wife, and an inscription dedicating them by Champion.
Lent by W. S. SALTING, ESQ.

**1538.** CHELSEA GROUP OF BOY AND GIRL MUSICIANS WITH PERFORMING DOGS IN AN ARBOUR OF WHITE JESSAMINE, gold anchor mark.
Lent by W. S. SALTING, ESQ.

**1539.** PORTRAIT OF BENJAMIN FRANKLIN, blue and white jasper.
Lent by GEORGE HARDING, ESQ.

*A SERIES OF PORTRAITS MADE BY JOSIAH WEDGWOOD, AFTER DESIGNS BY FLAXMAN, BACON, HACKWOOD, AND OTHER SCULPTORS.*

*LENT BY J. LUMSDEN PROPERT, ESQ., M.D.*

**1540.** JOHN FLAXMAN, R.A., 1755-1826, in terra-cotta, modelled by himself.

**1541.** LOUIS, DUKE OF ORLEANS, 1703-1752.

**1542.** PRINCE WILLIAM HENRY, afterwards William IV., 1765-1837.

**1543.** SIR FREDERICK WILLIAM HERSCHEL, Astronomer, 1738-1822.

**1544.** GEORGE WASHINGTON, 1732-1799, AND BENJAMIN FRANKLIN, 1706-1790.

**1545.** WILLIAM I., KING OF THE NETHERLANDS, HIS QUEEN AND FAMILY. (5 portraits on one plaque.)

**1546.** ADMIRAL LORD HOWE, 1725-1799.

**1547.** ADMIRAL LORD ST. VINCENT, 1734-1823.

1548. ADMIRAL LORD DUNCAN, 1731-1804.

1549. ADMIRAL LORD NELSON, 1758-1805.

1550. PRINCE EDWARD OF BRUNSWICK.

1551. CARDINAL PONIATOWSKI.

1552. LADY ELEANOR AUCKLAND, d. 1818.

1553. WILLIAM PITT, Statesman, 1759-1806.

1554. WILLIAM, EARL OF MANSFIELD, Lord Chief Justice, 1705-1793.

1555. DR. ERASMUS DARWIN, Physician, 1731-1802.

1556. DR. SAMUEL JOHNSON, Writer, 1709-1784.

1557. GEORGE IV. AS PRINCE REGENT, 1762-1830.

1558. MARIA I., QUEEN OF PORTUGAL.

1559. SIR WILLIAM HAMILTON, Diplomatist, 1730-1803.

1560. SIR JOSHUA REYNOLDS, P.R.A., 1723-1792.

1561. CATHERINE II., EMPRESS OF RUSSIA, 1729-1796. (The only portrait known of this colour.)

1562. THOMAS PITT, LORD CAMELFORD, 1737-1793.

1563. MR. MEERMAN, a friend of Wedgwood.

1564. FERDINAND I., KING OF THE SICILIES, 1751-1793.

1565. CHARLOTTE AUGUSTA, PRINCESS ROYAL, daughter of George III., 1766-1828.

1566. EDGAR BOURNE, one of Wedgwood's workmen; modelled by Flaxman.

1567. JOSIAH WEDGWOOD, 1730-1795. Coloured and glazed pottery, inscribed "Josiah Wedgwood, Esquire, Etruria, Potter."

1568. WILLS, EARL OF HILLSBOROUGH, AFTERWARDS MARQUESS OF DOWNSHIRE, Statesman, d. 1793.

1569. CHARLES, 1ST MARQUESS OF CORNWALLIS, Governor-General of India, 1738-1805.

1570. WARREN HASTINGS, Governor of India, 1733-1818.

1571. ADMIRAL VISCOUNT HOOD, 1724-1816.

1572. MARQUESS OF STAFFORD, 1721-1803.

1573. J. P. ELERS, early Staffordshire potter.

1574. LOUIS XVI. OF FRANCE, 1754-1793.

1575. ADMIRAL KEPPEL, 1725-1786.

1576. DR. JOSEPH BLACK, Chemist, 1725-1786.

1577. JOHN GASPER CHRISTIAN LAVATER, Swiss Physiognomist, 1741-1801.

1578. EDWIN LAW, 1ST EARL OF ELLENBOROUGH, Lord Chief Justice, 1748-1818?

1579. JONAS HANWAY, Traveller, 1712-1786; he is said to have introduced umbrellas into England.

1580. GENERAL G. A. ELLIOT, LORD HEATHFIELD, Defender of Gibraltar, 1718-1790.

1581. ALEXANDER ADAM, LL.D., Antiquary, 1741-1809.

1582. GOVERNOR FRANKLIN, 1731-1813.

1583. W. T. FRANKLIN, son of Governor Franklin.

1584. SILVER-GILT PALETTE, a prize awarded by the Society of Arts to John Flaxman, aged 11 years and 5 months, for a model in clay," Class 117; Anno 1767." With Wedgwood scroll ornament.

**1585.** MALE PORTRAIT, unknown.
**1586.** MALE PORTRAIT, unknown.
**1587.** MALE PORTRAIT, unknown.
**1588.**
**1589.**
**1590.**
**1591.** PORTRAITS, unknown.
**1592.**
**1593.**
**1594.**

The following four frames containing thirty-six portraits were mounted in a cabinet and presented by Wedgwood and Bently to George Engleheart, miniature-painter, in return for work done by him for the firm. Some of the portraits are not of the Hanover period; these have been included in order not to disturb the arrangement.

*LENT BY J. LUMSDEN PROPERT, ESQ., M.D.*

### 1595.—*Frame I.*
1. JOHN REINHOLD FORSTER, botanist, 1729-1798 (in centre).
2. DR. JOSEPH PRIESTLEY, scientist, 1733-1804.
3. CHARLES VON LINNÆUS, botanist, 1707-1778.
4. REV. J. WRAY, naturalist, 1628-1705.
5. DR. DANIEL CHARLES SOLANDER, botanist, 1736-1782.
6. CAPTAIN JAMES COOK, navigator, 1728-1779.
7. THOMAS PENNANT, naturalist, 1740-1790.
8. SIR JOSEPH BANKS, BART., naturalist, 1743-1820.
9. GALILEO GALILEI, astronomer, 1564-1642.

### 1596.—*Frame II.*
1. SIR HANS SLOANE, naturalist, 1660-1752.
2. WILLIAM SHAKESPEARE, dramatist, 1564-1616.
3. DR. HENRY PEMBERTON, physician, 1694-1771.

4. DAVID GARRICK, actor, 1716-1779.
5. CHARLES PRATT, 1ST EARL CAMDEN, Lord Chancellor, 1713-1794.
6. WILLIAM PITT, EARL OF CHATHAM, statesman, 1708-1778.
7. SIR ISAAC NEWTON, scientist, 1642-1727.
8. JOHN LOCKE, philosopher, 1632-1704.
9. JAMES WYATT, architect, 1743-1813.

### 1597.—*Frame III.*

1. QUEEN ELIZABETH, 1560-1602 (in centre).
2. CATHERINE II., EMPRESS OF RUSSIA, 1729-1796.
3. GUSTAVUS III., KING OF SWEDEN, 1771-1792.
4. GEORGE III., 1760-1820.
5. QUEEN CHARLOTTE, 1744-1818.
6. CHARLES IV., KING OF SPAIN, 1788-1808.
7. THE EMPEROR OF GERMANY.
8. HENRY IV., KING OF FRANCE, 1589-1610.
9. MAXIMILIER DE BETHUNE, DUC DE SULLY, French Minister, 1560-1641.

### 1598.—*Frame IV.*

1. WILLIAM PENN, 1644-1718 (in centre).
2. GEORGE EDWARDS, naturalist, 1693-1773.
3. CONYERS MIDDLETON, scholar, 1683-1750.
4. VOLTAIRE, French author, 1694-1778.
5. POPE PIUS VI., 1717-1799.
6. SIR WILLIAM HAMILTON, diplomatist, 1730-1803.
7. RICHARD MEAD, physician, 1673-1754.
8. DR. SAMUEL P. WOODWARD, geologist, 1665-1728.
9. ALGERNON SIDNEY, parliamentarian, 1617-1683.

## CASE X.—Central Hall.

### ARMS, ETC.

**1599.** FOUR CLAYMORE SWORDS AND TWO SPORRANS, from the field of Culloden.
Lent by MRS. HARVEY, of Ickwell-Bury.

**1600.** PENINSULAR GOLD CROSS.
Lent by The ROYAL UNITED SERVICE INSTITUTION.

**1601.** CAPTAIN COOK'S SWORD.
Lent by The ROYAL UNITED SERVICE INSTITUTION.

**1602.** GENERAL WOLFE'S SWORD.
Lent by The ROYAL UNITED SERVICE INSTITUTION.

**1603.** SASH with which Sir John Moore was lowered into his grave.
Lent by The ROYAL UNITED SERVICE INSTITUTION.

**1604.** SWORD of William IV. used by him when a naval officer.
Lent by The ROYAL UNITED SERVICE INSTITUTION.

**1605.** GOLD MEDAL, struck in 1745 to commemorate the Battle of Culloden. Given to General Wren, from whom it has descended to the present owner.
Lent by MAJOR HERBERT YOUNG

**1606.** THE HANGER with which Lord Byron slew Mr. Chaworth.

On Saturday, 26th January, 1765, a quarrel took place at the "Star and Garter" tavern in Pall Mall between William, 5th Lord Byron, and Mr. Chaworth of Nottinghamshire. The ground of the dispute was concerning the preservation of game. A duel ensued in a private room in the hotel, and Lord Byron mortally wounded his adversary. For this Lord Byron was tried by his peers, and found guilty of manslaughter, but claiming benefit of clergy, he was discharged on payment of a fine. The sword was given by the poet to Mr. Dearden, of Rochdale, by whose son it was bequeathed to the present owner. The blade is 24 inches long, and a small pistol is attached to the side, with the trigger within the sword guard.
Lent by The REV. T. E. WALDY.

**1607.** PISTOL carried by William, Duke of Cumberland, at the Battle of Culloden.

It was left by the Duke at Moy Hall, the castle of the MacIntosh, chief of the clan MacIntosh, where the Duke stayed after the battle. The pistol, which is of Italian work, is ornamented with a silver plate bearing the royal crest.
Lent by LIEUT-COL. R. RINTOUL.

**1608.** Fragment of King's Colour of the 57th Foot.
              Lent by Capt. W. R. Inglis.

**1609.** Remains of Regimental Colour of the 57th Foot.

These colours were carried in the Peninsula from the time that the 57th joined the army under Sir Arthur Wellesley in 1809 until the end of the war, and were present at all the principal engagements from Albuhera to Nive. At Albuhera the regiment and its colours suffered considerably; early in the day the staff of the King's colour was broken by a shot, and it was subsequently pierced by seventeen shots, whilst the regimental colour received twenty-two. The colours were presented to Colonel (afterwards Lieut.-General Sir Wm.) Inglis when full colonel of the regiment, from whom they came to the present owner, his grandson.
              Lent by Capt. Inglis, 2nd Norfolk Regiment.

**1610.** Gorget worn by Infantry Officers on Duty up to 1830.
              Lent by Harry Dillon, Esq.

**1611.** Parasol of green silk, which belonged to Georgiana, Duchess of Devonshire, and given to her by the servants on her birthday.
              Lent by John Cleland, Esq., of Stormont.

**1611a.** Pair of Pistols, flint locks, silver mounted.
              Lent by J. E. Collingwood, Esq.

**1612.** Case of Firearms, comprising a brace of pistols and a gun.
Given by Empress Catherine of Russia to the Rt. Hon. Charles James Fox.
              Lent by The Earl of Ilchester.

**1612a.** Hat worn by the Right Hon. Spencer Perceval when he was shot by Bellingham in the Lobby of the House of Commons, May 11, 1812, and showing where it was pierced by the bullet.
              Lent by The Earl of Egmont.

**1612b.** Pistol with which Bellingham shot the Right Hon. Spencer Perceval in the Lobby of the House of Commons, May 11, 1812.
              Lent by The Earl of Egmont.

**1612c.** Sketch of Napoleon's Guns, with certificate.
              Lent by Henry H. P. Cotton, Esq.

## SCULPTURE (North Gallery).

**1613.** MARBLE BUST OF ELIZABETH FARREN, COUNTESS OF DERBY, AS "THALIA," 1759-1829.
By The HON. MRS. DAWSON DAMER.
Lent by MRS. CAMPBELL JOHNSTON.

**1614.** MARBLE BUST OF ADMIRAL VISCOUNT NELSON, made at Vienna in 1801.
By Franz Thallor and Matthias Rarson. It was purchased by Mr. Herbert Agar of Admiral Small who had it from Lady Hamilton. It was given by Mr. Agar to the present owner.
Lent by The EARL NELSON.

**1615.** MARBLE BUST, life-size, of the Duke of Wellington.
By GEOGHEGAN.
Lent by The REV. T. E. WALDY.

**1616.** BUST OF ARTHUR, DUKE OF WELLINGTON, K.G.
It was executed by order of the Corporation in 1814.
By PETER TURNERELLI.
Lent by The CORPORATION OF THE CITY OF LONDON.

## SCULPTURE (Central Hall).

**1617.** "MATERNAL LOVE"; model by Flaxman.
Lent by ISAAC FALCKE, ESQ.

**1618.** "THE SUPPLICANT"; model by Flaxman.
Lent by ISAAC FALCKE, ESQ.

**1619.** ILLUSTRATION FROM THE LORD'S PRAYER, "LEAD US NOT INTO TEMPTATION"; model by Flaxman.
Lent by ISAAC FALCKE, ESQ.

**1620.** ILLUSTRATION FROM THE LORD'S PRAYER, "BUT DELIVER US FROM EVIL"; model by Flaxman.
Lent by ISAAC FALCKE, ESQ

**1621.** PANDORA CONVEYED TO EARTH BY MERCURY; model by Flaxman.
Lent by ISAAC FALCKE, ESQ.

**1622.** "THE GOLDEN AGE"; model by Flaxman.
Lent by ISAAC FALCKE, ESQ.

**1623.** BUST OF MERCURY in basalt, by Flaxman.
   Lent by ISAAC FALCKE, ESQ.

**1624.** MEDALLION, in plaster, OF JOHN KEATS, 1796-1820; executed at Rome after his death.
   Lent by The RIGHT HON. SIR C. WENTWORTH DILKE, BART.

## FURNITURE, ETC. (Central Hall).

**1625.** CABINET, OR CONSOLE TABLE, which belonged to Mrs. FitzHerbert, containing twenty-nine miniatures of naval and other celebrities, *temp.* George III. and IV. Also a large miniature of George IV., and another of Her Majesty the Queen, aged eleven years, by Mrs. Ince, and wax medallions of George III., Pitt, and Fox by Miss Andras.
   Lent by The BARON DE WORMS.

**1626.** THE LIBRARY CHAIR which belonged to George IV., and which he always used.
   Lent by JOHN CLELAND, ESQ., of Stormont.

**1627.** DR. JOHNSON'S WRITING DESK.
   Lent by the MASTER AND FELLOWS OF PEMBROKE COLLEGE, OXFORD.

**1628.** HANDEL'S HARPSICHORD.
   This is a single keyboard harpsichord. Externally it is covered with paper much discoloured, but showing a delicate pattern. Above the keyboard is inscribed the maker's name, "Andreas Rukers, 1640." On the inside of the lid are the following inscriptions in Roman characters: "*Concordia Musis amica,*" and "*Musica letitiæ comes medicina dolorum.*" The interior of the instrument is decorated with flowers and birds in oil-painting.
   This instrument was given by Dr. Burney, the author of the *History of Music,* to his friend, the Rev. Thomas Twining, Rector of St. Mary's, Colchester, the "Country Clergyman of the Eighteenth Century," himself a musician. It has always remained in the possession of the Twining family, and with it the tradition has been handed down that it was used by Handel in the composition of his works.
   Lent by MRS. A. B. DONALDSON.

**1629.** CHAIR, used by Lord Nelson on board the *Victory.*
   The following account of this chair dated 7th December, 1883, is given by Mr. Henry Thompson, of Andover, from whom it came to its present owner: "It was given by the

late Captain Thomas Wm. Hardy to my aunt, Isabella Thompson, and landed out of the *Victory* in 1805, after Trafalgar, and taken to my grandfather's house in Chapel Row, Portsea. After various removals it was given by my aunt to me. I would add that my aunt once told Captain Hardy that he kept the Admiral's chair and gave her the one he used himself, upon which Sir Thomas assured her, and with a nautical oath confirmed 'that he'd be d . . . . d if that was not the Admiral's chair, its fellow in which he himself sat was broke in clearing the ship for action.' It has never been repaired but only loosely covered, and is to be given at my decease to the present Earl Nelson or his heirs." (Signed) Henry Thompson. In the right arm a piece has been removed and stuffed for the stump to lean upon.

Lent by The EARL NELSON.

**1630.** CORONATION CHAIR AND STOOL OF GEORGE III.

Lent by COUNT KIELMANSEGG.

**1631.** CHAIR WORKED BY THE ELECTRESS SOPHIA OF HANOVER, mother of George I.

Lent by COUNT KIELMANSEGG.

**1632.** A BAROMETER, which belonged to George III.

On a paper pasted on to the back is written, " This barometer was the property of his late Majesty King George the third, and hung in the Queen's dressing-room at Weymouth and was purchased for me in the sale which took place there on Saturday, the 15th July, 1820." (Signed) Thos. Hardwick. Thomas Hardwick was the well-known architect, and father of Philip Hardwick, R.A. The barometer came into the possession of the present owner through Mr. P. C. Hardwick, grandson of Thomas Hardwick.

Lent by S. J. NICHOLLS, ESQ.

**1633.** A SCREEN, with Portraits of George III., Queen Charlotte and Family, and Portrait of George IV. as Prince of Wales, after Gainsborough.

Lent by LADY CHARLOTTE SCHREIBER.

**1633.\*** A CHINESE WORK-TABLE with the crown and initials of Queen Adelaide.

Lent by MISS REID.

## AUTOGRAPHS, ETC.

### CASE AA—Balcony.

#### ROYAL LETTERS, ETC.

**1634.** LETTER from ERNEST AUGUSTUS, BISHOP OF OSNABURG, afterwards Elector of Hanover, Father of George I., and GEORGE WILLIAM OF BRUNSWICK LUNE-BERG, afterwards Duke of Zelle, to Count ————, requesting permission for three regiments sent to aid the Venetians in Candia to pass through his dominions. Dated $\frac{20}{30}$ Nov., 1668. *Autograph signature. German.*

Lent by G. MILNER GIBSON CULLUM, ESQ.

**1635.** LETTER from JOHN FREDERICK OF BRUNSWICK-LUNEBURG, Duke of Calenburg, Uncle of George I., to Rudolf Augustus, Duke of Brunswick-Luneburg, respecting the payment of the interest of 6000 reichsthalers, borrowed by the town of Brunswick. Dated Hanover, 29 Nov., 1672. *Autograph Signature. German.*

Lent by G. MILNER GIBSON CULLUM, ESQ.

**1636.** DRAFT in French of the first Speech of GEORGE I. at the opening of Parliament, with corrections and alterations. The speech comments in general terms on, the state of affairs, the dangers to be apprehended from "le Pretendant" (*i.e.* King James III.), and other similar matters, the only definite suggestions being a demand for increased revenues for himself and his son. March, 171$\frac{4}{5}$.

Lent by ALFRED MORRISON, ESQ.

**1637.** Two Translations of the above into English.

Lent by ALFRED MORRISON, ESQ.

**1638.** LETTER from GEORGE LOUIS, ELECTOR OF HANOVER, afterwards GEORGE I., to the Duke of Leeds, thanking him for his professions of attachment, and referring to the visit of Lord Danby and his brother to Hanover. Dated Hanover, 22 Dec., 1710. *Autograph signature. French.*

Lent by ALFRED MORRISON, ESQ.

**1639.** LETTER from GEORGE I. to ——————, with congratulations for the New Year. Dated St. James's, $\frac{7}{18}$ Jan., 1715. *Autograph signature. German.*

Lent by G. MILNER GIBSON CULLUM, ESQ.

**1640.** LETTER from GEORGE AUGUSTUS, ELECTORAL PRINCE OF HANOVER, afterwards GEORGE II., to a lady, with expressions of civility and respect. Dated du Camp de Werwick, 27 July [1710?]. *Holograph. French.*

Lent by ALFRED MORRISON, ESQ.

**1641.** WARRANT under Sign Manual of GEORGE II. for the payment to John Scrope of £8000 "for our secret service, without account." Countersigned " H. Pelham " and "G. Lyttelton." Dated Kensington, 24 May, 1751.

Lent by G. MILNER GIBSON CULLUM, ESQ.

**1642.** LETTER from CAROLINE OF ANSPACH, wife of George II., to the Duchess of Dorsét [Elizabeth, wife of Lionel, 1st Duke], referring to the appointment of the Countess of Suffolk [Henrietta, wife of Charles, 9th Earl], as Mistress of the Robes. Dated Hampton Court, 29 June [1730?] *Holograph. French.*

Lent by ALFRED MORRISON, ESQ.

**1643.** LETTER from FREDERICK, PRINCE OF WALES, to Frederick, Duke of Saxe Gotha, with New Year's congratulations. Dated Leicester House, 18 Jan., 1746. *Autograph signature. German.*

Lent by G. MILNER GIBSON CULLUM, ESQ.

**1644.** LETTER from AUGUSTA OF SAXE GOTHA, PRINCESS OF WALES, mother of George III., to her brother Frederick, Duke of Saxe Gotha, with New Year's congratulations. Dated " Pell Mell House," 12 Jan., 1742. *Autograph signature. German.*

Lent by G. MILNER GIBSON CULLUM, ESQ.

**1645.** LETTER from WILLIAM HENRY, DUKE OF GLOUCESTER, son of Frederick, Prince of Wales, to Mr. Perigeaux, banker, Paris. Dated Lyons, May 30, 1785. *Holograph.*

Lent by G. MILNER GIBSON CULLUM, ESQ.

**1646.** LETTER from WILLIAM AUGUSTUS, DUKE OF CUMBERLAND (known as the "Butcher") containing New Year's congratulations. Dated St. James's 29 Dec., 1747. *Autograph signature. German.*

Lent by G. MILNER GIBSON CULLUM, ESQ.

**1647.** LIST of the Names of the Persons chosen by ANNE, PRINCESS OF ORANGE daughter of George II., "Omme te dienen als scheepenen van de Dorpen en Heerlykheeden van Ginneken en Bavel voor den Jaare 1757." Dated "Op ons, Hof d'Orange Zaal," 5 Sept., 1757. *Autograph signature. Dutch.*

Lent by G. MILNER GIBSON CULLUM, ESQ.

**1648.** LETTER from FREDERICK V., KING OF DENMARK, husband of Princess Louisa, daughter of George II., to Frederick, Duke of Saxe-Gotha, with New Year's congratulations. Dated Christiansburg, Copenhagen, 6 Jan. 1749. *Autograph. signature. German.*

Lent by G. MILNER GIBSON CULLUM, ESQ.

**1649.** LETTER from CHRISTIAN VII., KING OF DENMARK, son of Frederick V. and Louisa, daughter of George II., to Frederick, Duke of Saxe-Gotha. . Copenhagen, 26 Mar., 1770. *Autograph signature. German.*

Lent by G. MILNER GIBSON CULLUM, ESQ.

## CASE BB.

### ROYAL LETTERS, ETC.

**1650.** LETTER from GEORGE III. to Lord Ashburton, signifying that he had "taken the bitter potion of appointing the seven Ministers named by the Duke of Portland." These seven were the Duke of Portland, C. J. Fox, and Lords Stormont, Carlisle, Keppel, North, and John Cavendish, and formed the "Coalition Ministry." Dated Queen's House, 2 April, 1783. *Holograph.*

Lent by ALFRED MORRISON, ESQ.

**1651.** LETTER from GEORGE III. to the Queen of Sweden respecting the recall of his Minister. Dated St. James's, 23 Dec., 1808. With *autograph signature,* written after the King had become blind. *French.*

Lent by ALFRED MORRISON, ESQ.

**1652.** ORDER by GEORGE III. for a Court Martial on Thomas Williams, "Private Soldier in our Shropshire Regiment of Militia," for desertion. Dated St. James's, 7 July, 1809. Signed by the King and countersigned by the Earl of Liverpool.

Lent by A. KEILY, ESQ.

**1653.** COLLECTION OF LETTERS from GEORGE III., Edward Duke of York, William Henry Duke of Gloucester, Princess Sophia, and others, to Earl Harcourt. The letters of George III. begin in 1751. Mostly *holograph.*

Lent by E. W. HARCOURT, ESQ.

**1654.** COLLECTION OF LETTERS from CHARLOTTE OF MECKLENBURG-STRELITZ, wife of George III., to Earl and Countess Harcourt, 1769-1817. *Holograph.*

Lent by E. W. HARCOURT, ESQ.

**1655.** LETTER from CHARLOTTE OF MECKLENBURG-STRELITZ, wife of George III. Dated St. James's, 14 Jan. 1766. *Autograph signature. German.*

Lent by G. MILNER GIBSON CULLUM, ESQ.

**1656.** LETTER from CHARLOTTE OF MECKLENBURG-STRELITZ, wife of George III., to Richard Hurd, Bishop of Lichfield (afterwards of Worcester). The letter begins— " My Lord, it will be difficult to decide whose conduct deserves the most to be criticised, my eldest daughter's in sending you a present of a young lady, or mine in encouraging her to do so," and continues in the same strain. Dated.Queen's House, 26 January, 1781. *Holograph.*

Lent by ALFRED MORRISON, ESQ.

**1657.** LETTER from CHARLOTTE OF MECKLENBURG-STRELITZ, wife of George III., to Lady Charlotte ——— ———, containing congratulations and good wishes on her marriage. The letter ends, " Receive the Blessing of yr affectionnate Queens Charlotte." Dated Windsor, 28 Mar., 1799.

Lent by ALFRED MORRISON, ESQ.

**1658.** LETTER from ADOLPHUS FREDERICK, Duke of Cambridge, to the Rev. Thomas Morgan, telling him that he has presented his letter to Lord Liverpool. Dated Calais, Aug. 16, 1820. *Holograph.*

Lent by A. KEILY, ESQ.

**1659.** LETTER from AUGUSTUS FREDERICK, DUKE OF SUSSEX, son of George III. forwarding a letter received by the Duke of Kent respecting a nephew of the Master of the Rolls. Dated Kensington Palace, Sep. 12, 1812. *Holograph.*

Lent by G. MILNER GIBSON CULLUM, ESQ.

**1660.** LETTER from EDWARD, DUKE OF KENT, to Major-General Alured Clarke : " The information you give me that His Majesty had said he would consent to my returning to England very soon is by much the most comfortable news I have received for many years. . . . . Every account we have from the States confirms the idea that the French have it seriously in contemplation to attack us here this summer. Our fortifications are in a ruinous state, our garrison excessively weak, and I am confident if we were to be attacked by any serious force, we should be able to give a very poor account of ourselves." Dated Halifax, May 26, 1795, *Holograph.*

Lent by ALFRED MORRISON, ESQ.

Q

1661. LETTER from EDWARD, DUKE OF KENT, to the Earl of Buchan respecting the political situation of the day. Dated Kensington Palace, 1 Dec., 1810.
Lent by A. KEILY, ESQ.

1662. LETTER from ERNEST, DUKE OF CUMBERLAND, afterwards KING OF HANOVER, to William Battini. He says, "Pray does Lady A—— intend to recriminate? is she become mad? Otherwise I do not understand what she means by retaining any lawyer." Dated St. James, Friday afternoon. *Holograph.*
Lent by ALFRED MORRISON, ESQ.

1663. LETTER from ERNEST, DUKE OF CUMBERLAND, afterwards KING OF HANOVER, declining an invitation to dinner on the grounds that he cannot absent himself from headquarters "for fear of anything particular occurring which might demand an immediate answer." Dated Bristol, 8 Sept., 1813. *Holograph.*
Lent by G. MILNER GIBSON CULLUM, ESQ.

1664. LETTER from FREDERICK, DUKE OF YORK, to Richard Hurd, Bishop of Worcester, thanking him in the King's name for his letter, and expressing his Majesty's pleasure at finding the Bishop's sentiments coincided with his own on the question of the emancipation of the Catholics. Dated Horse Guards, March 9, 1801. *Holograph.*
Lent by ALFRED MORRISON, ESQ.

1665. LETTER of WILLIAM FREDERICK, DUKE OF GLOUCESTER, as Chancellor of Cambridge, on University matters. Dated Croome, Dec. 13th, 1823. *Autograph.*
Lent by ALFRED MORRISON, ESQ.

1666. LETTER of WILLIAM FREDERICK, DUKE OF GLOUCESTER, to the Rev. George Vanburgh. Dated Bagshot Park, June 19, 1834. *Holograph.*
Lent by G. MILNER GIBSON CULLUM, ESQ.

1667. LETTER from PRINCESS AMELIA, the youngest daughter of George III., to her mother, Queen Charlotte. Undated. *Holograph.*
Lent by G. MILNER GIBSON CULLUM, ESQ.

1668. LETTER from PRINCESS AUGUSTA SOPHIA, daughter of George III., to General Charles FitzRoy, husband of her sister Amelia. Undated. *Holograph.*
Lent by G. MILNER GIBSON CULLUM, ESQ.

1669. LETTER from CHARLOTTE, DUCHESS (afterwards QUEEN) OF WÜRTEMBERG, daughter of George III., to Frederick, Duke of York, begging him to use his influence to obtain for the Duke of Würtemberg the "indemnifications for the severe losses he had suffered during the war," which according to the treaty concluded with the Duke for his troops, Great Britain promised to obtain for him. Dated Louisbourg, 22 May, 1802. *Holograph.*

Lent by ALFRED MORRISON, ESQ.

1670. LETTER from CHARLOTTE, QUEEN OF WÜRTEMBERG, eldest daughter of George III., to her brother, George IV., expressing her sorrow at not seeing him before leaving England. Dated St. James's Palace, October 7, 1829. *Holograph.*

Lent by G. MILNER GIBSON CULLUM, ESQ.

1671. LETTER of ELIZABETH, LANDGRAVINE OF HESSE-HOMBURG, daughter of George III. Dated Hanover, Jan. 11, 1830. *Holograph.*

Lent by G. MILNER GIBSON CULLUM, ESQ.

1672. LETTER from MARY, DUCHESS OF GLOUCESTER, daughter of George III., to Mrs. Nepean (Anne, daughter of Sir Herbert Jenner Fust, and wife of the Rev. E. Nepean, Incumbent of Grosvenor Chapel), inviting her and her husband to dinner, "though I know that Thursday is the day the family meet at your Father's." [*Circ.* 1850.] *Holograph.*

Lent by G. MILNER GIBSON CULLUM, ESQ.

1673. LETTER from PRINCESS SOPHIA, daughter of George III., to her father, written when a child, in French. Undated. *Holograph.*

Lent by ALFRED MORRISON, ESQ.

1674. LETTER from PRINCESS SOPHIA, daughter of George III., to Mr. Bridge, jeweller, respecting some alterations to be made in some jewellery and the price of a pair of pearl bracelets. Dated Tuesday morning, April 17. *Holograph.*

Lent by G. MILNER GIBSON CULLUM, ESQ.

1675. "Address to the Deity," copied out by GEORGE AUGUSTUS FREDERICK, PRINCE OF WALES, afterwards George IV., written in copy-book hand at the age of twelve. Dated 1774. *Holograph.*

Lent by ALFRED MORRISON, ESQ.

1676. LETTER from GEORGE IV., which begins, "You may easily imagine, warm and sincere as my affections are towards you, I have had but little rest since we separated last night. Let me implore of you to come to me ... for I shall hate myself until I have the opportunity of expressing *personally* to you those true and genuine feelings of affection for you which will never cease to live in *my Heart* so long as that Heart itself continues to beat. I am much too unhappy to say more."—Dated, C[arlton] H[ouse], 3 o'clock, July 11, 1822. *Holograph.*

Lent by ALFRED MORRISON, ESQ.

**1677.** LETTER from GEORGE IV. to the Duke of Wellington offering him the command of the army. The letter begins " My dear Friend," and ends " Your sincere Friend G.R." Dated Royal Lodge, 15 Aug. 1827. *Holograph.*
Lent by ALFRED MORRISON, ESQ.

**1678.** WARRANT under sign manual of GEORGE, PRINCE REGENT, afterwards GEORGE IV., appointing David Morier, Consul-General in France, and James Drummond, a Commissary-General of the Army, to be Commissioners of Deposit in accordance with the provisions of the Treaty of Paris of 25 April, 1814, and subsequent conventions for the settlement of claims of British subjects on the Government of France. Dated Carlton House, 15 June, 1818. *Autograph Signature.*
Lent by CAPTAIN TELFER, R.N.

**1679.** ANSWER to the above from the DUKE OF WELLINGTON accepting the command. Dated Kington Hall (?) 17 Aug. 1827. *Holograph.*
Lent by ALFRED MORRISON, ESQ.

**1680.** LETTER from CAROLINE OF BRUNSWICK, wife of George IV. to ———— summoning him to England to give evidence at her trial. Dated London, 8 July, 1820. *Holograph. Italian.*
The name of the person to whom the letter was sent has been carefully erased.
Lent by ALFRED MORRISON, ESQ.

**1681.** " A COPIE of the letter which the Princess of Wales has written to Mr. Brougham." This copy, which is in the handwriting of CAROLINE, PRINCESS OF WALES, wife of George IV., asks Brougham for "detail upon what new grand fresh attaque can be made after the declaration of the House of Commons," and encloses a copy of a letter to Lord Liverpool, desiring him to deliver a letter to Princess Charlotte. Dated Naples, 2 Jan. 1815.
Lent by A. KEILY, ESQ.

**1682.** LETTER from MARIA ANNE FITZHERBERT, written at the Prince's desire, respecting some arrangements to be made about warming a house. *Holograph.*
Lent by ALFRED MORRISON, ESQ.

**1683.** LETTER from MARIA ANNE FITZHERBERT to George, Prince of Wales, afterwards George IV. She complains that her last letter is unnoticed, and says, " Do not, Sir, by contemptuous silence compel me for my own justification to appeal to the opinions of impartial persons by showing them my letters to you on this occasion, that they may judge whether or not I have said anything in them to merit the treatment I have met with." Dated, 25 Oct., 1812. *Holograph.*
Lent by the HON. GERALD PONSONBY.

## CASE CC.

### ROYAL AND POLITICAL LETTERS.

**1684.** LETTER from PRINCESS CHARLOTTE OF WALES to Mr. Bridge respecting a ring. Dated 31st, Bognor, 1811. *Holograph.*

Lent by G. MILNER GIBSON CULLUM, ESQ.

**1685.** LETTER from PRINCESS CHARLOTTE OF WALES to Miss Hayman, giving details of her movements and those of her mother. She says also "The visit of the P.R. took place and they met again last Wednesday. She goes again to-morrow. I should not wonder at all to see him again. As to the K., I understand he is as mad as puss, and no chance I believe whatever of his recovery." Dated 7 May [1813?] *Holograph.*

Lent by ALFRED MORRISON, ESQ.

**1686.** LETTER from WILLIAM, DUKE OF CLARENCE, afterwards WILLIAM IV. to Captain J. Wright, respecting a case of noyeau which had been sent him as a present. Dated St. James, Dec. 15, 1801. *Holograph.*

Lent by CAPT. HENRY WRIGHT.

**1687.** LETTER from WILLIAM, DUKE OF CLARENCE, afterwards WILLIAM IV., to Captain J. Wright. Dated Bushey House, April 22nd, 1803. *Holograph.*

Lent by CAPT. HENRY WRIGHT.

**1688.** LETTER from WILLIAM, DUKE OF CLARENCE, afterwards WILLIAM IV., to Captain J. Wright, thanking him for some pheasants. He also remarks in the letter, "As for this rascal Bonaparte, I wish he was at the bottom of the sea. All naval officers think invasion improbable, and that is clearly my opinion." Dated Bushey House, Dec. 15, 1803. *Holograph.*

Lent by CAPT. HENRY WRIGHT.

**1689.** LETTER from WILLIAM, DUKE OF CLARENCE, afterwards WILLIAM IV. to Captain J. Wright. Dated Bushey House, Thursday night. *Holograph.*

Lent by CAPT. HENRY WRIGHT.

**1690.** LETTER from WILLIAM, DUKE OF CLARENCE, afterwards WILLIAM IV., to Mr. Vincent, respecting a change of tutors for his son, Lord Augustus FitzClarence, and explaining his reasons for making the change. Dated Bushey House, March 1st, 1826. *Holograph.*

Lent by ALFRED MORRISON, ESQ.

**1691.** LETTER from WILLIAM, DUKE OF CLARENCE, afterwards WILLIAM IV., to Mr. Powell, expressing the pleasure he will have in hearing that "Chambers" is a free man again, and hoping that both will be more prudent for the future. Dated Bushey House, Thursday night. *Holograph.*
Lent by H. SPENCER WALPOLE, ESQ.

**1692.** LETTER from HENRY ST. JOHN, VISCOUNT BOLINGBROKE to the Duke of Marlborough (?), respecting "the most scandalous and malicious falsities relating to our affairs" that had recently appeared in the *Ghent Gazette.* He directs the Duke to seize the author and make him divulge his authority. Dated Whitehall, 14 Oct., 1712. *Holograph.*
Lent by H. SAXE WYNDHAM, ESQ.

**1693.** LETTER from HENRY ST. JOHN, VISCOUNT BOLINGBROKE to the Marquis de Trivie, announcing the death of Queen Anne and the accession "de nostre auguste Roy George." Dated Whitehall, 7 August, 1714. *Holograph. French.*
Lent by ALFRED MORRISON, ESQ.

**1694.** LETTER from HENRY ST. JOHN, VISCOUNT BOLINGBROKE to his brother Lord St. John, respecting some pictures which he had left at his brother's house. On the back is the draft of Lord St. John's reply. Dated Battersea, 14 July, 1744. *Holograph.*
Lent by ALFRED MORRISON, ESQ.

**1695.** COPY, in the handwriting of EDMUND BURKE, of the finding of the Court-Martial on Admiral Keppel in 1778.
Lent by ALFRED MORRISON, ESQ.

**1696.** PROMISSORY Note for £100 from EDMUND BURKE to Samuel Athawes. Dated 16 Mar., 1782. *Holograph.*
Lent by G. MILNER GIBSON CULLUM, ESQ.

**1697.** LETTER from GEORGE CANNING to the Prince de Polignac [French Ambassador in England], referring to negotiations for a treaty with France. He states that Mr. Huskisson is of opinion that the omission of the article respecting Jersey and of another article respecting "European dominions" will reduce the treaty "à très peu de chose," and be "a considerable source of squabble and appeal." Dated Foreign Office, 18 Jan., 1826. *Holograph.*
Lent by ALFRED MORRISON, ESQ.

**1698.** LETTER from CHARLES JAMES FOX to R. B. Sheridan. Speaking of the taking of Pondicherry, he says: "I do not think it possible to depreciate the importance of it, but to take away the merit of it from the Ministers, and to show that we do not owe it to any activity or wisdom of theirs, I believe is easy." Undated [probably 1793, the date of the third taking of Pondicherry]. *Holograph.*
Lent by ALFRED MORRISON, ESQ.

**1699.** LETTER from CHARLES JAMES FOX to the Prince de Tallyrand. He informs the Prince that his colleagues in the Cabinet agreed with him " sur l'affaire en question," also " lorsque je contois à sa majesté ce que j'ai eu l'honneur de vous communiquer, Elle montra une emotion aussi vive que naturelle ; " but he adds, " Je vous dis ceci, monsieur, sous le sceau du secret, parceque je scais bien que sa majesté s'approuveroit nullement qu'on divulgerât ce qui s'est passé tête-à-tête entre elle et son Ministre dans un entretien confidentiel quel qu'en ait été le sujet." Dated Downing Street, 20 Feb., 1806. *Holograph. French.*

Lent by ALFRED MORRISON, ESQ.

**1700.** LETTER from SIR STEPHEN FOX to John Taylor relating to Orders of Loan which were deposited in the hands of the latter as security for John Knight, late cashier of the Customs, making clear his accounts. Dated Whitehall, 6 March, 1698. *Holograph.*

Lent by H. SAXE WYNDHAM, ESQ.

**1701.** LETTER from the RIGHT HON. GEORGE GRENVILLE to George, Lord Lyttelton, answering a letter of condolence on the death of Lord Egremont. Also saying that he has received the draft for a thousand pounds upon Mr. Hoare, and that he will leave Lord Lyttelton's bond with him when he receives the money. Dated Downing Street, Sept. 20, 1763. *Holograph.*

Lent by The VISCOUNT COBHAM.

**1702.** LETTER from PHILIP YORKE, 2ND EARL OF HARDWICK, to George, Lord Lyttelton, on current politics of the day, informing him that Lord Egremont has the seals of the Southern Province. Dated Grosvenor Square, Oct. 17, 1761. *Holograph.*

Lent by The VISCOUNT COBHAM.

**1703.** LETTER from ROBERT HARLEY, afterwards EARL OF OXFORD, to ———— sending him a " Saxon transcript " and a picture. Dated 27 July, 1699. *Holograph.*

Lent by H. SAXE WYNDHAM, ESQ.

**1704.** BILL for stationery and books delivered to ROBERT HARLEY, Speaker of the House of Commons, afterwards EARL OF OXFORD. Dated Oct. 24, 1704. *With autograph acknowledgment.*

Lent by G. MILNER GIBSON CULLUM, ESQ.

**1705.** LETTER from GEORGE, afterwards LORD LYTTELTON, and his father, Sir Thomas Lyttelton, Bart., expressing his pleasure at the praise his father bestowed upon his speech, and giving him the last news from the seat of war in Holland, which is, that the Prince of Orange was on Wednesday last declared Statdholder of the Netherlands. Dated April 25, 1747. *Holograph.*

Lent by The VISCOUNT COBHAM.

**1706.** LETTER from WILLIAM MURRAY, EARL OF MANSFIELD, to George, Lord Lyttelton who had made a request respecting a vacant Bishopric which he wishes to be bestowed on his brother Charles. Lord Mansfield fears that to give this "lift" "won't do at present, and improper to attempt." Dated Kenwood, Oct. 12, 1759. *Holograph.*
Lent by The VISCOUNT COBHAM.

**1707.** LETTER from THOMAS PELHAM, DUKE OF HOLLES AND NEWCASTLE, to George afterwards Lord Lyttelton, congratulating him on his success at Bewdley, and setting forward his own contributions to that success. Dated Newcastle House, 2 Oct. 1744. *Holograph.*
Lent by the VISCOUNT COBHAM.

**1708.** LETTER from The RIGHT HONORABLE HENRY PELHAM to Lord Lyttelton, about the appointment of a Mr. Forbes to a military post, and respecting foreign politics and the movement of the troops upon the Continent. Dated Sep. 24, 1747. *Holograph.*
Lent by The VISCOUNT COBHAM.

## CASE DD.

### *POLITICAL, NAVAL AND MILITARY.*

**1709.** LETTER from RIGHT HON. SPENCER PERCEVAL to a lady named "Margaret," enclosing a draft for £200, which he assures her it gives him more pleasure to send than it can her to accept. Dated Hampstead, Oct. 27, 1803. *Holograph.*
Lent by H. SPENCER WALPOLE, ESQ.

**1710.** LETTER from WILLIAM PITT, afterwards EARL OF CHATHAM, to Sir George, afterwards Lord Lyttelton, announcing his engagement to Lady Hester Grenville, he remarks, "To whom has it happened but to me, to receive the object of his whole heart, from the hands of a family whose alliance a Duke of Bedford would ambition with every endearing and flattering circumstance of preference and joy." Dated, Bath, Oct. 22, 1754. *Holograph.*
Lent by The VISCOUNT COBHAM.

**1711.** LETTER from WILLIAM PITT, EARL OF CHATHAM, to Lord ——— [probably Charles Sackville, Earl of Middlesex, afterwards 2nd Duke of Dorset], thanking him for his letter, "by which I have two satisfactions, one of knowing that Knole is safe, and the other that England may be so, from rioters at least, if gentlemen will follow the example you have shown." He goes on to inform him of the recent movements of the Fleet. Dated 7 Oct., 1757. *Holograph.*
Lent by ALFRED MORRISON, ESQ.

**1712.** LETTER from CHARLES WATSON WENTWORTH, MARQUIS OF ROCKINGHAM, to George, Lord Lyttelton. He says, "I am so fully satisfied with the conduct your Lordship, the Chancellor, and the five Lords took last night, that indeed for one I could wish to enter our short line of argument in a protest." Dated Grosvenor Square, Friday, P.M. 1 o'clock. *Holograph.*
Lent by The VISCOUNT COBHAM.

**1713.** LETTER from RICHARD, 1ST EARL TEMPLE, to George, Lord Lyttelton. He says among other things, "All my philosophy could scarce furnish me with the smallest mite of patience whilst the Princess [of Wales] was here: Rainy weather and not one gleam of sun, the days very fine before she came and since she has left us." Also, "As to Wilkes's affair by the Post I may say but little and less of what relates to No. 45 [of the "North Briton"] but a year's imprisonment and five hundred pounds fine . . . is I own to me very astonishing." Dated Stowe, 5 July, 1768. *Holograph.*
Lent by The VISCOUNT COBHAM.

**1714.** LETTER from the Right Hon. CHARLES TOWNSHEND to George, Lord Lyttelton, enclosing a copy of his letter to the Duke of Newcastle. He says, "I dined yesterday at Devonshire House and . . . I took the opportunity of asserting the necessity of union and immediate activity; union declaredly with Mr. Pitt and Mr. Yorke and activity both in a summer and a winter plan. Mr. Conway and Mr. Walpole were present, the Duke made strong general profession: Mr. Conway seem'd to think with me and Mr. Walpole went before me in many points." Dated Grosvenor Square, 2 May, 1764. *Holograph.*
Lent by The VISCOUNT COBHAM.

**1715.** SIR ROBERT WALPOLE'S banking account with Robert Mann from 1714 to 1718, settled and signed by Sir Robert Walpole.
Lent by H. SPENCER WALPOLE, ESQ.

**1716.** BIBLE used by SIR ROBERT WALPOLE at college, and given by him to his son Horace. Autograph note by Horace Walpole on fly leaf at end.
Lent by H. SPENCER WALPOLE, ESQ.

**1717.** Ædes WALPOLIANA, or "a description of the collection of pictures at Houghton Hall, in Norfolk, the seat of the Right Honourable Sir Robert Walpole, Earl of Orford." *Manuscript.*
Lent by H. SPENCER WALPOLE, ESQ.

**1718.** LETTER from SIR ROBERT WALPOLE, afterwards EARL OF ORFORD, putting off an appointment because Lord Townshend has sent him word that he wishes to talk with him on matters of business. Dated Arlington Street, Monday, 3 o'clock. *Holograph.*
Lent by ALFRED MORRISON, ESQ.

**1719.** LETTER from GEORGE WASHINGTON to Mr. Wolcott, thanking him for his account of a meeting which took place in the State House yard. He will receive with satisfaction all information respecting the sentiments of the people upon the Treaty with Great Britain. "It is an interesting subject, and to know the sense of the people generally on it, and that of cool, dispassionate men who are judges of the subject without prejudice or partiality, would be very agreeable to me.' Dated, Mount Vernon, 29th July, 1795. *Holograph.*

Lent by ALFRED MORRISON, ESQ.

**1720.** LETTER from GEORGE WASHINGTON to the Emperor [Francis II.], begging that the Marquis de la Fayette might be set at liberty and allowed to come to America. Dated Philadelphia, 15th May, 1796. *Holograph.*

Lent by ALFRED MORRISON, ESQ.

**1721.** MEMORIAL by SIR RALPH ABERCROMBY recounting his services during 32 years of military service. "It was his lot," he says, "to bring into order the worst regiment of cavalry in the army." He complains bitterly of his treatment in the matter of raising a regiment of infantry in 1781. "After 32 years service, after spending in the purchase of commissions near six thousand pounds, and after seeing many junior officers go over his head, he is indeed a general officer, but without employment, and with an income not forty pounds a year better than the day he entered the service." Dated 9th April, 1788. *Holograph.*

Lent by ALFRED MORRISON, ESQ.

**1722.** LETTER from NAPOLEON BONAPARTE to Louis XVIII. in answer to a letter respecting the return of the King. He says "Vous ne devez plus souhaiter votre retour en France ; il vous faudrait marcher sur 100,000 cadavres. Sacrifiez votre interet au repos et au bonheur de la France. L'histoire vous en tiendra compte." Dated Paris, 20 Fructidor, An. 8 [*i.e.* 7 Sept., 1800.]. *Holograph. French.*

Lent by ALFRED MORRISON, ESQ.

**1723.** "EXTRAIT d'une letre particulière de Constantinople du 4 fevrier 1801 (12 pluvoise an. 9)," containing news of the landing of the English in Egypt and of the attitude of the Turks. The letter is corrected, and passages added and suppressed in the handwriting of NAPOLEON BONAPARTE. The passage added by Napoleon reads "Ils [the Turks] ont aussi l'éveil et calculent très bien que l'Egypte entre les mains des Anglais serait un coup plus funeste pour la puissance ottomane qu'entre les mains des Français."

Lent by ALFRED MORRISON, ESQ.

**1724.** LETTER from CUTHBERT, LORD COLLINGWOOD, to Lord Robert Fitzgerald, Ambassador at Lisbon. The Ambassador had forwarded to him a note from the Portuguese Minister, respecting British ships at Lagos. Lord Collingwood states that it is very rarely that any of our ships go to Lagos, and gives an opinion that the complaint is the "prelude to their following the example of Prussia and shutting their ports altogether." Dated Ocean, 26 April, 1806. *Holograph*.

Lent by ALFRED MORRISON, ESQ.

**1725.** LETTER from CHARLES, 1ST MARQUIS CORNWALLIS, to B. Roebuck, stating that he has sent Capt. Kyd, Surveyor-General and Lieut. Robinson, his aide-de-camp, "to obtain every information in their power, previous to my arrival, of the future means of carrying on the war." He recommends Lieut. Robinson to Mr. Roebuck. Dated Calcutta, 10 Nov. 1790. *Holograph*.

Lent by ALFRED MORRISON, ESQ

**1726.** LETTER from CAPTAIN JAMES COOK to Captain John Walker, of Whitby. He begins, "I should have answered your last favour sooner but waited to know whether I should go to Greenwich Hospital or to the South Sea. The latter is now fixed upon; I expect to be ready to sail about the latter end of April with my old ship the Resolution and the Discovery." Dated Mile End, London, 14th February, 1776. *Holograph.*

Lent by ALFRED MORRISON, ESQ.

**1727.** LETTER from PRINCE EUGENE OF SAVOY to the Count de Wrangel, respecting the disorders caused in Brussels "par une Trouppe seditieuse des Vagabonds," and a question of parole. Dated Vienna, 22 Feb. 1719. *Autograph Signature*. *Fr nch*.

Lent by H. SAXE WYNDHAM, ESQ.

## CASE EE.

### *NAVAL AND MILITARY AND LITERARY.*

**1728.** LETTER from JOHN CHURCHILL, DUKE OF MARLBOROUGH, written at the siege of Tournay. He says: "This army has never at any sieges til this meet with mynes, so that our Ingeniers moue very slowly by which they give the soldiers time to accustum themselves to be blowen up." Dated August, 1709. *Holograph*.

Lent by ALFRED MORRISON, ESQ.

**1729.** LETTER from JOHN CHURCHILL, DUKE OF MARLBORUGH, to ——— [probably to Lord Godolphin]. He is sorry that an augmentation of troops will meet with great difficulty, and gives information respecting the probable increase of strength on the part of the French during the next year "so that if 38 [*i.e.* Godolphin himself] thinkes it practicable for him to continue in the service he may be the better able to advise what is fitt to be done." He mentions resolutions of the States respecting the sending of the "Pallatin" troops to King Charles [claimant to the Spanish Crown against Philip of Anjou, afterward the Emperor Charles VI.]. These resolutions he has sent to "Mr. Sec. Harley." He advises that Mr. St. John should prepare estimates for the Saxon troops and the regiment of Bothmar. In conclusion he desires that the letter should be burnt "if you find that 38 has a mind to retier." Dated Helchin, 26 Sept., 1707. *Holograph.*

Lent by ALFRED MORRISON, ESQ.

1730. LETTER from JOHN CHURCHILL, DUKE OF MARLBOROUGH, to Queen Anne, full of strong remonstrance. "I am in my judgment persuaded that if you do not alter the resolution you seem to have taken, by which you will make it impossible for 10 [Lord Godolphin] to serve you with any success, you will not only disturb the quiet of your own life but also ruin the prodistant Religion and all the libertys of Europe." Dated Hague, Oct. 4th, 1707. *Holograph.*

The letter is in the handwriting of the Duke, but the tone of it, and the fact that the writer takes the cypher 40 to represent himself or herself, while the Duke in another letter of 1708 uses 39 for himself, make it seem probable that it is a letter of the Duchess. It is endorsed by Lord Godolphin, "D. of Marlb: to the Q."

Lent by ALFRED MORRISON, ESQ.

1731. LETTER from HORATIO, VISCOUNT NELSON, to Captain Collingwood, giving news of the Fleet, the sortie from Mantua, that "Genl. Buonaparte is wounded in the thigh," etc. He adds, "Mr. Pitt seems as strong as ever, what have we to do with the Princess [of Wales] private amours, the world say, there is faults on both sides—like enough, thank God I was not born in high life." Dated *Captain,* Leghorn Roads, 1 Aug. 1796. *Holograph,* written with the right hand.

Lent by ALFRED MORRISON, ESQ.

1732. LETTER from HORATIO, VISCOUNT NELSON, to Captain Horte, enclosing a note to Lord Melville asking him to attend to his sincere wishes for Captain Horte's employment afloat. Dated *Victory,* Oct. 12, 1804. *Holograph.*

Lent by H. SPENCER WALPOLE, ESQ.

1733. LETTER from HORATIO, VISCOUNT NELSON, to Lady Hamilton, written off Dunmore. He says, "We have fair wind, and God, I hope, will soon grant us a happy meeting." Dated off Dunmore, Sep. 16, 1805, 11 A.M. *Holograph.*

Lent by EDWARD WALFORD, ESQ.

1734. LETTER from ADMIRAL GEORGE BRYDGES RODNEY, afterwards LORD RODNEY, to George, Lord Lyttelton, congratulating him on the invasion from the port of Havre being suspended for the winter and all the troops having left the town. Dated, In the Road of Havre, Nov. 3, 1759. *Holograph.*

Lent by the VISCOUNT COBHAM.

**1735.** LETTER from HORATIO, VISCOUNT NELSON, to Lady Hamilton. He says: "A frigate is coming down which we take to be the *Decade* from the fleet off Cadiz, if the battle has been fought I shall be sorely vext, but I cannot help myself." Dated *Victory*, 30 leagues S.W. from Scilly, 20 Sept. 1805. *Holograph*, written with the left hand.

Lent by ALFRED MORRISON, ESQ.

**1736.** LETTER from HENRY MORDAUNT, EARL OF PETERBOROUGH, to Lord ———— defending himself at great length against "the double accusation of lavishing the public money, and not giving itt to the support of the King of Spaine as I ought." Dated "Abord the *Resolution* off Genoa, 12 Dec., 1706. *Holograph*.

Lent by H. SAXE WYNDHAM, ESQ.

**1737.** LETTER from ARTHUR WELLESLEY, afterwards 1ST DUKE OF WELLINGTON, to J. H. Piele, respecting treasure alleged to have been concealed in certain villages in the neighbourhood of Bangalore, when Hyder Ali first seized the place. Dated Seringapatam, 6 Aug., 1801. *Holograph*.

Lent by ALFRED MORRISON, ESQ.

**1738.** LETTER from ARTHUR WELLESLEY, DUKE OF WELLINGTON, to the Marchioness of Salisbury thanking her for her congratulations on the battle of "Victoria," and informing her of a battle [one of those in the Pyrenees] just gained after a much harder fight. He says he was never so hard pressed as on the 25th of the last month, but on the 27th and 28th he gained a great victory. "I never saw the soldiers fight so well." Dated August 3rd, 1813.

Lent by ALFRED MORRISON, ESQ.

**1739.** LETTER from JOSEPH ADDISON to Ambrose Phillips, praising a pastoral and an essay on pastoral by the latter, though rather faintly. He goes on to give items of literary news :—" Mr. Row has promised ye Town a farce this winter, but it dos not yet appear." "Mr. Dennis has a Tragedy that is now in its first run of Acting. It is called Liberty Asserted, and has ye Whiggs for its patrons and supporters." Dated London, 10 March, 1703 [4], *Holograph*.

Lent by ALFRED MORRISON, ESQ.

**1740.** LETTER from JOSEPH ADDISON to John Taylour, promising to remind the Lord Lieutenant of his promise to two clergymen recommended by the latter, and to take care that "our votes, speeches, and any other public transactions that appear in print" should be sent to him. Dated Dublin Castle, 7 May, 1709. *Holograph*.

Lent by H. SAXE WYNDHAM ESQ.

**1741.** LETTER from WILLIAM BECKFORD, author of *Vathek*, to Mr. Clarke of 38 Bond Street. He refers to the sale of the "Bedford Missal" [now Add, MS., 18,850 in the British Museum], which he thinks "might have been worked up higher." In a

. postscript he says "I find G. Mannering most admirable; as far as I have read even preferable to Waverley. At page 309, the author alludes to the tale of *Vathek*." Dated Salisbury, 12 April, 1815. *Holograph.*

              Lent by ALFRED MORRISON, ESQ.

**1742.** LETTER from JAMES BOSWELL to Thomas Percy, afterwards Bishop of Dromore. "Dr. Johnson and your humble servant and some more people whom you will be glad to see are to sup this evening at the 'Crown and Anchor' in the Strand. If you return in time pray be with us." Dated Saturday, 13 April ——. *Holograph.*

              Lent by ALFRED MORRISON, ESQ.

**1743.** ORIGINAL DRAFT by GEORGE GORDON NOEL BYRON, LORD BYRON, of the poem entitled "The Farewell," beginning:

"Fare thee well—and if for ever,
Still for ever fare thee well."

With many alterations and corrections. Written 18 March 1816.

              Lent by ALFRED MORRISON, ESQ.

**1744.** LETTER from LORD BYRON to R. B. Hoppner, announcing his determination to go to Switzerland, "this country being in a state of proscription, and all my friends exiled or arrested," "and the Guiccioli menaced with a convent." He says also: "I have sent two dramas to England," one upon "Sardanapalus," the other upon "The Two Foscari" (a Venetian story), both in five acts. Dated Ravenna,' 23 July, 1821. *Holograph.*

              Lent by ALFRED MORRISON, ESQ.

**1745.** "Εὐριπίδου 'Εκάβη. Euripidis Hecuba ... Edidit R. Porson. Cantabrigiæ, 1802." Belonged to LORD BYRON. It contains translations of words in his handwriting, and was bequeathed by him "to the Monitor's Library prior to his leaving Harrow. Tuesday December 4th, A.D. 1804."

            Lent by The HEADMASTER OF HARROW SCHOOL.

**1746.** REVELATION viii. 7, written by LORD BYRON at the end of one of his poems.

              Lent by JOHN MURRAY, ESQ.

**1747.** LETTER from LADY BYRON to the Hon. Augusta Leigh (Lord Byron's sister). She thanks her for her help and comfort, and says that there was no cause to be alarmed about Lord Byron's health. Dated 23 June, 1816. *Holograph.*

              Lent by ALFRED MORRISON, ESQ.

**1748.** NOTE by the HON. AUGUSTA LEIGH respecting Lord Byron's memoirs. She relates how, after negotiations with Mr. Thomas Moore, Mr. Hobhouse, and Mr. John Murray, the publisher, the MSS. were by the advice of Mr. Hobhouse destroyed at Mr. Murray's house on the 17th of May, 1824. *Holograph.*

              Lent by ALFRED MORRISON, ESQ.

## CASE FF.

*LITERARY (Continued).*

**1749.** AUTOGRAPH MS. of the poem by ROBERT BURNS, "On turning up a mouse in her nest in the beginning of the winter 1785, with the plough." Beginning:
"Wee, sleeket, cowrin', tim'rous beastie,
O what a panic's in thy breastie,
Thou need na start awa sae hasty
          Wi' bickerin' brattle;
I wad be laith to rin an' chase thee
          Wi' murd'ring pattle."
*Lent by* ALFRED MORRISON, ESQ.

**1750.** LETTER of Sylvander [ROBERT BURNS] to Clarinda [Mrs. Maclehose, *née* Agnes Craig]. Beginning "The Impertnence of fools." Letter No. 25. [Date 1788].
*Lent by* ALFRED MORRISON, ESQ.

**1751.** LETTER from THOMAS CAMPBELL to Mons. Billing, containing an invitation to a party at his house. Dated Saturday, 23rd May. *Holograph.*
*Lent by* G. MILNER GIBSON CULLUM, ESQ.

**1752.** LETTER from PHILIP DORMER STANHOPE, 4TH EARL OF CHESTERFIELD, to his son, expressing delight in the boy's progress in languages and especially in Greek, and going on to a definition of poetry, and a short dissertation on metre. Dated Bath, 26 April, 1739. *Holograph.*
*Lent by* ALFRED MORRISON, ESQ.

**1753.** LETTER from PHILIP DORMER STANHOPE, EARL OF CHESTERFIELD, to George, afterwards Lord Lyttelton, expressing his indignation at the order in Council ordering the Peers to go into mourning for Queen Caroline, when a former order had forbidden the Peers to wear mourning for their own near relations. He says, "This new order of Council seems to me to be a declaration that no public marks of regard, tenderness, and affection shall be shown in this kingdom, but for the sacred persons of the Royal family." Dated Bath, Nov. 20, 1737. *Holograph.*
*Lent by* The VISCOUNT COBHAM.

**1754.** AUTOGRAPH poem by HARTLEY COLERIDGE, beginning:
"Where dwells she now? That life of joy
Which seem'd as age would ne'er destroy."
*Lent by* G. MILNER GIBSON CULLUM, ESQ.

**1755.** Letter from Samuel Taylor Coleridge to Mary Evans, written when the poet was an undergraduate at Cambridge. He gives an amusing account of a mishap which befel Mr. Newton, the Mathematical Lecturer, at Jesus College, describes his own attempts at learning the violin. He ends with a song, the "Complaint of Nina-thoma." Dated Jesus College, Cambridge, 7 Feb., 1793. *Holograph.*
Lent by Alfred Morrison, Esq.

**1756.** Receipt from William Congreve to John Warner & Co. for £40. Dated 8 Dec., 1719. *Holograph.*
Lent by G. Milner Gibson Cullum, Esq.

**1757.** Letter from William Cowper to his cousin, General Cowper, with a poem entitled "The Negro's Complaint." Dated Weston Underwood, 14 April, 1788 *Holograph.*
Lent by Alfred Morrison, Esq.

**1758.** Letter from William Cowper to his brother, regretting to hear of his indisposition, and informing him that he is going to be accountable to docket for a new electrical machine. Dated Weston, Nov. 17, 1793. *Holograph.*
Lent by G. Milner Gibson Cullum, Esq.

**1759.** Letter from Daniel Defoe to Lord ———. He refers to the attempted assassination of Harley by Guiscard, "The Person with whom I endeavoured to plant your interest has been strangely taken up since I had that occasion, viz. First in suffering the operation of the surgeon to heal the wound of the assassin, and since on accumulating honours from Parliament, Queen and People. On Thursday evening her Majesty created him Earl Mortimer, Earl of Oxford, and Lord Harley of Wigmore." Dated Newington, 29 May, 1711. *Holograph.* Bears an autograph note by Sir Walter Scott.
Lent by Alfred Morrison, Esq.

**1760.** Letter from George Crabbe to John Robinson, asking him to send the money due to him, as he has bills to pay. Dated Parham, July 13, 1795. *Holograph.*
Lent by G. Milner Gibson Cullum, Esq.

**1761.** Letter from Henry Fielding to George, afterwards Lord Lyttelton, congratulating him on his marriage to Elizabeth, daughter of Sir Thomas Rich, Bart. Dated Bow Street, 29 Aug. 1849. *Holograph.*
Lent by The Viscount Cobham.

**1762.** Bill from J. H. Thylman, of Lausanne to Edward Gibbon, with the words "Bon pour £30 : 16 sur quittance générale E. Gibbon, ce 1 Janvier, 1786" at the end.
Lent by G. Milner Gibson Cullum, Esq.

**1763.** LETTER from EDWARD GIBBON relating to the trust of Mr. Bagnall Clarke's estate, in which he says that "it would give me great pleasure to contribute to the relief and benefit of Mr. Clarke's family." Dated Sheffield Place, Dec. 18, 1793. *Holograph.*

Lent by ALFRED MORRISON, ESQ.

**1764.** LETTER from OLIVER GOLDSMITH to David Garrick about a play of his which Garrick refuses acting by the advice of Mr. Colman. Goldsmith says, "Upon mature deliberation and the advice of a sensible friend, I begin to think it indelicate in me to throw upon you the odium of confirming Mr. Colman's sentence. I therefore request you will send me my play by my servant back." Undated. *Holograph.*

Lent by ALFRED MORRISON, ESQ.

**1765.** LETTER from THOMAS GRAY to the Rev. James Brown, Master of Pembroke Hall, Cambridge, informing him that he is sending him an early copy of "Caractacus," and asking him not to lend it, as they hope to sell the more of them. Undated. *Holograph.*

Lent by ALFRED MORRISON, ESQ.

**1766.** LETTER from THOMAS HEARNE, Antiquary and Nonjuror, to —————, relating to the classification, &c., of the coins in the Ashmolean Museum. Dated Oxford, March 25, 1707. *Holograph.*

Lent by H. SAXE WYNDHAM, ESQ.

**1767.** LETTER from FELICIA HEMANS to Mrs. Graves. Undated. *Holograph.*

Lent by G. MILNER GIBSON CULLUM, ESQ.

**1768.** LETTER from LEIGH HUNT to his brother, inclosing for the *Examiner* some verses by Lord Byron, who gives leave to "do what you please with them—omit words, or passages, or whole stanzas together; and of course you will do so, as the libellousness is abundant and can afford pruning." Dated Pisa, July 6, 1822. *Holograph.*

Lent by ALFRED MORRISON, ESQ.

**1769.** LETTER from LEIGH HUNT to Edward Moxon, asking him to discount a bill for £11 10s., and to let him have the money in cash. Dated Kensington, April 22. *Holograph.*

Lent by G. MILNER GIBSON CULLUM, ESQ.

**1770.** LETTER from DAVID HUME to his publishers respecting the publishing of his *History of Religion*, and stating that he has begun a new work, a *History of England from Henry VII.*, and much wishing he had begun from the first at that period, as it is the commencement of modern history, and he would have obviated many objections to his *History of the Stuarts* by taking matters so high. Dated Edinburgh, May 25, 1757. *Holograph.*

Lent by ALFRED MORRISON, ESQ.

**1771.** PRAYER in the handwriting of DR. SAMUEL JOHNSON. Dated Ashbourn, 18 Sept., 1784.
              Lent by ALFRED MORRISON, ESQ.

**1772.** LETTER from DR. SAMUEL JOHNSON to William Strahan, referring to a passage in the first edition of the *Journey to the Western Highlands*, which contained "a severe censure of the Clergy of an English Cathedral" [according to Dr. Birkbeck Hill, Lichfield]. The passage occurred in the description of the Cathedral of Elgin, and the leaf (pp. 47, 48) was cancelled for the reason given in this letter, "for the Dean did me a kindness forty years ago." Dated Nov. 30, 1774. *Holograph.*
              Lent by ALFRED MORRISON, ESQ.

**1773.** LETTER from DR. SAMUEL JOHNSON to William Strahan. "Having now done my *Lives [of the Poets]*, I shall have money to receiue, and shall be glad to add to it what remains due for the Hebrides, which you cannot charge me with grasping very rapaciously. The price was two hundred guineas or pounds. I think first pounds then guineas, I have had one hundred." Dated March 5, 1781. *Holograph.*
              Lent by ALFRED MORRISON, ESQ.

**1774.** LETTER from DR. SAMUEL JOHNSON to William Henry Lyttelton, Lord Westcote, afterwards Lord Lyttelton, asking that a short life of the brother of the latter, George, 1st Lord Lyttelton, should be written under his direction by any friend whom he might be willing to employ. Dated, Bolt Court, Fleet Street, July 27, 1780. *Holograph.*
              Lent by The VISCOUNT COBHAM.

**1775.** VERSE, in the handwriting of JOHN KEATS, written by him in pencil on the cover of a fellow-student's lecture-book during their attendance together at hospital lectures.
              Lent by G. MILNER GIBSON CULLUM, Esq.

**1776.** "MILTON'S *Paradise Lost*. A New Edition. Adorned with beautiful plates. Volume II. Edinburgh, Printed for W. and J. Deas. 1807. 12°."

Given to Mrs. Dilke by JOHN KEATS. It contains MS. notes, and on the fly-leaf a sonnet "To Sleep" in his handwriting.
              Lent by The RIGHT HON. SIR CHARLES W. DILKE, BART.

**1777.** "MR. WILLIAM SHAKESPEARE'S Comedies, Histories, & Tragedies, published according to the true originall Copies. London, Printed by Isaac Jaggard and Ed. Blount, 1623" Fol.

The facsimile reprint of the first folio. Belonged to JOHN KEATS, and contains MS. notes, a sonnet "On sitting down to read King Lear once again," and an ode "On seeing a lock of Milton's hair," in his handwriting.
              Lent by The RIGHT HON. SIR CHARLES W. DILKE, BART.

**1778.** "THE POETICAL WORKS of William Shakespeare, London, printed for Thomas Wilson, 1806, 8vo."

Given to JOHN KEATS by John Hamilton Reynolds. It contains MS. notes and two sonnets in his handwriting. One of the sonnets, beginning " Bright Star, would I were steadfast as thou art," was, according to a note by Sir C. W. Dilke, the last poem of Keats.

Lent by The RIGHT HON. SIR CHARLES W. DILKE, BART.

**1779.** LETTER from JOHN KEATS to Miss Brawne at Hampstead, in which he apologises for not coming to see her, and says, " I cannot resolve to mix any pleasure with my days . . . I love you too much to venture to Hampstead ; I feel it is not paying a visit but venturing into a fire . . . Knowing that my life must be passed in fatigue and trouble, I have been endeavouring to wean myself from you . . . I cannot bear the pain of being happy, it is out of the question : I must admit no thought of it." Dated Fleet Street, Monday Morning. *Holograph.*

Lent by ALFRED MORRISON, ESQ.

**1780.** LETTER from JOHN KEATS to C. W. Dilke expressing his resolution to take to magazine writing, and to try and push his way in the literary world. He says " I should a year or two ago have spoken my mind on any subject with the utmost simplicity. I hope I have learnt a little better, and am confident I shall be able to cheat as well as any literary Jew of the market. . . . I am fit for nothing but literature . . . I have no trust whatever on poetry. I don't wonder at it—the marvel is to me how people read so much of it." Undated. *Holograph.*

Lent by The RIGHT HON. SIR CHARLES W. DILKE, BART.

**1781.** LETTER from JOHN KEATS to C. W. Dilke written while he was staying with an artist friend in the Isle of Wight. Keats relates his arguments with his friend, as to his method of painting, and how one day they had a competition in drawing Shanklin church. The tone of the letter is very bright, airy, and fanciful. Dated Shanklin, Saturday Evening. *Holograph.*

Lent by The RIGHT HON. SIR CHARLES W. DILKE, BART.

**1782.** LETTER from JOHN KEATS to C. W. Dilke, asking him to send him " Sybilline Leaves" by Bearer. Dated Nov. 1817. *Holograph.*

Lent by The RIGHT HON. SIR CHARLES W. DILKE, BART.

**1783.** LETTER from JOHN KEATS to C. W. Dilke, written shortly before he died, telling him that he has a choice of going to South America, or as surgeon to an Indiaman, which last he thinks will be his fate. Date 1820. *Holograph.*

Lent by The RIGHT HON. SIR CHARLES W. DILKE, BART.

**1784.** LETTER from JOHN KEATS to Mrs. Brawne, written while in quarantine in the Bay of Naples. He expresses his admiration of the Bay, and regrets that he does not feel himself sufficiently a citizen of this world to be able to give a worthy account of it. He says: "I feel a spirit in my brain would lay it forth pleasantly. What a misery it is to have an intellect in splints!" He has been much depressed on his voyage by a young lady in consumption being on board, and evidently marks and fears his own symptoms in noting hers. Dated Naples Harbour, Oct. 24, 1820. *Holograph.*

Lent by The RIGHT HON. SIR CHARLES W. DILKE, BART.

## CASE GG.

### *LITERARY (Continued).*

**1785.** LETTER from CHARLES LAMB to S. T. Coleridge regretting that he cannot obtain leave from his office to pay him a visit, and containing a parody of some dactyls which Coleridge had sent him. Undated. *Holograph.*

Lent by ALFRED MORRISON, ESQ.

**1786.** LETTER from CHARLES LAMB to Messrs. Ollier respecting the disposal of some of his books, and containing a list of the names of his friends he wishes copies to be sent to. In a postscript he says: "I think Southey will give us a lift in that damn'd Quarterly." Dated 18th June, 1818. *Holograph.*

Lent by ALFRED MORRISON, ESQ.

**1787.** LETTER from CHARLES LAMB to B. Montague calling his attention to the fact that a Miss B. is in want of money and is too modest to ask for it, and asking Montague to procure it for her. Dated Monday. *Holograph.*

Lent by G. MILNER GIBSON CULLUM, ESQ.

**1788.** LETTER from CHARLES LAMB to S. T. Coleridge, telling him that "My poor dear, dearest sister, in a fit of insanity, has been the death of her mother. I was at hand only time enough to snatch the knife out of her grasp. . . . . God has preserved to me my senses—I eat and drink and sleep, and have my judgment I believe very sound. My poor father was slightly wounded and I am left to take care of him and my aunt . . . . write as religious a letter as possible, but no mention of what is gone and done with. With me the former things are passed away and I have something more to do than to feel. Mention nothing of poetry. I have destroyed every vestige of past vanities of that kind." Undated. *Holograph.*

Lent by ALFRED MORRISON, ESQ.

**1789.** LETTER from HANNAH MORE to Mr. Cadell, informing him that she is not disposed to part with her poems for less than the sum of forty guineas, and mentioning that the "Search" has brought her in one hundred pounds. Dated Bristol, Oct. 29th, 1775. *Holograph.*

　　　　　　　　　　　　Lent by G. MILNER GIBSON CULLUM, ESQ.

**1790.** LETTER from THOMAS MOORE, asking that a parcel belonging to his wife may be forwarded to her. Dated Sloperton, April 12, 1844. *Holograph.*

　　　　　　　　　　　　Lent by G. MILNER GIBSON CULLUM, ESQ.

**1791.** LETTER from ALEXANDER POPE to Samuel Buckley, written by the side of Lord Peterborough's couch where he lay ill. Pope remarks of Lord Peterborough, "I really think it worth no man's while to do any great or good action for any other motive than the inward satisfaction of his own conscience in the good done." Dated Southampton, Aug. 26. *Holograph.*

　　　　　　　　　　　　Lent by ALFRED MORRISON, ESQ.

**1792.** LETTER from ALEXANDER POPE to ————, relating his expeditions in the country and on various other small topics. Dated Chiswick, 25 Oct. *Holograph.*

　　　　　　　　　　　　Lent by H. SAXE WYNDHAM, ESQ.

**1793.** LETTER from ALEXANDER POPE to George, afterwards Lord Lyttelton, expressing his pleasure in the quiet he finds at his present residence and saying, "Tho I let the world alone at my very entrance into it I found as much envy and opposition as if my ambition had been to overwhelm it; and since I chanced to succeed in my own Low Walk, as much solicitation and vile flattery as if I had places and Preferment to bestow. I never deserved nor desired either." Dated Bath, Dec. 12, 1739. *Holograph.*

　　　　　　　　　　　　Lent by The VISCOUNT COBHAM.

**1794.** LETTER from MATTHEW PRIOR to Lord Godolphin (?), thanking him for the continuance of his pension, complaining of his circumstances, and asking for employment. Dated "West<sup>r</sup>" July 28th, 1709." *Holograph.*

　　　　　　　　　　　　Lent by H. SAXE WYNDHAM, ESQ.

**1795.** LETTER from SAMUEL RICHARDSON to his sister in answer to her having sent him, at his request, her criticism on "Sir Charles Grandison," in which he gently chides her for not finding more faults. He is interrupted in writing this letter by the news of the death of his brother, to whom he was tenderly attached. Dated April 9th, at night. *Holograph.*

　　　　　　　　　　　　Lent by ALFRED MORRISON, ESQ.

**1796.** AUTOGRAPH MS. of a critique by Sir Walter Scott in the *Edinburgh Review* of "Women; a Pour et Contre." A Tale by the Author of "Bertram," &c. [　　　　Mathurine.] 1818.

　　　　　　　　　　　　Lent by A. CONSTABLE, ESQ.

**1797.** POEM, by Sir Walter Scott, entitled, "The Sheriff's Fancy," to a tune so-called, sent to Miss Smith. *Autograph.*

Lent by ALFRED MORRISON, ESQ.

**1798.** TWO SONGS from *Rokeby*, "Hail to thy cold and clouded beam," and "Brignal's Banks," in the handwriting of SIR WALTER SCOTT.

On the other half of the sheet is a letter to Dr. J. Clarke, giving the author's opinion as to the style of music to which the last should be set. "Being quite unmusical I can only say the tune should have a mixture of wild lightness and melancholy capable in short, by the taste of the singer dwelling on particular notes, to be made either gay or sad as the words require." Dated Edinburgh, 16 Nov., 1812. *Holograph.*

Lent by ALFRED MORRISON, ESQ.

**1799.** LETTER from SIR WALTER SCOTT to Dr. J. Clarke, Professor of Music at Cambridge, in answer to a question respecting the professorship of music at Edinburgh.

After disparaging remarks on the probable management of the matter, "on that quiet snug mode of management called jobbery," and "upon the true national principle of keeping our own fishguts for our own seamaws," he goes on to speak of "some exquisite songs in Miss Baillie's third volume of plays on the passions now just coming out. An outlaw's song in particular is one of the wildest and most fanciful things I remember. I hope you will set it. Something of a wild bugle-horn note in the last line but one would have a fine effect." The song in question is the well-known "Chough and Crow," afterwards "set" by Sir H. Bishop. Dated Ashetiel, 22 Dec., 1811. *Holograph.*

Lent by ALFRED MORRISON, ESQ.

**1800.** LETTER from SIR WALTER SCOTT to Sir William Knighton. A long discourse on the condition of political parties in Scotland, and especially of Scottish Toryism and its subdivisions. The letter is dated, "Abbotsford, 14 Nov.," but the year is probably 1825. *Holograph.*

Lent by ALFRED MORRISON, ESQ.

**1801.** LETTER from SIR WALTER SCOTT to Sir W. Knighton, referring to the death of George IV., whom he praises in strong terms. Dated, Abbotsford, Melrose, 14 July, 1830. *Holograph.*

Lent by ALFRED MORRISON, ESQ.

**1802.** LETTER from PERCY BYSSHE SHELLEY to Lord Byron respecting a desire on the part of "Clare" [Jane Clairmont] that Byron should allow Allegra [her daughter by Byron] to visit her in Italy. Shelley while excusing Clare's manner of writing agrees with Byron that Allegra should not be sent to her. Dated, Pisa, 17 Sept., 1820. *Holograph.*

Lent by ALFRED MORRISON ESQ.

**1803.** AUTOGRAPH MS. of part of "The Revolt of Islam," by Percy Bysshe Shelley. Stanzas 16, 17, and part of 15 and 18.
            Lent by G. MILNER GIBSON CULLUM, ESQ.

**1804.** LETTER from RICHARD BRINSLEY SHERIDAN to Miss N. Ogle, telling her to expect him in Southampton the next day. Dated George Inn, Winchester [22 Aug. 1813]. *Holograph.*
            Lent by H. SAXE WYNDHAM, ESQ.

**1805** LETTER from RICHARD BRINSLEY SHERIDAN to Mrs. Van Hutcheson, asking for an appointment for the following day to arrange about the remaining mortgages due to the estate of the late Mr. Garrick. Dated, Old Burlington Street, Friday, Feb. 27. *Holograph.*
            Lent by ALFRED MORRISON, ESQ.

**1806.** LETTER from TOBIAS SMOLLETT to Dr. Macauley, regretting that he is in such a hampered situation, and saying that he had hoped to have had good news from the East Indies, but everything has thwarted him; he has not credit enough in England to raise the sum his friend requires, were it to save himself from a jail. If he were able to borrow the money even at 50 per cent. he would raise it and send to his friend, but never before has he been so harassed by duns as now, which he owes to the detention of the remittance from Jamaica. Dated Chelsea, Saturday, Nov. 16, 1754. *Holograph.*
            Lent by ALFRED MORRISON, ESQ.

**1807.** MEMORANDUM of an agreement between TOBIAS SMOLLETT and Robert Dodsley James Rivington, and William Strahan. Smollett is to write a new collection of voyages and travels, to be published in seven duodecimo volumes, the whole to contain about one hundred sheets. He is to be paid at the rate of one guinea and a-half per sheet. Dated May 5, 1753. Signed by T. Smollett, R. Dodsley, James Rivington, Will. Strahan.
            Lent by ALFRED MORRISON, ESQ.

**1808.** LETTER from ROBERT SOUTHEY expressing his detestation of Malthus's theory, and his pleasure at his name being coupled with the writer of a work against Malthus, concluding with : "Time was when those persons were not considered singular who took religion for their pole star and the Scriptures for their chart, and its standard of right and wrong for their compass. Statesmen and philosophers who steer by any other will be wrecked at last." Dated Keswick, 19 June, 1830. *Holograph.*
            Lent by G. MILNER GIBSON CULLUM, ESQ.

**1809.** LETTER from LAURENCE STERNE to " Mons. Foley et Pauchard," written at Florence. " I have been a month passing the plains of Lombardie, stopping in my way at Milan, Parma, &c., with weather as delicious as a kindly April in England ; and have been three days in crossing the Apennines, covered with thick snow—sad transition! I stay here three days and dine with our Plenipo—Lord Litchfield and Cowper—and in five days shall tread the Vatican, and be introduced to all the saints in the Pantheon. I stay but 14 days to pay these civilities, and then decamp for Naples." Dated Florence, Dec. 18, 1765. *Holograph.*

Lent by ALFRED MORRISON, ESQ.

**1810.** LETTER from LAURENCE STERNE to the Rev. G. Blake, relating to family matters. Undated. *Holograph.*

Lent by ALFRED MORRISON, ESQ.

**1811.** LETTER from FRANÇOIS MARIE AROUET DE VOLTAIRE to George Lord Lyttelton, in English, containing a long critique on Thomson's "Seasons," and other works, with a dissertation on poetry generally, in which he says, "Give me leave to say that the taste of your politest countrymen in point of tragedy differs not much in point of tragedy from the tastes of the mob at bear gardens; 'tis true we have too much of words, if you have too much of action." Dated Paris, May 17, 1750. *Holograph.*

Lent by The VISCOUNT COBHAM.

**1812.** LETTER from WILLIAM WARBURTON, afterwards BISHOP OF GLOUCESTER, to George afterwards Lord Lyttelton, respecting his controversy with Dr. Middleton on the theory of the latter as to the Pagan origin of Roman Catholicism. Dated 1 Nov. 1741. *Holograph.*

Lent by The VISCOUNT COBHAM.

## CASE HH.

### *LITERARY AND ARTISTIC.*

**1813.** AUTOGRAPH MS. of a letter by JONATHAN SWIFT, Dean of St. Patrick's, containing advice to a lady on her marriage. It is supposed that this letter was written either on Lady Betty Moore's marriage with George Rochfort or for that of Mrs. John Rochfort, daughter of Dr. Staunton.

Lent by ALFRED MORRISON, ESQ.

**1814.** LETTER from JONATHAN SWIFT, Dean of St. Patrick's, to Alderman Barber, introducing Mr. Loyd of Coleraine: "It seems your Society hath raised the Rents of that Town and your lands adjoining about three years ago to four times the value of what they formerly paid, which is beyond all I have ever heard even among the most screwing landlords of this impoverished kingdom." After a discussion on rents, he says, "For I am as much convinced as I can be of anything human, that the wretched oppressed country must of necessity decline every year." Dated Dublin, 30 Mar., 1737. *Holograph.*

Lent by ALFRED MORRISON, ESQ.

**1815.** LETTER from JONATHAN SWIFT, Dean of St. Patrick's, to Alderman Barber, complaining of his loss of memory and other ailments. "I have for almost three years past been only the shadow of my former self with years and sickness and rage against all publick Proceedings, especially in this miserable oppressed country." He commends Mr. Richardson, a member of the Irish Parliament, to the Alderman, and asks for a church living in his gift, "which is now held by one Doct. Squire, who is so decayed that he cannot possibly live a month," to be bestowed on Mr. William Duncan, in case of Dr. Squire's death. Dated Dublin, 17 Jan., 1737. *Holograph.*
Lent by ALFRED MORRISON, ESQ.

**1816.** LETTER from JONATHAN SWIFT, Dean of St. Patrick's, to Alderman Barber, who is about to set out for London. The Dean tells him that Mr. Richardson is to go with him; complains of his ailments, and begs the Alderman to "visit the few Friends I have left . . . as my Lord and Lady Oxford, my Lord Bathurst, the Countess of Granville, my Lord and Lady Cartret, my Lady Worsley, my dear friend Mr. Pope and Mr. Lewis." He also says, "Let me know what is become of my Lord Bolingbr——, how and where he lives, and whether you ever expect he will come home." Dated Dublin, 31 Mar. 1738. *Holograph.*
Lent by ALFRED MORRISON, ESQ.

**1817.** "THE PROCEEDINGS in the House of Commons touching the impeachment of Edward late Earl of Clarendon." Printed in 1700. Belonged to JONATHAN SWIFT, Dean of St. Patrick's. There are two notes in his handwriting to the Preface, one "A silly tedious Irony," the other "A very foolish Preface, J. S."
Lent by The RIGHT HON. SIR CHARLES W. DILKE, BART.

**1818.** LETTER from WILLIAM WORDSWORTH to the Rev. R. Bamford congratulating him on the testimony he had received of Dr. Bell's esteem. Dated Rydal Mount, May 28, 1825. *Holograph.*
Lent by G. MILNER GIBSON CULLUM, ESQ.

**1819.** LETTER from DR. EDWARD YOUNG to Mrs. Haviland congratulating her on a safe journey to Dundee, and telling her that the papers say that only three regiments are to continue in Scotland, and that the rest are soon to go to Ireland. Dated, Wellwyn, Nov. 3, 1748. *Holograph.*
Lent by ALFRED MORRISON, ESQ.

**1820.** LETTER from JOHN FLAXMAN to Miss Denman (afterwards Mrs. Flaxman), containing an offer of "tender and honourable affection, which remains undiminished altho' I have not been able to see you more than once these six months: consider this I entreat you as a proof that my disposition is not changeable, and let this earnest of my constancy incline you to grant me permission to see you." Undated. *Holograph.*
Lent by ALFRED MORRISON, ESQ.

**1821.** LETTER from JOHN FLAXMAN to William Hayley respecting a pupil of Flaxman's, stating the terms of the agreement entered into about his board, lodging, and work. Dated London, Sep. 25th, 1796. *Holograph.*
Lent by G. MILNER GIBSON CULLUM, ESQ.

**1822.** LETTER from THOMAS GAINSBOROUGH to the Rev. William Dodd, D.D., thanking him for Mrs. Dodd's present to his wife of an elegant silk dress, and wishing he could express his gratitude with his pencil instead of his pen, as he would be better able to express it in that manner. Dated Bath, Nov. 24th, 1773. *Holograph.*
Lent by ALFRED MORRISON, ESQ.

**1823.** RECEIPT by WILLIAM HOGARTH for one Guinea from George Scotts for a sett of Prints call'd the *Harlot's Progress.* Dated 10 May, 1745. *Holograph.*
Lent by ALFRED MORRISON, ESQ.

**1824.** "THE No Dedication," by WILLIAM HOGARTH, supposed to be intended for his *Analysis of Beauty*, published in 1753. The book is humorously dedicated "to nobody." *Holograph.*
Lent by ALFRED MORRISON, ESQ.

**1825.** LETTER from JOHN HOPPNER to Thomas Stodhart acquainting him with the intention of the Prince of Wales of visiting his studio the next day. Undated. *Holograph.*
Lent by G. MILNER GIBSON CULLUM, ESQ.

**1826.** LETTER from ANGELICA KAUFFMANN (Mrs. Zucchi) to Dr. (afterwards Sir) William Fordyce informing him of her having been commissioned to paint the Royal Family at Naples, and expressing her desire of meeting him and other friends again. Dated Rome, December 28th, 1782. *Holograph.*
Lent by ALFRED MORRISON, ESQ.

**1827.** RECEIPT from SIR GODFREY KNELLER for £20, being for six months' interest for £500 "Lent unto her Majesty upon the credit of an Act of Parliament," on an Exchequer bond. Dated 28 Nov., 1707. *Autograph Signature.*
Lent by G. MILNER GIBSON CULLUM, ESQ.

**1828.** LETTER from SIR THOMAS LAWRENCE to Mrs. Wolff, giving an account of the death of Sir Alexander Gordon, brother of Lord Aberdeen, who in leading his troop forward under Lord Wellington's command, received a severe wound in the thigh, which checked him for a moment, but he led his men on, and returned to Lord Wellington, and saying that the orders were executed, died almost immediately. Dated Russell Square, July 24th, 1815. *Holograph.*
Lent by ALFRED MORRISON, ESQ.

**1829.** LETTER from SIR THOMAS LAWRENCE to Davies Gilbert, expressing his gratification at the honour done him by the society [probably the Royal] of which Gilbert was a member, at his instigation. Dated Norfolk Square, Dec. 2nd, 1829. *Holograph.*

Lent by G. MILNER GIBSON CULLUM, ESQ.

**1830.** LETTER from HENRY RAEBURN to D. Colnaghi respecting a portrait which he is willing to sell of a member of the Brougham family by Sir Thomas Lawrence. Dated Howden House, by Midcalder, 28th Dec. 1842. *Holograph.*

Lent by G. MILNER GIBSON CULLUM, ESQ.

**1831.** LETTER from SIR JOSHUA REYNOLDS to Mr. Cunynham about two pictures by Rubens which he is desirous of purchasing from the Capuchins at Lisle. Reynolds offers £300 for the two pictures, which are in bad condition, but which he hopes to clean and restore. Dated London, Nov. 25, 1788. *Holograph.*

Lent by ALFRED MORRISON, ESQ.

**1832.** LETTER from GEORGE ROMNEY to Lady Hamilton, relating to pictures for which she had sat to him. Undated, *circ.* 1795. *Holograph.*

Lent by ALFRED MORRISON, ESQ.

**1833.** LETTER from JOSIAH WEDGEWOOD to J. Crisp respecting a circular sent to him having reference to parliamentary petitions connected with the Potteries. Dated Etruria, Jan. 16. *Holograph.*

Lent by G. MILNER GIBSON CULLUM, ESQ.

**1834.** LETTER from SIR DAVID WILKIE to Mr. M. Nutter, regretting that he is unable to assist the patriotic exhibition at Carlisle by contributing any of his pictures. Dated 1 Circus Place, North Edinburgh, Sep. 11, 1834. *Holograph.*

Lent by A. KEILY, ESQ.

## CASE II.

### SCIENTIFIC AND DRAMATIC.

**1835.** LETTER from JEREMY BENTHAM to John Miller, speaking of letters received from General Miller, and advising that the general should go to Guatemala to help the "new formed political state" to put its affairs in order. Dated Queen's Square Place, Westminster, 24 March, 1832. *Holograph.*

Lent by ALFRED MORRISON, ESQ.

**1836.** LETTER from SIR HUMPHREY DAVY. It contains the following statement: "I have called the basis of Potass, Potassium, that of Soda, Sodium." Dated 9 April, 1808. *Holograph.*

Lent by ALFRED MORRISON, ESQ.

**1837.** LETTER from BENJAMIN FRANKLIN to his wife, which he sends to her by the hand of a friend, Mr. Neave, in which he tells her that he has been ill of a cold and fever. Dated London, July 3, 1767. *Holograph.*

Lent by ALFRED MORRISON, ESQ.

**1838.** LETTER from SIR FREDERICK WILLIAM HERSCHELL to Sir J. Banks asking him to solicit the King's aid in a pecuniary sense to erect a larger telescope than the one of twenty feet reflector, the making of which has exhausted the astronomer's means. The latter gives a short dissertation on the properties of the telescope, and mentions some of the hitherto unknown stars and nebulæ which he has discovered by means of the existing telescope, and his hopes of obtaining much greater results from one of greater power. Dated Clay Hall, near Windsor. *Holograph.*

Lent by ALFRED MORRISON, ESQ.

**1839.** LETTER from JOHN HUNTER to Dr. Edward Jenner, in which he says, "whatever *was* my opinion about people living under water, it is now that the actions of life can be suspended for hours, even days, and put into action again. . . . I have been extremely busy these few days past in dissecting an elephant; it is a strange beast, not like anything on the earth, nor in the water under the earth." Dated London, May 22. *Holograph.*

Lent by ALFRED MORRISON, ESQ.

**1840.** LETTER from DR. EDWARD JENNER to a physician in Vienna, giving him a detailed account of the process and symptoms attending vaccination, and an account of his theory respecting it, with observations on the nature of cow-pox. He mentions that he incloses with the letter some virus for the use of the physician, and states that nothing has occurred to lessen the confidence he first held out, but that fresh and convincing evidence of the power of the vaccine disease in destroying the effects of the variolum is constantly flowing in. Dated Berkeley, November 27, 1799. *Holograph.*

Lent by ALFRED MORRISON, ESQ.

**1841.** LETTER from SIR ISAAC NEWTON respecting a book he has read by Captain Newhouse, entitled *The Whole Art of Navigation*, which he highly approves of and desires to see printed. Dated Cambridge, July 3, 1684. *Holograph.*

Lent by G. MILNER GIBSON CULLUM, ESQ.

**1842.** LETTER from SIR ISAAC NEWTON to Sir John Newton, asking him to employ a certain undertaker for the funeral of a Mr. Cook, as the undertaker had married a near kinswoman of his own. Undated. *Holograph.*

Lent by ALFRED MORRISON, ESQ.

**1843.** NOTE of the inscription to be placed on the foundation stone of Eddystone lighthouse, with notes on the back as to the measurements and progress of the work, in the handwriting of JOHN SMEATON. Dated August 24th, 1759.

Lent by ALFRED MORRISON, ESQ.

## Autographs, Etc.

**1844.** LETTER from ADAM SMITH in which he goes into the question of the relative amounts of custom duties paid in Scotland in that and former years. Dated Custom-house Edinburgh, December 22nd, 1785. *Holograph.*

Lent by ALFRED MORRISON, ESQ.

**1845.** LETTER from JAMES WATT to Mr. A. Weston, relating to a dispute about a patent, and giving Watt's reasons for the plea of prior invention set up against him being false and worthless, and saying that a writ commanding him to appear in the Court of Chancery has been served upon him. Dated Heathfield, Sunday, June, 1795. *Holograph.*

Lent by ALFRED MORRISON, ESQ.

**1846.** DOCUMENT signed by ROBERTS WILKS, BARTON BOOTH, and COLLEY CIBBER, as managers of Drury Lane Theatre, allowing to each of them £1 13s. every acting day for their "daily attendance, management, and acting." Dated, 23 Sept., 1721.

Lent by G. MILNER GIBSON CULLUM, ESQ.

**1847.** LETTER from KITTY CLIVE [Catherine Raftor] to David Garrick, complaining in strong terms of the stoppage of her salary. Dated, Oct. 14, 1765. *Holograph.*

Lent by ALFRED MORRISON, ESQ.

**1848.** LETTER from DAVID GARRICK to Dr. John Hoadley, referring to the play of the *Rehearsal* He also gives an epitaph on Hogarth which he had written at the request of Mrs. Hogarth. Dated, London, 4 [  ] 1772. *Holograph.*

Lent by ALFRED MORRISON, ESQ.

**1849.** LETTER from EDMUND KEAN to — Whiston, manager of Drury Lane Theatre, remonstrating with him on his cruelty in wishing a dying man to appear on the stage, and saying that he shall retire to France if wearied any more with importunities to return. He leaves an excellent "succedaneum" in the brilliant talents of Mr. Macready. Dated, Brighton, May 18th, 1844. *Holograph.*

Lent by ALFRED MORRISON, ESQ.

**1850.** LETTER from JOHN PHILIP KEMBLE to Professor J. D. Levade, of Lausanne, respecting a controversy between C. L. de Haller, a convert to Catholicism, and J. L. H. Manuel, a Swiss Protestant pasteur. Dated, Beausite [Lausanne], 25 Nov., 1821. *Holograph.*

Lent by ALFRED MORRISON, ESQ.

**1851.** LETTER from CHARLES KEMBLE, enclosing a note for ten pounds in payment for a ticket for the Dramatic Fund. Dated 29 Soho Square, Feb. 11, 1825. *Holograph.*

Lent by A. KEILY, ESQ.

**1852.** LETTER from CHARLES MATHEWS, respecting a dramatic piece which he returns with the remark, "You do not seem to be aware that the license for the Adelphi Theatre confines us to the performance of burlesques." Dated Adelphi Theatre, October 16. *Holograph.*

Lent by A. KEILY, ESQ.

**1853.** LETTER from SARAH SIDDONS to Miss Bird, in which she laments the illness of a friend. She says, "I am afraid she is greatly altered. Good God! if it is to enable me to disguise emotions which no preparation can prevent! but I am a wretched actress *off the stage*." Undated. *Holograph.*

Lent by MRS. MOSS COCKLE.

**1854.** LETTER from SARAH SIDDONS to Miss Bird, asking how a friend is, and saying, "I am acting Lady Macbeth almost without consciousness of what I say or do." Undated. No signature. *Holograph.*

Lent by MRS. MOSS COCKLE.

**1855.** LETTER from SARAH SIDDONS, giving an account of the burning of Drury Lane Theatre and the loss of all the dresses, laces, and jewels that she had been collecting for thirty years, and her gratitude that her brother did not know of the fire until it was over, or he would certainly have been injured in endeavouring to save something from the horrible catastrophe. She particularly laments the loss of a piece of lace which had belonged to the poor Queen of France, "It could never have been bought for a thousand pounds, but that's the least regret, it was *so* interesting!" Undated. *Holograph.*

Lent by ALFRED MORRISON, ESQ.

## CASE JJ.

### *MISCELLANEOUS.*

**1856.** LETTER from GEORGIANA, DUCHESS OF DEVONSHIRE [Daughter of John, Earl Spencer], to ————. Undated [circ. 1790]. *Holograph.*

Lent by The HON. GERALD PONSONBY.

**1857.** CERTIFICATE of the Baptism of "Amyly Daughter of Henry Lyon of Nesse" [*i.e.* EMMA HART, LADY HAMILTON], May 12, 1765. Copied from the Register of Neston, by R. Carter, Curate, Dec. 19, 1781.

Lent by ALFRED MORRISON, ESQ.

**1858.** TRANSCRIPT in the handwriting of EMMA, LADY HAMILTON, of a letter originally in cypher, from Charles IV., King of Spain, to Ferdinand IV., King of the Two

Sicilies, dated San Ildefonso, Aug. 11, 1795, announcing that he had made peace with the French Republic. Endorsed by Sir William Hamilton. *Italian.*

This letter, which was obtained by Lady Hamilton from the Queen of the Two Sicilies, was sent to the English Government. Nelson, in the last codicil to his will, says, " She (Lady Hamilton) obtained the King of Spain's letter to his brother, the King of Naples, acquainting him of his intention to declare war against England, from which letter the Ministry sent out orders to Sir John Jervis to strike a stroke, if opportunity offered, against either the arsenals of Spain or her fleet."

Lent by ALFRED MORRISON, ESQ.

**1859.** LETTER from JOHN HOUGH, BISHOP OF WORCESTER, to Sir Thomas Lyttelton, thanking him for sending him Dr. Warburton's Legation, &c., and referring with praise to the " Observations on the Life of Cicero" by the same author. Dated 9th Sept. 1741. *Holograph.*

Lent by The VISCOUNT COBHAM.

**1860.** LETTER from SELINA, COUNTESS OF HUNTINGTON, to the Rev. Mr. Green [minister of her chapel at Howick], congratulating him and herself on the opinions they hold, and relating that when on her travels after health in Glamorganshire, she came to several places where the gospel had not been preached, accordingly some of her suite preached to the people. One of her people has joined the Baptists, and she hopes they will keep him in better order than she could. Dated Oct. 8, 1784. *Holograph.*

Lent by ALFRED MORRISON, ESQ.

**1861.** LETTER from MRS. DOROTHY BLAND JORDAN to the effect that the Duke of Clarence (afterwards William IV..), has settled a liberal provision on her and his children, and she trusts that everything will now sink into oblivion. Dated St. James's, Tuesday. *Holograph.*

Lent by ALFRED MORRISON, ESQ.

**1862.** POWER of Attorney from EHRENGARDA MELUSINA VON SCHULEMBERG, DUCHESS OF KENDAL, Mistress of George I., to Arnold Rosenhagen of Isleworth to sell South Sea Stock. Dated 29 July, 1732. *Autograph Signature.*

Lent by G. MILNER GIBSON CULLUM, ESQ.

**1863.** LETTER from SARAH, DUCHESS OF MARLBOROUGH to the Duke of Newcastle on the subject of a dispute with the Duke of St. Alban's respecting the privilege of driving in Windsor Park. The Duke of St. Alban's being Constable of the Castle had received a key from the Duke of Marlborough, and had had other keys made from it to distribute as he pleased, and had also driven in his coach through the Park, a privilege reserved for the Royal Family and the Ranger (*i.e.* the Duchess herself). Dated Marlborough House, 25 Aug. 1735. In the handwriting of the Duke of Marlborough.

Lent by ALFRED MORRISON, ESQ.

1864. LETTER from SARAH, DUCHESS OF MARLBOROUGH, to Mrs. Godolphin, wife of Dr. Henry Godolphin, Provost of Eton. She says : " I don't know whether you will have the news of this day in print and therefore I venture some repetition rather than not tell you that 'tis certain the P. [*i.e.* James III.] is landed with some few officers in Scotland. To any one that does not know the whole design, I believe it will appear a very hopeless undertaking." Dated London, 5 Jan. 1715. *Holograph.*
                   Lent by ALFRED MORRISON, ESQ.

1865. LETTER from LADY MARY WORTLEY MONTAGUE to her husband, Edward Wortley Montague, telling him of her difficulties in getting her English guineas passed in France, and expressing her desire to avoid the crowds of English, who are spread all over France. She speaks of Dijon as an agreeable town, but far too dear for her to reside in. Dated Dijon, Aug. 27, 1739. *Holograph*
                   Lent by ALFRED MORRISON, ESQ.

1866. LETTER from ROBERT WALPOLE (4th son of Horatio, 1st Baron Walpole, of Wolterton), Envoy Extraordinary to Portugal, to Thomas Walpole, relating, among other things, to the late junction of the Spanish and Dutch in the West Indies, and its probable results. Dated Lisbon, 7 Aug. 1780. *Holograph.*
                   Lent by H. SPENCER WALPOLE, ESQ.

1867. LETTER from HORACE WALPOLE to the Hon. Thomas Walpole, condoling with him on a domestic bereavement. Undated. *Holograph.*
                   Lent by H. SPENCER WALPOLE, ESQ.

1868. LETTER from HORACE WALPOLE to Charles Lyttelton, afterwards Bishop of Carlisle, describing a visit to Oxford and Cambridge, and breaking into verse at the end. Dated King's College, Cambridge, 22 May, 1736. *Holograph.*
                   Lent by The VISCOUNT COBHAM.

1869. LETTER from HORACE WALPOLE to Sir J. Cullum, Bart., in answer to a question, which he is unable to solve, respecting the name of a sculptor whose cypher appears on some tomb. Dated Arlington Street, 26 Nov. 1767. *Holograph.*
                   Lent by G. MILNER GIBSON CULLUM, ESQ.

1870. LETTER from JOHN WESLEY to his wife, containing much good advice to her as to her doing with diligence all that came to her to do, yet not fretting herself, but in quietness and patience possessing her soul. It contains an allusion to his letter to the " stewards," which he believes will " stir them up." Dated Liverpool. April 24, 1757. *Holograph.*
                   Lent by ALFRED MORRISON, ESQ.

BALCONY.] *Autographs, Etc.* 257

**1871.** LEDGER of the PUBLIC ADVERTISER from January 1765 to December 1771, showing the effect of the publication of the Letters of Junius on the sale of the paper. In the handwriting of H. S. Woodfall.
Lent by Sir CHARLES W. DILKE, Bart.

**1872.** "SEAL of Safety" of Joanna Southcott, to George Newman. [*Circ.* 1810.] *Autograph Signature*
Lent by MRS. A. J. HIPKINS.

**1873.** "PROCÉS VERBAL constatant que la France est entièrement libérée de tous les engagemens qu'elle a pris pour l'acquittement de l'indemnité pecuniaire de sept cents millions stipulée au profit des puisances alliées par l'art. 4 du traité de Paris du 20 Novembre 1815." Signed and sealed by the Baron de Barbier on the part of Austria, James Drummond on the part of Great Britain, the Chevalier Piautaz on the part of Prussia, the Baron de Merian de Salkach on the part of Russia, and by Baron Monnier, Mons. de Rayneval, Baron Ramond and Baron Hely d'Oissel on the part of France. Dated Paris, 28 Sept. 1821.
Lent by CAPTAIN TELFER, R.N.

**1874.** HANDBILL announcing a Main of Cocks to be fought at the Cockpit Royal, the south side of St. James's Park, on Monday the 20th and Tuesday the 21st instant," between the Gentlemen of Winchmore Hill and Suffolk [*Circ.* 1800].
Lent by H. SAXE WYNDHAM, ESQ.

**1875.** HANDBILL announcing a Main of Cocks to be fought in the Manchester Hall, Wrexham, 22nd and 23rd of June, 1818, between the Gentlemen of Montgomeryshire and Flintshire.
Lent by H. SAXE WYNDHAM, ESQ.

**1876.** CORONATION TICKET OF GEORGE III. (d. 1830).
Lent by G. MILNER-GIBSON-CULLUM, ESQ.

**1877.** CORONATION TICKET OF WILLIAM IV. (d. 1837).
Lent by G. MILNER-GIBSON-CULLUM, ESQ.

**1878.** FUNERAL TICKET OF WILLIAM PITT (d. 1806).
Lent by G. MILNER-GIBSON-CULLUM, ESQ.

**1879.** FUNERAL TICKET OF LORD NELSON (d. 1805).
Lent by G. MILNER-GIBSON-CULLUM, ESQ.

**1880.** TICKET OF ADMISSION TO THE TRIAL OF WARREN HASTINGS, 1788-1795.
Lent by G. MILNER-GIBSON-CULLUM, ESQ.

**1881.** TICKET OF ADMISSION TO THE TRIAL OF LORD MELVILLE, 1805.
Lent by G. MILNER-GIBSON-CULLUM, ESQ.

S

## CASE KK.

*COINS AND MEDALS LENT BY JOHN GLOOG MURDOCH, ESQ.*

## COINS.

### GEORGE I. 1715—1727.

1. (*Gold*) FIVE GUINEAS, 1717.
2. TWO GUINEAS, 1717.
3. GUINEA, 1717.
4. HALF-GUINEA, 1725.
5. QUARTER-GUINEA, 1718.
6. (*Silver*) CROWN, 1716.
7. HALF-CROWN, 1717.
8. SHILLING, 1725.
9. SIXPENCE, 1723. Struck for the South Sea Company.
10-13. MAUNDY SET, consisting of GROAT, THREEPENCE, HALF-GROAT, AND PENNY for 1717.
14. (*Copper*) HALFPENNY, 1717.
15. HALFPENNY, 1723.
16. FARTHING, 1717.
17. FARTHING, 1719.

## GEORGE II. 1727—1760.

**18.** (*Gold*) FIVE GUINEAS, 1729.

**19.** TWO GUINEAS, 1739.

**20.** GUINEA, with young head, 1732.

**21.** GUINEA, with old head, 1759.

**22.** HALF-GUINEA, with young head, 1734.

**23.** HALF-GUINEA, with old head, 1746.

**24.** (*Silver*) CROWN, 1741.

**25.** HALF-CROWN, 1739.

**26.** SHILLING, 1735.

**27.** SIXPENCE, 1732.

**28-31.** MAUNDY SET for 1746. (See Nos. 10–13.)

All the foregoing silver pieces have the young bust of the King.

**32.** CROWN, 1746.

**33.** HALF-CROWN, 1745.

**34.** SHILLING, 1746.

**35.** SIXPENCE, 1746.

The last four coins bear on the obverse the older bust of the King, and below it the inscription LIMA, denoting that they were coined from silver captured by Admiral Anson in the great Spanish Acapulco Galleon during his famous voyage round the world, 1740-1744.

**36.** (*Copper*) HALFPENNY, 1754.

**37.** FARTHING, 1744.

## GEORGE III., 1760—1820.

**38.** (*Gold*) PATTERN FOR FIVE GUINEAS, 1770.

**39.** PATTERN FOR TWO GUINEAS, 1768.

**40.** PATTERN FOR FIVE POUNDS, 1820.

Only twenty-five specimens of this coin were struck. It is said that Pistrucci, having completed the dies, left orders at the Mint that proofs should be struck on the morrow On his way home, however, he heard the bell at St. Paul's tolling for the death of the King. Upon this he immediately hurried back to the Mint and caused the twenty-five copies to be at once struck.

**41.** PATTERN FOR TWO POUNDS, 1820.

**42.** GUINEA, 1777.

**43.** HALF-GUINEA, 1786.

**44.** QUARTER-GUINEA, 1762.

**45.** SPADE GUINEA, 1798.

**46.** SPADE HALF-GUINEA, 1788.

**47.** GARTER GUINEA, 1813.

**48.** GARTER HALF-GUINEA, 1804.

**49-50.** SEVEN SHILLING PIECES, 1803 and 1804.

**51.** SOVEREIGN, 1820.

**52.** HALF-SOVEREIGN, 1821.

**53.** (*Silver*) SHILLING, 1763.

Known as the "Northumberland Shilling." These were struck to the amount of £100, for the purpose of being distributed amongst the populace, when the Earl of Northumberland made his first public appearance in Dublin as Lord-Lieutenant of Ireland.

54. SHILLING, 1787.

55. SIXPENCE, 1787.

56. PATTERN FOR SIXPENCE, 1790.

57. CROWN, 1818, by PISTRUCCI.

58-59. HALF-CROWNS FOR 1817 and 1820.

60. SHILLING, 1816.

61. SIXPENCE, 1817.

62—65. MAUNDY SET FOR 1820. (See Nos. 10-13).

66. PATTERN BANK OF ENGLAND DOLLAR, 1804.

67—68. THREE SHILLINGS BANK TOKENS, FOR 1811 and 1813.

69—70. EIGHTEEN PENCE BANK TOKENS, FOR 1812 (two types).

71. NINEPENCE BANK TOKEN, 1812.

72—75. (*Copper*) THE "BROAD BAND," TWO PENCE, PENNY, HALFPENNY AND FARTHING, 1797. This is the only instance of the Twopence being struck in copper.

76—78. PENNY, HALFPENNY, AND FARTHING, 1806.

## GEORGE IV., 1820-1830.

79. (*Gold*) SOVEREIGN, 1821.

80. HALF-SOVEREIGN, 1821.

81. PATTERN FIVE POUNDS, 1826.

82. PATTERN DOUBLE SOVEREIGN, 1826.

**83.** Sovereign, 1826.

**84.** Half-Sovereign, 1826.

**85.** (*Silver*) Crown, 1821. By Pistrucci.

**86.** Half-Crown, 1820.

**87.** Shilling, 1821.

**88.** Sixpence, 1821.

**89-92.** Maundy Set for 1828 (see Nos. 10-13).

**93-96.** Proofs of the Crown, Half-Crown, Shilling, and Sixpence for 1826. The bust on the obverse marks the second coinage of this reign.

**97-99.** (*Copper*) Proofs of the Penny, Halfpenny, and Farthing of 1826.

## WILLIAM IV., 1830-1837.

**100.** (*Gold*) Pattern Double Sovereign, 1831.

**101, 102.** Proofs of the Sovereign and Half-Sovereign, 1831.

**103.** (*Silver*) Pattern Crown, 1831.

**104-106.** Proofs of the Half-Crown, Shilling, and Sixpence, 1831.

**107-110.** Maundy Set (Proofs), 1831 (see Nos. 10-13).

**111-113.** (*Copper*) Proofs of the Penny, Halfpenny, and Farthing, 1831.

## MEDALS.

*Coronation Medals of:—*

114. GEORGE I., 1714. Gold. By T. CROKER.
115. GEORGE II., 1727. Gold. By T. CROKER.
116. GEORGE III., 1761. Gold. By L. NATTER.
117. QUEEN CHARLOTTE, 1761. Gold. By L. NATTER.
118. GEORGE IV., 1826. Gold. By B. PISTRUCCI.
119. WILLIAM IV., 1831. Gold. By W. WYON, R.A.
120. QUEEN ADELAIDE, 1831. Gold. By W. WYON, R.A.

### GEORGE I., 1714-1727.

121. ACCESSION TO THE CROWN OF ENGLAND, 1714. Silver.
122. ARRIVAL OF THE KING IN ENGLAND, 18 Sept. 1714. By T. CROKER. Silver.
123. BATTLE OF SHERIFFMUIR AND DEFEAT OF THE STUARTS, 1715. By T. CROKER. Silver.
124. TAKING OF PRESTON, 1715. By T. CROKER. Silver
125. NAVAL ACTION OFF CAPE PASSARO AND DEFEAT OF THE SPANIARDS, 1718. By T. CROKER. Silver.
126. JOHN LAW THE FINANCIER. His scheme ridiculed, 1720. Silver.
127. SIR THOMAS DEREHAM, SCHOLAR AND ADHERENT OF THE STUARTS, d. 1739. By ANTONIO SELVI. Copper.
128. SIR CHRISTOPHER WREN, ARCHITECT, 1632-1723. Silver.

129. DANIEL WRAY, ANTIQUARY, d. 1783. Copper.

130. SIR ISAAC NEWTON, 1642-1727. By T. CROKER. Silver.

## GEORGE II., 1727-1760.

131. GEORGE II., QUEEN CAROLINE, AND THE ROYAL CHILDREN, 1732. By T. CROKER. Silver.

    This medal was struck for special presentation by the King.

132. MARRIAGE OF WILLIAM, PRINCE OF ORANGE, AND PRINCESS ANNE, 1734. By M. HOLTZHEY. Silver.

133. TAKING OF PORTO BELLO BY ADMIRAL VERNON, 1739. Copper.

134. THE DUKE OF ARGYLE AND SIR ROBERT WALPOLE: the Excise Bill satirized. 1741.

135. FREDERICK, PRINCE OF WALES, AND PRINCESS AUGUSTA. Birth of Princess Elizabeth Caroline, 1740. By J. C. KOCH. Silver.

136. MARRIAGE OF FREDERICK, PRINCE OF DENMARK, AND PRINCESS LOUISA, 1743. By D. HAESLING. Silver.

137. BATTLE OF CULLODEN, 1746. By R. YEO. Silver.

138. BATTLE OF CULLODEN, 1746. By R. YEO. Silver.

    This medal, or badge, is said to have been presented to some of the officers who were present at the battle. Gold and copper specimens are scarce, but this specimen in silver is unique.

139. BATTLE OF CULLODEN: View of the Battle, 1746. Copper.

140. ADMIRAL LORD ANSON: Defeat of the French Fleet off Cape Finisterre, 1747. By J. PINGO. Silver.

141. FREDERICK, PRINCE OF WALES: Free British Fishery Society founded 1750. By L. KOCH. Silver.

142. VICTORIES OF 1758. Silver.

143. BATTLE OF MINDEN, 1759. Silver.

144. TAKING OF QUEBEC, 1759. Silver.

145. DEFEAT OF THE FRENCH OFF BELLEISLE, 1759. Silver.

146. SIR ROBERT WALPOLE, afterwards 1st Earl of Orford, 1741. Silver.

147. ALEXANDER POPE, THE POET, 1741. Memorial by DASSIER. Copper.

148. WILLIAM CHESELDEN, EMINENT SURGEON, 1688-1752. Copper.

149. RICHARD MEAD, EMINENT PHYSICIAN, 1673-1754. By L. PINGO. Silver.

## GEORGE III., 1760-1820.

150. GEORGE III. AS PRINCE OF WALES: Coming of Age, June 4th, 1759. By T. PINGO. Silver.

151. GEORGE III.: his Accession, 1760. By COLEBERT. Silver.

152. CHARLES PRATT, LORD CAMDEN, LORD CHANCELLOR, 1766. Silver.

153. PRINCESS CAROLINE MATILDA, daughter of Frederick, Prince of Wales. Her marriage to Christian VII. of Denmark, 1767. By J. H. WOLFF. Silver.

154. JOHN WILKES. His election for Middlesex, 1768. Copper.

155. GEORGE III. Portrait medal, *circ.* 1770.
This medal was struck for special presentation to the American Indian chiefs.

156. DEPARTURE OF CAPTAIN COOK in the *Resolution* and the *Adventure*, 1772. Silver.

157. CAPTAIN COOK. The Copley medal of the Royal Society. Silver.

158. CAPTAIN JOHN PAUL JONES, AMERICAN ADMIRAL. Destruction of English vessels off the Coast of Scotland, 1779. By G. DUPRÉ. Silver.

159. SIEGE OF GIBRALTAR, 1779–1783. Silver.

160. ADMIRAL ELLIOT. Siege of Gibraltar raised, 1783. By J. C. REICH. 1783.

161. FREDERICK, DUKE OF YORK, and FREDERICA OF PRUSSIA. Marriage 1791. By J. STIERLE. Silver.

162. GEORGE IV. (Prince of Wales) and PRINCESS CAROLINE OF BRUNSWICK. Marriage 1795. Silver.

163. BATTLE OF THE NILE, 1st AUG., 1798. Silver-gilt.

164, 165. SIR RALPH ABERCROMBIE, K.B. Death 1801. Silver.

166. UNION WITH IRELAND, 1801. Silver.

167. BATTLE OF TRAFALGAR, 21st Oct., 1805. Pewter.

168. UNION WITH SCOTLAND, Centenary of, 1807. By T. WYON. Silver.

169. CAPTURE OF THE BRITISH FLEET ON LAKE ERIE, 10th Sept., 1813. Copper.

170. CENTENARY OF THE ACCESSION OF THE HOUSE OF HANOVER, AUG. 12, 1814. By W. MOSSOP. Silver.

171. THE WATERLOO MEDAL, 18th June, 1815. Silver.

172. PRINCESS CHARLOTTE. Death 1818. Silver.

173. DUKE OF WELLINGTON. His victories. Copper.

174. JOHN WESLEY. Death 1791. By CARTER. Silver.

175. DR. EDWARD JENNER. Death 1796. Silver.

176. WILLIAM WILBERFORCE. Slave Trade Abolished, 1807. Copper.

177. DR. HENRY QUIN, PHYSICIAN. By W. MOSSOP. Silver.

178. JOHN KEMBLE. The O. P. Riots. Pewter.

179. MATTHEW BOULTON. Memorial 1809. Copper.

## GEORGE IV., 1830–1837.

180. CORONATION, 1821. Silver.

181. ROYAL VISIT TO HANOVER, 1821. Silver.

182. DEATH OF THE KING, 1830. Silver.

183. GEORGE CANNING. Death 1827.

## WILLIAM IV., 1830–1837.

184. ACCESSION, 1830. By W. WYON. Silver.

185. FREDERICK, DUKE OF CAMBRIDGE AS COLONEL OF THE GUARDS. Pewter.

186. FREDERICK, DUKE OF YORK. Badge. Silver.

187. SIR JOHN SOANE. The Soane Museum Founded, 1834. By W. WYON. Copper.

188. SIR FRANCIS CHANTREY, SCULPTOR, 1782-1841. Silver.

189. SIR WALTER SCOTT, 1771-1832. Silver.

190. ANOTHER. Memorial. Copper.

## PICTURES.

**1882.** VICTORIA MARY LOUISA, DUCHESS OF KENT.
Lent by HER MAJESTY THE QUEEN (Windsor).

**1883.** GEORGE IV. AS PRINCE REGENT (1762-1830). By H. Bone.
Lent by H.R.H. THE DUKE OF CAMBRIDGE.

**1884.** WILLIAM IV. (1830-1837). By Sir W. J. Newton.
Lent by the EARL OF MAYO.

**1885.** QUEEN ADELAIDE. By Sir W. J. Newton.
Lent by MRS. NEWTON.

**1886.** WILLIAM PITT, 1ST EARL OF CHATHAM.
Lent by G. P. BOYCE, ESQ.

**1887.** CHARLES JAMES FOX. (Enamel.) By C. Muss.
Lent by the EARL OF ILCHESTER.

**1888.** GEORGE CANNING. By H. Bone.
Lent by JOHN TUDOR FRERE, ESQ.

## DRAWINGS AND ENGRAVINGS.

### In the Balcony.

**1889.** MRS. FITZHERBERT.   Pencil Drawing.
By COSWAY.           Lent by The HON. F. B. MASSEY MAINWARING.

**1890.** A SKETCH.   Pencil Drawing.
By COSWAY.           Lent by The EARL of CARLISLE.

**1891.** SKETCH OF A LADY.   Pencil.
By COSWAY.           Lent by The EARL OF CARLISLE.

**1892.** GEORGE IV. AS PRINCE OF WALES.
By COSWAY.           Lent by SIR P. CURRIE, K.C.B.

**1893.** HORATIO, LORD NELSON, drawn in 1800.
By KESTOR.           Lent by The EARL NELSON.

**1894.** SAMUEL JOHNSON, LL.D.   Mezzotint.
           Lent by UNIVERSITY COLLEGE, OXFORD.

**1895.** MRS. SIDDONS AND HER BROTHERS, JOHN AND CHARLES KEMBLE.   Water-colour Drawing.
By SIR W. T. NEWTON.   Lent by MRS. H. LLEWELLYN BIRD.

**1896.** ALEXANDER POPE.   Pencil Drawing.
By G. VERTUE.   Lent by The RT. HON. CHARLES WENTWORTH DILKE, BART.

**1897.** BEAU BRUMMEL, 1778-1840.
By DIGHTON.           Lent by JULES JOUBERT, ESQ.

## ENGRAVINGS LENT BY HARRY THORNBER, ESQ.

1898. ROBERT, VISCOUNT CASTLEREAGH, 1769-1822.
By C. TURNER, after Lawrence.

1899. ROBERT BURNS, 1759-1796.
By W. WALKER and S. COUSINS, after Nasmyth.

1900. SIR HENRY RAEBURN, 1756-1823.
By W. WALKER, after Raeburn.

1901. MRS. ABINGTON, 1731-1815.
By J. WATSON, after Reynolds.

1902. KITTY CLIVE AS PHILIDA, 1711-1785.
By J. FABER, after Van Bleeck.

1903. ELIZABETH FARREN, COUNTESS OF DERBY, 1759-1829.
By BARTOLOZZI, after Lawrence.

1904. MRS. JORDAN AS HYPPOLITA
By JONES, after Hoppner.

1905. MRS. OLDFIELD, 1683-1730.
By E. FISHER, after Richardson.

1906. MRS. SIDDONS, 1755-1831.
By R. GRAVES, after Gainsborough.

1907. JAMES WATT, 1736-1819.
By C. TURNER, after Lawrence.

**1908.** Royal Visit to the Royal Academy in 1787.
By Martini, after Ramberg.　　　　Lent by John Harley, Esq.

**1909.** Royal Visit to the Royal Academy, 1788.
By Martini, after Ramberg.　　　　Lent by John Harley, Esq.

### In Central Hall.

**1910.** Pedigree of the Royal House of Guelph, founded principally on *L'Art de vérifier les Dates*, with a few modern notes compiled by W. A. Lindsay, Portcullis.

---

*MINIATURES OMITTED FROM*

### CASE K—North Gallery.

*LENT BY J. LUMSDEN PROPERT, ESQ., M.D.*

**1911.** Mary, Duchess of Montagu, daughter of John, Duke of Marlborough.
Unknown.

**1912.** David Garrick, Actor, 1716–1779.

**1913.** Mrs. Robinson as "Perdita," 1758–1800.
By Miss O. Palmer.

**1914.** Richard Brinsley Sheridan, Statesman, &c., 1751–1816.
By G. Engleheart.

**1915.** Mrs. C. J. Fox and Child.
By Ozias Humphry, R.A.

**1916.** Lady Anne Duckett.
By Ozias Humphry, R.A.

**1917.** FRANCES BURNEY (MADAME D'ARBLAY), 1752-1840.
By S. SHELLEY.

**1918.** LADY PRIDEAUX AND CHILD.
By S. SHELLEY.

**1919.** GEORGE ROMNEY, 1734-1802.
By HIMSELF.

**1920.** LADY MARY WORTLEY MONTAGU, 1690-1762.
By a TURKISH ARTIST.

**1921.** ELIZABETH FARREN, COUNTESS OF DERBY, 1759-1829.
By J. NIXON.

**1922.** MRS. HARLOWE, Actress, 1765-1852.
By J. NIXON. *Signed.*

**1923.** JACK BANNISTER, Actor, 1760-1836.
By H. EDRIDGE.

**1924.** ELIZABETH, COUNTESS GROSVENOR.
By SIR T. LAWRENCE, P.R.A.

**1925.** MARIA THERESA, EMPRESS OF GERMANY, 1717-1780.
By J. S. LIOTARD.

**1926.** TALLEYRAND, 1736-1821.
By J. P. G. AUGUSTIN.

**1927.** HARRIET BOYLE, LADY O'NEILL, d. 1793.
By W. HAMILTON, R.A.

**1928.** GEORGE PONSONBY.
By N. PLIMER.

# INDEX OF PICTURES.

*(Indexed under pages.)*

A NEW WAY TO PAY OLD DEBTS, 65
Abercromby, Sir R., 112
Addington, Henry, 1st Viscount, 33
Addison, J., 72, 104
Adelaide, Queen, 27
Aikman, William, 97
Amelia, Princess, daughter of George III., 7, 10, 17, 21
Amherst, William, 1st Earl, 119
Anne, Princess, 7, 11
Anson, George, Lord, 12
Anspach, Elizabeth, Lady Craven, Margravine of, 26
Arkwright, Sir R., 49
Augusta, wife of Frederick, Prince of Wales, 13
Augusta, Princess, 13
Augusta, Sophia Princess, daughter of George III., 21

BACELLI, Mad. Giovanna, 49
Banks, Sir J., 64
Bannister, John, 90
Beckford, Hon. Mrs. Peter, 53
Beckford, William, 37
Bentley, Richard, 78
Billington, Mrs. Elizabeth, 81
Blackstone, Sir William, 38
Bligh, Captain, 45
Blücher, Marshal L. Von, 53
Bolingbroke, Henry St. John, Viscount, 2
Boscawen, Admiral Edward, 32
Boston, Lord, 13
Boswell, James, 108
Boyce, William, 103
Boyle, Lady Elizabeth, 9
Boyle, Lady Henrietta, 9
Boyle, Lady Juliana, 9
Bristol, Augustus John, 3rd Earl of, 54

Bridport, Admiral, 1st Viscount, 41
Burdett, Sir Francis, 101
Burke, Edmund, 34, 110
Burlington, Richard Boyle, 3rd Earl, 6, 9
Burney, Dr. Charles, 93
Burney, Frances (Mad. D'Arblay), 90
Burton, as "Subtle," 109
Bute, John, 3rd Earl of, 35
Bute, John, 4th Earl and 1st Marquis, 35
Byng, Admiral John, 3
Byron, George, 6th Lord, 74

CAMBRIDGE, Adolphus Frederick, Duke of, 26
Camden, Charles, 1st Earl, 57
Campbell, Thomas, 74
Canning, George, 35
Canova, Antonio, 97
Carlisle, Frederick Howard, 5th Earl of, 29
Caroline, Queen, wife of George II. 10
Caroline, Queen, wife of George IV., 23
Cavendish, Lady Caroline, 46
Cavendish, Lord Frederick, 46
Cavendish, Lord George, 46
Charlotte, Princess (Queen of Würtemberg), 17
Charlotte, Princess Royal, 25
Charlotte, Queen, 18, 23
Chatham, Hester, Countess of, 59
Chatham, William Pitt, 1st Earl of, 25, 39
Chatterton, T., 68
Chesterfield, Anne, Countess of, 32
Chesterfield, Philip Dormer Stanhope, 4th Earl of, 11
Chesterfield, Philip, 5th Earl, 39
Cibber, Colley, 89
Clive, Robert, Lord, 16
Coleridge, Samuel T., 79
Collingwood, Cuthbert, 1st Lord, 47
Commons, House of, 14, 30

T

## Index of Pictures.

Congreve, William, 78
Constable, John, 92
Conway, —, 101
Conway, Field-Marshal G. H., 114
Cook, Captain James, 60
Coram, Capt. T., 110
Cosway, R., 84
Coutts, Thomas, 30, 107
Coventry, George William, 6th Earl of, 105
Coventry, Maria (Gunning), Countess of, 46, 105
Cowper, William, 76, 105, 120
Crabbe, Rev. G., 78
Craven, Lady Elizabeth, 26
Croft, William, 93
Crotch, William, 109
Cumberland, Anne Lutrell, Duchess of, 15, 36
Cumberland, Ernest Augusta Duke of (King of Hanover), 25
Cumberland, Henry Fred., Duke of, 106
Cumberland, William, Duke of, 7, 10, 115

D'ARBLAY, Frances Burney, Madame, 90
Darlington, Countess of, see Kielmansegg, &c.
Derby, Edward, 12th Earl of, 20
Devonshire, Eliz. (Foster) Dchss. of, 52, 66
Devonshire, Georgiana Spencer, Dchss. of, 29, 53, 114, 115
Devonshire, William, 3rd Duke, family of, 46
Devonshire, William, 4th Duke, 46
Devonshire, William, 5th Duke of, 57, 118
Dibdin, Charles, 93
Dorset, Arabella, Diana, Duchess of, 44
Dorset, John Frederick, 3rd Duke of, 36
Dorset, Lionel Sackville, 1st Duke of, 14
Duncan, Adam, 1st Visct., 119

EDWARD, Prince, 13
Eldon, John, Earl of, 59, 114
Elizabeth, Princess, daughter of George III., 7, 19
Exmouth, Edward, 1st Visct., 60

FAWCETT, John, 81
Feilding, Anne Cath., Visctss. of, 51
Fielding, Henry, 77
Fisher, Kitty, 82
Fitzharding, Lady, 2
Fitzherbert, Mrs., 26, 114
Flaxman, J., 98
Fleet, Trial of Governor of, 41

Folkes, Martin, 96
Foote, Samuel, 81, 108; as "Major Sturgeon," 109; as the "President," 109
Fox, Charles J., 30, 39
Franklin, Benjamin, 64
Frederick, Prince of Wales, 7, 12
Frere, Right Hon. J. H., 116

GAINSBOROUGH, T., 94
Garrick, David, 86; and his wife, 88; 103, 109, 113
Garrick, Mrs. 88, 103, 106
Gay, John, 72, 107
George I. 3, 4
George II. 7, 11
George III. 13, 16, 17
George IV., 18, 24, 27
Gibbon, Edward, 67, 105
Girtin, T., 99
Gloucester, Maria Walpole, Duchess of, 22, 30
Gloucester, William, see Frederick, 2nd Duke of, 24
Gloucester, William Henry, 1st Duke of, 22
Glynn, J., 111
Godolphin, Francis, 2nd Earl, 9, 21
Godwin, William, 79
Goldsmith, Oliver, 73
Gordon, Jane Maxwell, Duchess of, 104
Gordon, Jane, Duchess of, 43
Gower, Hon. J. L., 33
Grafton, Charles, 2nd Duke, 4
Granby, John Marquess of, 18
Gray, Thomas, 71
Grenville, Right Hon. George, 22
Grenville, William Wyndham, Lord, 20, 103
Guildford, Frederick, 2nd Earl of, 33

HAMILTON, Alexander, 10th Duke, 34
Hamilton, Douglas, 8th Duke of, 61
Hamilton, Lady, 83, 90, 101
Hamilton, Lady Anne, 13
Hamilton and Argyll, Elizabeth, Duchess of, 42
Handel, G. F., 94, 97
Hansard, L., 64
Harcourt, George, 2nd Earl of, 56
Harcourt, Simon, 1st Viscount, 5
Harcourt, Simon, 1st Earl, 48
Hardy, Adm. Sir Charles, 45
Hardwick, Philip Yorke, 1st Earl of, 10
Hartley, Mrs. Elizabeth, 86

## Index of Pictures.

Hastings, Francis, 1st Marq. of, 55
Hastings, Warren, 37
Hawkins, Sir J. 91
Haydn, F. J., 96
Hayes, as "Sir Jacob Jollup," 108
Heathfield, George Augustus, Lord, 58
Herbert, Mrs., 13
Hervey, John Lord, 104
Hogarth, Miss Anne, 8
Hogarth, W., 82
Holland, Henry Fox, 1st Lord, 13
Holland, Mary, Lady, 51
Hood, Adm. Sir Samuel, 46
Hood, Samuel, 1st Viscount, 42
Hoppner, J., 97
Howard, John, 112
Hunt, J. H. Leigh, 80
Huntly, George, Marquis of, 43

ILCHESTER, Stephen Fox, 1st Earl, 118

JOHNSON, Samuel, 70
Jordan, Mrs., 99

KAUFMANN, Angelica M. C., 100
Kean, Edmund, 65, 111
Keats, John, 77
Keith, George, Visct., 116
Kemble, Charles, 100
Kemble Family and Henry VIII., 100
Kemble, Stephen, 100
Kent, Edward, Duke of, 24
Kent, Victoria Mary Louisa, Duchess of, 24
Keppel, Augustus, Viscount, 31
Kerr, Lord Robert, 54
Kielmansegg, Baron, 14
Kielmansegg, Charlotte Sophia, Baroness, 13
Kneller, Sir G., 84
Knyvett, Charles, 100

LADY, Portrait of, 83
Lamb, Charles, 77
Lawrence, Sir Thomas, 100
Lee, John, 31
Ligonier, John, 1st Earl, 59
Louise, Princess, 7
Lyttelton, George, 1st Lord, 48
Lyttelton, Thomas, 2nd Lord, 52

MACCLESFIELD, George, 2nd Earl, 118
"Mall, The," 15
Marlborough, John, 1st Duke, 4
Marlborough, Sarah, Duchess of, 2
Mary, Princess, Duchess of Gloucester, 7, 21, 121
Mason, Rev. W. M., 75
Mathews, Charles, 63
Mathews, Mrs. Charles, 66
Mellon, Harriet, Duchess of St. Albans, 89
Melville, Henry Dundas, Viscount, 38
Midnight Modern Conversation, 107
Montagu, Edward Wortley, 6, 111, 117
Montagu, Lady Mary Wortley, 87, 111
Moore, Adm. Sir Graham, 58
Moore, Edward, 69
Moore, Gen. Sir John, 57, 61
Moore, Sir John, 61
Moore, Thomas, 95
Morland, G., 98
Murray, John, 92

NAPOLEON I., 51
Nelson, Horatio, Viscount, 44, 48; death of, 60, 106
New Way to Pay Old Debts, 65
Newcastle, Thomas Pelham, Duke of, 14
Newton, Sir Isaac, 75, 112
Nollekens, J., 65
North, Lord Frederick, 2nd Earl of Guildford, 33
Northcote, James, 63
Nuneham, George Simon, Visct., 56

OPIE, J., 110
Orford, Horace Walpole, 4th Earl of, 88, 108, 113
Orford, Sir Robert Walpole, 1st Earl, 7, 12, 118
Oxford, Edward Harley, 2nd Earl of, 3, 15

PALMER, John, as "Face," 109
Pelham, Right Hon. Henry, 15
Pembroke, Eliz. Spencer, Ctss. of, 45
Pembroke, George, 11th Earl, 45
Pembroke, Henry, 10th Earl of, 43
Penn, Lady Juliana, 39
Penn, Thomas, 32
Perceval, Rt. Hon. Spencer, 62
Peterborough, Charles Mordaunt, 3rd Earl, 2
Pitt, Right Hon. William, 34, 38, 119

## Index of Pictures.

Pope, A., 69
Porson, R., 113
Powys, Mrs., 51
Prior, Matthew, 67, 87
Pritchard, Mrs. Hannah, 89
Punch Bowl, 107

QUIN, James, 83

RAMSAY, Allan, 91
Reynolds, Sir Joshua, 84, 96
Richardson, Samuel, 76
Richmond, Charles, 3rd Duke of, 22, 115
Ridge, Miss, 53
Robertson, W., 68
Robinson, Mrs. Mary, 87
Rockingham, Charles, 2nd Marquis, 37
Rodney, George, Lord, 42
Rogers, Samuel, 79
Romney, Frances, Ctss. of, 47
Romney, George, 94
Romney, John, 94
Rutland, Charles, 4th Duke, 56
Rutland, Elizabeth H., Dchss. of, 115

SACKVILLE, George, Viscount, 20
Scott, Sir Walter, 75
Selwyn, George Augustus, 29
Seward, Anna, 80
Shelley, P. Bysshe, 73
Siddons, Mrs., 85, 100, 120
Sidmouth, Henry Addington, 1st Viscount, 33
Sheridan, Mrs., 55
Sheridan, Richard Brinsley, 17, 49, 68
Sloane, Sir Hans, 92
Sophia Dorothea, wife of George I. 5
Sophia Dorothea, Princess (Queen of Prussia), 6
Sophia, Electress of Hanover, 1
Sophia, Matilda of Gloucester, Princess, 27
Sophia of Gloucester, Princess, 30
Sophia, Princess, daughter of George III., 18, 21
Southey, R., 72
Spencer, Margaret Georgiana, Ctss. of, 19, 114
Stanhope, James, 1st Earl, 5
St. Albans, Harriet (Mellon) Duchess of, 89
St. James's Park, View of, 15

St. Vincent, John, 1st Earl, 40
Steele, Sir Richard, 15, 76
Stephens, Mrs., 100
Sterne, Rev. Lawrence, 71, 105
Stowell, William, Lord, 116
Strahan, W., 66
Suffolk and Berkshire, Henry, 12th Earl of, 19
Sumner, Mrs. (née Gambier), 36
Sussex, Augustus Fred., Duke of, 23
Swift, Jonathan, 79

THOMSON, James, 91
Thurlow, Edward, Lord, 54
Tonson, Jacob, 95
Tooke, J. Horne, 111
Torrington, 1st Visct., 117
Trial of the Governor of the Fleet, 41

VANBRUGH, Sir J., 68
Vernon Admiral, Edward, 40

WALPOLE, Horace, 4th Earl of Orford, 88, 108, 113
Warwick, Charlotte, Countess of, 8
Watson, as "Dr. Last," 109
Watson, R., Bp. of Llandaff, 66
Wedgwood, Jos., 98
Wellesley, Richard, Marquess of, 61, 111
Wellington, Arthur, Duke of, 50, 52
West, Benjamin, 91
Westmoreland, John, 10th Earl of, 105
Weston, Mrs., 117
Whitehead, W., 82
White, H. Kirke, 104
Wilberforce, William, 28
Wilkes, J., 111
Wilkie, Sir D., 99
William IV., 27, 112
Williams, Mrs. John, 57
Windham, William, 50
Woffington, Peg, 101
Wolfe, General James, 8
Wordsworth, W., 65

YORK, Frederick, Duke of, 23

# INDEX OF EXHIBITORS.

*(Indexed under pages.)*

HER MAJESTY THE QUEEN, 6, 11, 13, 15, 16, 17, 18, 19, 21, 23, 24, 36, 42, 44, 83, 86, 88, 96, 106, 116, 121, 122, 268

H.R.H. THE PRINCE OF WALES, 122, 143

H.R.H. THE PRINCESS LOUISE, MARCHIONESS OF LORNE, 24, 123

H.R.H. THE DUKE OF CAMBRIDGE, 22, 23, 24, 25, 26, 123, 124, 143, 144, 145, 146, 268

ADDISON, W., 8, 104
Admiralty, Lords of the, 46, 60
Alexander, Major-General Sir Claud, Bart., 30
Amherst, W. A. Tyssen, M.P., 129
Arkwright, F.C., 42
Aston, W. W., 137, 138

BAGOT, Lord, 2
Baker, W. R. 4, 9, 68, 72, 76, 78, 84, 95
Balliol College, Oxford, 105
Bathurst, Earl, 38
Beck, Rev. J., 137, 182, 183
Bird, Mrs. H. Llewellyn J., 269
Bischoffsheim, H. L., 27, 81, 190
Bishop, Mrs. W. Follen, 129
Bligh, Hon. and Rev. E. V., 24
Bodleian Library, Oxford, 33, 38, 79, 97
Bolton, Mrs., 201
Boxall, W. Percival, 76, 80, 89, 98, 110
Boyce, G. P., 11, 63, 77, 83, 105, 268
Bristol, Marquess of, 54, 104, 158, 180, 181
Burdett-Coutts, Lady, 22, 30, 63, 65, 66, 74, 75, 89, 98, 101, 107, 111, 140, 141, 183, 184, 187
Burney, Rev. H., 90, 185

Burney, the Ven. Archdeacon, 110
Butler, Charles, 82
Buzzard, Miss, 128
Byron, Major-General J., 191

CARLISLE, Earl of, 2, 29, 41, 61, 108, 109, 114, 115, 147, 148, 269
Carnarvon, Earl of, 32, 39, 47
Chaplin, Clifford, 8
Chichester, Earl of, 4, 10, 14, 15, 23, 118
Christ Church, Oxford, 22, 119
Clanrikarde, Marquess of, 35
Clark, Mrs. Godfrey, 201, 202
Cleland, John (of Stormont), 27, 130, 133, 163, 218, 220
Clerk, Sir G. D., Bart., 91, 98
Cobham, Viscount, 39, 48, 52, 91, 231-233, 236, 239, 240, 242, 245, 248, 255, 256, 257
Cockle, Mrs. Moss, 129, 131, 254
Cole, Miss Emily, 131
Collingwood, J. E., 128, 129, 139, 158, 159, 162, 163, 193, 218
Constable, Archibald, 245
Cotton, Henry H. P., 133, 140, 160, 161, 181, 183
Coventry, Earl of, 105
Crawford, Earl of, 28, 34, 98, 102
Cripps, Wilfrid, C.B., 155, 156
Cullum, G. Milner-Gibson, 132, 137, 142, 159, 160, 163, 222-227, 229, 231, 239, 240-242, 244, 245, 247, 249, 250-253, 255, 256, 257
Currie, Sir Philip H. W., K.C.B., 269
Cust, Lionel, 114

DALTON, Mrs., 142
Dartrey, Earl of, 181, 182

## Index of Exhibitors.

Davis, Charles, 134
De L'Isle & Dudley, Lord, 27, 112
Denbigh, Earl of, 51, 132
Denny, E. Collingwood, 47
Dent, Mrs., of Sudeley, 156, 157
Derby, Earl of, K.G., 20, 137
Devonshire, Duke of, K.G., 19, 29, 46, 52, 66, 97, 103, 151, 152, 160
De Worms, Baron, 220
Dilke, Rt. Hon. Sir C. W., Bart., 77, 136, 139, 142, 160, 162, 193, 194, 220, 242-244, 249, 257, 269
Dillon, Harry, 218
Dillon, Viscount, 164
Donaldson, Mrs. A. B., 220
Drake, H., 151, 163
Drake, The late Sir W., 127, 128
Dundas, Robert, of Arniston, 38

EDINBURGH, University of, 68
Egmont, Earl of, 218
Eldon, Earl of, 59
Ellis, H. H. Dynes, 154, 155, 156, 157
Ellis, Rev. F. R., 141
Engleheart, P. G. D., C.B., 138
Estcourt, G. Sotheron, 33
Eton College, Provost of, 39, 103, 111
Evans, John, P.S.A., 131, 132, 139, 158
Evans, W. H., 115

FALCKE, I., 141, 142, 194, 195, 196, 209, 212, 219, 220
Fane, Rt. Hon. Sir S. Ponsonby, 105, 139
Fetherstonhaugh, Hon. Mrs., 188
Fife, Duke of, K.T., 3, 5, 11
Fishmongers' Company, 26
Fitzhenry, J. H., 209
Fitzherbert, B., 152, 153
Fitzwilliam, G. C. W., 37
Follett, Colonel, 154, 155, 156
Fortescue, Earl of, 20, 25, 26
Fortnum, C. Drury E., 163
Fortnum, Miss, 153
Foster, H., 193
Frere, John Tudor, 116, 146, 147, 268

GARRICK CLUB, Committee of, 65
Gell, Mrs. E. S. Hamilton, 133

Gibbons, Rev. B., 30
Gibbs, H. H., 131
Girtin, G. W. H., 99
Glyn, G. Carr, 198, 199, 200, 201
Goldsmid, Sir Julian, Bart., 184, 185
Gower, J. Leveson, 32, 33
Grafton, Duke of, K.G., 57
Green, W. S., 105
Grueber, Mrs. H. A., 154, 191
Gwyn, A. W. S., 129, 131
Gwyn, W. R. Harcourt, 132, 133, 187

HAMILTON, Dr. E., 69, 106, 133
Hamilton, Duke of, K.T., 34, 37, 42, 46, 53, 139
Harcourt, E. W., 5, 48, 56, 69, 82, 87, 89, 224, 225
Harding, G. R., 212
Hardy, Mrs. H., 157, 160
Harley, John, 112, 271
Harrow School, Head-Master of, 192, 238
Hartington, Marquess of, M.P., 6, 7, 9, 10, 11, 57, 115
Hartshorne, A., 134, 158
Hartshorne, Miss, 159
Harvey, Mrs., of Ickwell-Bury, 83, 129, 217
Helyer, H. A., 117
Hill, Miss, 129
Hinckley, Frederick, 117
Hipkins, Mrs. A. J., 257
Hipkins, Mrs. J. Souter, 159
Holtby, Miss, 135, 162
Hood, Viscount, 41, 42, 46
Hotham, Lord, 191
Howard, J. J.

ILCHESTER, Earl of, 13, 51, 79, 95, 118, 137, 141, 153, 218, 268
Inglis, Captain W. R., 218
Irving, Henry, 51, 81, 111

JACKSON, J., 142, 155, 157, 163
Johnson, H. R. V., 120
Johnson, Jas. Henry, 193
Johnson, Junr., Rev. W. Cowper, 193
Johnson, Rev. W. Cowper, 193
Johnston, Mrs. Campbell, 114, 180, 218
Jones, Charles A., 132, 134, 156, 163
Jones, Sir Lawrence, Bart., 153

## Index of Exhibitors.

Joseph, E., 186, 190
Joseph, Felix, 194, 195
Joubert, J. A., 269

KEILY, A., 224—226, 228, 251—253, 253, 254
Kennedy, C. Storr, 164—167
Kielmansegg, Count, 13, 14, 130, 137, 141, 161, 221
Kinnoul, Earl of, 15

LANSDOWNE, Marquess of, 71
Laurence, Miss, 80
Lee, Mrs. J. Hutchinson, 90
Lee, Rev. Dr. F. G., 161, 193
Leeds, Duke of, 21, 186
Lees, C. E., 136, 140
Le Fanu, Mrs., 140
Lemon, Mrs. Arthur, 66
Lewis, Miss, 130, 160, 163, 164
Logie, Mrs., 192
Lomax, A. C., 192, 193
London, Corporation of, 23, 40, 58, 119, 219
Lothian, Marquess of, K.T., 18, 54, 56
Loudoun, Earl of, 37, 55, 72
Lowndes, Miss A. T. Selby, 140
Lowther, Hon. Mrs. W., 130, 137

MACKENZIE, General, 99
Mainwaring, Hon. F. B. Massey, 31, 45, 87, 96, 118, 269
Malet, Col. H., 137
Malmesbury, Earl of, 94
Marlborough, Duke of, 1, 2, 4, 180
Marsh, S. C., 134, 161
Maxwell-Scott, Hon. Mrs., 82, 131, 136, 159, 161, 187, 188
Maxwell, Sir Herbert, Bart., 43
Mayo, Earl of, 132, 137, 139, 268
Merchant Taylors' Company, 191
Middleton, Viscount, 154, 191
Milman, H. S., 142
Montague, S., M.P., 154
Moore, J. Carrick, 57, 58, 112
Morrison, A., 112, 222—256
Morrison, Mrs., 101, 107
Mowatt, J. L. G., 149
Munster, Countess of, 146

Murdoch, J. Gloog, 258—267
Murray, John, 72, 74, 78, 79, 92, 238

NAYLOR, R. C., 209
Nelson, Earl, 44, 48, 188, 189, 219, 220, 269
Newton, Mrs., 268
Nicholls, S. J., 130, 163, 221
Norman, P., 108
Nottingham, Art Museum, 104

ONSLOW, Earl of, K.C.M.G., 14
Oxenham, Rev. F. Nutcombe, 132
Oxford, Earl of, 129, 136, 159
Oxford, University of, 91, 93, 113

PEMBROKE COLLEGE, Cambridge, 71, 75
Pembroke College, Oxford, 220
Pembroke, Earl of, 43, 45
Pfungst, H. T., 130
Ponsonby, Hon. Gerald, 77, 129, 130, 150, 186, 228, 254
Portarlington, Earl of, 114, 125, 126, 127
Portland, Duke of, 3
Powerscourt, Viscount, K.P., 84, 134, 150, 160
Propert, J. Lumsden, M.D., 177—180, 212—216, 271, 272
Pym, Horace N., 49, 84

QUILTER, W. Cuthbert, M.P., 92

RANFURLY, Earl of, 32, 39, 134
Reid, Miss, 8, 156, 201, 221
Richmond, Duke of, K.G., 7, 12, 104, 115, 119
Rintoul, Lieut.-Colonel R., 217
Rodwell, B. J. H., 40
Rothschild, A. de, 11, 53
Royal Academy, 91, 100
Royal Academy of Music, 102
Royal Society, 64, 92, 96, 97, 118
Royal United Service Institution, 217
Rutter, Mrs., 164

SACKVILLE, Lord, 14, 20, 34, 36, 44, 49, 55, 70, 73, 81, 101, 113
Salters' Company, 190, 191
Salting, W. S., 212
Scarsdale, Lord, 107

## Index of Exhibitors.

Schreiber, Lady Charlotte, 202, 204, 221
Sharpe, Mrs. William, 94
Shaw, Mrs. F., 68
Sheffield, Lord, 67
Shelley, Lady, 73, 79
Southampton, Corporation of, 93
St. Albans, Duchess of, 53, 87, 140
St. John's College, Cambridge, 65
Stanhope, Earl of, 5, 59, 64, 152
Stationers' Company, 15, 64, 67, 76
Sterry, J. Ashby, 131, 210
Stowe, Alfred, 186
Strafford, Earl of, 3, 117
Stuart, W. Johnston, 162, 210
Suffolk and Berkshire, Earl of, 19
Sumner, Miss G., 139, 158, 162
Sutherland, Duke of, K.G., 59, 110

TAYLOR, Harry, 68
Telfer, Captain, 139, 162, 228, 257
Thornber, Harry, 270
Thurlow, T. Lyon, 36, 50, 54, 129, 140, 160
Trinity College, Cambridge, 75, 78, 113, 142

UNIVERSITY COLLEGE, Oxford, 50, 114, 116, 269

WALDEGRAVE, Earl, 124, 125, 128
Waldy, Rev. T. E., 12, 100, 217, 219

Walford, E., 16, 236
Walpole, H. Spencer, 7, 12, 62, 88, 108, 113, 162, 230, 232, 233, 236, 256
Ward, T. Humphrey, 111
Warwick, Earl of, 94, 120
Wass, C. Wentworth, 197, 198
Watson, C. Knight, 66
Wayne, Mrs. E. F., 134
Weigall, H., 52, 130, 159, 185, 186, 187, 190, 191
Wellesley, Gerald E., 187
Wellington, Duke of, 52, 53, 61, 137
Wemyss, Earl of, 90, 101
Wertheimer, A., 190, 191
Westminster, Duke of, K.G., 85, 86
Wharncliffe, Earl of, 6, 35, 87, 117, 130, 151
Whatman, Mrs., 105
Wheatley, Colonel Moreton, 57
White, Henry, 133
Whitehead, Jeffery, 168, 169, 171-176
Wilkie, Colonel D., 92
Willett, H., 204-208
Willoughby de Eresby, Lord, 148, 149, 161, 162
Wing, W. H., 131
Wright, Captain H., 229
Wyndham, Henry Saxe, 230, 231, 235, 237, 241, 245, 247, 257

YOUNG, Major H., 217

www.ingramcontent.com/pod-product-compliance
Lightning Source LLC
Chambersburg PA
CBHW032052230426
43672CB00009B/1571